W9-AEM-562

ISLAM, SECTARIANISM AND POLITICS
IN SUDAN SINCE THE MAHDIYYA

GABRIEL WARBURG

Islam, Sectarianism and Politics in Sudan since the Mahdiyya

THE UNIVERSITY OF WISCONSIN PRESS

WINGATE UNIVERSITY LIBRARY

The University of Wisconsin Press
1930 Monroe Street
Madison, Wisconsin 53711

www.wisc.edu/wisconsinpress/

Copyright © 2003 Gabriel Warburg
All rights reserved

5   4   3   2   1

Printed in Scotland by Bell & Bain Ltd, Glasgow

Library of Congress Cataloging-in-Publication Data
Warburg, Gabriel.
    Islam, sectarianism, and politics in Sudan since the Mahdiyya / Gabriel
    Warburg.
    p. cm.
    Includes bibliographical references and index.
    ISBN 0-299-18290-8 (cloth: alk. paper)–ISBN 0-299-18294-0 (pbk: alk.
    paper)
    1. Sudan–History–19th century. 2. Sudan–History–20th century.
    3. Islam and politics–Sudan.
I. Title.
DT156.4 .W375 2002
962.404–dc21
                                  200267595

*In loving memory of Rachel
and with love to our grandchildren
Guy, Tal, Ron, and Timon*

CONTENTS

Preface and Acknowledgements   *page*   ix

Abbreviations   xiv

Part I. ISLAMIZATION   1

1. Sufism and Holy Families   1
2. Islam and State under the Turkiyya, 1820–81   6
3. Social, Economic and Geopolitical Factors Leading to Revolt   12

Part II. THE MAHDIST STATE, 1881–98   22

4. Background to the Mahdiyya   22
5. The Path Leading to Revolt   27
6. Muhammad Ahmad b. 'Abdallah, the Mahdi   30
7. The Mahdist State under the Khalifa 'Abdullahi   43
8. Laying the Foundations of Mahdist Administration   50
   Military and administrative hierarchy   50
   Economics and finances   51
   The administration of justice   55

Part III. RELIGIOUS POLICY UNDER
THE CONDOMINIUM   57

9. Laying the Foundations, 1899–1918   57
   The Impact of Wingate and Slatin   57
   Orthodox or popular Islam   59
   The Shari'a courts and the selection of 'Ulama' and Qadis   64
   Religious education   68
   The Waqf and the building of government mosques   71
   The pilgrimage   73
   Fears of Mahdist 'revival', 1899–1914   74
   The First World War and the revision of policy   76

10. The Emergence of Neo-Mahdism   81
    Sayyid 'Abd al-Rahman al-Mahdi, 1885–1959   81
    The years of ambivalence, 1925–38   87
    The recruitment of the Ansar   94
    Neo-Mahdist ideology   99

11. The Path to Independence, 1939–55   104
     The 1936 Anglo-Egyptian Treaty and its impact on Sudan   104
     The Graduates' General Congress   110
     The emergence of al-Ashiqa' and al-Umma   119
     The two Sayyids on the eve of independence   128
     The Southern question   138

Part IV. INDEPENDENT SUDAN, 1956–89   142

12. Statehood and Constitution-Making   144
13. The Islamic Path, 1977–85   152
     The implementation of the Shari'a   155
     The trial and execution of Mahmud Muhammad Taha   160
     The Shari'a laws and the South   165

14. The Ansar-Umma in Politics, 1956–86   170
15. The Muslim Brothers and Numayri   178
     Early years   178
     From opposition to collaboration   183
     The army and the economic system in Ikhwan politics   189

16. The Third Democratic Interlude, 1986–9   194

Part V. ISLAMISM AND DEMOCRACY   202

17. The Islamist Coup and the NIF–Military Coalition   205
18. Islam and Democracy   222

Bibliography   227
Index   239

MAPS

The Egyptian Sudan   xvi
The Modern Sudan   xvii

PREFACE AND ACKNOWLEDGEMENTS

This book has been in preparation for many years and I will share with you some of the reasons that led to it. Shortly before I completed *The Sudan under Wingate*, in 1971, I was invited to an international conference at the Hebrew University in Jerusalem by my mentor and friend the late Professor Gabriel Baer. I was at the time somewhat at a loss as to what direction my future research should take. I had almost decided to resume my work on Egypt, my first love, and to undertake a research project on the role of the peasants in the 'Urabi revolt of 1882, which I had planned in 1965 as a topic for my PhD dissertation. Gabriel Baer, however, made a different suggestion. The paper I had presented to the conference mentioned above was on " 'Ulama', Popular Islam and Religious Policy in the Northern Sudan, 1899–1916".[1] Baer thought that the problem of religion and politics in Sudan, raised both in that paper and in my PhD dissertation, was of such importance that it warranted further attention and more time. Sudan, he argued, presented a unique opportunity to undertake such a study since the Mahdiyya of the nineteenth century was one of the only examples of an Islamic state that had succeeded in driving out foreign rulers and had been a success story until British imperial interests brought about its premature destruction. Furthermore, the revival of Mahdist ideology and politics in Sudan during the twentieth century coincided with Islamic resurgence in the Muslim world. It was therefore more than likely that political Islam was going to remain with us for some time to come. Islam in a modern state thus became the centre of my research in the years to come and I have pursued it ever since with minor deviations. Although I later undertook research on a variety of topics, such as the Nile in Egyptian–Sudanese relations or on the 1906 Taba Incident between Britain and the Ottoman Empire, I have always returned to my central topic of research, which involved the question of religion and politics in modern Sudan.

My second book, *Islam Nationalism and Communism in a Traditional Society: The Case of Sudan*, published in 1978, thus set me on a path along which I have travelled ever since. The present volume therefore represents the condensed results of over three decades of research and study on this

[1] Warburg, *'Ulama'*, 89–119.

topic. If I ever had doubts as to whether I had chosen the right direction, they were banished by President Ja'far Numayri, in September 1983, when he decided to implement the shari'a in Sudan and establish an Islamic state with him as its *imam*. Since I was living in Egypt in 1984–7, I was in a position to follow the new developments more closely. Moreover, I had all the relevant secondary sources, especially Sudanese and Egyptian newspapers, journals and new books, within easy reach. I realized that it fitted in with my main thesis – namely, that in Sudan Islam and politics were so intertwined that they could not be separated, at least in the foreseeable future. Consequently I decided to devote a major study to this topic. My book *Historical Discord in the Nile Valley*, which examined most of the secondary sources dealing with this topic, especially those written by inhabitants of the Nile Valley, was a by-product of the present study.[2]

However, resurgent Islam was gaining force not only in Sudan and Egypt but also throughout the Muslim world. This trend has dominated the Middle East ever since the mid-1960s, when it rejected – either totally or partly – secularism and other ideologies imported from Europe, such as socialism, nationalism, or positive neutralism. All of these had flourished during the post-World War period, boosted by the Cold War, and had reached a new peak after the Free Officers, headed by Jamal 'Abd al-Nasser assumed power in Egypt in July 1952. When Wilfred Cantwell Smith wrote *Islam in Modern History* in 1957, it was the heyday of nationalism and socialism throughout the Muslim world and especially in the Arab world under the impact of Nasserism. Yet Smith wrote:

Islam is today living through that crucial, creative moment in which the heritage of the past is being transformed into the herald of its future . . . For both outsiders and Muslims the most important, most interesting chapter in Islamic history so far is the one that is today in process of being enacted.[3]

Gustav von Grunebaum, who published his *Modern Islam* a couple of years later, reiterated similar thoughts when he stated:

It is the persistence of the Muslim political community and the growth of a Muslim civilizational area expanding in the face of political fragmentation which emerge as phenomena peculiar to the Islamic development and as such call for consideration.[4]

In other words, both Smith and von Grunebaum realized at that time that a most important phase in Islamic history was about to unfold, while many scholars, both in the region itself and in the West, were predicting its demise and its replacement by secular democratic nationalism.

In 1898 Lord Cromer, then British Agent and Consul-General in Cairo,

[2] Warburg, *Historical Discord*.
[3] Smith, *Islam*, 11.
[4] Grunebaum, *Modern Islam*, 3.

dictated to Egypt the terms according to which Anglo-Egyptian Sudan was to be governed. The terms of this so-called Condominium Agreement, slightly modified, became the blueprint for post-Mahdist colonial Sudan. The Turco-Egyptian rulers of Sudan had been defeated in the 1880s and had been forced to evacuate Sudan by a political Islamic movement, which had established an Islamic Mahdist state. It was therefore logical that the colonial power which had now reconquered Sudan was determined to remove Islam from politics or, to use Western terminology; 'to separate Church and State'. Muslims were to be allowed to conduct their religious affairs and to establish their own shari'a courts, in which matters relating to personal status were to be adjudicated. But Sudan was to be governed by a secular government, composed primarily of British officials, with a sprinkling of Egyptians and others thrown in for good measure. As for the future, which was not yet in sight, it was predicted that a system of democratic government, not dissimilar to that in Westminster, would gradually evolve in Sudan as well as in other countries that were at the time under British colonial rule. We are well aware that this prediction has not been realized and that, as seen from the West, it has failed dismally. However, the question remains as to whether it really was a failure or whether, perhaps, the very concept of separating politics and religion was a contradiction in terms in Muslim societies. To express it more bluntly, it seemed that the Muslim world was neither ready nor willing to absorb Western-style secular democracy as propagated by its colonial rulers.

This is the main topic with which the present study will attempt to deal and although it is limited to Sudan, it has repercussions throughout the Muslim world. In another volume, which I co-authored with Aharon Layish, we limited our examination to the Islamist state under Numayri and to the Islamic laws implemented in Sudan in September 1983.[5] It will therefore not be a central topic in my present study, nor will other important aspects of Sudanese history. Instead, I will limit myself to an attempt to explore the role of Islam in Sudanese politics since the Mahdiyya and will examine the part played by the colonial administration in 1899–1956 in enhancing the functions of Islam in Sudan, despite its desire to separate religion and politics. My writings on the Mahdist period rely heavily on Professor Peter Holt's extended research on the Mahdiyya, and on the Mahdist archival documents published and annotated by Dr Muhammad Ibrahim Abu Salim. As for the Anglo-Egyptian colonial period I have benefited from numerous studies of many Sudanese and western scholars and relied on my own previous research.

Historically, the study of independent Sudan is far more problematic than that of the colonial period, in particular because, in multi-ethnic and multi-religious societies such as Sudan, contemporary studies tend to be

---

[5] Layish and Warburg, *Reinstatement.*

intertwined with controversial political agendas. In addition, it seems that historians have on the whole concentrated on the story of the majorities in these societies and thus the problems faced by ethnic or religious minorities in such societies have been studied by default by members of the minorities themselves.[6] Moreover, most of the primary sources relevant to this period are unfortunately not yet available and hence the ground covered in the section dealing with the post-independence period is based primarily on secondary sources. Finally, despite my lasting interest in Sudan and my love of its people, I have never been able to go there and gain a firsthand impression of the land and its people. However, despite these shortcomings I decided to undertake this task primarily because it is to be my last major work on the topic. I therefore decided that it should encompass the entire period, starting with the nineteenth-century Mahdi and ending with the Islamist state as conceived by Sudan's Islamist regime since 1989. I have written numerous papers on independent Sudan and have by and large been told by fellow Sudanese scholars who attended my lectures or read my papers that they appreciated my ability to grasp the essential problems of the country as it is today. It would therefore have been cowardly if I had opted out of dealing with the present only because future scholarship may prove my shortcomings.

In this study I have used several sources that I have utilized previously. Also, as can be noted in the bibliography, I have relied on my previous research and publications dealing with the topic of this study in preparing certain sections of the present book. This is especially true with regard to the study of the Condominium, in which I relied to a large extent on primary sources deposited in the Public Record Office in London and in the Sudan Archive deposited in the library of Durham University. With regard to the latter, I wish to apologize for not having updated the documents according to the new catalogue system, especially of the Wingate and Slatin papers. I would like to thank the keepers of the archives, as well as the publishers and editors of my previous publications, for enabling me to use these publications for my current study.

As already mentioned, the work leading to this volume was started many years ago and most of that research was undertaken during sabbatical leaves spent at various institutes, which fortunately enabled me to pursue my study in great comfort and in relative relaxation. I started my study at the Annenberg Research Institute in Philadelphia in 1989–90, and during the following year I enjoyed the hospitality of St Antony's College, Oxford, where I also completed my book on *Historical Discord in the Nile Valley*. Finally I owe a major debt to several institutions of higher learning in Berlin.

---

[6] Volkov, *Minorities*, 7.

First, I was invited in 1991–2 by the Wissenschaftskolleg zu Berlin to spend a year as its Fellow. I later revisited it for prolonged periods in 1997–9, with the help of a Minerva Fund stipend. While in Berlin I also enjoyed the hospitality of the Centre for Islamic Studies of the Freie Universität and of the Zentrum Moderner Orient. To all of these and to my own University of Haifa I feel deep gratitude.

My acknowledgements cannot be concluded without mentioning Rachel, who passed away in April 2000 just as I was about to conclude this book. Rachel was my wife and my best friend for more than fifty years. She was also an ardent and critical reader of everything I ever wrote. This is my only book which goes to press without being read by her and without the benefit of her wise and critical comments. She was with me when I started to undertake the research leading to its writing in Philadelphia in 1989, and she accompanied me to Oxford in 1991. Finally we spent a very happy and fruitful period at the Institute for Advanced Study in Berlin in 1992 and in 1997–9, when I completed my research and started to write. I hope that she would have given her approval to the final version since I have always cherished her verdict.

Haifa, May 2002   G. W.

ABBREVIATIONS

BSOAS	*Bulletin of the School of Asian and African Studies*
DUP	Democratic Unionist Party
FO	Foreign Office Archive at the Public Record Office, London
GGR	*Reports on the Finances, Administration, and Conditions of the Sudan* (Confidential)
ICF	Islamic Charter Front
IJMES	*International Journal of Middle Eastern Studies*
ILM	Islamic Liberation Movement
JMAS	*Journal of Modern African Studies*
KUSU	Khartoum University Student Union
MES	*Middle Eastern Studies*
NCC	National Constitutional Conference
NDA	National Democratic Alliance
NF	National Front
NIF	National Islamic Front
NUP	National Unionist Party
PDF	Popular Defence Force
PDP	Peoples' Democratic Party
PIAC	Popular Islamic and Arabic Conference
RCC	Revolutionary Command Council
SAD	Sudan Archive in Durham University's library
SCP	Sudan Communist Party
SDF	Sudan Defence Force
SDG	*Sudan Democratic Gazette*
SIR	*Sudan Intelligence Report*
SMIS	*Sudan Monthly Intelligence Summary*
SNR	*Sudan Notes and Records*
SPIS	*Sudan Political Intelligence Summary*

SPLA	Sudan's People Liberation Army
SPLM	Sudan's People Liberation Movement
SPS	Sudan Political Service
SRP	Socialist Republican Party
SSIR	*Sudan Secret Intelligence Report*
SSU	Sudan Socialist Union
TMC	Transitional Military Council

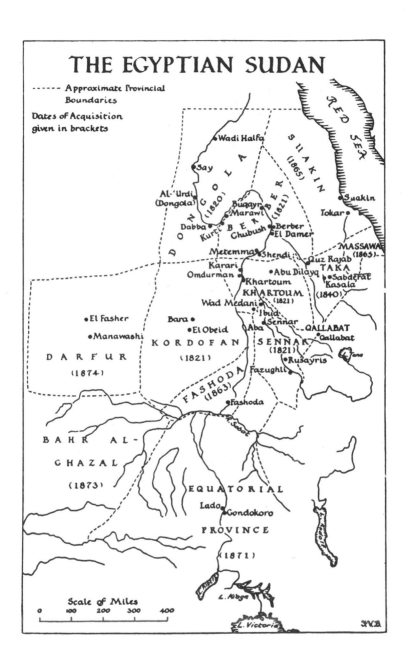

THE EGYPTIAN SUDAN

----- Approximate Provincial
Boundaries

Dates of Acquisition
given in brackets

RED SEA

Wadi Halfa

Say

S U A K I N
(1865)

Al-'Urdi
(Dongola)
(1820)

D O N G O L A

Buqayr
Marawi

Suakin

Dabba

B E R B E R
(1821)

Berber
El Damer

Tokar

Kurti

Chubush

Metemma

Shendi

Quz Rajab

MASSAWA
(1865)

Karari

Omdurman

Abu Dilayq

TAKA

Khartoum

Sabderat
Kasala
(1840)

KHARTOUM
(1821)

Wad Medani

Ibud

Aba

Sennar

QALLABAT

El Fasher

Bara

El Obeid

SENNAR
(1821)

Qallabat

Manawashi

KORDOFAN
(1821)

Rusayris

L. Tana

DARFUR
(1874)

Fazughli

FASHODA
(1863)

Fashoda

R. Sobat

BAHR AL-

GHAZAL
(1873)

E Q U A T O R I A L

Lado
Gondokoro

P R O V I N C E

(1871)

L. Kioga

Scale of Miles

0   100   200   300   400

L. Victoria

J.V.B.

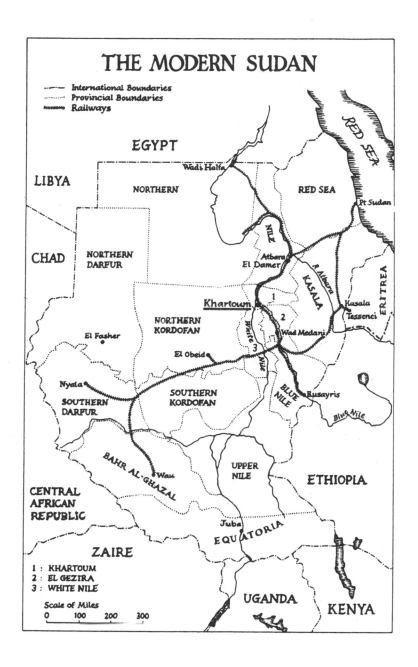

THE MODERN SUDAN

- –·–·– International Boundaries
- ············· Provincial Boundaries
- ~~~~~ Railways

EGYPT

LIBYA

NORTHERN

Wadi Halfa

RED SEA

Pt. Sudan

CHAD

NORTHERN
DARFUR

NILE

Atbara
El Damer

R. Atbara

KASALA

ERITREA

Khartoum

Kasala
Tessenei

1

2

Wad Medani

El Fasher

NORTHERN
KORDOFAN

White Nile

3

El Obeid

Nyala

SOUTHERN
DARFUR

SOUTHERN
KORDOFAN

BLUE
NILE

Busayris

Blue Nile

BAHR AL-GHAZAL

Wau

UPPER
NILE

ETHIOPIA

CENTRAL
AFRICAN
REPUBLIC

Juba

EQUATORIA

ZAIRE

1 : KHARTOUM
2 : EL GEZIRA
3 : WHITE NILE

UGANDA

KENYA

Scale of Miles
0   100   200   300

Part I

ISLAMIZATION

1

SUFISM AND HOLY FAMILIES

In order to comprehend the role of Islam in the emergence of Sudan as a political entity we have to examine briefly the process of Sudan's Islamization during the preceding centuries. Both Sudanese and other scholars have fortunately undertaken studies of this process and this study will be limited to a brief examination of some central issues.[1] The great success of Sufism and of the 'holy families' in the Funj Sultanate of Sinnar, between the fifteenth and eighteenth centuries is one of the issues that have a direct bearing on the central topic of this book. *Sufi* shaykhs and other Muslim holy men had a great following in Sudan for a number of reasons. First, although the process of Islamization by Muslim jurists had started earlier, Sufism was far more popular and easier to comprehend than its orthodox counterpart. Secondly, by the sixteenth century, Sufism had reached a rather low ebb and was tainted with many superstitions. Hence its absorption into a superficially Islamized population, such as that of the Sultanate of Sinnar, was much easier because local customs and superstitions were simply assimilated by the *sufi* orders. Thirdly, saint cult and *baraka* (divine blessing) were both heritable and appealed to Sudan's tribes since they offered the population intermediaries with God. Consequently, the *fuqara'* (dervish), or *fikis* (a corruption of *faqih*, Muslim jurist), as they were locally known, were better understood and more popular than the learned and knowledgeable *fuqaha'* or *'ulama'*. An important element of this Islamic penetration for the Hijaz was the introduction of the Qadiriyya and the Shadhiliyya orders into Nilotic Sudan. Neither of them was centralized at the time and hence they were easily absorbed within the cult of holy men and their *zawiyas* who presented 'the embryonic Islamic civilization in a pagan environment'.[2] The Qadiriyya succeeded in Sudan because 'it adapted itself readily to the peculiarities and idiosyncrasies of whatever

---

[1] Hasan, *Islam*; Hasan, *Islamization of Sudan*, 73–86; Holt, *Holy Families*; Trimingham, *Islam*.

[2] Trimingham, *Islam*, 101.

1

society it penetrated'.[3] In an article on the role of the *'ulama'* in spreading Islam in the Sudan, Muhammad Ibrahim Abu Salim stated the following. First, in Sudan, unlike in other Muslim states, there was no class of *'ulama'* who fulfilled special religious, cultural or social functions, as distinct from other religious leaders. Secondly, the Sudanese *'alim* was first and foremost a loyal member of a *sufi* order, since Sufism was regarded in Sudan as the confirmed path to piety. Finally, Sudanese esteem, as far as men of religion were concerned, preferred *tasawwuf* over *'ilm*. The Sudanese *'alim* was therefore in most cases, a *sufi* who having studied the *Qur'an*, had decided to devote himself to further religious studies.[4]

Among those who introduced Islam into the Funj Sultanate there were 'holy families', who settled among the tribes, established their own Qur'an schools, and gained both influence and wealth.[5] The Awlad Jabir were one of the holy families who played an active role in the Islamization of Sudan from the beginning of the Funj sultanate. They established schools in the Nilotic Sudan as well as in Dar Fur and Wadai, and accumulated considerable wealth and social standing. The graduates of their schools became teachers in various parts of Sudan.[6] The Awlad Jabir also provide a good example of the accumulation of wealth and economic power in the hands of some of holy families. Like many riverain tribesmen stemming from the Ja'aliyyin and the Danaqla, who were driven from the Nile Valley to seek their fortunes in western Sudan, the Awlad Jabir, also established branches of their family in Dar Fur and Wadai probably as part of this migration. But unlike the riverain tribesmen, who sought occupation primarily in trading, the Awlad Jabir, apart from their teaching activities, enhanced their positions as major landowners and administrators. Their estates differed in size and value and in some cases included whole villages, as well as numerous slaves.[7] Another holy family which may serve to illustrate the religious, social and economic impact these holy men had under the Funj was the Majdhubiyya. They were a religious clan, from among the Ja'aliyyin, who established a *khalwa* at al-Damir (al-Damar) probably in the mid-seventeenth century. As a Ja'ali clan, the Majadhib claimed descent from 'Abbas, the Prophet's uncle. The founder of the Majdhubiyya was a Ja'ali *faqih*, Hamad ibn Muhammad al-Majdhub (b.1693/4), who studied the *Maliki* legal treatises in Sudan and later made the pilgrimage to Mecca, where he studied and joined the Shadhiliyya *sufi* order. Upon his return he reorganized the community of al-Damir, which was thereafter, dominated by

[3] Karsani, *Beyond Sufism*, 136, quoted from McHugh, *Holy Men*, 130.

[4] Abu Salim, *Dawr al-'ulama'*.

[5] For details see the contemporary chronicle written by *katib al-shuna* known as 'The Funj Chronicle', in Holt, *Funj Chronicle*; also *idem. Holy Families*.

[6] For details of their history and their religious teachings, see Holt, *Sons of Jabir* in Holt, *Studies*, 88–103; and *idem, Holy Families*.

[7] O'Fahey & Abu Salim, *Land in Dar Fur*, 18–19; see also Klein, *Awlad Jabir*.

himself and his offspring. During that period Sinnar was in decline, but Islamic beliefs and institutions had gradually overcome traditional African ones and consequently al-Damir, under the influence of the Majadhib, became a flourishing religious centre. When James Bruce visited it in 1774, he described it as 'a town *belonging* to Fakir Wed Madge Doub [*sic* – wad Majdhub]', who is worshipped by the Ja'aliyyin. When, in 1814, Burckhardt visited the town, he wrote that all power was vested in al-Faqih al-Kabir, while *baraka* was no longer confined only to the head of the Majadhib but had spread to other members of the family and even to some who were not related to it. Many of these *faqih*s had their own chapels next to their houses. But, according to Burckhardt 'Friday prayers were always performed in the great mosque' of the Majadhib which also included a *madrasa* (a school of Islamic studies). The *madrasa* emphasized the training of students from as far away as Kordofan and Dar Fur, in Islamic law. The teachers were mostly Majadhib '*ulama*' who had studied in Cairo or Mecca. Al-Damir thus became a known centre for the administration of justice, according to Islamic law. The office of *al-faqih al-kabir* (the great jurist) remained hereditary within the Majdhubiyya and his powers were considerable. Opposition to the Majadhib, even among the nomads in al-Damir's vicinity seems to have been negligible and their power, though derived from their religious standing, soon embraced all aspects of al-Damir's political, social and economic life.[8]

In order to comprehend the Islamic background of the Mahdiyya and the *Weltanschauung* of Muhammad Ahmad, its founder and first leader, an understanding of Sudan's larger, centralized *sufi* brotherhoods is also required. The intellectual innovations of the eighteenth- and nineteenth-century *sufi* orders, primarily attributed to Shaykh Ahmad ibn Idris, are not the concern of the present study nor are they particularly relevant to the impact of the *sufi* heritage in Sudan on the Mahdiyya.[9] Within a study of the Mahdiyya it is however relevant that some of these orders, notably the Sammaniyya and the Khatmiyya, introduced new organizational structures that paved the way for gaining cross-tribal support within wider territories. This pattern of expansion entailed the incorporation of pre-existing religious centres into this new *tariqa* network. The Sammaniyya was the first of these new supra-national *sufi* brotherhoods. Muhammad b. 'Abd al-Karim al-Samman (1718–75), the founder of the new order, was initiated into the Khalwatiyya while on a visit to Cairo in 1760. Both he and his

---

[8] Spaulding, *Heroic Age*, 173–4, quoted from Bruce, *Travels*, 451, also Burckhardt, *Travels*, 236. According to Hofheinz, *Internalising Islam*, 22, Hamad b. 'Abdallah b. Muhammad founded the first *khalwa* of the Majdhubiyya as early as the mid-seventeenth century. I am grateful to Hofheinz for sending me a copy of his dissertation in February 2001. However, since by then I had completed the final draft of this work, I was unable to make full use of his new findings.

[9] O'Fahey and Radtke, *Neo-Sufism*, 52–87; also O'Fahey, *Enigmatic Saint*.

successors continued to live in al-Madina and it was through their *khulafa'* that their message was propagated in Indonesia, Malaysia and Sudan. One of these was Ahmad al-Tayyib wad al-Bashir, who had also been initiated into the order while on a pilgrimage to al-Madina, in about 1764. He succeeded in recruiting Sudanese followers especially in the Gezira, south of Omdurman, where the Hamaj Regent Nasir b. Muhammad Abi Likaylik, joined the order and granted him an estate. Furthermore, several of the religious shaykhs of the earlier *sufi* orders such as the Halawiyyun, the Ya'qubab, and the Qadiriyya, also joined the Sammaniyya. The importance of this development lay in the fact that the prevailing trend in Sudanese Sufism had been one of small and rather diffused orders that had very little influence outside their limited circle of followers.[10] The arrival of more centralized and better-organized supranational orders, of which the Sammaniyya was a forerunner, helped to create an Islamic establishment whose impact exceeded tribal or regional boundaries and hence had wider political implications. However, the Sammaniyya lost its impact soon after its founder's death. Ahmad al-Tayyib wad al-Bashir died in 1824, shortly after the Turco-Egyptian conquest of Sudan, without nominating his successor. Consequently the followers of the order split into several groups under the leadership of Muhammad Sharif Nur al-Da'im (d.1908/9), al-Qurashi wad al-Zayn (d.1878) and Ahmad al-Basir (d.1830). Hence the Sammaniyya, instead of assuming the stature of a centralized order with branches in several regions, split into numerous autonomous suborders, due to clashes of personality as well as ethnic and regional loyalties.[11] This diffusion was exploited successfully by Muhammad Ahmad, the future Mahdi.

The Khatmiyya was another such supranational order. It was first introduced into Sudan by Muhammad 'Uthman al-Mirghani (1793-1852), a member of a Sharifian family who had studied under Ahmad ibn Idris. He toured the Funj Sultanate on al-Idrisi's behalf in 1815–19, namely on the eve of its conquest by the Turco-Egyptian army. In 1816 he entered Kordofan, which was then a province of the Sultanate of Dar Fur, and laid the foundations of his *tariqa*. His attempt to establish a foothold in Sinnar in 1817 largely failed and it was only in 1819 that he established his first mosque and school in al-Matamma in Ja'aliyyin country. While on the Nile, Muhammad 'Uthman realized that the Egyptian invasion was advancing and instead of moving north, where he would have encountered the Egyptian army, he left for Massawa on the Red Sea and by 1822 was back in Mecca.[12] Following the death of Ibn Idris, in October 1837, Muhammad 'Uthman sent his son Muhammad al-Hasan al-Mirghani, to found a Khatmiyya branch in what had become Turco-Egyptian Sudan and acquired immediate government

[10] For details see Karrar, *Sufi Brotherhoods*, especially 42–72.
[11] *Ibid.*, 43–8.
[12] For details see O'Fahey, *Enigmatic Saint*, 142–9; also Hofheinz, *Internalising Islam*, 156–8.

support from the new regime. Al-Sayyid al-Hasan al-Mirghani was born in Bara in Kordofan in 1819 and was later sent to Mecca where he memorized the Qur'an and studied with his father a wide range of Islamic topics. Following his graduation he was ordered by his father to return to Sudan, which was already ruled by Muhammad 'Ali's agents, and to act as his representative (*khalifa*) in that country. Sayyid al-Hasan started an intensive missionary campaign in the riverain and eastern regions of northern Sudan. He appointed agents from among Khatmiyya supporters, including several contemporary holy men, as well as previous followers of the Shadhiliyya order, who had transferred their allegiance to him. The Khatmiyya's great success in Sudan probably resulted from the following factors. First, due to its superior organization it was able to face challenges to its influence and did not suffer from internal splits like those which, as noted above, afflicted the Sammaniyya. Secondly, the Khatmiyya was the first among the new *sufi* orders of the Idrisi tradition to arrive in Sudan and hence its message was more coherent and less tainted by local superstitions. Thirdly, and probably most importantly, Sayyid al-Hasan exploited the fact that the older and smaller *sufi* orders had been largely discredited and partly destroyed by Sudan's Egyptian rulers. He thus came to the riverain tribes, such as the Sha'iqiyya, as the charismatic holy man in whose *tariqa* they could find a substitute for their traditional institutions and superstitious *fikis*. Lastly, the Khatmiyya benefited from its association with Sudan's new rulers, namely the Turco-Egyptians, whose conquest of Sudan coincided with the expansion of their *tariqa*. It is important to note that al-Sayyid al-Hasan al-Mirghani associated with the Turco-Egyptian rulers at the explicit wish of his father, who probably realized the political advantages of such an association.[13] Thus on the eve of the Turco-Egyptian conquest, the political, economic and social power of the new *sufi* orders and the well-established holy families was superior to that of central government in the disintegrating Funj sultanate.

[13] Karrar, *Sufi Brotherhoods*, 75–6. According to Karrar neither Ibn Idris nor Muhammad 'Uthman al-Mirghani had previous relations with the Turkish rulers but his orders to al-Hasan stated explicitly that he should not follow in his footsteps in this regard but should establish close relations with the Turks.

2

ISLAM AND STATE UNDER
THE TURKIYYA, 1820–81

The annexation of Sudan to Egypt was undertaken in two stages. The first, in 1820–2, under Muhammad 'Ali the Ottoman *wali* of Egypt and Egypt's de facto ruler until 1848, embraced primarily central northern Sudan. The second stage of this conquest was completed under his grandson, the Khedive Isma'il during the 1870s, when he extended Egyptian rule to the Great Lakes in Central Africa and to Bahr al-Ghazal and Dar Fur in western Sudan. In the history of Sudan this period became known as the First Turkiyya. The term Turkiyya is not really arbitrary since Egypt itself was an Ottoman province, ruled by an Ottoman (Albanian) dynasty. Moreover, most of the high officials and army officers serving in Sudan were of Ottoman rather than Egyptian origin. Lastly, though Arabic made considerable headway during the second half of the nineteenth century in Sudan's daily administrative usage, the senior officers and officials continued to communicate in Ottoman Turkish, since their superior – the *khedive* – was of Ottoman origin and Turkish was the language of the ruling elite. The Egyptian army brought with it three *'ulama'*, belonging to the *shafi'i, hanafi* and *maliki* schools. Of the three only the *maliki qadi*, Ahmad al-Salawi, played a significant role since most of the Sudanese were *maliki*s. He supported their schools, befriended their *'ulama'* and granted young Sudanese graduates employment opportunities in the newly founded shari'a courts and in other government offices. He was also the first to encourage Sudanese *'ulama'* to put pen to paper and consequently we have to thank him for Ahmad Abu 'Ali's history of the Kings of Sinnar, known as 'The Funj Chronicle' (*katib al-shuna*), which is a primary source of knowledge of the period.[14]

Although the conquered regions of northern Sudan were Arabicized and superficially Islamized, the new rulers badly needed a local élite with whom they could communicate and whom they could trust to act on their behalf in fulfilling certain administrative functions, hitherto unknown in the newly annexed territories. The Sudanese elite at the time of the invasion consisted primarily of two elements: tribal shaykhs and heads of holy families and *sufi* orders. The Ottoman Egyptians viewed neither of these groups

---

[14] Abu Salim, *Dawr al-'ulama'*, 81; see also Holt, *Funj Chronicle*, fn. 4.

as fully trustworthy, since both were naturally loyal to their local adherents
and in the case of the *sufi*s and *fiki*s, their mysticism – tainted with local
superstitions – was abhorrent to the new rulers. They therefore looked for
possible allies who seemed to be more dependable and hence could act as
trustworthy collaborators. Among the tribal population their choice fell on
the Sha'iqiyya, one of the northern riverain tribes whose villages were
spread along the Nile south of the Egyptian border. They had fought against
the Egyptian army when it first invaded northern Sudan, in 1820, but following their defeat had become trustworthy allies of the new rulers. The
Sha'iqiyya supplied the government with irregular soldiers (*bash buzuq*)
who acted as tax collectors among the other tribes and were in return
exempt from taxation. Military raids led by the Sha'iqiyya became a regular
method of tax collection. Thus in 1830, when the governor-general of
Sudan Khurshid Pasha, could not pay his troops for lack of income, he set
out with the Sha'iqiyya to raid the tribes in the vicinity of al-Qadarif in order
to pay his troops and compensate his allies. Another tribe whose interests
seemed at first to coincide with Sudan's new rulers were the Ja'aliyyin, who
were leading *jallaba* (traders) and hence benefited from the newly established order. The Ja'aliyyin *jallaba*, as well as traders from other riverain
tribes, engaged in barter trading especially during slack agricultural seas-
ons when their small farms could be left in the hands of their families and
their slaves. They initially welcomed Turkish rule since in addition to
security it also led to greater prosperity through the establishment of military posts and improved communications. However, heavy taxation soon
drove many of the smaller riverain farmers from their lands, since they were
in no position to pay the hitherto unknown taxes. Furthermore, shortage of
cash with which to pay these taxes forced them to hand over their cattle and
their house slaves on whom their agricultural production depended. The
Egyptian historian Muhammad Fu'ad Shukri thus lists the heavy taxes,
which in numerous cases exceeded the value of the taxed article, as a major
cause for discontent which ultimately led to the Ja'aliyyin revolt in 1822–
3. He also emphasized the brutality and corruption involved in the extrac-
tion of these taxes by the Sha'iqiyya tax collectors. In fact the mass escape
of oppressed peasants who could not pay their taxes from riverain Sudan
to the outlying regions of western Sudan such as Dar Fur, the Nuba Mountains and Bahr al-Ghazal, created a new class of migratory *jallaba* who
thrived in these regions and became involved in ivory and slave trading.
Most of them made their livelihood as small merchants hoping to return to
their homes once they struck rich. But this happened to only a few of them,
primarily to those who engaged in large-scale ivory or slave trading. Others
became pedlars and middlemen and could barely make ends meet.[15]

The Turco-Egyptian conquest thus established a relatively modern

[15] Shukri, *Al-Hukm al-Misri*, 221–42; Spaulding, *Land Tenure*, 17–19; see also Bjorkelo,
Turco-Jallaba Relations, 84–9.

administrative system in Sudan with which neither the old holy families nor the *sufi* orders could compete. Within the traditional Islamic elite there consequently emerged a feeling of hostility, leading to identity or solidarity transcending both tribes and villages, against the Turkiyya as the common enemy. Those who rebelled, such as the Ja'aliyyin and the Majdhubiyya, suffered defeat and the latter's mosque in al-Damir was burnt. Those, who collaborated with the new administration, such as the Sha'iqiyya and the Khatmiyya, succeeded in breaking out of their confined regions and becoming part of the state system, creating centralized organizations throughout the Sudan.[16] In a study published in 1988 and entitled 'The Fallacy of Egyptian Colonization of Sudan', the Egyptian historian 'Abd al-'Azim Ramadan, goes one step further.[17] He described Sudan as 'Egypt's strategic depth', and claimed that Egypt provided Sudan with similar strategic advantages. Ramadan stated that, historically, there were never any borders between Egypt and Sudan, rulers of one region often ruled the other and territories frequently changed hands. Since nationalism was unknown in either Egypt or Sudan, it was only natural that Egyptian *'ulama'* from al-Azhar had asked Muhammad 'Ali, a foreigner, to rule over them. Similarly, it did not seem wrong for Sudanese Muslim leaders to ask the Egyptian *wali* to rule in their region. Not unlike the Azharite *'ulama'* in Egypt, they were motivated predominantly by Islam and hence the ethnic origin of the ruler was of little consequence.[18] In contrast to the conclusions of many European, Egyptian and Sudanese historians, that Turco-Egyptian rule in Sudan had imperialist–colonial motives, Ramadan claimed that Egypt's control of Sudan was on the whole benevolent. It introduced orderly government, reduced taxes – when they seemed excessive – and appointed Sudanese notables to central administrative positions. It constituted a 'legitimate extension' of the borders of Egypt, just as the United States extended its dominions in the nineteenth century to the south and the west of the American Continent.[19] Arriving at another important aspect of Egyptian rule in Sudan, namely that of the slave trade, Ramadan stated that slavery was not an Egyptian invention and had been practiced extensively in the Sudan, under the Funj Sultanate, by European traders as well as by others.[20]

The Khatmiyya was, as mentioned above, the only well-organized *sufi* order that fully collaborated with the Turco-Egyptian rulers. Not unlike the government, the Khatmiyya encouraged a more centralized 'orthodox' Islam rather than the diffused *fiki*-orientated Sufism that had prevailed in the Funj Sultanate. It therefore found natural allies in the Turco-Egyptian rulers. The religious centres of the Khatmiyya were not only tolerated, but

[16] Voll, *Stateness*, 15–18.
[17] Ramadan, *Ukdhubat*.
[18] *Ibid.*, 24–6.
[19] *Ibid.*, 59–66; compare with Rafi'i, *'Asr*, 171–2.
[20] Ramadan, *Ukdhubat*, 10–11.

were even subsidized by the new rulers, who also exempted the Khatmiyya shaykhs from taxation. As for the older generation of holy clans and *sufi* orders, several methods were employed in order to undermine their leadership, although with varying degrees of success. The introduction of shari'a courts and government-subsidized Qur'an schools (*khalwas* or *kuttab*s) was aimed at curtailing the *sufi* hold over their adherents. In certain cases, sons of *sufi* leaders were sent to al-Azhar to study and were later appointed to government posts as teachers or *qadi*s. However, the Turkiyya failed in its attempts to replace *sufi* orders or local *fiki*s with its newly imported Azharite *'ulama'*. This was the result of the popularity of local holy men among the rural population. The *fuqara'*, as they were called, did not perform a merely religious function, they also played a dominant social role in spheres such as education and health within their societies. Hence, even after the introduction of educated *'ulama'*, shari'a courts, government schools and modern clinics, the majority of the rural Muslims continued to prefer their local 'holy men' since they were imbued with *karama* (saintliness) and *baraka* (blessing). People who suffered from government oppression, taxation and forced labour could hardly be expected to trust the Azhar-trained *qadi* or *'alim*, who were after all government employees. Instead they remained loyal to the *fuqara'* who had healed them and guided them through previous calamities and who shared similar interests.[21]

Relations between the Khatmiyya and the government were not always cordial and after Sayyid al-Hasan al-Mirghani's death several Khatmi agents were arrested and their privileges were abolished. Thus, when attempting to explain the success of the Khatmiyya's missionary campaign, emphasis should also be placed on the appeal of its spiritual message, on the one hand, and on the charisma of Sayyid al-Hasan, on the other. Sayyid al-Hasan died on 18 November 1869 and his son, Sayyid Muhammad 'Uthman al-Mirghani II, was recognized by the family and the principal agents of the Khatmiyya as his successor. He had to face several challenges following his appointment. There was, as mentioned above, a change in the attitude of the government towards the order which brought about the arrest of several Khatmiyya leaders and the cancellation of their privileges. It affected especially the northern regions of Dongola and Berber, both strongholds of the Khatmiyya. Luckily for Sayyid Muhammad 'Uthman II, the change in government policy was a temporary setback and after 1873 cordial relations were once again resumed.[22] A further challenge to the Khatmiyya emerged at that time due to the arrival in the Sha'iqiyya region of numerous additional followers of Shaykh Ibn Idris who founded the new Ahmadiyya Idrissiyya order in that region. There is no evidence that al-Mirghani's claim that the Khatmiyya was the 'seal' of Sufism, namely the

[21] Gaddal, *Religion*, 51–3.
[22] Karrar, *Sufi Brotherhoods*, 86–7, 88–91.

ultimate *tariqa* and that he was the last of the *awliya'* from whose descendants the expected *mahdi* would appear, was connected with these challenges.[23] It is therefore hardly surprising that when Muhammad Ahmad made his manifestation as *al-mahdi al-muntazar* (the expected Mahdi), in June 1881, Sayyid Muhammad 'Uthman II sent out messages in which he denounced the Mahdi as an impostor and the Mahdiyya as a 'blind and deaf sedition whose advocates were at the gates of hell'.[24] Both the Tijaniyya and the Khatmiyya claimed the ranks of *qutb al-aqtab* (Lord of the Saints) and seal of all *sufi* orders, on the basis of direct prophetic sanction.[25] Their denunciation of Muhammad Ahmad's claim to be the *mahdi* was therefore a natural outcome. According to some accounts the Mahdi even offered Muhammad 'Uthman II the post of one of his four *khulafa'* but the latter declined. Instead he helped to recruit anti-Mahdist forces among his followers in eastern Sudan. In June 1884, when it became clear that the Mahdiyya was gaining ground, Muhammad 'Uthman escaped with his younger son, 'Ali al-Mirghani, via Massawa to Sawakin, from where he proceeded to Egypt and continued to make propaganda against the Mahdiyya until the Mahdist state was destroyed in September 1898. It is therefore no wonder that when the Khatmiyya headquarters near Kassala was conquered by the Mahdist *amir* 'Uthman Diqna, its central mosque and Sayyid al-Hasan al-Mirghani's tomb were both destroyed.[26]

Muhammad Ahmad b. 'Abdallah, the future *mahdi*, was initiated into the Sammaniyya at an early stage of his life. Muhammad Sharif Nur al-Da'im, the founder's grandson, was his first *sufi* teacher but the latter expelled him from the *tariqa* following a dispute. Muhammad Ahmad then transferred his allegiance to al-Qurashi wad al-Zayn, a Sammani shaykh of a rival branch, and later married his daughter. He stayed with his new teacher until 1878 and helped to erect Shaykh Qurashi's tomb following his death in the same year. It concequence the Sammaniyya under al-Qurashi wad al-Zayn and his successor Muhammad al-Tayyib al-Basir, to whom Muhammad Ahmad remained loyal, joined the Mahdiyya at the outset, while his first Sammani teacher, Shaykh Muhammad Sharif Nur al-Da'im and his followers continued to oppose him. The internal leadership quarrels, within the Sammaniyya tend to prove that unlike the Khatmiyya order which arrived at a later stage, the Sammaniyya lost its impact within a rather short time due to the lack of central leadership, on the one hand, and ethnic and regional disputes, on the other. The Sammaniyya may therefore be

[23] O'Fahey and Radtke, *Neo-Sufism*, 82; a similar claim was made by al-Qurashi wad al-Zayn, a shaykh of the Sammaniyya, a few years later (see below).

[24] O'Fahey and Radtke, *Neo-Sufism*, 83, quoted from the Bergen photographic collection; NI 298, 15/26; for further details on the Khatmiyya's relations with the Mahdiyya see Karrar, *Sufi Brotherhoods*, 93–102.

[25] Cited in O'Fahey and Radtke, *Neo-Sufism*, 67.

[26] Dhaher, *Al-Mirghani*, 3–12.

considered 'a halfway house between the older orders and the new centralized ones'.[27] The Mahdi inadvertently benefited from the fragmentation of
the Sammaniyya since, in a centralized order under one shaykh recognized
by all followers, he would hardly have succeeded in his claim to be the expected *mahdi*. The Mahdiyya needed a centralized Islamic structure to
enable it to spread its message. But, unlike the Khatmiyya, Mahdist revivalism was intertwined with the social and economic transformation of the
state, which made cooperation with the rulers impossible. The socio-
economic policies adopted by the Turco-Egyptian rulers, especially with
regard to the slave-trade, played into the Mahdi's hands since, as a result
of this policy, the people of Sudan were 'ready to hear and participate in
the mission of "reviving" Islam in their area.'[28]

[27] Karrar, *Sufi Brotherhoods*, 48.
[28] Voll, *Revivalism*; the reference is quoted from 177–8.

3

SOCIAL, ECONOMIC AND GEOPOLITICAL FACTORS LEADING TO REVOLT

As already noted the Mahdist revolt also owed its success to administrative, social, economic and financial factors. The growth of Khartoum as the seat of the Turkish government was one of the most striking phenomena of the Turkiyya. A small village, at the time of the Turkish conquest, Khartoum was chosen for its strategic importance, being situated at the confluence of the Blue and White Niles. 'Uthman Bey Jarkas al-Birjini, who was appointed to command the troops in Sudan, came to the conclusion that Wad Madani was unsuitable as the capital and selected Khartoum instead. Thus in 1833 Khartoum became the capital of Sudan and started to develop rapidly at the expense of other traditional urban centres such as Sinnar, Wad Madani, Shendi, al-Matamma or al-Damir. After the opening of the White Nile for merchants, coinciding with the abolition of the monopolies in the 1840s, Khartoum attracted many foreign trading companies and was thus in a position to offer employment to a relatively large number of migrant wage-earners. These included many of the previous *saqiyya* (water-wheel) farmers who, as already mentioned, had abandoned their lands due to high taxation and the new system of land tenure. The growth of Khartoum and other new towns, both in the east and in the west, was also facilitated by the increase in military and administrative centres under the Turkiyya. In these new centres the influence of the older established holy families and *fuqara'* was naturally diminished. El-Obeid, provincial capital of Kordofan, became an administrative as well as a commercial centre for the west. Many of the Danaqla, the Ja'aliyyin and other riverain tribes made their way as *jallaba* to Kordofan in search of a better living. El-Obeid became their centre of activity and, once the monopolies were abolished trading links both with foreign firms and with their riverain kinsmen developed rapidly. Foreign firms brought their merchandise to Khartoum and other market towns while the *jallaba*, who were their agents, sold these goods throughout Sudan. The old overland routes from the Nile through Kordofan to southern Dar Fur became important for this trade.[29]

[29] Björkelo, *Turco-Jallaba Relations*, 90–1; Hill, *Egypt in Sudan*, 19; Stiansen, *Imperialism*, 38–58.

One of the major hardships in Sudan was the shortage of cash and hence the difficulty of paying the newly imposed taxes. Peasants, who were not in a position to pay, became indebted to the *jallaba* or to tax collectors, while nomadic tribes, such as the Baqqara, became dependent on the *jallaba* for similar reasons. In the 1840s, when shipments of cattle to Egypt were brought to an end, the *jallaba* stepped in as intermediaries. The Baqqara, unable to provide cash continued to pay their annual tribute in cattle. The cattle were sold to the *jallaba* for cash, and they then resold them to the Baqqara in exchange for slaves. Towards the end of the Turkiyya, this chain of exchange was refined. The *jallaba* in Kordofan paid the Baqqara's annual tribute directly to the tax collectors and were rewarded by them with a regular supply of slaves. Many of these slaves were then transported to the Nile Valley where they were employed in agriculture by the riverain tribes. If we remember that most of the *jallaba* in western Sudan were Ja'aliyyin or Danaqla who belonged to the same riverain tribes as the farmers, the economic advantage gained by these tribes becomes self-evident.[30]

Turco-Egyptian rule thus brought to Sudan its first experience with orderly centralized government and laid the foundation of a Sudanese state. In addition to increased taxation, it introduced modern methods of agriculture and trade. However, this proved a mixed blessing since it involved competition of Egyptian and European entrepreneurs with local businessmen. Trade had existed in Sudan prior to the Turkiyya, though on a rather small scale. The rulers of Dar Fur and Sinnar employed agents to act on their behalf in trading with Egypt. Thus Shendi, seat of the *makk* (king) of the Ja'aliyyin, was an important market town with a population of some 6,000, prior to the Turkish conquest. Though it was destroyed following the Ja'aliyyin uprising against the Turks in 1822–3, it resumed its former position as a trading centre later in the nineteenth century, when it became the last station for the pilgrimage caravans leading to Sawakin on the Red Sea.[31]

The ownership of land and slaves was a precondition for prospering in nineteenth century Sudan and the emerging middle class, consisting mainly of riverain tribes, achieved this by collaborating with the Turkish ruling élite. Since each *saqiyya* (water-wheel) was taxed at a fixed rate, labour intensive production was essential for obtaining high profits. Slave labour therefore predominated quite early in the more fertile lands adjacent to the Nile. Tax in these regions was imposed on *saqiyya*s and was assessed in accordance with the area they irrigated. Excessive taxation brought about a rapid decrease in the number of the *saqiyya*s operated. Thus, a survey undertaken in Berber province in 1827 revealed that only 796 out of 2,437 *saqiyya*s were in full operation. Another land tax, called *jad'a* (an

---

[30] Björkelo, *Turco-Jallaba Relations*, 92–5.
[31] Warburg, *Social and Economic Aspects*, 778–9.

area of about 5¹/₃ acres), was imposed on other cultivated lands, regardless of the harvest, which, of course, differed from one year to another. This, yet again, brought about a decline in cultivation as many farmers escaped in order to avoid taxation. But, since the village was responsible for payment, the remaining farmers had to pay the difference, which in turn resulted in a further decline in cultivation and resentment of central government by the farmers. Tribal and religious leaders were in many cases exempt from taxation in return for their loyalty and willingness to collect taxes. They included among others both the Sha'iqiyya tribe and the Khatmiyya *sufi* order which as noted above, were consequently resented by others.[32]

The more moderate methods implemented in later years in order to induce farmers who had escaped out of government reach to return to their lands apparently had some favourable effect. Many of the Ja'aliyyin and the 'Arakiyyin who had escaped from their lands following their rebellion in 1822–3 returned and resumed cultivation in the late 1830s, once taxes were decreased to meet their demands. However, when in 1879 Muhammad Ra'uf Pasha – then Governor-General – suggested a reform of Sudanese taxes, the situation was apparently unacceptable. In the ten years 1869–79, taxes for Sudan had been assessed at £E3,840,175, while only £E2,962,711 were in effect collected. According to Carl Giegler, then deputy governor-general, five out of eleven provinces were governed at a loss in 1878. The deficit in Dar Fur amounted to £E113,000, in Equatoria £E39,000, Khartoum £E18,385, Sinnar £E22,209 and Somali Coast £E14,241. Ra'uf suggested lowering taxation, which he considered a major evil since it continued to lead to the abandonment of agricultural lands and hence to the loss of revenue. His suggestion was rejected by Cairo on the grounds that he had produced insufficient evidence to support his case. Egyptian authorities cited inefficiency, rather than overtaxation, as the major reason for the discrepancy between their assessment of taxes and those collected.[33]

In 1863, following the return of Speke and Grant from their historic journey to discover the sources of the Nile, British public and official opinion became concerned with the slave trade in Sudan. Six years later Samuel Baker was entrusted by Khedive Isma'il with what he called 'the greatest expedition of our times'. Between Baker's first expedition in 1862 and his second in 1869–73, slave hunting and trading had increased greatly throughout Sudan. Yet Baker claimed that, within four years of his second expedition, he had succeeded against enormous odds in suppressing the slave-trade completely. His claim that 'should the slave-trade recommence

[32] *Ibid.*, 773–8; also Spaulding, *Land Tenure*, 1–20.

[33] Hill, *Egypt in Sudan*, 37–42; see also Hill, *Giegler Pasha*, 141–57. Carl Christian Giegler Pasha, of German origin, served in the Sudan telegraph service from 1873–83; he was also Deputy Governor-General of Sudan under Gordon, Ra'uf and 'Abd al-Qadir Hilmi.

when I leave, it will be the fault of the Soudan Authorities'[34] could not be corroborated. In July 1873 Khedive Isma'il, while on a visit to Istanbul, submitted to the British Ambassador, Sir Henry Elliot, the draft of a convention for the suppression of the slave-trade. The timing was not a coincidence since, on 8 June of that year, Isma'il had gained from the Ottoman Sultan – with British help – yet another concession. The new *firman* codifying all Isma'il's previous concessions since 1866, granted the Khedive and his successors the continued rule, not only of Egypt and Sudan, but also of Sawakin, Massawa and their environs. What concerned Britain primarily was the increased-trade in the Red Sea in slaves originating from West Africa, which they believed could only be stopped if the British Navy were allowed to search Egyptian ships and boats in that region. Since all Egyptian vessels sailed under the Ottoman flag, the Khedive could not grant this concession without Ottoman consent, even had he so desired. In September 1874 the British consul in Cairo proposed the appointment of British consular officers in Sawakin and Massawa, which, he stated, could virtually suppress the export of slaves from Sudan. However, it was only in January 1876 that following agreement with the Ottoman Sultan, the British Foreign Office finally instructed its Consul in Cairo to take up the matter of an anti-slave-trade convention with the Khedive. Isma'il tried once again to exploit the negotiations in order to gain further concessions in the Red Sea, as well as continued control of the Somali coast and the demarcation of Egypt's border with Zanzibar. The Convention for the Suppression of Slave Trade was finally signed by the Egyptian and British governments on 4 August 1877. Under this convention boats of either signatory – suspected of being involved in slave-trade could be seized by the authorities of the signatories in order to be searched, and, if found guilty, those responsible would be brought to trial.[35] However, the convention was quite ineffective since Khedive Isma'il was forced to abdicate in 1879, before the convention was implemented. Thereafter, central administration in both Egypt and Sudan deteriorated rapidly and the slave-trade continued to flourish.

Hit by General Charles Gordon's anti-slavery measures in the 1870s, the proclamation made by Muhammad Ahmad al-Mahdi that slavery was once again a legitimate institution was greeted by Egyptian and Sudanese *jallaba* with relief and, not surprisingly, they joined him in great numbers. However, some *jallaba* had made their fortunes in collaboration with Egyptian merchants and depended on free trade between Dongola and Egypt. Hence the Mahdist revolt threatened their livelihood and some of them went into exile with their Turco-Egyptian trading partners. The importance of the *jallaba* association with the rulers during the Turkiyya is

---

[34] Abbas, *Slave Trade*, 43–5; the quotation is from an interview with Samuel Baker published in *The Times*, 13 Aug. 1873.

[35] Abbas, *Slave Trade*, 89–95.

thus manifold. With the abolition of the government monopolies and the lifting of trade restrictions in the late 1840s, some of the *jallaba* struck rich not only as a result of their association with foreign trading companies but also because they found profitable ways in which to associate with the Turkish administration and its army. Some of them achieved important administrative positions since they were, by and large, the most educated segment of Sudanese society. Most notable among these was Ilyas Umm Birayr, a Ja'ali merchant who was appointed Governor of Kordofan, with the title of Pasha, in 1878. Some *jallaba* also joined punitive and slave-raiding campaigns where they could purchase booty and slaves at low prices or in exchange for goods, which they provided *en route*. Since the Turkish soldiers were often paid in slaves, the *jallaba* were in a position to dictate their price. The importance of *jallaba* association with the rulers during the Turkiyya was thus considerable.[36] However, in this case too, the sword followed the trade. It was the greatest Ja'ali *jallab*, al-Zubayr Rahma Mansur, who, having erected his own slave kingdom in south-western Sudan, later handed both Bahr al-Ghazal and Dar Fur to the Khedive Isma'il.[37]

Dar Fur was of prime importance in this regard since it provided a safe haven for slave traders during the second half of the nineteenth century, along *darb al-arba'in* (the forty-days route). The first description of *darb al-arba'in* dates from 1698, though it is known to have existed earlier. Its prime use during the nineteenth century was for the slave-trade and it owed its popularity to its remoteness and hence its relative safety. It was estimated that between 5,000 to 6,000 slaves were transported annually from Dar Fur to Egypt along the *darb al-arba'in*.[38] However, during the late eighteenth and nineteenth centuries the more direct route from Dar Fur to Sudan gradually assumed an important role also for the pilgrimage to Mecca. The first to traverse this route were pilgrims from Dar Fur and Wadai who, being poor, could not afford the trip along the safer but longer *darb al-arba'in*. They were soon joined by poor pilgrims from Bornu and the Hausaland, who established the first village of so-called *fallata* in Sudan in the mid-eighteenth century at Ras al-Fil. The famous Swiss traveller John Burckhardt described the alternative routes of the pilgrimage from Dar Fur to the Hijaz at the beginning of the nineteenth century. Apart from the traditional northerly route leading to Egypt along the 'forty-day-road', there were two routes to the east. The first headed to Sinnar and from there to Gondar and Massawa. The second, and more frequented one, led north on the Nile to Shendi or Berber and from there, eastward to Sawakin. Most of these pilgrims were, according to Burckhardt, destitute and made their way through Sudan by begging or by performing

[36] Hill, *Egypt in Sudan*, 141–52, Björkelo, *Prelude to the Mahdiyya*, 143–5.
[37] Björkelo, *Prelude to the Mahdiyya*, 123–4, 142–3.
[38] O'Fahey, *Religion and Trade*, 92–3.

manual labour. However, some of these pilgrims, once familiar with the new route, realized its trading potential and joined the caravans on a regular basis, thus establishing a trade route between Dar Fur, Kordofan and the Hijaz. Pilgrims also engaged in trading in merchandise such as books, ivory and slaves, though only on a small scale. The writing of amulets was their most favoured source of livelihood, since Sudanese Muslims believed that amulets written by West African 'holy men' possessed greater virtue than those written by their own *fikis*.[39] Some *'ulama'* and notables from West Africa continued to use the Nile Valley route in the nineteenth century, but, on the whole, the affluent pilgrims favoured the more costly and safer route via Egypt. However, in the second half of the nineteenth century the new route gained in popularity. French rule in West and North Africa enabled pilgrims to take the new route through the Turkish-dominated Sudan in relative safety. Until the mid-nineteenth century the number of pilgrims probably did not exceed 500 per annum but from then onwards it gradually increased.[40] The more expensive 'forty-days road' from Dar Fur to Egypt thus gradually lost ground to the cheaper overland route through Kordofan to Sinnar and thence, via Berber, to Sawakin. This route, though not quite as safe, also enabled pilgrims to settle and work in agricultural settlements or even in towns for prolonged periods, while making their way eastward. This was true especially after many West Africans settled in Nilotic Sudan, thus providing shelter and a source of livelihood for other *fallata* pilgrims. Consequently the route through the Nile Valley 'probably drained most of the poor foot-traveler traffic from the desert routes during the course of the nineteenth century'.[41]

On the Red Sea shores, Sawakin and Massawa monopolized most of the African trade with the Arabian peninsula. Their proximity to Jedda and hence to Mecca made them the centre of African Muslims performing their pilgrimage to the holy places of Islam. Moreover, since the pilgrimage season attracted traders, both from the African continent and from the Arab provinces and the Indian sub-continent, these two Red Sea ports prospered more than other regions of Turkish Sudan. Following the Egyptian conquest of the Hijaz in 1811–18 it seemed only natural that Muhammad 'Ali would seek to dominate the Red Sea and its African shore. Thus his interest in Massawa and Sawakin predated his decision to conquer Sudan. However, apart from certain periods when control over the Red Sea province was granted to Muhammad 'Ali – the two ports remained under direct Turkish control from Jedda until the Khedive Isma'il's venture into Africa in 1865. This was the first time that they came under Egyptian control for a relatively long period. Isma'il supervised their development personally, realizing that their strategic and economic importance

[39] Naqr, *Dirasat*, 113, quoting from the 1819 edition of Burckhardt, *Travels*, 364–5.
[40] Birks, *Pilgrimage*, 14–15; Warburg, *Social and Economic Aspects*, 788–91.
[41] Naqr, *Dirasat*, 107.

exceeded that of his other African possessions. Isma'il's 'civilizing mission' in Africa was based on the belief that Egypt's superior civilization, as well as its adoption of modern technology, legitimized its conquests and made Sudan – its 'southern province' – an integral part of upper Egypt. Sawakin's position was also enhanced by the fact that in November 1865 the 'Aziziyya Misriyya Steamship Company, which sailed from Suez to Jedda and back, regularly called at Sawakin, thereby linking it with Egypt both administratively and commercially. As of August 1866, a special 'Aziziyya boat departed from Suez every Tuesday and went directly to Sawakin, carrying mail to Sawakin and Massawa as well as to the rest of Sudan, thereby enhancing control and trade even further.[42]

Between 1867 and 1871 Sawakin was under the jurisdiction of Ahmad Mumtaz Pasha, first as Governor and later as *hukumdar* of eastern Sudan, which included Kassala, Sawakin, Massawa and the Somali coast. Under Mumtaz, attention was paid to cotton-growing projects in the Kassala region and Sawakin's economic and political position benefited therefrom. Between 1871 and 1879, the Khedive Isma'il vacillated constantly between centralizing his administration of Sudan and decentralizing it. But regardless of the form of administration, Sawakin and Massawa received his utmost attention, since Isma'il believed in the economic profits to be derived, especially from Sawakin and the Kassala plateau. His great concern with Egypt's image in European eyes also added importance to the two ports, since they were more exposed to foreigners than the Sudanese hinterland. This led at an early stage to the setting up of clinics in each of the ports with Egyptian doctors and nurses, since it was clear that any outbreak of an epidemic in either of them or even a rumour to that effect would become a great setback to both trade and economic development. Since the pilgrimage to Mecca and Medina was also of major concern, an Egyptian medical team was sent to Jedda too.[43]

Khedive Isma'il's concern with Massawa and Sawakin was also connected with the opening of the Suez Canal in 1869. He believed that once the Suez Canal became fully operative, an era of prosperity would prevail in the Red Sea, with the 'Aziziyya Company shipping the produce of the fertile Sudanese provinces through Suez to Europe. Hence his emphasis on large-scale cultivation of cotton in Sudan and on improving internal communications so that it could be easily transported to Sawakin. The reasons for the failure of these ambitious plans are tied up with the general bankruptcy of Egypt, which reached its climax in 1875. Also, inadequate management of capital investments at exorbitant interest rates and the constant replacement of one Governor by another prevented the development of projects from being fully accomplished. There were scores

---

[42] Hill, *Egypt in Sudan*, 82–4, 87, 114–16.
[43] Talhami, *Suakin*, 80–5.

of blueprints for the development of cotton growing, salt-mines, railways etc. between Sawakin and its hinterland, none of which were ever implemented, despite their soundness. But even those projects that were realized fell into disrepair once their initiators were removed from office. Thus, for example, under Ahmad Mumtaz Pasha the Shatta dam was constructed and large-scale cotton growing was started in eastern Sudan. Even a spinning and ginning factory was established in Kassala at great cost. The tribal population of the region was constantly complaining against Mumtaz, accusing him of arbitrarily forcing them to work. The population was simply not ready for the fast development initiated by the German-educated Mumtaz and other officials influenced by Western education. Once the modernizing Governor was removed in 1872, the tribes gladly withdrew from the scene of his profitable projects and returned to their traditional economy. Resentment against the government was so deep that in 1874 Isma'il issued an order forbidding forced labour among the population. Another example planning at a forced pace was the Sudan railway, which was inaugurated in February 1875, after prolonged and costly planning only to be stopped three months later due to lack of funds and the reluctance of the population to endure the hardships of building it.

Khedive Isma'il seems to have been in two minds regarding the rapid development of Massawa and Sawakin and their linkage with the Nile Valley. He knew the economic potential of Sudan and realized the advantages of fast transportation to European markets. However, he hesitated on several accounts. First, Sawakin and Massawa were never ceded to the Khedive on a permanent basis and their development could thus become an impediment to future negotiations with the Ottoman Sublime Porte. Secondly, in opening the direct route from Massawa and Sawakin through Suez, the eastern Sudan gained a considerable trading advantage over the Mediterranean ports of Egypt. Thus, the Egyptian government's ivory and other goods that were transported north on the Nile route and then via Alexandria, reached London markets six months later than those transported directly from Sawakin in Sudan via the Suez Canal. Thirdly, direct export from Sawakin to Europe also entailed a considerable loss of revenue to Egyptian customs, especially since Egypt did not share in the profits of transit through the Suez Canal.[44]

Both Sawakin and Massawa had the characteristics of Red Sea, rather than African, towns. This was evident in their architecture, mixed populations, clothing and mode of living. It was only after they were ceded to the Khedive Isma'il in 1865 that they were forced to rely on the African hinterland for their economic development. In the case of Sawakin, the fertile lands of the Gash delta, comprising some 46,000 square miles and

---

[44] Hill, *Egypt in Sudan*, 123–4.

inhabited by the Beja tribes, were also affected since the opening of trade through a Sudanese port offered new incentives to the Beja farmers of Kassala. The route to Sawakin through Kassala or Berber was also favoured by West African pilgrims to Mecca and Medina, as mentioned above. The dichotomy between the urban, non-tribal inhabitants of Sawakin and the Beja of the Kassala plateau, enhanced Egypt's ability to control Sawakin and exploit it to its own advantage. Islam became predominant in Sawakin at a much earlier stage than among the Beja of the hinterland. The rest of the population, referred to as 'Suakinis', were a mixture of Beja tribes intermarried either with the Hadariba, a tribe of mixed Arab and Beja origin, or with the Turkish soldiers who had been stationed in Sawakin in the sixteenth century. In the 1850s the town's population received both Egyptian and Greek traders, lured by the prospects of a booming trade after the monopolies were abolished. The final *firman* ceding Sawakin and Massawa to the Khedive was issued in 1866. Proof had been furnished by the British foreign office to the Ottoman Sultan that the flourishing slave trade between the two ports and Jedda was undertaken with the encouragement of the Ottoman Wali in Jedda. Following British pressure the Ottomans granted Khedive Isma'il the new territory for his lifetime, at an annual tribute of 2,500 bourses of gold paid to the Jedda treasury. Thus, strategic considerations, combined with trade and 'morals', determined the eastern borders of Turco-Egyptian Sudan.[45]

While the 'civilizing mission' of Khedive Isma'il included the introduction of orthodox Islam into the newly acquired regions, this seems to have been primarily motivated by political and economic ambitions rather than by religious zeal. In order to acquire additional regions on the Red Sea, Isma'il exploited the threat of Christian missionaries so as to persuade the Sultan to cede them to permanent Egyptian rule. Similarly, his setting up of shari'a courts in Sawakin and its hinterland, with Azharite *qadis*, stemmed from his desire to subjugate the semi-pagan Beja and introduce orderly government, rather than from the purely religious belief in the superiority of orthodox Islam. Khedive Isma'il and his Armenian Prime Minister Nubar Pasha had both been educated in France and were imbued with its secular ideology. They sought to create a Europeanized Egyptian empire in Africa, in which Islam would play a role but would never be allowed to interfere with Isma'il's political and modernizing ambitions. Yet this civilizing mission, by which Islam was granted only a limited political role, came to an end as a result of the fact that since the mid-1870s the efficiency of Turco-Egyptian administration had declined whereas its oppressiveness had grown. Furthermore, the expanded means of communication and security enabled small merchants and preachers, such as the

[45] Talhami, *Suakin*, 20–33; on the evolution of trade during these years see also Björkelo, *Prelude to the Mahdiyya*, 114–20.

future Mahdi Muhammad Ahmad, to travel to western Sudan with relative ease. The anti-Turkish message that the Mahdi and other holy men
preached was, as a result of the economic and administrative decline,
practically all-embracing and appealed to an ever-expanding audience.
Muhammad Ahmad, like other *sufi* leaders and Sudanese tribal shaykhs
and merchants, was expressing the anti-Turkish feelings of a large segment of the population.[46]

Sudan was therefore ready for the *jihad* led by Muhammad Ahmad
the Mahdi against what he and many Sudanese viewed as a corrupt Muslim Turkish rule, just as Egypt, hit by massive bankruptcy, was ready for
the 'Urabi revolt which subsequently led to its conquest. Unlike 'Urabi's
revolt in Egypt, which Great Britain viewed as a threat to its interests, the
Mahdist conquest of Khartoum and the rest of Sudan was tolerated by
Britain, as long as Sawakin and its environs remained under Anglo-Egyptian administration. The reason was that British strategic interests could
not have tolerated Mahdist supremacy on the Red Sea shore, in close
vicinity to the Suez Canal, which since 1875 was primarily owned by
Great Britain and served British strategic and commercial interests. However, Sawakin and its environs were isolated from Sudan's hinterland by
the Red Sea mountains, in which the Mahdists – under 'Uthman Diqna,
reigned supreme. These mountains were under pro-Mahdist control because the hostile Beja tribes and the no less hostile followers of the
Majdhubiyya had supported the Mahdi since 1883. Sawakin therefore retained its special status under Egypt throughout the Mahdiyya, though
with hardly any economic benefits to Egypt, Britain or Sudan. Trade and
pilgrimage came to a virtual standstill since Sawakin was in fact besieged
and cut off from the Nile Valley till 1898.

[46] Voll, *Stateness*, 19.

Part II
THE MAHDIST STATE, 1881–98

4
BACKGROUND TO THE MAHDIYYA

The Sunni doctrine of the *mahdi* is a synthesis of two distinct beliefs. The first has Christian origins namely the belief in the second coming of Christ and the subsequent appearance of Antichrist, (*al-dajjal*).[1] These are an exegesis of a single reference in the Qur'an that associates Jesus with the Day of Resurrection and Judgement. The second element in the Mahdist belief has to do with political conflicts within the Muslim community in the first century of Islam. In the *shi'a* this belief was the result of political suppression and frustration. However, redemption developed in Islam as a marginal phenomenon based on foreign influences. Of these the most important one is the belief in a *mahdi*, based primarily on the eschatology of Islam and influenced by Christian and Zoroastrian beliefs. The word *mahdi* (the guided one) does not appear in the Qur'an but in the *hadith* and is sometimes identified with the Prophet Jesus (*nabi 'isa*). In some traditions Jesus is called *al-mahdi* or, following Shi'ite tradition, *al-imam al-mahdi*, indicating the impact of Shi'ism on Sunni eschatological beliefs. Thus, from a charismatic religious–political leader the *mahdi* developed into a redeemer of the *umma*, who 'will fill the earth with justice'. The appearance of a *mahdi* happened again and again in different Shi'ite and Isma'ili communities but only very rarely in Sunni Muslim communities, where the concept lacked any messianic connotations.[2] The *mahdi* in *shi'i* doctrine was connected with the return of the hidden *imam*, who according to this faith is in occultation. However, it is the *sunni mahdi* who concerns us when dealing with the Sudanese Mahdiyya. The expected *mahdi*, according to Sunni belief is not a historical personage returning from 'concealment', but 'a man from the People of the House' (*ahl al-bayt*), i.e. a descendant of the Prophet and preferably of 'Ali and Fatima.[3] As noted the Mahdist doctrine rests mainly on the extra-Qur'anic writings known as *hadith* (traditions).

---

[1] Holt, *Islamic Millenarianism*, 337–47.

[2] Lazarus-Yafeh, *Redemption in Islam*, 168–70.

[3] Holt, *Islamic Millenarianism*, 338–9; see also Hajj, *Al-Mahdiyya wa'athruha*, in Abu Salim, *Ma'alim*, 91–104, especially 96.

22

Since the portrayal of the *mahdi* varies in these traditions, it is no wonder that claimants to the title mushroomed throughout Muslim history, which conversely made it relatively easy for central governments to oppose their claims and to dispose of them before they gathered a following.

The rise of the Mahdiyya and the creation of an Islamic state in Sudan in the years 1881–98 can only be understood against the background of the Turco-Egyptian period. It was in effect an indigenous Muslim protest movement against foreign domination, be it by a Muslim ruler or, even worse, delegated to European Christian agents hired by the Egyptian Khedive. As mentioned above the revolutionary situation in Turco-Egyptian Sudan that evolved during the sixty years preceding the outbreak of the Mahdiyya was the result of profound changes that had affected the way in which traditional society and Islam had coexisted in Nilotic Sudan.[4] Muhammad 'Ali Pasha's conquests in Sudan in 1820–1 ended the independence of numerous sedentary and nomadic groups. His establishment of a centralized and autocratic administrative system with its unaccustomed fiscal burdens (undoubtedly aggravated by corruption and extortion) had a traumatic effect. Moreover, the increasing demand for qualified personnel in Egypt, as a result of rapid modernization, meant that officials in Sudan were rarely of high quality or integrity. One group of traditional Sudanese leaders whose political and social status declined under the Turkiyya was that of the indigenous men of religion called *fuqara'*, who during the previous three centuries had fulfilled a range of functions as teachers of the Qur'an and shari'a, leaders of *sufi* orders, arbitrators, and intercessors with the rulers. Among the *fuqara'* there also evolved a group of so-called saints, healers, miracle-makers and those pretending to possess religious wisdom, generally known in Sudan as *fikis*. The establishment of an orthodox hierarchy of *'ulama'*, serving in government mosques and integrated into the newly established judicial system, created a rival group of religious leaders. Although individual members of the old and more learned holy families took advantage of the offer of the opportunities to study at al-Azhar and enter the official hierarchy, there remained a fundamental incompatibility between the *fikis* and the government-supported *'ulama'*, whom the Mahdi was later to designate as evil (*'ulama' al-su'*). According to 'Uthman Sayyid Ahmad Isma'il, the Turkish conquest of Sudan introduced a new brand of Islam, which was alien to the vast majority of Sudanese Muslims. Moreover many of them opposed their invasion by a Muslim conqueror which they viewed as anathema to Islam. The Majdhubiyya as a Ja'ali clan, fought against this invasion alongside the Ja'aliyyin, following their revolt in 1822–3. This ultimately led to their support for the Mahdi and to the heroic fight of the Mahdist amir 'Uthman Diqna at the Mahdi's and later the Khalifa's side.[5]

---

[4] Holt, *EI*, 1247–52.
[5] 'Uthman, *Al-din wa'l-siyasa*, 21–2.

In the case of Sudan a situation of crisis and conflict therefore evolved which reached its peak in the second half of the nineteenth century. Its components were as follows. First, politically the country had been subjected to alien rule. While intertribal conflicts continued to flourish, Egyptian–European domination was increasingly resented since it interfered with local traditions and power structures, and involved growing dependence on and collaboration with European Christian powers, which added to its unpopularity. Secondly, social and economic instability increased as a result of taxation and the dislocation of tribes. This applied especially to the riverain tribes who consequently migrated from the Nile as a result of demographic and economic pressures and settled in Dar Fur and Bahr al-Ghazal in the western Sudan to avoid government administration and taxation. There they formed a new élite, based on their superior education, and some of them rose to prominence as government officials and traders (*jallaba*) in slaves and ivory. The ban on the slave trade, imposed by the government in the 1870s, was thus a major cause for discontent, both for this group and for other tribes. Increased urbanization under Egyptian rule was an additional cause for the breakdown of tribal structures. With the opening of new trade routes tribesmen escaped from taxation and army service with greater ease, and headed for the growing new towns to pursue a more lucrative and safer career. A collaborating élite, consisting of tribes such as the Sha'iqiyya, the *awlad al-balad* of the dispersion, or the Khatmiyya *sufi* order, played leading roles in this transformation and contributed to internal conflicts.[6] Finally, the attempt to impose Azharite orthodoxy on a Muslim community largely led by popular Islamic beliefs, created frictions within both *sufi* and tribal élites. Shari'a courts threatened tribal authority while the new government Qur'an schools (*kuttabs*), under trained '*ulama*', threatened the local *fuqara'*.[7]

In Islamic society the definition of state institutions is, in itself, part of a religious–ideological matter. Thus in Muslim society 'God alone is the real sovereign; all others are merely his subjects' and hence final authority cannot be vested in a person, class or group, or even in the entire population of the state as a whole. The legitimacy of the ruler(s) in Islamic societies therefore rests ultimately on their association with God. Since in Islam religion and politics are not separable, Islamic revivalism is often concerned with the religious corruption, in the eyes of the revivalist, of a politically successful Muslim ruler. This also resulted from the fact that Muslims were generally dissatisfied with the piety of their rulers:

[P]erhaps the heart of Muslim revivalism in Islamic history is the 'religious' critique of 'politics'. When things were prospering for the state, the leaders could be

[6] For details on the emergence of the new sufi orders, see Chapter 1; see also O'Fahey & Radtke, *Neo-Sufism*, 52–87.

[7] Dekmejian & Wyszomirski, *Charismatic Leadership*, 193–214.

condemned for their luxury and called 'caesars' . . . Leaders were always forced into a position of trying to prove their Islamic validity and worth.[8]

The reason was that they sought legitimization in Islam and were generally accepted by the Muslim establishment, since in Islam 'one hundred years of tyranny is better than a day of anarchy'. This was true of the Ottomans too, who constantly struggled with the problem of legitimizing their power. However, it should be emphasized that legitimacy is questioned only when political leadership is particularly inept and when social transformation calls for revivalism.

As for the 'state', its definition as a 'constant' or 'absolute' can, according to Isma'il al-Faruqi, therefore hardly be applied to Muslim societies. However, viewing the state as a conceptual variable enables us to analyse Muslim states too. Here we have to distinguish between two critical dimensions: the so-called 'eternal and unchanging', on the one hand, and the 'historical', on the other. In Muslim society the primary unit of social identity is the *umma*, embracing all Muslims regardless of ethnic or cultural background. The *umma* has its institutions, schools and courts of law, whereas the state is the political framework within which the *umma* functions. Consequently, the state that emerged was neither universal nor sovereign, since its creation was the *umma*'s prerogative. It was often dominated by military groups and enjoyed a 'relatively low degree of stateness'.[9]

However, there has been another mode of political operation in Islam, one that evolved around charismatic leadership. The sovereignty of God was in these cases associated with the leader and the political structure created by him. Since the divinely guided leader, usually called *mahdi*, limited the *umma* of believers to those who accepted his divine leadership, the political framework that emerged had a higher degree of 'stateness' than traditional forms of Islamic social order. However, it remained an 'Umma-oriented Mahdist state' rather than the prevailing territorial or nation-state.[10] The shift from the local *fiki* to the state-creating mode of Islamic leadership reflects the basic processes of social change in modern Sudan. This process took place during the last phases of the Funj Sultanate when, instead of the local *fiki*, there emerged holy families such as the Awlad Jabir or the Majdhubiyya, who as mentioned above exploited the decline of central government in order to create alternative institutions of authority. The larger neo-Sufi orders, which appeared in the eighteenth century, also played an important role in the shift to new modes of Islamic political institutions. This evolution was interrupted by the Turco-Egyptian conquest, which sought to create a comparatively modern style of government.

[8] Voll, *Revivalism*, 168–80, quoted from 175.

[9] Voll, *Stateness*, 6–7. The references are from Isma'il R. al-Faruqi, *Islam* (Niles, Il: Argus Communications, 1979), 61–5.

[10] Voll, *Stateness*, 8–9.

It was based on the Egyptian model and may be defined as pseudo-secular. Holy families, such as the Majadhib, who had achieved a great measure of power during the Funj decline, were consequently opposed to this new centralized authority and were crushed in attempting to resist it. Other *sufi* orders, such as the Khatmiyya, realized the futility of resistance, on the one hand, and the advantages of collaboration, on the other, and decided to cooperate with the new rulers and support the state. The degree of state control thereby increased after the conquest. It implied government control in regions hitherto left to their own devices, such as the Beja tribes in the Red Sea region, or the Baqqara tribes of Kordofan and Dar Fur. It also allowed central authority to become involved in tribal administration and leadership as well as in all matters concerning taxation.

Under Turco-Egyptian rule a military force was formed, stronger than any previous one, which enabled the government to impose its will by force on groups seeking to loosen their ties with central authority and to resist it. The emerging state also helped in creating a common identity for the Sudanese and in providing them with a common enemy, identified as 'Turks'. On the other hand, improved lines of communication enabled northern Sudanese Muslims to interact and even collaborate with each other. A kind of 'national' élite, consisting of tribal and *sufi* groups associated with central government, established complex trade networks both within the Sudan and with the outside world. Thereby an order like the Khatmiyya succeeded in establishing a central organization, hitherto unknown in Sudan, which controlled or coordinated the activities of its members from the Red Sea hills to Kordofan. The leaders of such orders, with a foot in both worlds, realized the advantages of a well-organized and geographically diffused *sufi* order for their commercial endeavours. The Khatmiyya's concentration in commercial centres, rather than in rural areas, and its support by a growing middle class were a natural outcome.[11] On the other hand the increased mobility of merchants, religious teachers and others also enabled the Sudanese to mobilize forces against oppressive government orders. These included, for instance, the suppression of the slave-trade in the 1870s, which affected many of them adversely. The travels of Muhammad Ahmad b. 'Abdallah, the future Mahdi, to Kordofan and other regions in search of support for his future mission as *mahdi* can also be seen against this background of general discontent. But instead of a 'nationalist' movement, such as that which emerged in Egypt in the wake of the 'Urabi revolt, Sudan turned to a Mahdist-type Islamic state with minor proto-nationalist attributes.[12]

---

[11] For details see Gaddal, *Religion*, 49–56.
[12] Voll, *Stateness*, 17–20.

5

THE PATH LEADING TO REVOLT

Developments in the two decades preceding the Mahdiyya heightened the tension between the Turkiyya and the inhabitants of Sudan. The autocracy of Khedive Isma'il (1863–79) made the power of central government felt once more after the comparative laxity that had begun in Muhammad 'Ali Pasha's last years and continued under his successors, 'Abbas and Sa'id. Under Khedive Isma'il the upper regions of the White Nile as well as the former sultanate of Dar Fur were annexed to Sudan by force in the 1870s. Since the middle of the century, traders seeking ivory and slaves had penetrated into the unexplored regions of Bahr al-Ghazal, outside the Muslim and Arabicized northern Sudan and beyond the control of the Turco-Egyptian government. The slave-trade that was fed from these regions was viewed as evil by leading circles in Europe, which in turn put pressure on the Khedive to bring them under his administration and thereby to suppress the slave-trade. The implementation of this policy would in any event have antagonized vested interests, particularly those of the diaspora of northern Sudanese riverain tribes, the Danaqla and the Ja'aliyyin, who were involved in the slave-trade and who ranged from petty dealers to merchant princes such as al-Zubayr Rahma Mansur, the master of the western Bahr al-Ghazal and the conqueror of Dar Fur. The situation was rendered even more critical by the Khedive's recruitment of Europeans and Americans to carry out his plans. The appointment of Christians to high government positions offended the conservative piety of the Sudanese. Chief among these expatriates was the British officer Charles George Gordon who, as Governor of the Equatorial province (1873–6) and Governor-General of Sudan (1877–80) played a leading part in the attempts to establish Khedivial administration in the south and to suppress the slave trade. With their inadequate resources Gordon and his colleagues attained only limited success. The deposition of Isma'il in June 1879 was followed by Gordon's resignation in 1880 and the comparative feebleness of their successors in Cairo and Khartoum facilitated the drift towards insurrection in the Sudanese provinces.[13]

In November 1981 an international conference was held in Khartoum dedicated to studies on the Mahdiyya in commemoration of its centurry.[14]

[13] Holt, *EI*, 1247–52; see Moore-Harell, *Gordon*; Hill, *Frontiers*, 206–16.
[14] Naqr, *Dirasat*.

In a paper presented by Al-Hajj Hamad Muhammad Khayr and Maymuna Mirghani Hamza, two of the participants, a critical reassessment of the pioneering works of Peter Holt and Mekki Shibeika on the Mahdiyya was presented. The authors criticized Holt who, in their view, did not accept the view that the prime reason for the Mahdist revolt was Turkish maladministration. They also claimed that Holt neglected the most important aspect of the Mahdist revolution, namely the transfer of power from the indigenous ruling classes and their local collaborators to the revolutionary class.[15] However, Holt's studies on the Mahdiyya are largely ignored in this study. Thus for instance the authors failed to mention that Holt, not unlike Na'um Shuqayr, highlighted the attempt to suppress the slave trade as a major reason for discontent embracing practically all classes of society and every part of the country. Moreover, Holt did not dismiss Turkish maladministration as a major cause for discontent. But he rejected the emphasis on this factor, to the exclusion of others and rightly insisted on an examination of the local factors that also contributed to the Mahdi's success.[16] As for Shibeika, according to Khayr and Hamza, he erred in analysing the causes leading to the revolt by exaggerating religious aspects. The authors believe that the Mahdist revolution should be viewed as a series of local upheavals rolled into one. This, they claim, is of importance since the socio-economic conditions prevailing in the various regions were crucial for understanding their revolutionary potential.[17]

There are historians, especially in Egypt who dismiss the notion that the corrupt Egyptian rule was responsible for the Mahdist revolt. One of them is Ahmad 'Izzat 'Abd al-Karim, who published his views on this topic in 1959.[18] He claimed that basically the aims of Ahmad 'Urabi in Egypt and Muhammad Ahmad al-Mahdi in Sudan were the same since both sought to expel the foreign unbelievers (*al-kufra*) who were governing them. In fact Yahya regards the two movements as different aspects of Islamic union (Pan-Islam) and sees proof in the fact that 'Urabi sought a united front with 'Abd al-Qadir al-Jaza'iri and Muhammad Ahmad al-Mahdi against Christian invaders. Indeed, while in exile, 'Urabi wrote that he had intended to appoint the Mahdi as governor of Sudan and, according to Yahya, the Mahdi also regarded the liberation of Egypt from the foreign unbelievers as a first step leading to a united Islamic, Mahdist

---

[15] Al-Haj Hamad Muhammad Khayr wa-Maymuna Mirghani Hamza, 'Al-dirasat al-akadimiyya wa'l-thawra al-mahdiyya', in Naqr, *Dirasat*, 99–110. This criticism of Holt's views, which are summarized on 101–3, is based primarily on Holt and Daly, *History of Sudan* and ignores his studies on the Mahdiyya.

[16] Holt, *Mahdist State*, 32–3.

[17] Naqr, *Dirasat*, 103–6. While the two authors seem to propagate a Marxist approach to the study of the Mahdiyya, their assessment of the reasons leading to the revolt is on the whole rather conservative.

[18] For details on his views, elaborated below, see Yahya, *Al-thawra*, 6, 38–41.

world. Yahya therefore dismisses all claims as to Turco-Egyptian malad-ministration being responsible for the revolts and tends to view the Mahdiyya as part and parcel of a grand Islamic uprising against Western colonialism.[19] Muhammad Ahmad al-Hajj, in his study 'al-mahdiyya wa'athruha al-dini fi al-Sudan', concludes that, despite its brief rule the Mahdiyya had a lasting effect on Sudan. First, it acted as a melting pot for Sudanese society thereby laying the foundations of Sudanese nationalism and determining that Islam is the religion of the state. Secondly, the sim-plicity and clarity of the Mahdist message forced Sudanese *sufi*s to over-come their tendency of exceeding their proper boundaries and to submit to one supreme Muslim authority. It also enabled Muslims to study their religion and not to limit its learning to '*ulama*' and *fuqaha*'; thereby the Mahdiyya became a popular movement of reform. Lastly and probably most importantly, the Mahdiyya created a firm link between Islam and politics in Sudan. The role played by the two great sects, the Ansar and the Khatmiyya, in Sudan's struggle for independence in the twentieth century would probably not have been possible without the Mahdiyya.[20]

The reasons leading to the eruption of the Mahdist revolt were of course complex and one must take into account religious, political, social and economic components. But its success was due to Egypt's weakness, on the one hand, and to the fact that tribes and sultanates, which had enjoyed a semi-independent status in the southern Nile Valley under the nominal rule of the Funj sultans, had been forcefully united into a rather artificial state by the Egyptian conquerors. Hence it is quite appropriate that mod-ern historians continue to regard Turco-Egyptian Sudan as a 'prelude to the Mahdiyya'. In a study dealing primarily with the northern riverain Ja'aliyyin, Anders Björkelo concluded: 'the Turkiyya struck the final blow at the political and economic vitality of the Nile Valley north of Khar-toum'.[21]

[19] *Ibid.*, 38–40.
[20] Hajj, *Al-Mahdiyya wa'athruha*, 102–4.
[21] Björkelo, *Prelude to the Mahdiyya*, 137–47, quotation from 147.

6

MUHAMMAD AHMAD b. 'ABDALLAH, THE MAHDI

Muhammad Ahmad b. 'Abdallah, the Mahdi of nineteenth century Sudan, was the founder of an Islamic messianic movement that sought to implement pure incorrupt Islam under the banner of revivalism and renewal (*ihya wa-tajdid*). The most comprehensive biography of the Mahdi is the *sira*, or biographical chronicle, describing the life and campaigns of Muhammad Ahmad al-Mahdi, as written by Isma'il b. 'Abd al-Qadir, one of his contemporary adherents, on orders from the Mahdi's Khalifa 'Abdullahi al-Ta'aishi. The *sira*, in a condensed version translated and annotated by Haim Shaked, is of great significance since it presents us with a Sudanese nineteenth-century point of view of both the Turkiyya and the Mahdist state.[22] The Mahdi, as *khalifat rasul allah*, played a central role within the Mahdist movement. Without the attributes of a *mahdi*, which Muhammad Ahmad was convinced he possessed, such a movement could not have started, let alone succeeded. Mahdism was modelled, to a large extent, on the historical heritage of the Prophet and the four just caliphs (*al-khulafa' al-rashidun*), which was the only period in Islamic history when the *umma* was undivided and followed a path leading to the establishment of a just community of believers, based on the Qur'an and the *Sunna*. Muhammad Ahmad presented himself as having been appointed to the supreme succession (*al-khilafa al-kubra*) as Successor of the Apostle of God (*khalifat rasul allah*), while his leading disciples were the successors of the rightly-guided caliphs. Three of these were appointed soon after his manifestation. 'Abdullahi b. Muhammad al-Ta'aishi's status was recognized in his title of *Khalifat al-siddik*, i.e. the successor of Abu Bakr. An early follower of the Mahdi, 'Ali b. Muhammad Hilu ('Ali wad Hilu) was appointed the successor of 'Umar (*khalifat al-faruk*), and the Mahdi's young son-in-law, Muhammad Sharif b. Hamid, was appropriately named the successor of 'Ali (*khalifat al-karrar*). The appointment of the successor of 'Uthman was offered by the Mahdi in

---

[22] Shaked, *Sudanese Mahdi*. Isma'il b. 'Abd al-Qadir, the author of this biography, was born in El Obeid in 1844 and was a grandson of Isma'il al-Wali, head of the Isma'iliyya and one of the Mahdi's first supporters; a copy of the manuscript is in the Sudan archive at Durham University library.

May 1883, to the contemporary head of the Sanusiyya order, Muhammad al-Mahdi, whose cooperation Muhammad Ahmad was anxious to obtain, but was ignored.[23]

When announcing his manifestation, on 29 June 1881, Muhammad Ahmad based his claim largely on his reputation as a *sufi* shaykh of the Sammaniyya order, with considerable following in the White Nile region. The Sammaniyya had predicted that the *mahdi* would be one of its adherents and one of its leaders Shaykh al-Qurashi Wad al-Zayn had, as noted, stated that his tomb would be erected by the future *mahdi*. Thus following the erection of this tomb by Muhammad Ahmad, the latter advised Shaykh Muhammad al-Tayyib al-Basir and other Sammani leaders of the Hala-wiyyin tribe to free themselves 'of all worldly affairs and be in readiness for a Godly mission'. On the day of his manifestation Muhammad Ahmad wrote once again to Shaykh al-Basir informing him that the Prophet had instructed him 'to shoulder the honourable mission of the expected mahdi'. In his letter the future Sudanese Mahdi described a vision in which the Prophet Muhammad addressed him and several saints, mostly of the Sammaniyya order, telling them that: 'whoever does not regard his [Muhammad Ahmad's] Mahdiship as true is an unbeliever in God and His Apostle'.[24] It was further emphasized that the Mahdi's office was eternal since, like the Prophet, he was created out of the 'sacred light of God'. Moreover, the announcement, which was made during a Prophetic colloquy (*hadra nabawiyya*), emphasized that Muslims who did not follow the Mahdi or rejected his mission were heretics. The Mahdi therefore claimed to possess all the requirements and attributes (*al-shurut wa'l-awsaf*) demanded of the historic *mahdi*, according to the Maghribi school. Muhammad Ahmad claimed that the Mahdiyya was one of the pillars of Islam, that those who refused to follow him were *kuffar* (unbelievers) and that his doctrine and judicial verdicts thereby became infallible.[25] The Mahdi styled himself as the Prophet's successor, (*khalifat rasul allah*), but did not attempt to cite proof texts from the Qur'an or the *hadith* to buttress his claim. It was only in later letters that such texts were cited, but even then Muhammad Ahmad's *sufi* background remained predominant. This was used against him by both Egyptian and Sudanese *'ulama'* who, ridiculed him for failing to comply with the criteria indicated in the traditions, (*hadith*) regarding the expected *mahdi*. Moreover, the *'ulama'* also attacked Muhammad Ahmad for declaring *jihad* against the Turks, which they viewed as a

---

[23] Holt, *EI*, 1248–9. According to some sources the title of Khalifat 'Uthman was also offered to Muhammad 'Uthman al-Mirghani II, who ignored the honour.

[24] *Manshurat* II, 2; Abu Salim, *Athar*, I, 76–83; Shuqayr, *Ta'rikh*, 643; see also Holt, *Islamic Millenarianism*, 340–1; *idem*, *Mahdist State*, 105.

[25] Ahmed Uthman, *Ideology*, 30–2, quoting from Manshurat I, 12. Thus a wife who had embraced Mahdism would be granted a divorce on the grounds that her husband who had rejected the Mahdi was an unbeliever.

reprehensible slaughter of Muslims.[26] The *'ulama'* who opposed the Mahdi
based their arguments primarily on the absolute legitimacy of Ottoman
rule, which embodied the Caliphate to which obedience of all Muslims
was unquestionable. They rejected Muhammad Ahmad's claims to the
Mahdiship declaring that since there was a legitimate Caliph in office 'a
bay'a to another person was null and void and had no effect whatsoever'.
Muhammad Ahmad refuted these arguments stating that the office of the
Caliphate had stopped to exist long ago and the present rulers in Turkey
and Egypt must be deposed since they had 'turned away from the law of
the Lord of the messengers'.[27] Isma'il b. 'Abd al-Qadir, the author of the
Mahdi's biography, ridiculed the anti-Mahdist claims of Egyptian *'ulama'*
and compared their support for 'Urabi's revolt with their rejection of the
Mahdi's mission. The fact that they issued *fatwas* against the Khedive
Tawfiq and his allies 'rendered the fighting against the Turks obligatory
on all the Muslims, let alone the Mahdi, whose very mission was to do
away with the Turks'.[28] It is also significant that the author portrays the
Turks as *a'da' al-din* – the enemies of faith –and even as enemies of God
and *kuffar*, while the Christians in general and the British in particular received much less attention and were treated more gently. His portrayal
of Turkish wickedness reiterated many of the Mahdi's own criticisms of
Sudan's foreign rulers:

[The land] was filled with oppression and tyranny by the Turks, who profaned the
sacrosanctities of the Religion and imposed the poll-tax on the Muslims. Falsity and
infamy spread amongst them and they obeyed Satan and rebelled against the
Merciful [God]. They hastened to obliterate the traces of Islam and they did not
fear Allah . . .[29]

In his paper on revolutionary aspects in the Mahdi's ideology, Muhammad Sa'id al-Qaddal emphasized the fact that the Mahdi divided the world
into two: that of the Mahdiyya and that of the Turkiyya. The dividing line
between them was the acceptance of the Mahdi's *da'wa*. All those who
refused were unbelievers *(kufar)* and hence belonged to the non-Muslim
Turkish world, whose blood should be shed in the forthcoming *jihad* and
whose possessions were legal booty for the community of true believers.
According to al-Qaddal the purpose of this revolutionary approach was
rather pragmatic since the Mahdi had to overcome the Turco-Egyptian
enemy and total *jihad* was both justified and necessary under these circumstances. However, as in many revolutionary ideologies, this too proved to
be an obstacle in later developments since it dictated the perpetuation of

[26] Holt, *Islamic Millenarianism*, 342–6; for details of this controversy, see Shuqayr, *Ta'rikh*,
651–4
[27] Peters, *The Mahdi*, 409–20 quoted from 414–15.
[28] Shaked, *Sudanese Mahdi*, 93, quoting from 108–9 of the manuscript.
[29] *Ibid.*, 202–3, quoted from the *Sira*, 12/11–15.

jihad both against Egypt and Ethiopia, even after the enemy had been expelled from Sudan's boundaries. Consequently, this endless war undermined the economic and political stability of the Mahdist state, leading to military defeats and economic disaster. In the final analysis, al-Qaddal concludes, this facilitated the European penetration into the region.[30]

Faithfulness, as expressed in the Mahdist *bay'a* was based on the oath of allegiance, first enunciated by the Prophet. It was also adopted, with variations, by the heads of numerous *sufi* orders. However, the Mahdi realized at an early stage that he had to define his movement and its supporters in a distinctive way so as to differentiate between them and the many other *sufi* orders scattered throughout Sudan. While in the initial stages of his movement the support of the *sufi* shaykhs and their followers was essential, it later became intolerable since in the Mahdiyya there could be only one central authority namely the Mahdi and later the Khalifa 'Abdullahi. The Mahdi's followers, who in the early stages of the revolt were still called *fuqara'* or *darawish*, following *sufi* custom, were thereafter renamed *ansar* in line with the precedent of the Prophet's supporters. The Mahdi's ostensible reason in issuing this decree was that since his followers were promised paradise as a reward for their faithful devotion and willingness to die in *jihad*, they could not go by their previous *sufi* titles, which indicated poverty. However, those who refused to join the Mahdi continued to be known as *fuqara'* or *darawish* since they did not deserve paradise.[31]

As noted, *sufi* traditions played a predominant role in Sudanese Islam. However, the new *sufi* orders founded since the eighteenth century were more outgoing and missionary in their approach but, at the same time, less flexible in their attitude to pre-Islamic traditions or local superstitions. Their emphasis on the *da'wa* also helped them to surpass the older-established orders. It was thus crucial for the Mahdi to gain the support of these well-organized and centralized orders, especially during the early stages of his movement since he could exploit their organizations in order to spread his own *da'wa* among their members. First he relied on the support of his fellow members in the Sammaniyya and he persuaded some of the order's shaykhs to attend his colloquy. He then recruited followers of the Tijaniyya and Isma'iliyya orders, when he set out to spread his mission in western Sudan. The Isma'iliyya order in Kordofan is a good example of this wise policy, since it was from Jabal Qadir in southern Kordofan that the Mahdi intended to start his *jihad*. Led by Muhammad Isma'il al-Makki, the Isma'iliyya, which had been oppressed by the Turkish administration, embraced the Mahdi as the expected saviour even

---

[30] Qaddal, *Ru'ya Thawriyya*, 74–88.
[31] Abu Salim, *Athar*, II, 310–12, quoting messages addressed to *al-ahbab* in Mar.–Apr. 1884; Trimingham, *Islam*, 150–7; Dietrich, *Der Mahdi*, 199–288.

before his manifestation as *al-mahdi al-muntazar*, in June 1881. This support, combined with that of the powerful Baqqara tribes in Kordofan and Dar Fur, provided the Mahdi with the popular base required for his campaigns in the west. As to the eastern Sudan, the Majdhubiyya, who had also suffered from Turkish oppression ever since the Ja'aliyyin rebellion in 1822, helped him in gaining support among the Beja tribes in the Red Sea region.[32] When the Mahdist troops threatened al-Qadarif in April 1884, the Majadhib were allegedly involved in bringing about the peaceful surrender of the town. Initially, the Mahdi permitted the continuation of Qur'anic education in al-Qadarif, but in his letter to Ahmad b. al-Hajj 'Ali al-Majdhub he clearly stated that precedence had to be given to the *jihad* and that Qur'anic teachings were only allowed as long as the Mahdist *amir* responsible for the area did not personally go on a military campaign.[33] Ahmad b. Hajj 'Ali al-Majdhub served as *imam* and teacher in al-Qadarif for some time after the Mahdist revolt. However, continuing war, drought, and hunger led to a disruption of studies and the school had to be closed. Among the Mahdi's early adherents there were, not surprisingly, many *sufi* shaykhs and members of their orders who believed that the Mahdist militant brand of popular Islam would help them to get rid of the *'ulama'*, imported by the Turco-Egyptian rulers from al-Azhar, and thus help them to regain their previous standing. The Khatmiyya alone, among the large important *sufi* orders, did not join the Mahdist movement despite the Mahdi's repeated appeals. First, this was because of its claim regarding the status of Muhammad 'Uthman al-Mirghani, who was created out of the Prophet's light. Secondly, as part of the new urban class, the social and economic interests of the Khatmiyya adherents were largely linked with those of the Egyptians. Offshoots of the Khatmiyya such as the Isma'iliyya in Kordofan as well as Khatmiyya adherents in that region were, as mentioned, among the earliest supporters of Muhammad Ahmad al-Mahdi. However, although the Khatmiyya leaders and most of its followers believed in the coming of a *mahdi* they refused to recognize Muhammad Ahmad as such. Indeed, Muhammad 'Uthman II and Muhammad Sirr al-Khatim II maintained their anti-Mahdist propaganda throughout the existence of the Mahdist state, both within Sudan and from their exile in Egypt. Muhammad 'Uthman II used the Khatmiyya headquarters near Kassala as an anti-Mahdist centre and travelled throughout the region in order to gather as many anti-Mahdists as possible around him. Even General Gordon, during his last mission in Sudan, used Muhammad 'Uthman II in order to correspond with the outside world

---

[32] Hill, *Egypt in Sudan* 127; see also Abu Salim, *Athar*, I, 76–81, in which the Mahdi orders Muhammad al-Tayyib al-Basir to give the *bay'a* to his brethren in the Sammaniyya order and to make the *hijra* to jabal Qadir; Karrar, *Sufi Brotherhoods*, 93–102; see also Johnson, *Religious Paradigms*, 159–78.

[33] Abu Salim, *Athar*, IV, 212.

from the besieged Khartoum. But finally Muhammad 'Uthman was forced to withdraw, first to Sawakin and later to Egypt, where he died in 1886. His son Sayyid 'Ali al-Mirghani travelled to Egypt a year later and came to Cairo with Sirr al-Khatim II to study at al-Azhar. Following their departure from Sudan, al-Bakri al-Mirghani became the leader of the Khatmiyya at Kassala where he and his followers swore allegiance to the Mahdist state, now led by the Khalifa 'Abdullahi. However, al-Bakri continued to oppose the Mahdiyya and even took part in military actions against the Ansar. Several prominent Khatmiyya leaders, including Maryam bint Hashim al-Mirghani, were imprisoned during the Mahdiyya and remained under arrest until after the Anglo-Egyptian conquest.[34]

The Mahdist state later turned even against its most loyal *sufi* allies since it refused to tolerate their divided loyalties and demanded complete submission first to the Mahdi and later to the Khalifa. In a proclamation issued by the Khalifa, early in 1884, he denounced in the Mahdi's name all *sufi* orders as divisive and called upon their adherents to disband them and grant their undivided loyalty to the Mahdiyya.[35] The Mahdi himself also dealt in some detail with the relationship between Sufism and the Mahdist *da'wa*. He compared *sufi* beliefs to 'water wells' from which the adherents drank so as to quench their spiritual thirst. However, now that a great sea of water, namely the Mahdiyya, had covered all these wells, it no longer made any sense to drink from the small wells (the *sufi* orders), now engulfed within this sea. Quoting from Ahmad al-Tayyib wad-al-Bashir, the Mahdi expressed this in a letter he wrote to the Sammaniyya shaykh, Muhammad al-Tayyib al-Basir:

> In the *tariqa* there are humility, contrition, scant eating and drinking, forbearance (patience), and pilgrimage to the masters (*al-sadat*), making six [items]. In the *mahdiyya* there are also six [items]: warfare, discretion, determination, trust [in God], reliance upon God, agreement in doctrine. And these twelve joined together for no one but for you.[36]

The Mahdi styled himself as the Prophet's successor but as noted did not attempt to cite proof texts from the Qur'an or the *hadith* to buttress his claim. This can be partly explained by Muhammad Ahmad's *sufi* background. His was a charismatic leadership in which *baraka*, implying an active power of holiness, played an important role. The citing of texts from the *hadith* was therefore of lesser significance to him and to the majority of both *sufi* shaykhs and followers in Sudan than to his antagonists the Azharite trained *'ulama'*. The Mahdi denounced them as evil (*'ulama' al-su'*), because of their exclusive dependence on the written

---

[34] Karrar, *Sufi Brotherhoods*, 99–102.

[35] Abu Salim, *Manshurat*, 61–5; the Mahdi also banned the use of *sufi* flags and forbade their ceremonial *dhikr*.

[36] Abu Salim, *Athar* I, 78; Sadiq, *Yas'alunaka*, 173.

texts and their failure to accept him. He stated that 'texts cannot bind
God's will' and accused them of having become subservient to forms
while ignoring the content. He did not forgive them for allying themselves
with non-Muslims and acting in defiance of Islam at the behest of their
alien masters. According to the Mahdi they refrained from implementing
the shari'a and even sanctioned breaking the fast of *Ramadan* by the pro-
government troops in Khartoum, so that they could fight against the Ansar,
their excuse being that the Prophet had sanctioned the conquest of Mecca
under similar circumstances. The Mahdi stated that he did not oppose the
'ulama' for their learning but for their subservience to texts, which they
misused to denounce his mission and to justify their support of a corrupt
government. In other words he contended that most of the *'ulama'*, limited by their scientific methods, lacked the tools inherent in Sufism to
comprehend his mission.[37] It is noteworthy that his opponents among the
'ulama' did not reject the idea of a *mahdi* but concentrated on proving
that Muhammad Ahmad was a pretender. They did not denounce the
concept of the *mahdi* as heretical, probably because this belief prevailed
in Sudan's *sufi* traditions. On the other hand, there were, according to al-
Sadiq al-Mahdi, the Mahdi's great grandson, many *'ulama'* both in Sudan
and Egypt who justified the Mahdi's call for a *jihad* against the Sultan (*al-
khuruj 'ala al-sultan*) from the very beginning for the following reasons.
First, they regarded Khedive Tawfiq as unfit to rule and hence the Mahdi,
like 'Urabi in Egypt, had a duty to fight against the Egyptian attempt to
conquer Sudan. Secondly, every Muslim had a duty to rise against the
Ottoman Sultan 'Abd al-Hamid II who had betrayed Islam through his
support of Christian foreigners. The duty of Muslim unity and submission
to the legitimate ruler therefore no longer applied and the Mahdist uprising was fully justified. Thirdly, Islam required an active leader who would
implement the laws of religion. It was immaterial whether this role was
fulfilled by the Mahdi of Sudan or by someone else. Among the *'ulama'*
who sent messages of support to the Mahdi was Shaykh Ahmad al-'Awwam,
one of Ahmad 'Urabi's supporters, who had been exiled to Sudan and
was later imprisoned in Khartoum by General Gordon. His message of
support was sent to the Mahdi from the besieged city in 1884 but failed to
reach him until after the Mahdist conquest of Khartoum in January 1885.[38]
Similar views were expressed by Jamal al-Din al-Afghani and Muhammad
'Abduh and published in their journal *al-'urwa al-wuthqa* while they were
living in Paris.[39]

[37] Sadiq, *Yas'alunaka*, 225–6; Abu Salim, *Haraka*, 80–1; Holt, *Mahdist State*, 108.
[38] Abu Salim, *Nasihat al-'Awwam*.
[39] Al-Sadiq al-Mahdi summarized the views of the *'ulama'* opposing the Mahdi in Sadiq,
Yas'alunaka, 145–9, and of those supporting him on 149–53; in Abu Salim & Vikör, *The Man
Who Believed*, 29–52, the authors tell of a Moroccan *'alim*, Ahmad b. 'Abdallah al-Fasi, who
expressed his pro-Mahdist views in 1888–9, and rejected all doubts raised against the Mahdi

At a much later stage this debate was picked up by the Mahdi's son, Sayyid 'Abd al-Rahman al-Mahdi, who sought to present a more balanced view of the Mahdi and the Mahdiyya than the one presented by the West or by Egypt and simultaneously to boost his own prestige. He therefore invited a well known Muslim Yemenite scholar, al-Jabri, to come as his guest to Omdurman and to undertake a study of the Mahdiyya. 'Abdel Rahman Ibn Hussein al-Jabri was born in San'a and arrived in Sudan after fifteen years of travels in Arabia and North Africa. His arrival coincided with the anti-Mahdist turn in British policy, in 1925–6, which brought about a curtailment of Sayyid 'Abd al-Rahman's activities and the banning of the recruitment of Ansar into the newly founded Sudan Defence Force. While in Sudan al-Jabri wrote the history of the Mahdist movement in order to 'meet a want long felt in Arabia, Egypt, Syria, India, Constantinople and Mesopotamia'. But the British authorities regarded the book as seditious and confiscated the manuscript.[40] Al-Jabri's book deals with the movement's history and its justification in the *hadith*. It includes many of the Mahdi's letters (*manshurat al-Mahdi*) and sermons, as well as a copy of his *ratib* (prayer-book), elaborating its significance.[41] However, it must be regarded as a laudatory book aimed at glorifying the Mahdi and his twentieth century successor, Sayyid 'Abd al-Rahman, who was his host in Omdurman.

Mekki Shibeika listed a long line of local *sufi* leaders who fought against superior government forces in the Gezira and other regions only because of their deep belief in the Mahdi and his mission. But Shibeika admits that some of these orders joined the Mahdiyya only after its initial military victories, especially the annihilation of Colonel Hicks's expedition at Shaykan in 1883. But on the whole the impact of those who denied the Mahdiyya on religious grounds was relatively negligible, due to its predominance in Sudanese society. Consequently, according to Shibeika, the government inspired anti-Mahdist propaganda had little impact on the Sudanese, who were quite prepared to believe in the Mahdi's propaganda and dismiss that of his antagonists. Furthermore, Shibeika claims that the government underestimated the Mahdi's appeal and thus inadvertently played into his hands. The most ignorant and hence most negligent

---

by Azharite and Sudanese '*ulama*'. On al-'Awwam's message see Abu Salim, *Haraka*, 67–71; Abu Salim states that al-'Awwam, Muhammad 'Abduh and al-Afghani did not support the Mahdi's religious message but welcomed his military victories over British forces; see Abu Salim, *Nasihat al-'Awwam*, which deals with the relationship between the two revolts. I am grateful to Prof. R.S. O'Fahey for enabling me to use his copy of Abu Salim's manuscript; on al-'Awwam see also *ALA* I, 332–3.

[40] Beshir, *El Jabri*, 136–9; a copy of the manuscript (about 700 pages) was saved and is preserved at the University of Khartoum library.

[41] Beshir, *El Jabri*, 137–9. In 1925–6 Sulaymän Dawood Mandil, the son of a Sudanese Jew who converted to Islam during the Mahdiyya, published two cheap editions of the *ratib* in Cairo.

role was played, according to Shibeika, by Giegler Pasha, who was Acting Governor-general following Muhammad Ra'uf Pasha's dismissal and prior to the arrival of 'Abd al-Qadir Hilmi. Following his appointment, Giegler telegraphed to Cairo not to send reinforcements, as requested by his predecessor, since he could easily deal with the Mahdi's revolt with the forces at his disposal. This, according to Shibeika, was the result of Giegler's being a Christian who was ignorant of the religious significance of the Mahdi's mission and hence underrated his appeal. Furthermore, the Egyptian lack of response to the continuous appeals by 'Abd al-Qadir for reinforcements resulted from the complacency of Britalin because, following the conquest of Egypt in 1881, it was in a position to dictate to the Khedive Tawfiq how to handle the Mahdist uprising. Britain was concerned with the security of Egypt and the Suez Canal and had practically no interest in defending Kordofan or Dar Fur against the Mahdi.[42] Consequently, one of the reasons for the Mahdi's early success was a result of the fact that the authorities underestimated his challenge, but, when a small military expedition sent to arrest him was beaten in August 1881, the matter was taken more seriously. The Mahdi and his *ansar* meanwhile undertook the *hijra* to Jabal Qadir in the Nuba Mountains in order to escape from government revenge, just as the Prophet and his followers had undertaken the *hijra* to Yathrib (Medina) in flight from their enemies some 1250 years earlier. The Mahdi's supporters were now named *ansar*, just as were those of the Prophet. The Mahdi's call for *jihad* was also modelled on that of the Prophet. It was a holy war seeking to convince the unbelievers, whether corrupt Muslims, Christians or pagans, that there was only one just cause. Those who refused to join the true religion, as propagated by the Mahdi, were either imprisoned, killed in battle or exiled from Sudan. They included many of the leading *'ulama'*, as well as heads of *sufi* orders and tribal shaykhs. However, the *jihad* aimed to liberate not only Sudan but all the domains ruled by the corrupt Ottoman Sultan, starting with Egypt.[43] While the pre-*hijra* stage was largely dominated by Muhammad Ahmad's *sufi* allies, headed by Muhammad al-Tayyib al-Basir and the Sammaniyya order, the following post-*hijra* stage diminished the *sufi* connection and strengthened the position of western tribes, such as the Baqqara, on the one hand, and the Nuba kingdoms, on the other. The alliance with King Adam 'Umar, the independent ruler of Jabal Taqali, was crucial in enabling the safe arrival of the Mahdi and his followers at Jabal Qadir, on 1 November 1881 (7 *dhu al-hijja* 1298). Thus the western regions had already become the main source of Mahdist support already at an early stage of the movement and its natural area for gaining new adherents and

---

[42] Shibayka, *Sudan fi qarn*, 138–42, 154–69; Shibeika, *British Policy* 32–40; see also Hill, *Giegler Pasha*, 177. Giegler told Ra'uf Pasha, following the Mahdi's *hijra* to Qadir, that the best thing to do was nothing.

[43] Abu Salim, *Athar* I, 153–4; also Holt, *EI*, 1249.

territories was in Dar Fur and Bahr al-Ghazal, while the Nile regions and the Gezira had to wait for a later stage. It was in the west that the Mahdi's Ansar had their first decisive military triumphs in December 1881 and May 1882.

Following the victory over Yusuf Hasan al-Shalali, on 30 May 1882, the Mahdi declared the implementation of his governing laws. In a way, this may be viewed as the beginning of independent Sudanese statehood. It was at Qadir that he organized his government and appointed his *khulafa'* to govern in various regions. He also divided the army into three commands or flags, the Red Flag under Muhammad Sharif his cousin, the Green under 'Ali wad Hilu and the Blue (or Black), under 'Abdullahi al-Ta'aishi, in addition there was the white command flag, carried by the Mahdi's brother Muhammad 'Abdallah. He appointed his close friend Ahmad Sulayman as head of the newly constituted treasury (*amin bayt al-mal*), while Ahmad Jubara was named *qadi al-Islam*.[44]

Although the Mahdi's early victories over government troops were viewed as the final proof of the validity of his mission, he soon met with a new obstacle. The government troops were capable of prolonged resistance in fortified positions and an attempt to storm El Obeid (al-Ubayyid), the provincial capital of Kordofan, on 8 September 1882 was a complete failure. Thereafter the Mahdi relied upon siege-tactics, and the tribal forces were supplemented with a corps known as the *jihadiyya*, largely recruited from captured government troops of southern Sudanese origin and of the ex-slave armies who were also southerners and who had joined the Mahdi with their previous commanders. They were provided with firearms, which the Mahdi was anxious to keep out of the hands of the undisciplined tribal warriors. The surrender of El-Obeid on 19 January 1883 gave the Mahdi an urban administrative centre and Kordofan formed the first nucleus of a territorial Mahdist state. In the meantime, Khedivial control had been further weakened by the British occupation of Egypt in September 1882 and the reluctance of the British government to undertake any further administrative or military commitments in Sudan. An Egyptian expeditionary force was, however, organized, with Colonel William Hicks, a retired Indian Army officer, as chief of staff. Advancing through difficult terrain from the White Nile into Kordofan, it was annihilated by the Ansar at Shaykan, on 5 November 1883. The Mahdi was now the master of the west. Dar Fur and Bahr al-Ghazal were evacuated or surrendered by their European Governors, the Austrian, Rudolf von Slatin and the Italian Romolo Gessi, in December 1883 and April 1884, respectively.[45] Meanwhile, 'Uthman Diqna, a descendant of a mercantile family in Sawakin, had been sent in May 1883 to raise the revolt among the Beja of the Red

---

[44] Abu Salim, *Haraka*, 19–23; for the Mahdi's letter to Muhammad Ra'uf see Abu Salim, *Murshid*, document 19.

[45] Hill, *Slatin*, 18–20; Keown-Boyd, *Good Dusting*, 17–18.

Sea province, a mission in which he was supported by the influential leader of the disgruntled Majdhubiyya holy clan, Shaykh al-Tahir al-Majdhub. Consequently, by the end of February 1884, the Red Sea region was also under Mahdist control and only Sawakin remained in Egyptian hands.[46]

Khartoum and the riverain areas to the north were consequently directly threatened by the Ansar. At this juncture General Charles Gordon, who had been Governor-General of Sudan in 1877–80, was sent out by the British government, primarily to report on the military situation and to advise on the withdrawal of the Egyptian army. He was also appointed, at his own request, as Governor-General of Sudan by the Khedive. Arriving in Khartoum in February 1884, he produced a succession of plans for the future of Sudan while the Ansar were rapidly closing in on the city. 'Uthman Diqna's success closed the route from the Red Sea to the Nile, while the fall of Berber to an army of Ansar in May 1884 put an end to traffic along the Nile to Egypt. Military pressure on Khartoum itself was increasing, and between April and October 1884 the Mahdi brought up his main forces from El-Obeid to Omdurman where they set up camp opposite the capital. Weakened by siege, the city fell on 25 January 1885, Gordon being killed in the fighting.[47]

From his new seat of government in Omdurman, legislation was undertaken by the Mahdi after the fall of Khartoum. He revised some of his earlier formulations and intended to compile them into a comprehensive legislative body, a task that was, however, interrupted by his sudden death. In order to achieve his goals the Mahdi had to create a unique legal methodology that provided him with unlimited authority to enact positive rules without interference from orthodox *'ulama'*. This implied meeting custom and tribal law halfway while maintaining puritanism in matters pertaining to morality and ethics. It also enabled a charismatic leader, namely the Mahdi, to outmanoeuvre his antagonists and solve the daily political and social problems within the Mahdist theocracy without undue interference.

The Mahdi's legal methodology, though simple and unsophisticated, seems to have been effective in enabling him to achieve his goals. He ignored all schools of law (*madhahib*) and disregarded their legal literature, thus releasing himself from the burden of *taqlid*, and the positive law as consolidated within these schools.[48]

The Mahdi acknowledged three sources of law in the following order: the *Sunna*, the *Qur'an*, and the *ilham* (inspiration) transmitted to him by the Prophet. In this he agreed with other reformist or revivalist movements, such as the Wahhabiyya and the Sanusiyya, who emphasized the

---

[46] Jackson, *Osman Digna*, 24–8.
[47] Keown-Boyd, *Good Dusting*, 71–4.
[48] Layish, *Legal Methodology*, 37–66; quoted from 39.

Sunna and the Qur'an as sources of law, and replaced *qiyas* (analogical reasoning) with direct inspiration (*ilham*) from the Prophet. Since such inspirations were not subject to *ijma'* (consensus) of the *'ulama'*, it gave him greater freedom in establishing the Islamic law in accordance with the dictates of his movement. *Ijtihad* (independent judgement), in which customary law also played a significant role, was reserved for the Mahdi alone. It was a personal *ijtihad* in which *ilham* (inspiration) played a role exceeding that allowed by analogical reasoning (*qiyas*). To this one should add the impact of the Mahdi's *sufi* background, both within the Sammaniyya order and through the teachings of Ahmad ibn Idris, on his judgement. Ibn Idris influenced the Mahdi's thinking through his emissary 'Abdullahi al-Dufani, who was one of Muhammad Ahmad's teachers prior to the latter's proclamation as Mahdi.[49]

Finally, it is important to re-emphasize that in the Mahdiyya there could be no separation between religion and state. The Mahdist state embraced all matters pertaining to government or administration and rejected any attempt to regard political matters as being separate from religion. The creation of an Islamic society was ordered by God and could not be regarded as a political entity, such as a kingdom or a *bashawat*, both of which were by definition divorced from religion. The mistaken attempt to separate religion from state was, according to the Mahdi, the reason for the deterioration of the Turkish Empire and the Egyptian Khedivate.

The bases for a righteous Islamic society were asceticism and the renunciation of worldly things (*taqashshuf wa-zuhd*). Muhammad Ahmad's tendency to abolish the *sufi* orders and the four schools (*madhahib*) of Sunni Islam probably preceded his manifestation as *mahdi* and was part of his belief in the unity of God (*tawhid*). It implied the indissoluble basis of the Mahdist state which is to be founded solely on the Prophetic principles. The first written expression we have to this effect is the Mahdi's letter to Shaykh Muhammad al-Amin al-Hindi, written in Sha'aban 1299 (June/July 1882), in which he urges him to follow only the Qur'an and the *Sunna*. After the *hijra* to Jabal Qadir, where *sufi* traditions were much weaker than in the Nile Valley, total opposition to the four Sunni schools (*madhahib*) and the Sufi orders (*turuq*) prevailed in the Mahdi's writings. In a letter written to *al-faqih* Balal Sabun and his followers the Mahdi explicitly stated that the Qur'an and the *Sunna* were the sole source of all that mattered regarding the *tawhid* and the *fiqh*.[50] But, according to Abu Salim, the most elaborate treatment of this subject is to be found in an undated letter written by the Khalifa 'Abdullahi to the Mahdi's followers in the first few months of 1884 (mid AH 1301). In this letter the Khalifa explicitly reminds them that the Mahdi has ordered all followers to abolish the *sufi*

---

[49] *Ibid.*, 44.

[50] Abu Salim, *Haraka*, 44–5; the letters are quoted from *idem, Murshid*, Document 44 on p. 24 and Document 879 on p. 412.

orders since he is the 'Seal of all the Saints' (*khatim al-awliya*).[51] This superior status also applied to tribal leaders who had supported the Mahdi in the early stages of his revolt but were later discarded because of their leadership ambitions.

---

[51] Abu Salim, *Haraka*, 45–8; the Khalifa's letter refers exclusively to the Tijaniyya order.

7

THE MAHDIST STATE UNDER THE KHALIFA 'ABDULLAHI

The Mahdi's death, on 22 June 1885 (8 *Ramadan* 1302)[52] confronted the Ansar with two problems, one practical, the other ideological. First, who was to take the Mahdi's place as a ruler of the emerging Mahdist state? Secondly, how was the Mahdi's death to be explained, since he had claimed a universal mission to restore Islam but had achieved only a partial conquest within the boundaries of Turco-Egyptian Sudan? The problem of the succession was seemingly quickly resolved when a council of notables met in the Mahdi's house immediately after his death and gave their oath of allegiance (*bay'a*) to the Khalifa 'Abdullahi b. Muhammad (al-Ta'aishi). Already in the critical period of political evolution, following the fall of El-Obeid in 1883, the Mahdi had conferred plenary powers on the Khalifa 'Abdullahi, who was thereafter known as *khalifat al-mahdi*, although he did not use this title until after the Mahdi's death. He was also the commander of the black (Blue) flag (*al-ra'ya al-zarqa*), the largest body of tribal warriors concentrated in Omdurman. His political and military superiority were recognized in his election as the Mahdi's successor. This event suggested how the ideological problem arising from the Mahdi's death could be handled. A proclamation stressed the parallel between Abu Bakr al-Siddiq's succession of the Prophet and that of *khalifat al-Siddiq*'s succession of the Mahdi, and urged all the Ansar to follow the example of the early Muslims who had fought for their faith after the Prophet's death. There was other propaganda, much of it of a visionary or mystical nature, to legitimize 'Abdullahi's succession as *khalifat al-mahdi*. However, it may be concluded that the Mahdi's death ended the so-called millennarian stage of this religious movement. The task of consolidating the territories liberated in the *jihad* and of setting up the autocratic state that was to follow was left to *khalifat al-Siddiq*, 'Abdullahi al-Ta'aishi.[53]

---

[52] Abu Salim, *Haraka*, 41.

[53] Shuqayr, *Ta'rikh*, 934. Shuqayr claims that 'Abdullahi al-Ta'aishi succeeded the Mahdi in mid-June 1885 while the latter was still alive, on the basis of the Mahdi's *manshur al-raha* (letter of respite). However, according to al-Sadiq al-Mahdi, this was ordered by the Mahdi only because he did not want to be disturbed by worldly problems during *Ramadan*; Sadiq, *Yas'alunaka*, 188–9, quotes from the Mahdi's letter to the *umara'*, written on 22 *Sha'ban* 1302 (June 1885); Holt, *EI*, 1249–51.

The Khalifa 'Abdullahi's supremacy was by no means surprising though it was resented by many of the *ashraf*, the Mahdi's direct relations and by their associates. There were two other candidates who could have taken over the movement's leadership, namely the Khalifa 'Ali Muhammad wad Hilu, representing the core supporters of the movement, *abkar al-mahdiyya*, or the Khalifa Muhammad Sharif Ibn Hamad, representing the *ashraf* and the riverain tribes. However, their title never implied actual succession or inheritance. These *khulafa'*, as well as the commanders of the armies (*al-umara'*), were occasionally summoned in order to take part in the supreme consultative council (*al-majlis al-a'la li'l-shura*). The *ashraf*, as well as other sections of the riverain tribes resented the supremacy of the Baqqara, whom they regarded as backward and primitive. However, since the *hijra* to Jabal Qadir in western Sudan, the Baqqara had supplied crucial support for the Mahdist *jihad* and hence had to be rewarded. The *ashraf* also resented the fact that the Khalifa 'Abdullahi, whom they regarded as ignorant and primitive, would be the head of the Islamic state instead of a learned Muslim *'alim*, preferably one of their own number. But the Mahdi had denounced the *ashraf* publicly, in the central mosque of Omdurman, shortly before his death accusing them of attempting to usurp power as if "the Mahdia is for them alone". Therefore, while the choice of the Khalifa 'Abdullahi to the leadership was opposed by certain groups with vested interests, it probably gained the support of the vast majority of the movement's adherents and, more important that of the Council of Elders, which included many of the Mahdi's first supporters. Though this so-called Council of Elders had existed since the early days of the Mahdiyya, there are only a few indications as to its exact functions. It was called upon by the Mahdi when he sought advice and it intervened in cases in which there were disputes with regard to authority or succession. In a way this informal body may be compared with a *shura* council as mentioned above.[54]

Within twelve months of his succession, the Khalifa defeated a conspiracy hatched by the *ashraf* in Omdurman with one of their kinsman Muhammad Khalid, the governor of Dar Fur. Thereafter the Khalifa's fellow-tribesmen or their clients replaced the Mahdi's appointees in all provincial governorships, with the exception of 'Uthman Diqna, who was essential for handling the Beja tribes in the Red Sea province. In 1888–9 the Khalifa enforced a mass migration of his own tribe, the Ta'aisha, from the western Sudan to the centre and settled them in Omdurman and in the Gezira. Although *awlad al-balad* continued to be indispensable in the civil service and the judiciary of the Mahdist state, because of their superior education and training, they had lost political power and the rift opened

---

[54] Details of this event were related by Yusuf Mikha'il, the son of a Coptic tax collector whose family was brought to Sudan during the Turkiyya; Holt, *Mahdist State*, 135–7; quoted from Dietrich, *Der Mahdi* 262–3.

between them and the ruling Baqqara persisted. Following the Mahdi's death the Khatmiyya became the centre of opposition to the Khalifa 'Abdullahi. Many previous supporters of the Mahdi now joined the opposition against the autocracy of *awlad al-'arab*, probably referring to the Baqqara tribes of Dar Fur and Kordofan. These new opposition forces included the *ashraf*, the *awlad al-bahr* (riverain tribes) and many *sufis* who had previously been allies of the Mahdi. This opposition to the Khalifa was also the result of the intolerant attitude of the Mahdists towards any Islam that did not correspond with 'true Islam', namely Mahdism. Indeed, they defined such Muslims as unbelievers or *dukhala'* and thereby alienated many of their erstwhile supporters.[55] In addition to the complex problem of replacing a blessed religious leader such as the Mahdi, the Khalifa was also burdened by the fact that following the movement's successful *jihad*, which had liberated Sudan from alien rule, the *mujahiddin* were now expecting to reap the material benefits of victory which had so far failed to materialize.[56]

In the sphere of foreign relations the Mahdi managed, in the few months following the fall of Khartoum and before his death, to send letters propagating his mission to the people of Fez, Marakesh, Mali and Mauritania. Similarly he addressed personal messages to the Khedive of Egypt, the Emperor of Abyssinia, al-Sanusi of Libya and Hayatu Ibn Sa'id of Sokoto. On 22 June 1885, a few days before his death, the Mahdi received a delegation from the Hijaz and appointed 'Uthman Nur al-Din as the region's Mahdist commander. It was thus quite clear that the Mahdi regarded the liberation of Sudan only as the first step in implementing his message in other parts of the Muslim world.[57] A pronouncement made by the Mahdi following the conquest of El Obeid in 1883 is overwhelming evidence that the universal mission of the movement was foremost in his mind and that he did not regard the minor skirmishes in remote parts of Sudan as the main aim of his *jihad*:

The Apostle of God gave me good tidings in the prophetic vision and said to me "As thou didst pray in El Obeid, thou shalt pray in Khartoum, then thou shalt pray in the mosque of Berber, then thou shalt pray in the Holy House of God, then thou shalt pray in the mosque of Yathrib, then thou shalt pray in the mosque of Cairo, then thou shalt pray in the mosque of Jerusalem, then thou shalt pray in the mosque of al-'Iraq, then thou shalt pray in the mosque of al-Kufa." O God, let us to be of those who pray in these mosques and thereafter make us to be of the martyrs slain at the hands of the vile unbelievers. Amen.[58]

[55] 'Uthman, *Al-din wa'l-siyasa*, 24–6; the terms *awlad al-'Arab* and *awlad al-Bahr* are those used by the author.

[56] Abu Salim, *Haraka*, 30–1; for details see below.

[57] *Ibid.*, 27–30.

[58] Holt, *Mahdia and Outside World*, 276–90, quoted from 278; the quotation is from MS Nujumi. The reference to Yathrib, Medina's name before the *hijra*, is in line with the Mahdi's attempts to portray parallels between his career and that of the Prophet.

Following a detailed examination of the Mahdi's and the Khalifa's letters to the outside world, Yusuf Fadl Hasan concluded that their repeated calls, aimed at neighbouring Muslim leaders to join in the *jihad* failed to produce any meaningful results. The reason, according to Hasan, was that neither the Mahdi nor the Khalifa was familiar with the conditions prevailing in the countries surrounding Sudan let alone in the international arena. Having exploited successfully the circumstances in their own country, where their call for a *jihad* against the Turks, the British, and others, met with eager approval, they were misled into believing that similar results could be expected in other regions – in West Africa, the Maghrib, Egypt or the Arabian Peninsula. Thus the *manshurat* were dispatched and when there was no response it only led to additional letters requesting compliance. But, while a lack of reaction by internal antagonists was often followed by a military campaign, this was not the rule in relations with the outside world, except in the cases of Egypt and Abyssinia.[59] There was, however, a growing impact of the Sudanese Mahdiyya on Mahdism in western Africa in the 1880s and 1890s, especially in the Sokoto Caliphate. A demand by Muhammad Ahmad, following the capture of El Obeid in 1883, for support from Sokoto and Bornu was at first refused. However, Hayatu ibn Sa'id, a grandson of Muhammad Bello, was appointed Mahdist *'amil* (agent) in Sokoto. Secondly, a Fulani named Mallam Jibril Gaini established in 1885 a Mahdist state based on Bormi, on the Sokoto–Bornu frontier. Thirdly, Rabih ibn Fadl Allah (Zubayr), a one-time assistant of al-Zubayr in Bahr al-Ghazal, established a Mahdist state in Bornu (1894-1900) which, despite its ambiguous relations with the Mahdist state in Sudan, fought under the Mahdist flag and declared its adherence to the Mahdist ideology. These Mahdist beliefs in Central and West Africa led to the proposed *hijra* to the East which was undertaken by leaders of this movement following the French conquest. Ahmadu Shehu – son of Hajj 'Umar ruler of Segu – moved to Sokoto after the French conquest of Bandiagara in 1898. His son Bashir continued the *hijra* with the deposed Caliph of Sokoto – al-Tahir Ahmad – after the fall of Sokoto in March 1903 and moved to the Mahdist town Burmi – where they made their final stand against the European conquerors in July 1903 (700 were killed in battle). The *hijra* to British-dominated regions in the east continued under al-Tahir's son Muhammad Bello Mai Wurnu, and thousands of western Mahdist believers migrated and established new settlements there. This massive *hijra* culminated in the Satiru rebellion of 1906.[60]

It was only to be expected that having established his authority within Sudan the Khalifa sought to fulfil the program of *jihad* and conquest that had been cut short by the Mahdi's death. This *jihad* was actively pursued

[59] Hasan, *Masar al-da'wa*, 166–82.

[60] Hodgkin, *Mahdism*, in Hasan, *Sudan in Africa*, 113–16. On the continuation of the *hijra* of the *fallata* and its impact on neo-Mahdism during the Condominium, see below.

for several years after the Mahdi's death, at heavy cost to a people suffering from the effects of the revolutionary war and population movements. The Christian kingdom of Ethiopia under John IV was a principal theatre of the *jihad*, although the fighting should be seen in the historical context of conflicts going back to the Funj period. A successful raid by Hamdan Abu 'Anja, one of the Khalifa's *umara'*, penetrated as far as Gondar in January 1888 and took booty and slaves. In the following year, after Abu 'Anja's death, King John was killed in battle at al-Qallabat (March 1889), a victory that was widely publicized by the Khalifa. These, however, were merely border conflicts resulting in no significant territorial gains, but they were hailed as major victories in the *jihad*. The second objective of the *jihad* was Egypt, now firmly under British military and political control. An invasion had been planned before the Mahdi's death, under the command of the Ja'ali *amir* 'Abd al-Rahman al-Nujumi. The project was postponed for several years, however, although al-Nujumi had made his headquarters at al-'Urdi (New Dongola) as early as 1886. The Khalifa's mistrust of *awlad al balad* led to encroachments on al-Nujumi's command which he was compelled to share with a Ta'aishi commander. In the summer of 1889 a large Mahdist force at last advanced on Egypt, but it was annihilated at Toski (Tushki), north of Wadi Halfa, on 3 August 1889, and al-Nujumi himself was killed in battle. Thereafter the *jihad* against Egypt in effect ended. There were continued military raids, sometimes serious, into Egyptian-held territory, but these were border skirmishes rather than a bona fide *jihad*. A similar stalemate developed in the west and the south. The Fur, as expected, had never been reconciled to the loss of their independent Sultanate and after the withdrawal of the Mahdist *amir* Muhammad Khalid in 1887, a member of the old royal Fur clan, Yusuf Ibrahim, sought to re-establish the independent Sultanate of Dar Fur. He was, however, overthrown by the newly designated governor, 'Uthman Adam, a young kinsman of the Khalifa 'Abdullahi, who in the following year suppressed a still more dangerous revolt in western Sudan. This was headed by a charismatic leader known as Abu Jummayza, who claimed the vacant position of successor of the third Khalifa 'Uthman. Abu Jummayza's death from smallpox, following his initial success, somewhat relieved the position of the Ansar, who had defeated the insurgents outside El Fasher the provincial capital of Dar Fur, in February 1889. 'Uthman Adam showed himself to be a competent governor, but on his early death, in September 1890, the combined provinces of Dar Fur and Kordofan passed into the less capable management of yet another of the Khalifa's kinsmen, Mahmud Ahmad, and from then onwards the whole region suffered from mismanagement and gradually sank into decay.[61]

The pagan regions in douthern Sudan, which had been brought under

---

[61] Holt, *Mahdist State*, 165–84.

the Khedivial administration only in the 1860s and 1870s, were never really integrated into the Mahdist state. Although Bahr al-Ghazal had surrendered to the Mahdi as early as 1884, its Governor Karamallah Muhammad Kurkusawi, a Dunqulawi trader by origin, withdrew his troops from the region in October 1885 in order to fight the Rizayqat Baqqara of Dar Fur, who had revolted after the Mahdi's death. Thereafter Bahr al-Ghazal drifted gradually out of Mahdist control. The Equatorial province was even more remote from the centre of the Mahdiyya. Its Governor since 1878 had been Emin Pasha (Eduard Schnitzer), of Silesian Jewish origin, the last survivor of Khedive Isma'il's expatriate officials who in spite of a mutiny led by some of his Egyptian troops and two Mahdist invasions, in 1885 and 1888, held out until he was forcibly "rescued" by Sir Henry Stanley in 1889. The Mahdist invading force that arrived in the region in 1888 succeeded in establishing a garrison at al-Rajjaf, which maintained sporadic contacts with the Mahdist centre of government in Omdurman by steamer. However, Mahdists held little more than the river line, and their position was constantly challenged by former government troops who had refused to be evacuated by Stanley and who were led by Fadl al-Mawla Muhammad, an officer of southern Sudanese origin. The next Mahdist *amir* to arrive in Equatoria was al-Hajj Muhammad 'Uthman Abu Qarja, who was sent by the Khalifa because he was a strong commander whom he did not really trust, and hence his banishment to Equatoria was a way of removing him as far away from Omdurman as possible. Indeed several of the Baqqara who accompanied him to Rajjaf were supposedly instructed by the Khalifa to assassinate him at the earliest opportunity. However, Abu Qarja discovered the plot and succeeded in fleeing to the Nuba Mountains. Although the Mahdist contingent continued to hold nominal power in the region, one can hardly regard Equatoria as having formed part of the Mahdist state.[62]

The year 1889 thus marks the end of the militant phase of the Mahdiyya which, as has been noted, can hardly be viewed in terms of *jihad* but rather as an armed intertribal conflict under a new guise. The following period saw the stabilization of the Khalifa's autocracy within a territorial state limited for all practical purposes to the Muslim and Arabicized regions of northern Sudan. An additional factor in the decline of Mahdist militancy was the great famine of 1888–90, the effects of which were aggravated by the migration of the Ta'aisha to Omdurman, mentioned above. In November 1891 the Khalifa's authority was challenged by a second revolt of the *Ashraf* in Omdurman under the leadership of the fourth Khalifa Muhammad Sharif. After some desultory firing and a few casualties, a formal reconciliation was effected by *khalifat al-faruk* 'Ali wad Hilu on terms advantageous to the *Ashraf*. However, once the danger was past, the Khalifa ʿAbdullahi proceeded to destroy his opponents' base of power. Muhammad Sharif himself was arrested in March 1892, and sentenced to imprisonment by a special tribunal following which the Khalifa's autocracy went unchallenged. Thereafter, his only intimates in matters of government were his half-brother Yaʿqub ibn Muhammad, who acted as his *wazir* (but without the title), and his son ʿUthman, who was married to his cousin Yaʿqub's daughter. In order to avert envy, he received the honorific title of *shaykh al-din* and was trained for the eventual succession of his father as head of the Mahdist state.[63]

Under the Khalifa ʿAbdullahi the Mahdist state thus became a Taʿaishi autocracy. Most of the leading *ashraf* and practically all the *umara'* who had commanded the Mahdist armies in its victorious *jihad* were gradually eliminated by the Khalifa and replaced with those loyal to him, headed by his relatives and his close associates and later by his eldest son ʿUthman *shaykh al-din*. His period as absolute ruler ushered in the consolidation of the state, which entailed organizing its administration, including the treasury, and introducing a new system of taxation. As noted above, the *jihad* had more or less ended following the defeat the Egyptian army in the battle of Tushki in August 1889. If one adds to this the great famine in the years 1888–90, it is hardly surprising that in the British historiography of the Mahdist state, all evils and cruelties occurring in that state were attributed to the Khalifa ʿAbdullahi. Whereas the Mahdi was often portrayed as the charismatic leader of an Islamic revivalist movement, the Khalifa was depicted as an ignorant cruel dictator whose mismanagement of the Mahdist state led to its impoverishment and ultimate destruction.[64]

---

[63] Holt, *Mahdist State*, 208–9.

[64] See ʿAbbas, *British Views*, 31–46; also Holt, *EI*, 1249–51. These views were also influenced by the so-called 'Wingate Literature': see Daniel, *Islam & Europe*, 424–41.

8

LAYING THE FOUNDATIONS OF
MAHDIST ADMINISTRATION

Military and administrative hierarchy

Following the conquest of Khartoum in January 1885 the Mahdist centre
of learning and government was moved to the new capital Omdurman
(Umm Durman) – al-buq'a al-mubaraka. All the Mahdi's and the Khalifa's
orders, edicts and jurisdiction were written, classified and printed on the
only printing-press, which had been brought to Khartoum by the Egyptians for administrative purposes. They were then sent to religious, tribal
and other leaders and to provincial and military commanders (al-umara').
From the time of his manifestation in June 1881 until his death in June
1885, the Mahdi wrote and dictated some 1,000 letters, proclamations
(manshurat), warnings (indharat), visions (hadrat) and rulings (ahkam), on
legal military, political, religious and social issues. After the Mahdi's death,
the Khalifa ordered that all his writings be collected, catalogued and printed
at the stone-press in Omdurman. In addition, he ordered Muhammad al-
Tahir al-Tatli to assemble the talks and verdicts that had been delivered
by the Mahdi during the meetings of the assembly, and published them in
a volume entitled majalis al-mahdi.[65]

A second cultural centre emerged in eastern Sudan, under the leadership of Shaykh al-Tahir al-Majdhub and his son Muhammad Majdhub.
The Majadhib who became early adherents of the Mahdiyya, put all their
learning at the disposal of the movement and under the patronage of
'Uthman Diqna, continued to classify, edit and distribute the Mahdi's teach-
ings from their centre in Afafit until its conquest by the Egyptian army in
1891. A third centre emerged in Berber, where numerous books on the
Mahdi and the Khalifa were written during and immediately after the
Mahdi's reign. Of these the most important collection is that of 'Awad al-
Karim al-Muslimi, called al-fuyudat.[66]

---

[65] Abu Salim, Haraka, 53–5. The first book to be printed on that press was Ratib al-imam
al mahdi (the Mahdi's prayer-book). Other books or pamphlets included the Mahdi's letters
regarding the predominance of the Khalifa 'Abdullahi, published in several editions after the
Mahdi's death in order to counter the ashraf's hostile propaganda: ibid., 61–2; see also Layish,
Legal Methodology, VII; all the Mahdi's letters and proclamations have been gathered, edited
and annotated by Muhammad Ibrahim Abu Salim, in Al-athar al-kamila li'l-Imam al-Mahdi,
and were published in seven volumes at Khartoum University Press in 1990–4.

[66] Abu Salim, Haraka, 55–7. A copy of the Fuyudat (abundance, brilliance) is in the Sudan
Archive at Durham University's library; see also Hunwick and O'Fahey, ALA Vol. I, 306 ff.

The rapid development of the Mahdiyya, first into an armed rebellion and then into a territorial state, necessitated the improvisation, first, of a command structure and, secondly of an administrative system. During the lifetime of the Mahdi, the key position in all spheres was by definition occupied by the Khalifa 'Abdullahi. He commanded the Black (Blue) Flag (*al-rayya al-zarqa'*), the largest of the three divisions of the army, consisting of the western Baqqara tribesmen, and in addition he held the title of *amir juyush al-mahdiyya*, implying the overall control of the all the Mahdist fighting forces. His two colleagues commanded smaller divisions, the Khalifa 'Ali wad Hilu, the Green Flag (*al-rayya al-khadra'*) composed of Baqqara from Kordofan and the White Nile, and the Khalifa Muhammad Sharif the Red Flag (*al-rayya al-khamra'*), recruiting his troops from the riverain tribes (*awlad al-balad*). As previously mentioned, the Mahdi conferred plenary powers on the Khalifa 'Abdullahi as early as January 1883. The title of *amir* was held by subordinate officers, who in the early stages of the Mahdiyya had commanded virtually autonomous tribal or local contingents. In May 1884 the Mahdi ordered this term to be discontinued, probably because of its overtones of worldly rank, and substituted it by *'amil*. However, *amir* remained in popular usage until the Mahdist state's destruction. With the emergence of a territorial state these chief officers became military governors of provinces but continued to be called *umara'*.

Military and administrative institutions developed further during the reign of the Khalifa. A detachment of the *jihadiyya*, the regular corps first formed during the siege of El-Obeid, was stationed in the fort of Omdurman, named *Kara* during the Turkiyya. After the revolt of the Ashraf in 1891 the Khalifa felt the need of a reliable bodyguard. This was created by expanding a corps of orderlies (*al-mulazimiyya*). By 1895 it consisted of 9,000 or more troops under the command of 'Uthman *shaykh al-din*, the Khalifa's son. By then the fate of the Mahdist state had been decided elsewhere and the partition of Africa between contending European empires was well under way. The Mahdist state was destroyed at the battle of Karari, on 2 September 1898. It was the end of a long-planned reconquest which started with the invasion of Dongola by the Anglo-Egyptian army on 13 March 1896. It was in fact a British-planned conquest, conducted and executed in accordance with British imperial interests and under British command. Egypt was "allowed" to take part in the destruction of the Mahdist state and to pay its share of the expenses. Over 10,000 Ansar died at the battle of Karari alone, and thousands were slaughtered by machine-guns in other battles.

Economics and finances

Two main obstacles burdened the Mahdist economy. First, the infrastructure needed for trade and commerce was practically non-existent, since it had been destroyed during the fighting and was never reconstructed.

Secondly, both the Mahdist state's militant aims and its competition with its neighbours and with Western imperial powers, who were busily carving up the African continent, made trade and economic development practically impossible. The economy thus depended to an ever-growing extent on agriculture, but due to internal struggles between the riverain tribes and the Baqqara and because of long periods of drought, here too was a deterioration. It was a subsistence economy leading to misery and even disease which caused many of the Mahdi's erstwhile supporters to become disillusioned with the Mahdist message.[67]

A Civil Service recruited primarily from *awlad al-balad* and Copts, the only element within the population with the required qualifications, staffed the departments and treasuries of the capital and the provinces. Many of its members had held similar positions under the Turkiyya and some went on to serve under the Condominium during the twentieth century. Already in the Mahdi's time a regular chancery procedure had been established, and the surviving archives of the Mahdiyya as a whole have been estimated at 50,000 pieces. Dispatches were sometimes exchanged almost daily between the ruler and his provincial governors. The provinces fell into two categories in all financial matters too. An outer circle under military governors had their own fiscal and judicial establishments and garrison troops. The core of the metropolitan provinces, which were fiscal areas rather than administrative units, were tributary to the treasury in Omdurman.[68]

Bayt al-mal played a central role in the Mahdist state from the time of the *hijra* in 1881. It was founded at Jabal Qadir in 1882 under Ahmad Sulayman a close friend and supporter of the Mahdi. Its development from its primitive beginnings was determined by the following factors: the centralization of government, the militant nature of the state and its military victories and the commercial needs of the state. The newly established *bayt al-mal* was a place where the Ansar gathered following a victory in order to hand over to the treasury its part of the booty (*ghanima*). The sources of revenue at this stage were primarily two: booty and a levy on grain and cattle, to which the *zakat* was applied. The coinage in use included Ottoman, Egyptian, Austrian and Spanish coins, which had remained in circulation since the Turkiyya. After the conquest of Khartoum, the Mahdi ordered gold pounds and silver dollars to be minted and thus became the first Sudanese ruler to exercise this prerogative. However, other coinage also continued to be in circulation.[69] The Treasury also helped the Ansar and their families with their essential needs, such as food, clothing etc. The nature of *bayt al-mal* changed rapidly following

---

[67] Qaddal, *Siyasa iqtisadiyya*, 197–200.

[68] Holt, *Mahdist State*, 244–9, Abu Salim, *Haraka*, 51–62; Layish, *Legal Methodology*. On Kordofan during the Mahdiyya, see Stiansen & Kevane, *Kordofan Invaded*, 17–24.

[69] Appendix to Book IX, 'The Coinage of Mohammed Ahmed, the Mahdi of the Sudan' in Wingate, *Mahdiism*, 590–600.

the conquest of El Obeid in 1883. First, in comparison with the previous Mahdist conquests, El Obeid was rich and the booty included not only its Municipal Treasury but also considerable private fortunes, which all became part of the booty. Secondly, El Obeid was a central trading town and its financial needs and transactions required a professional financial approach. This led to the appointment of Ahmad Sulayman as the first Supervisor of the Treasury (*amin bayt al-mal*) and was followed by the appointment of two assistants, Muhammad 'Umar al-Banna and Ahmad al-Nur, to be responsible for the vast correspondence and the bookkeeping involved in this transformation. Anyone who acted without the explicit permission of Ahmad Sulayman was regarded as causing harm to the welfare of the Muslims and he was consequently imprisoned, flogged and dishonoured. As for the *amin* and his staff, according to Mahdist sources they were dedicated to their posts and preferred the welfare of the community to their own well-being.[70] The Mahdi himself was anxious to avoid any wrongdoing and even deposited all the personal presents he received in the Treasury. He viewed *bayt al-mal*'s main obligation to be the help it provided the warriors (*mujahidin*), their families and the poor, since many of those who had undertaken the *hijra* and the *jihad* in order to join the Mahdi had lost both their belongings and their incomes and were consequently destitute. It was in a way a communal form of financial aid to all those who required it and since the income of *bayt al-mal* was insufficient the Mahdi asked his followers to be patient and wait until their needs could be fulfilled. The Mahdi also advocated a life of subsistence for all his followers and asked them to lead a life of voluntary renunciation, as he did.[71] After the basic needs of the warriors and destitute were met, the largest part of funds was shared by the three Khalifas. In 1884 the Khalifa 'Abdullahi's Black Flag received 15,000 *riyal*, Muhammad Sharif's Red Flag 8,000 and 'Ali wad Hilu's Green Flag 7,000. In the following year the Khalifa 'Abdullahi received 20,000, the Red Flag 10,000 and the Green Flag 6,000, whilst a special grant of 5,000 *riyal* was made to 'Abd al-Rahman al-Nujumi, the Mahdist *amir al-umara'* (commander-in-chief). The reason given by the Mahdi for this disproportionate division of funds was that the Khalifa's Black Flag constituted half the Mahdist army. Regarding the destitute, who included orphans, widows, the wounded and the sick, Ahmad Sulayman reported in AH 1302 (1884/5) that *bayt al-mal* cared for 4,699 people who had asked for help. In some cases an order to provide assistance was handed down by the Mahdi himself, especially when help was required for warriors (*mujahidin*) who had lost their property or who could not repay former debts. The help provided by *bayt al-mal* sometimes exceeded 300 riyal per person.[72]

[70] Qaddal, *Siyasa iqtisadiyya*, 164–5; also Holt, *Mahdist State*, 56–7.
[71] Qaddal, *Siyasa iqtisadiyya*, 166–7.
[72] *Ibid.*, 168–9.

The history of the office of *amin bayt al-mal* after the Mahdi's death illustrates both its institutional complexity and the increasing autocracy of the Khalifa's reign. Ahmad Sulayman, the first *amin*, was a friend of the Mahdi and a partisan of the *ashraf* and was therefore disgraced and dismissed in April 1886, following the Mahdi's death. His successor, Ibrahim Muhammad 'Adlan, had been a merchant in El-Obeid. His reluctance to extort grain for the soldiery during the great famine led to a clash with the Khalifa and to his execution in February 1890. The next *amin*, al-Nur Ibrahim al-Djirayfawi, was also a former merchant and served until 1893/4. The tenure of office of the *amin*s of the Central Treasury thus became increasingly precarious; one was twice appointed and twice removed. The last year of the reign saw three treasurers: Ibrahim Ramadan, al-'Awad al-Mardi and Ahmad Yasin. The six Chancellors of the Mahdist Treasury (*umana' bayt al – mal*) were all members of riverain tribes. Thus it was the only important position in which the *awlad al-balad* survived after the Mahdi's death and the creation of the Ta'aishi autocracy. The reason is obvious; namely the fact that none of the Khalifa's closer allies from among the Baqqara possessed the necessary qualifications for this post.[73]

Under the Khalifa 'Abdullahi the organization of *bayt al-mal* and the division of its functions became more complex. First there was the central treasury in Omdurman (*bayt mal al-'umum*), which derived its income from *zakat*, *'ushr*, taxes on the Nile boats, land taxes and customs on gum arabic and other exports. Since the *jihad* was practically at an end, booty no longer constituted a major source of income. In addition, there were Provincial Treasuries, which were supposed to hand over a certain percentage of their income to the Central Treasury. This led to conflicts between the riverain tribes and the Khalifa's supporters, especially in the first period of the Khalifa's rule. The latter ordered that the commanders and provincial heads, most of whom were still of riverain origin, would thereafter have no say in the running and distribution of funds from *bayt mal al-'umum*. The Khalifa also declared that the Treasuries were independent and were not part of the political–military administration or of the ongoing struggle between *awlad al-balad* and their Baqqara rivals.[74]

Besides the Central and Regional Treasuries, there was *bayt mal al-mulazimin*, which served as a Treasury of the Khalifa's orderlies. This was founded in 1894 as a separate entity, under the direct supervision of the Khalifa and his half-brother Ya'qub. According to al-Qaddal, the income of this Treasury was derived from the Gezira, the most fertile part of Sudan, and exceeded that of other Treasuries. Thus in AH 1315 (1897/8) the income from the Gezira was 1,093,935 riyal in cash in addition to

---

[73] According to Holt, *Mahdist State*, 252–3. Between a quarter and a third of the 152 employees of *bayt al-mal*, who served during the Mahdiyya had previously been employed in the Turco-Egyptian administration.

[74] Qaddal, *Siyasa iqtisadiyya*, 169–71.

considerable quantities of dhura, cloth and other commodities. At the time of the Anglo-Egyptian conquest, this Treasury was also receiving revenues from the Abyssinian Frontier province. To care for his own needs and those of his family, the Khalifa founded an additional private Treasury in 1894, called *bayt mal khums al-khalifa* (the Khalifa's Privy Treasury). Its income was supposedly derived from one-fifth of the booty, but in reality it received its income from taxes on river-boats, ivory, ostrich feathers and other trade that had previously been part of the Central Treasury's Income. Thus a considerable part of the Mahdist state's income in its latter years provided for the Khalifa's private needs as well as for his immediate family and his bodyguard.[75] Furthermore, since many sources of revenue either dried up as a result of drought and the end of the *jihad*, while income from affluent regions, such as the Gezira, were allocated to the *mulazimin*, the General Treasury (*bayt mal al-'umum*) had to find new sources. *Zakat* continued to be levied, as was *fitr*, a poll tax paid at the end of *Ramadan*. To meet the decline of income al-Djirayfawi imposed a further 10 per cent on customs, which were taken at several points *en route*. The new sources also included fines for smoking and drinking, confiscation of offenders' goods and 'voluntary' contributions (*tabarru'at*) from the wealthy, applied mainly to *awlad al-balad*. Thus Ilyas Umm Birayr, was forced to contribute property valued at some $8,490, while, after the Ja'aliyyin revolt in al-Matamma, booty derived from the anti-Mahdist *ashraf* amounted to at least $100,000.[76]

The administration of justice

The Mahdi envisaged the restoration of the ideal Islamic *Umma*, which would legislate in accordance with the Qur'an and the *Sunna* and take upon itself all necessary jurisdiction, in compliance with the shari'a. However, he soon found himself obliged to give judicial decisions and to promulgate administrative regulations which were in effect legislative acts, all by himself. Many of these resulted from the revolutionary situation, namely rulings concerning broken marriages, irregular unions, inheritance and questions of land ownership. Customs that prevailed in Sudanese society but were regarded as repugnant to Islam were prohibited. The Mahdi's judicial functions were delegated to a specific judicial officer, with the title of *qadi al-Islam*. The first *qadi al-Islam* appointed by the Mahdi was Ahmad Jubara, a graduate of al-Azhar and a member of a Turkish family that had settled in Sudan.[77] After his death in the Friday battle of El Obeid in 1882

---

[75] *Ibid.*, 171–3; also Holt, *Mahdist State*, 238–42; the special Treasuries, except *bayt mal al-khums*, were apparently abolished in 1897.

[76] Qaddal, *Siyasa iqtisadiyya*, 161–93; Holt, *Mahdist State*, 240, 260. Holt relates that, as late as 1897 there were occasional windfalls of booty, arriving mainly from Dar Fur.

[77] Holt, *Mahdist State*, 116; Hill, *BD*, 34.

he was replaced by Ahmad 'Ali, who had been *qadi* of Shakka in Dar Fur under Slatin during the Turkiyya; he held office for twelve years under the Mahdi and the Khalifa, and was succeeded in 1894 as *qadi al-Islam* by Husayn Ibrahim wad al-Zahra, also a graduate of al-Azhar, whose over-zealous adherence to the principles of the shari'a led to a clash with Ya'qub, the Khalifa's brother. Following his arrest he was executed, probably in the summer of 1895, and the title of *qadi al-Islam* seems to have died with him.[78] Already during the tenure of Ahmad 'Ali, there was a deputy judge (*wakil al-mahkama*), and the two seem usually to have acted in concert. As early as November 1886, Sulayman al-Hajjaz was appointed as *wakil al-mahkama* and as Ahmad 'Ali's deputy filled a central position in the judiciary; most orders and decisions seem to have been given under both their seals. By the end of the Khalifa's reign the chief judge had six deputies (*nuwwab*), two of whom had special duties in connection with the Khalifa's bodyguard (*mulazimiyya*). In addition, there were special courts in Omdurman for cases concerning the market, shipping and the Treasury. Both in the capital and in the provinces, the judicial officers were dependent on the Khalifa and his Governors and were deferential to their wishes.[79]

A closer look at the way in which the Mahdist state functioned proves that Islam continued to play a central role even during the rule of the Khalifa 'Abdullahi. Although the state suffered from drought and poverty, its administrative, financial and judicial functions continued to be performed, more often than not by officials who held similar positions during the Turkiyya. The portrayal of 'Abdullahi as a cruel and ignorant dictator owes much to western sources and especially to Slatin Pasha, his prisoner and councillor until 1895, who according to many sources was well treated by the Khalifa. Furthermore, the norms of government applied during the Mahdiyya do not seem to compare unfavourably with those of their Turco-Egyptian predecessors.

[78] Hill, *BD* 29, 168-9; Holt, *Mahdist State*, 131-2.
[79] Holt, *EI*, 1251-2.

Part III
RELIGIOUS POLICY UNDER THE CONDOMINIUM

9
LAYING THE FOUNDATIONS, 1899–1918

The Impact of Wingate and Slatin

Three main principles guided the British authorities when they formulated the guidelines for their policy in Sudan. The first and most important principle, the separation of 'Church and State', as practised in Great Britain, was to be implemented in Sudan as it was throughout the British Empire. Secondly, Islam was to be encouraged to cope with all purely religious matters, including religious education and the enforcement of justice in matters concerning personal status. This implied the abstention of religious leaders from involvement in politics and a ban on popular Islamic movements such as Sufism or Mahdism, which were regarded as tending to fanaticism. Thirdly, there was encouragement of traditional tribal leadership which was to be empowered to cope with rudimentary administrative issues and the administration of justice in accordance with tribal customs, with minimum involvement of British officials. These principles were defined by Lord Cromer, the British Agent and Consul-General in Egypt, on his first visit to the reconquered Sudan in January 1899. In an address to the religious leaders of the Sudanese population Cromer stated that the authorities would not interfere in the religious life of the inhabitants and that they would permit the recognized Muslim leaders to conduct all the affairs that lay within their jurisdiction. He also promised that the new government would assist in building mosques and do all it could to bring about a rapid revival of the pilgrimage to the holy places in Mecca and Medina which had been brought to a halt during the Mahdiyya. But in his address Cromer also referred, both explicitly and implicitly, to certain things that would be prohibited. He stressed that the government would not allow *sufi* orders to restore the tombs of their saints and their mosques which had been destroyed during the Mahdiyya. It was therefore clear that the authorities would not recognize the traditional *fiki*s or the *sufi* leaders in the Sudan, but would assist the establishment of an orthodox Muslim hierarchy on the lines that existed in Egypt and which Egypt had introduced into Sudan in the years 1821–81.

Another area which Cromer touched on in his address was the extent to which Christian missionaries would be allowed to proselytize in Sudan. Here attention was focused on the division between northern and southern Sudan, with Fashoda (later renamed Kodok) as the line of demarcation between the two. In northern Sudan, which was a predominantly Muslim region, missionary activities were to be prohibited and, except in the fields of education and health, this prohibition was closely observed. The tribes inhabiting southern Sudan and at a later stage also those of the Nuba mountains in southern Kordofan were regarded by the British as pagan. Therefore, a different policy was adopted in these regions whereby Christian missionaries would be allowed to proselytize, Islamization, on the other hand would be prohibited. The south was divided into three regions, each assigned to a different missionary society which was allowed to found its own missionary schools in order to increase the numbers of its adherents.[1]

The methods used to win support in the Northern Sudan, which was fully Islamized, were determined by a number of assumptions made by the British administration. Perhaps the most basic of these was that 'a backward country is liable to paroxysms of fanatical agitation when the ruling authority is not of the same creed as the bulk of the inhabitants'.[2] This situation was believed to be especially difficult in Sudan because of the susceptibility of its people to religious fanaticism, as proved during the Mahdiyya. Most of the British top administrators during the early years of the Condominium had direct experience with the Mahdist movement. The first two Governors-General, Lord Kitchener and Sir Reginald Wingate, had long been involved in fighting the Mahdiyya. Rudolf von Slatin Pasha, the newly-appointed Inspector-General and Chief Adviser on Native Affairs, had been acquainted with many of Sudan's leaders since his days as Governor-General of Dar Fur and later as a prisoner of the Mahdi. The new government was therefore determined to draw what it viewed as the necessary conclusions from the success of the Mahdi, this implied that even a minor fanatical religious leader could spark a widespread rebellion. Consequently administrators were instructed to keep careful watch over local religious leaders and to act swiftly and decisively at the first signs of expanding influence or unrest. The British were for obvious reasons especially concerned about the possible revival of the Mahdiyya. For this reason

[1] 'Lord Cromer's speech to the Sheikhs and Notables of the Soudan', 4 Jan. 1899, FO 663/25. For further details see Hill, *Christian Missions*, 113; Warburg, *Wingate*, 95–123.

[2] *Reports on the Finance, Administration and Condition of the Sudan*, 1905; also R. Wingate, 'Memorandum by the Governor-General', 127, quoted in Voll, *Britain and the 'Ulama*, 212–28.

special restrictions were placed on members of the Mahdi's and the Khalifa's families and on their entourage.

Orthodox or popular Islam

The principles governing religious policy, as outlined by Lord Cromer in the address quoted above, constituted in effect the basis of government policy in this field up to the First World War and, with certain modifications remained in force until the end of the Condominium. They were principles based mainly on the views of Sir Reginald Wingate, Governor-General of Sudan in 1899-1916, and Sir Rudolph von Slatin, Inspector-General of Sudan up to the First World War. Wingate, who had headed the Intelligence Branch of the Egyptian Army during the Mahdiyya, regarded the superstitions that were prevalent among members of *sufi* orders in Sudan as dangerous and as leading to a revival of religious fanaticism as they had under the Mahdi. Slatin brought to bear the rich experience he had gained in Sudan, both as Governor of Dar Fur in 1875–83 and as a prisoner and orderly (*mulazim*) of the Khalifa 'Abdullahi in 1883-95. He had been greatly influenced by the suspicion with which both the Mahdi and the Khalifa had treated the heads of *sufi* orders, and consequently regarded them as superstitious and ignorant profit-seekers who could not be trusted and whose activities had to be kept under constant surveillance.[3] The conclusion they arrived at was that despite its shortcomings orthodox Islam should be fostered as it had been during the Turco-Egyptian period. Although they were convinced that the inflexibility of Islamic law had been a major reason for the 'stagnation' of the Islamic world, they nevertheless believed that the Azharite *'ulama'* possessed the prestige needed to overcome the fanatical inclinations of popular Islam. In establishing shari'a courts in Sudan they hoped to make the system flexible enough to introduce reforms relying primarily on the Azhar-trained *'ulama'*. They were to head the religious hierarchy and to prevent a revival of messianic movements such as the Mahdiyya. A network of shari'a courts headed by qualified *qadi*s was established so as to prevent the Sudanese Muslims from seeking the services of their *sufi* shaykhs or *fiki*s who were regarded by Azharite *'ulama'* as ignorant and superstitious. In addition, Wingate and Slatin attached great importance to the revival of the pilgrimage (*hajj*) to the holy places in the Hijaz, which had been stopped during the Mahdiyya. They also considered it necessary to build government subsidized mosques in important centres in northern Sudan so as to undermine the privately owned and operated *sufi zawiyas*.[4]

The authorities encountered three stumbling-blocks in attempting to

[3] Hill, *Slatin*, 85–90; further details in Wingate, *Wingate of the Sudan*.
[4] These principles were first enunciated in the 'Memorandum to Mudirs', enclosure in Cromer to Salisbury, 17 Mar. 1899, FO 78/5022.

carry out this policy. First, the Turco-Egyptian experience had proved that Sufism and other forms of popular Islam were so deep-rooted in Sudanese Islam that even sixty years of Turco-Egyptian rule had failed to leave a lasting mark in this field and had to all intents and purposes been wiped out during the Mahdiyya. Furthermore, although the Mahdi and the Khalifa 'Abdullahi had done everything in their power to weaken and suppress *sufi* leadership and to establish their interpretation of Islam as a factor uniting all Muslims, Sufism had been strong enough to withstand Mahdist rule. Secondly, Wingate believed that the antagonism between the Sudanese and the Egyptians was so deep-rooted that the penetration of Egyptian influence into Sudan had to be prevented at all costs. Even in the sphere of religion, in which he needed the help of Egyptian *'ulama'* and *qadi*s, because there were no Sudanese candidates of suitable calibre, he tried his utmost to limit their numbers and to prevent them from exerting undue influence. To do so he drew up an elaborate plan for the establishment of appropriate educational institutions, geared to training young Sudanese who would be able to replace the Egyptian *qadi*s and *'ulama'* as soon as possible. The third difficulty was economic. Until the First World War Sudan's deficits were covered by the Egyptian government, which as a partner in the condominium, was also entitled to supervise Sudan's budgets. It will therefore be readily understood that many plans, even in the field of religion, such as the building of mosques or the appointment of *imam*s and *qadi*s, suffered because of financial difficulties.[5] This was the situation at the turn of the century when Wingate and Slatin began to implement their policy for the restoration of orthodox Islam in northern Sudan.

One of the first steps taken by the authorities on the advice of Slatin was the establishment of a 'Board of Ulemas' whose function was to advise the Governor-General on all religious matters. In a letter to Cromer in 1901, Wingate informed him of the creation of the Board and concluded by expressing the hope that with the aid of its members, he would succeed in suppressing Sufism, whose influence had increased once again after the downfall of the Mahdist state.[6] The seven members of this Board were selected on Slatin's recommendation who as Inspector-General, assumed the responsibility for dealing with all problems relating to Islam. Until 1912 The Board of Ulemas was headed by Muhammad al-Badawi, a native of El-Obeid and a graduate of al-Azhar. During the Mahdiyya al-Badawi had at first served as a *qadi* in Berber, but after the Mahdi's death he had been removed from this office and had lived under the supervision of the Khalifa in Omdurman, where he had become friendly with Slatin. The other members of the Board included Muhammad al-Amim al-Darir, whose father had been Shaykh al-Islam of Sudan in the years preceding the

---

[5] For details see; Warburg, *Sudan & Egypt* 163–78.
[6] Wingate to Cromer, 13 June 1901, SAD/271/6.

Mahdi's revolt, and al-Tayyib Ahmad Hashim, a tutor of the Khalifa's son, who after the reconquest had been appointed *mufti* of Sudan. Al-Tayyib's brother, Abu al-Qasim Ahmad Hashim, who had served in the Mahdist state as one of the Khalifa's secretaries, was also appointed to the Board of Ulema and, after 1912, served as its head. It would therefore appear that Slatin trusted his acquaintances from the period of his imprisonment although they had served the Mahdist cause, rather than *sufi* shaykhs or prominent *'ulama'*, whom he did not know personally. It is also noteworthy that many of Slatin's old acquaintances reverted to their *sufi* loyalties, which they had to suppress during the Mahdiyya. Thus the two Hashim brothers and Muddathir al-Hajjaz, all prominent members of the Board of Ulema, re-established in Omdurman the Tijaniyya *sufi* order, to which they had adhered before the Mahdist revolt.[7]

The Board of Ulema was intended to give the official Muslim stamp to the decisions of the government, which was primarily Christian, and thus to render it unnecessary for European officials to interfere directly in Muslim religious affairs. The Board, however, had no real authority and its influence was limited to those cases in which the government needed its advice or stamp of approval. Its functions were never clearly defined, but from the evidence that remains of its work it would seem that most of its discussions and recommendations were instigated by the Governor-General or by Slatin and were not the result of any initiative on the part of the *'ulama'* themselves. An example of this procedure is a proclamation addressed to the Muslims of the Sudan, written by Slatin in May 1901, in which he urged them to cooperate with the authorities in strengthening the true Muslim faith. They were called upon to give up their superstitions and to desist from following their *sufi* leaders. This proclamation was submitted by Wingate to the Board of Ulema for discussion and only after its approval by the board was it distributed in thousands of copies throughout Sudan.[8] Another topic on which Wingate regularly consulted the members of the Board was the arraignment before the courts of those suspected of Mahdist activity or of stirring up religious fanaticism or revolt in any form. Already in 1900 'Ali 'Abd al-Karim and his followers had been arrested on suspicion of hostile religious activity. Since the Board of Ulema was not yet established at the time, the 'religious notables' of Sudan were consulted and they declared the sect to be dangerous and demanded its punishment. When members of the sect were released from prison in Wadi Halfa in 1907 Slatin, who had forgotten that the Board of Ulema was established only in 1901, protested that the Board should have been involved when they were first arrested.[9] In August 1901, it was asked to investigate the activities of Shaykh

[7] O'Fahey, *Sufism in Suspense*, 14–15.

[8] Slatin's diary, 26 May 1901, SAD/441; Wingate to Cromer, 17 Jan. 1902, FO 141/371. The proclamation was published in *The Egyptian Gazette*, 14 Nov. 1901.

[9] Wingate to Cromer, 1 Mar. 1900, FO 141/356; Slatin to Wingate, 24 July 1907, SAD/281/1.

al-Mudawwi 'Abd al-Rahman, who had returned to Omdurman after a lengthy exile. Al-Mudawwi, a graduate of al-Azhar, had visited the Mahdi at Jabal Qadir when his movement had just begun. He claimed to have examined the claims of the Mahdi and concluded that they were false. Therefore, at the first opportunity he had fled and joined the besieged garrison in Khartoum. During the Mahdiyya he had changed sides several times, and after the reconquest he had returned to the Sudan from his exile. Slatin instructed the Board to interrogate him and to keep watch over his activities, since he feared that al-Mudawwi would apply his same rigorous tests to the Islamic policy of the Condominium.[10]

The attitude adopted by the Board of Ulema in the investigation relating to the revolt of 'Abd al-Qadir Imam wad Habuba in the Masallamiyya region of the Blue Nile province in 1908 was of special interest. This revolt, in which a British inspector was killed, was considered the most serious to have taken place in the Sudan during the period between the reconquest and the end of the First World War. Wad Habuba and twelve of his followers were sentenced to death, but through the intervention of the British government the sentences were commuted. The Board of Ulema, which had approved the death sentences, claimed that it was the government's policy of compromise that was causing the many religious uprisings that were taking place. In a letter to Wingate the Board stated that even before 1901 it had demanded the execution of all Mahdist preachers and that if the government had acted on this advice, the uprisings would have ceased long ago.[11]

However, the gravest mistake of this policy was that it ignored the strength of Sufism in Sudan, a mistake that had been committed previously by both the Turkiyya and the Mahdiyya. Consequently, not much time elapsed after the reconquest before the *sufi* orders had reorganized themselves and set up new private mosques (*zawiyas*) and *sufi* schools (*khalwas*) for their adherents, despite the negative attitude of the authorities. Moreover, while restrictions were imposed on all *sufi* orders an exception was made in the case of the Khatmiyya, which, because of its consistent opposition to the Mahdi and the exile of its leaders to Egypt, was from the outset accorded special treatment. After the Anglo-Egyptian conquest the authorities felt that they had to recompense the Khatmiyya for its support. Sayyid 'Ali al-Mirghani, who had been appointed Shaykh of the *tariqa* after the death of his father in 1886, was awarded the CMG by Queen Victoria in 1900, the only Sudanese to receive a British decoration before the First World War. The principal mosque of the Khatmiyya in Kassala, which had been destroyed by the Mahdists, was rebuilt with government funds by the Public Works Department, in spite of the clear prohibition on the building of all *sufi zawiyas*. Even the subsidy which the Mirghani family had

---

[10] *SIR*, no. 85, Aug. 1901; see also Hill, *Slatin*, 88–9.

[11] Wingate to Stack (private), 12 May 1908, SAD/284/13; for details, see below.

received from Egyptian governments during their exile in Egypt was continued under the Condominium. When Lord Edward Cecil, Financial Adviser to the Egyptian government, proposed in 1916 that payment of the subsidy be stopped Wingate refused, stating that this would be tantamount to ingratitude to one of the very few families in Sudan who were consistently pro-British.[12] Wingate had good reason to be grateful to the Khatmiyya and its leaders. Sayyid 'Ali al-Mirghani supported Wingate by fighting on his side against growing Egyptian influence in Sudan. He insisted that all contact between Egypt and the Sudanese had to be prevented as far as possible.[13]

The official attitude of Sudan's authorities to other *tariqa*s remained one of suspicion bordering on hostility. This attitude was advocated by Slatin Pasha, who regarded the heads of the *sufi tariqa*s as persons who exploited their elevated status in order to deceive the masses for their own personal benefit. Stephen Butler, a British officer in the Intelligence Department, described Slatin's views as follows:

A busy morning with Slatin . . . Says Govt. should have nothing to do with these tarikas as the heads are really only after the monetary profits . . . they are really frauds and Govt. cannot be responsible for their activities. . . . The only religion recognized by Govt. is Orthodox Muhammedanism.[14]

At the same time Slatin was opposed to any interference in the internal affairs of *sufi* orders. When a British inspector in Dongola recommended the appointment of a new shaykh of the Idrisiyya, Slatin replied that since these fraternities and their leaders were not recognized by the government, there could be no intervention in their internal affairs.[15]

Slatin's views on Sufism greatly influenced the attitude of the provincial governors and the British inspectors, whose understanding of Islam or Sufism was extremely limited. *Sufi* customs and ceremonies, such as the *dhikr*, seemed to British-educated inspectors to be dangerous and leading to fanaticism. James Butler's description of a *sufi* celebration of *mawlid al-nabi* (the Prophet's birthday) clearly indicates this view:

[O]n all their face is a sort of 'far away', rapt expression, not a pleasant dreamy look, but a look that makes one picture them waving blood stained swords, as they hack their way through the forces of 'unbelievers' to the cry of 'Allah Akbar' . . . their barbaric discords adding to the weirdness of the scene, and the pious ecstasy of the religious maniacs.[16]

[12] Willis, *Religious Confraternities*; see also 'Khatmiyya Remuneration', Slatin's diary, 1903, SAD/441; Wingate to Cecil, 5 July 1916, SAD/201/2.
[13] Wingate to Cromer (private), 24 Feb. 1915, SAD/194/2; Ferguson to Wingate, 16 June 1902, SAD/272/4/2; quoted from a private conversation with Ferguson.
[14] S.S. Butler's diary, 21 Nov. 1911, SAD/400/10. Stephen S. Butler had served since April 1911 in the Intelligence Department in Khartoum.
[15] Slatin to Wingate, 3 Apr. 1913, SAD/186/1/1.
[16] Butler's Journal, 1911, SAD/422/12; James Butler, a graduate of Trinity College Dublin, served in Anglo-Egyptian Sudan from 1899 till 1913.

Despite their suspicion and their reluctance to recognize Sufism as an integral part of Islam, the British were gradually compelled by force of circumstances to change their attitude. The influence wielded by *sufi* orders and their leaders, especially in the outlying provinces, forced the British administrators to work in co-ordination with them. For example, the Isma'iliyya in Kordofan led by Muhammad al-Makki, one of the Khalifa's most prominent advisers, received special treatment despite its Mahdist past. Similarly, the leaders of the Majdhubiyya planned their activities in co-ordination with the Governor of the Red Sea province.[17] However, only after the outbreak of the First World War did a real change also take place in the official policy towards Sufism. Slatin's resignation and Wingate's desire to mobilize all possible support for Britain among Sudanese Muslims led to a more flexible policy and to the conversion of the *sufi* leaders from suspected fanatics into prospective allies.

The Shari'a courts and the selection of 'Ulama' and Qadis

The system of shari'a law courts had been established in Sudan by the Turco-Egyptian authorities. They sought to restrict the influence of the *fikis* and the *sufi* leaders who had carried out practically all the judicial functions which were not under tribal law, in the Funj Sultanate. The shari'a law courts established during the Turkiyya, followed the *hanafi madhhab* which predominated in Egypt and the Ottoman Empire, and not the *maliki* school which was generally followed in Sudan and in parts of Upper Egypt. However, the influence of the sahri'a courts remained limited both because of the tribal system of justice, relying on customary law ('*urf*), and because of the judicial reforms, leading to secularization, which had been undertaken by the Egyptian government.[18] In the Mahdist state all secular courts had been abolished while the four schools (*madhahib*) were declared obsolete. As noted, the Mahdi had declared that there was only one *Qur'an*, one *Sunna* and the Proclamations (*manshurat al-mahdi*) of the Mahdi himself, all of which were legally binding. The Mahdi and, after him, the Khalifa, had practically absolute powers in all matters of legislation, jurisdiction and the composition of the judiciary.

After the reconquest, an attempt was made to re-establish the network of shari'a law courts on the Egyptian model. 'The Sudan Mohammedan Law Courts Ordinance', promulgated in 1902, formed the basis of the Muslim judicial system in Sudan. One of the results of the re-establishment of the shari'a courts was that a number of interesting developments in

[17] Butler's diary, Oct-Nov. 1911, SAD/400/10; Slatin to Wingate, 3 Apr. 1911, SAD/186/1/1; further details below.

[18] 'Lieutenant-Colonel Stewart, Report on the Soudan', London, 1883, C. 3670.

shari'a reform promulgated in Egypt were introduced first in Sudan.[19] Thus the reform of the family law in Sudan preceded that in Egypt where the first reforms were enacted only in 1920.[20] Such reforms were viewed as necessary and were encouraged throughout the Condominium era. This policy was based on the assumption that the *'ulama'* in Sudan, both Egyptian and Sudanese, could be relied upon as far as the British administration was concerned. It was hoped that as the champions of a more progressive Islam the Sudan government would win local support. However, this policy never succeeded in having more than a marginal impact in Sudan.

The judiciary was headed by the Grand Qadi (*qadi al-qudat*) who, together with the *mufti* (official expounder of Islamic law) and two other members, constituted the Supreme Shari'a Court. Next came the provincial courts, in each of which there was one *qadi*. The authority of the shari'a courts applied to all matters of personal status affecting Muslims. They were also permitted to hear cases in which other matters were involved provided that all the parties concerned expressed their desire to be judged in accordance with Muslim law. In the event of a dispute between the shari'a courts and the secular judiciary, the matter was submitted for decision to a special committee composed of the British legal secretary, who headed the judiciary, the *qadi al-qudat* and one member appointed by the Governor-General.[21] In 1905 another ordinance was promulgated dealing with the organization of the shari'a law courts. This ordinance laid down that the *qadi al-qudat* could sit as a judge in any case involving matters of personal status affecting Muslims, no matter whether these were first brought before a provincial shari'a court or not. Furthermore, a tariff was drawn up for cases that came before the shari'a provincial courts, and it was decided that all cases were to be heard in the province in which the defendant was domiciled.[22] Instructions regarding procedure in the shari'a courts were promulgated in 1906. The main point in these instructions was that they made it incumbent on government officials and police officers to carry out the sentences passed by the shari'a courts.[23] However, reading the annual report of *qadi al-qudat* for the year 1912, it would seem that many government officials paid no attention to these instructions and in some cases even actively prevented court sentences from being executed.[24]

The most important ordinance dealing with the shari'a courts enacted during this period was the Mohammedan Law Courts Organization and Procedure Regulations, 1915. It authorized the *qadi al-qudat* to instruct

[19] For details, see Anderson, *Recent Developments*, 82–104.
[20] Anderson, *Law Reform*, 224.
[21] *Sudan Gazette*, 35 (May 1902); 61 (Apr. 1904).
[22] *Sudan Gazette*, 76 (May 1905).
[23] *Sudan Gazette*, 98 (July 1906).
[24] *GGR* – 1912 (Khartoum, 1913), 365.

the shari'a courts to deviate from the *Hanafi* school in certain cases and to adopt the principles of any of the four schools of Sunni Islam. Pursuant to this ordinance the first steps to reform the Muslim family law were undertaken in 1916, based in large measure on the opinions of the late Shaykh Muhammad 'Abduh and Shaykh Qasim Amin, both well-known Egyptian reformers of Islamic laws.[25]

The authority to issue instructions regarding the organization and procedure of the shari'a courts lay with the *qadi al-qudat*, who was subordinate to the British legal secretary. Throughout the entire period up to the end of the First World War, the office of *qadi al-qudat* was held by Egyptian *qadis*. In 1908 Shaykh Muhammad Mustafa al-Maraghi was appointed *qadi al-qudat* and served in this capacity till 1919. Shaykh Mustafa al-Maraghi had been a pupil and follower of Muhammad 'Abduh and had originally been appointed to his post in Sudan on the latter's recommendation. 'Abduh himself visited Sudan in 1904, one year before he died, at the explicit wish of Lord Cromer who held him in high esteem. 'Abduh also exerted an influence on the appointment of provincial *qadis* in Sudan, who up to 1918 were all of Egyptian origin, and was personally involved in the formulation and execution of Sudan's Islamic legal system. Not surprisingly it was al-Maraghi who initiated most of the reforms in the shari'a judicial system during this period. Muhammad 'Abduh had proposed many of these reforms in Egypt but most of them were rejected by the more conservative Azharite *'ulama'*.[26]

The extent to which the shari'a courts and *qadi al-qudat* himself were subordinate to the British administration is reflected in an exchange of correspondence between Cromer, Wingate and the Director of the Department of Education in Sudan. Muhammad Harun, who was *qadi al-qudat* in 1907, wrote a report regarding the syllabus in the seminary for *qadis* at Gordon College. On reading this report Cromer strongly criticized Harun's conservative views and especially his view that Islam needed no reforms. Harun was consequently opposed to the inclusion of any studies in the syllabus other than those dealing with Muslim law. In responding to Lord Cromer's objections, the British Director of Education made it clear that it was he who laid down the syllabus for the *qadis'* college and that the opinions of the *qadi al-qudat* carried no weight whatsoever.[27]

The *qadis* in the towns and provinces were also subordinate to British decision-makers. From the point of view of the administration, *qadis* were officials of the Department of Justice and were therefore under the supervision of British Provincial Governors and district inspectors. The request

---

[25] *Sudan Gazette*, 284 (Aug. 1915); Anderson, *Modernization*, 295–302.

[26] *GGR* – 1908, 148; Bishop L. Gwynne, 'Sheikh Maraghi as I knew him', n.d., SAD/466/9/8.

[27] Cromer to Wingate, 11 Feb. 1907, SAD/280/2; Currie to Wingate, 1 Mar. 1907, SAD/280/3; see also *Sudan Gazette* 98 (July 1906).

for leave by a provincial *qadi* was passed on to the governor of the province, while the inspectors sent confidential reports to the British Legal Secretary on the activities of the *qadis* in their districts.[28] Slatin, who as Inspector-General was in control of all issues concerned with Islam, was also responsible for the appointment and dismissal of *qadis*. Although he sometimes consulted Muhammad 'Abduh or Harry Boyle, Cromer's Oriental Secretary, the fact that the fate of the *qadis* ultimately rested with him enabled him not only to supervise their activities but also indirectly to influence their decisions.[29]

As part of the new administration, the shari'a courts also suffered because of financial difficulties. The salaries of *qadis* were extremely low, a circumstance that had its effect on their quality, since those who had the opportunity preferred their own legal practices. The budget was insufficient and hence the extension of the shari'a courts to remote regions was impossible. Many centres populated by Muslims were visited by a *qadi* only once a year.[30] In the years 1903–12 the number of provincial and regional shari'a courts grew from twenty-eight to forty-five. Nevertheless, many regions remained without a *qadi* even after World War I. Judicial functions were therefore carried out by British inspectors even in the field of Muslim law and questions of personal status, despite their ignorance of these matters.[31] Consequently the influence of the shari'a courts was confined primarily to the bigger towns. In the rural regions and in those inhabited by nomads, which constituted the larger part of Sudan, traditional *fikis* also continued to perform judicial functions that should have been under the jurisdiction of shari'a courts. In such cases the tomb of a saint, in which far greater faith was placed by ordinary Sudanese Muslims than in a *qadi* or a shari'a court, served as a place for taking oaths and passing sentences.[32]

The Sudanization of the lower ranks of the Civil Service, which included '*ulama*', *qadis*, *imams* etc., constituted a basic principle in British administrative policy after the reconquest. In his address in Khartoum on 28 January 1903 Lord Cromer expressed his confidence that the British government would do everything in its power to include Sudanese among the lower ranks in every branch of the Civil Service.[33] One of the first steps undertaken to implement this policy before Cromer's promise was the appointment of two '*ulama*', an *imam* and a *mu'adhdhin* (announcer of time for prayers) in each of the northern provinces of Sudan.[34] However, the

[28] *Civil Administrative Order*, no. 257, 10 Mar. 1905; no. 345, 20 Sept. 1905; see also Trimingham, *Islam*, 120–1.

[29] Slatin to Wingate, 9 Aug. 1907, SAD/281/1; Boyle to Wingate, 6 Dec. 1907, SAD/280/6.

[30] *GGR* – 1903, 79; 'Circuit of Kadis of Mohammedan Law Courts during 1911', *Sudan Gazette*, 208 (Dec. 1911).

[31] *GGR* – 1912, 94; Willis's diary, Kordofan, 1909–12, SAD/210/2.

[32] Trimingham, *Islam*, 122.

[33] Lord Cromer's speech in Khartoum, 28 Jan. 1903, FO 633/25.

[34] *GGR* – 1902, 114.

government failed to provide grants for the maintenance of the mosques and for the salaries of the *imams*, *mu'adhdhins* or *'ulama'*, as promised by Cromer. The sums allocated for these purposes were out of all proportion to the needs and were granted only to prove the goodwill of the authorities. The British Governor of Dongola province in 1902-22 complained that for over two years he did not receive an allocation from the government for the appointment of an *imam* and a *mu'adhdhin*, even though this had been promised him by Wingate himself.[35] Dongola was one of the more populated and civilized provinces, and its neglect proves that the government failed to implement its own policy because of lack of funds. *'Ulama'* who were appointed by the government as teachers or *imams* were paid a total of £E15-30 a year. Obviously, in the absence of adequate government remuneration they were forced to seek economic compensation for themselves elsewhere. The government tried to make good the lack in the financial sphere by conferring so-called 'religious robes of honour' on *'ulama'* and *qadis* of various ranks for their services.[36]

Religious education

Another step of even greater long-term significance was taken in the field of education, which was reorganized with the explicit aim of training local cadres for various government functions. The Qur'an schools (*kuttabs*) were utilized by the new administration for the purpose of spreading elementary education among the Muslim inhabitants. The function of the *kuttabs*, as seen by the government, was to teach as large a section as possible of the population the rudiments of reading, writing and arithmetic. The 'three Rs' were, according to Lord Cromer, sufficient for an understanding of basic features of government. In order to encourage *kuttabs* to broaden the narrow framework of their teaching, which had traditionally been to enable their pupils to recite the Qur'an, financial assistance was given to so-called 'model *kuttabs*', which included in their syllabus such new subjects as writing and arithmetic. By 1912 the number of these model *kuttabs* had reached only forty-two, hardly sufficient for a country as big as Sudan but none the less a step forward.[37]

The principle guiding the British government in Sudan, as in its colonies, was that the teaching of English or the establishment of a modern educational system was not only superfluous but also potentially harmful. Islam and Arabic were viewed as the religion and language of the population of northern Sudan and as paramount in the spheres of education and culture. Consequently the government saw the training of teachers for model *kuttabs* as one of its main duties and a seminary for teachers of religion was established in Omdurman in 1902. The students were carefully

[35] *GGR* – 1905, 63.
[36] *Sudan Gazette*, 36 (June 1902); Wingate to Herbert, 14 Feb. 1916, SAD/199/2.
[37] *GGR* – 1902, 75-6; *GGR* – 1912, 292.

selected by the authorities from among families of traditional tribal and religious notables, and after completing their course of studies – which, apart from Qur'anic studies and Arabic, also included mathematics – they were sent to the *kuttabs* as teachers. A year later a seminary for *qadis* was also set up as part of the Gordon College in Khartoum. The *qadis* and the *kuttab* teachers took the same courses during their first three years of studies, after which they were separated for a further two years of more specialized studies in accordance with their chosen future professions. The language of instruction in the two seminaries was Arabic while all other courses taught at Gordon College were in English. The reason for this, according to Wingate, was to keep the teachers and *qadis* away from harmful European influence since it was feared that it could lead to a breaking of their ties with the traditionalist Muslim population. However, when the authorities realized that the educational level of the *qadis* and teachers was too low, it was decided in 1908 to send future candidates first to government schools, where the language of tuition was English, so that they could receive an elementary education before their professional training as teachers or *qadis*. At the same time the Hashimab brothers and Muddathir al-Hajjaz, all members of the Board of Ulemas, were active in laying the cornerstone of *al-ma'had al-'ilmi* (the [Islamic] institute of learning) in Omdurman, with full approval of Slatin and Wingate. The main aim of this institute was to train teachers (*'ulama'*) for the *kuttabs*, as well as *ma'dhuns*, who were authorized by the *qadi* to perform marriages and other minor tasks. The training of *qadis* was later transferred from Gordon College to *al-ma'had al-'ilmi*, which also trained *imams* (preachers), jurists and teachers for the religious seminary itself. The length of the various courses and their syllabus corresponded to the syllabus of al-Azhar.[38]

Up to 1908 forty *qadis* and *'ulama'* had completed their training in Sudan and were appointed by the government to fulfil duties hitherto undertaken by Egyptians, who were consequently dismissed. The government thereby achieved two of its aims: first, it effected a considerable saving of funds; and, secondly, it rid Sudan of undesirable Egyptian influence which Wingate and his colleagues were determined to reduce as fast as possible.[39] An additional advantage of the seminary for *qadis* was that it helped the British to reduce the number of Sudanese *qadis* whom it had previously been compelled to send for specialized studies at al-Azhar. Basing themselves on past experience, the authorities feared that the Azharites returning to Sudan might bring with them pan-Islamic ideas or, even worse, might infect the Sudanese Muslims with the 'germ' of Egyptian nationalism. From a British point of view this would naturally disqualify them from continuing to serve as *qadis* or teachers in Sudan. Nevertheless, in 1911 Wingate suggested sending a limited number of Sudanese *qadis* to al-Azhar for specialized

<hr />

[38] Trimingham, *Islam*, 121–2. *Al-ma'had al-'ilmi* became the nucleus of the present Omdurman Islamic University: see O'Fahey, *Sufism in Suspense*, 15.

[39] *GGR* – 1908.

studies, since *al-ma'had al-'ilmi* required teachers of superior qualifications. His assumption was that the importation of Egyptian *'ulama'* as teachers in this institute was even more dangerous than the possible influence of
al-Azhar on the Sudanese students.[40] Thereafter the policy adopted was to
appoint Egyptian *qadis* to serve in Sudan only if there was no alternative.
When Edgar Bonham Carter, Sudan's first legal secretary, wanted to
appoint Egyptian *qadis* after 1906, he had to prove to Wingate that there
were no suitable candidates among Sudanese graduates.[41]

A good example of the complex problems involved in implementing
this policy is that of Majdhub Jalal al-Din (1887–1976), regarded as the last
inspiring religious figure who was universally recognized by the Majadhib
family.[42] He was raised by his maternal uncle, a pious Moroccan teacher
and memorized the Qur'an at the age of seven. He belonged to the first
generation of young Sudanese who were exposed to the government's
secular education. When, in 1902, the government urged rural leaders, to
send their sons to the newly-founded Gordon Memorial College, the
Majadhib, like other religious families, resisted. They feared that it would
lead their sons to *kufr* (unbelief) or, worse, to Christianity, and refused to
send them. After much persuasion by the Egyptian *ma'mur* (official in
charge of a subdistrict), who warned them that resistance might be interpreted as indicating continued support for their Mahdist beliefs, they
reluctantly decided to send an orphan from their family to the College.
They stated that this orphan was the son of their shaykh and they changed
his name to Majdhub Jalal al-Din to mislead the authorities. The career of
Majdhub, following his graduation from Gordon College, is of considerable interest since it shows the ability of students selected from holy families
to become part of the intelligentsia without losing their previous identities.
Majdhub joined the staff of Gordon College in 1921, and taught Arabic and
Islam until his retirement in 1944. He continued to teach for a while at *al-
ma'had al-'ilmi* in Omdurman but returned to al-Damir to build a *khalwa*,
combining school and mosque, in 1948–9. Following disagreements within
the Majadhib in 1950–1, he decided to build his own mosque and school,
called *ma'had al-Damir al-'ilmi* and modeled on the Omdurman *ma'had*.
In it he adopted modern methods of teaching while preserving the emphasis on religious education. Thus Majdhub Jalal al-Din, who opposed the
government's secular educational policy, exploited what he had learnt at
Gordon College both as student and teacher, as well as his teaching at the
ma'had in Omdurman. He even received government subsidies for education, in order to attract pupils to his own brand of modernized Islamic

[40] Wingate to Kitchener (private), 26 Oct. 1911, SAD/301/4; Kitchener had returned to
Egypt as High Commissioner in 1911.
[41] Bonham Carter to Wingate, 16 Jan. 1907, SAD/280/1; Wingate to Bonham Carter
(private), 28 Sept. 1916, SAD/201/8.
[42] Hofheinz, *Faki*, 1–2.

teachings. Among those who graduated from Majdhub's school were Sirr al-Khatm al-Khalifa, a future Minister of Education, who became Prime Minister of the transitional government in 1964–5.[43] But at the same time Majdhub also excelled in promoting Majdhubiyya *sufi* traditions. He collected and printed the special Majdhubiyya prayers and litanies (*awrad*), hoping to give them their own separate identity. He instituted a *mawlid* for Shaykh Hamad b. Muhammad al-Majdhub's anniversary (*hawliyya*). He thereby gave the order a more 'orthodox' image in line with Egyptian brotherhoods organized in the 'Supreme Sufi Council'. While he failed to form a separate centralized Majdhubiyya order, as he had hoped, he succeeded in turning the Majadhib centre in al-Damir and the tomb of Shaykh al-Majdhub into a religious centre of significance, shifting its centre from eastern Sudan, where it had been since the Ja'aliyyin revolt in 1822–3, to the Nile Valley.[44]

The Waqf and the building of government mosques

Another step taken by the authorities to promote orthodox Islam was that of providing assistance for the building and maintenance of public mosques. The purpose was to encourage and finance the building of public mosques with schools (*madrasas*) attached to them, in order to reduce the importance of private mosques, built and maintained by the *waqf* (religious endowment) and often owned by *sufi* orders, which were regarded as undesirable. This policy was only partially successful since the financial situation, following the reconquest, did not permit the government to allocate adequate sums for this purpose. Thus, entire provinces such as Kordofan and Kassala were left without a properly built and maintained mosque until 1905. Whenever central mosques were built in other provinces, they were subsidized by the *waqf* administration in Egypt or through donations from local inhabitants. As a result the government was compelled to moderate its hostile attitude towards private mosques that continued to be erected by the *sufi* orders with funds derived from family endowments (*waqf ahli*). Consequently, by the end of 1904 there were in Sudan 224 private mosques compared with only 189 public ones.[45] Even when the government did participate in building mosques, its financial contribution was only a token one. The Department of Public Works helped in the planning and construction of the mosques, while local inhabitants supplied labour. For example, the government contributed £E10 to the building of a mosque on the White Nile south of al-Dueim, while the mosque cost over £E700.[46]

---

[43] *Ibid.*, 3–4; Majdhub's *ma'had* in al-Damir became a regular government school, probably in 1973.
[44] Hofheinz, *Faki*, 4–5.
[45] *GGR* – 1904, 81.
[46] *GGR* – 1902, 298–9; *GGR* – 1905, 63; Wingate to Clayton, 13 Feb. 1911, SAD/300/2.

It should be noted that, before the Turco-Egyptian conquest there were few *waqf*s in Sudan. The Funj rulers used to make gifts of land to families of *'ulama'* and to heads of *sufi* orders, which became the private property of the recipients. In this manner, the Majdhubiyya, for instance, accumulated considerable landed property in al-Damir.[47] The scarcity of *waqf* in Sudan forced the Turco-Egyptian authorities after the conquest, to build a number of mosques in Sudan financed by the Egyptian *waqf*. At the same time, the authority of Shaykh al-Bakri, who was responsible for all *sufi* *tariqa*s in Egypt, was extended to Sudan. By virtue of his office Shaykh al-Bakri was nominally in charge of the administration of all *zawiya*s and *waqf*s of *sufi* orders, but in effect he wielded little influence in Sudan.[48] In 1901 Wingate ordered a survey to be made of all the *waqf*s in Sudan. The survey showed that only a small area of land and very few buildings were in fact designated as religious endowments and that most of these were neither properly registered nor were they being administered in an appropriate manner. Wingate aimed at transferring the administration of the *waqf*s to the shari'a courts so as to prevent interference by the Egyptian *waqf* administration,[49] an aim which was only partially realized. For example, in Kordofan the *waqf* continued to be administered by the provincial government, which built the principal market of El-Obeid on *waqf* land and used its revenues to erect the central mosque in the town. A similar situation evolved in Khartoum, where the revenues of the *waqf*, amounting to £E250 per annum, were used by the Governor to build mosques. It was only in 1911 that the administration of all *waqf*s was officially handed over to the shari'a law court.[50] Moreover, *waqf* administration was so disorderly that in 1907 it transpired that certain government buildings had been erected on *waqf* land without the authorities being aware of the fact. A proposal by the Legal Secretary that a Sudanese *waqf* administration be established was turned down by Wingate who, as noted, feared Egyptian interference.[51]

This policy did not prevent the authorities from accepting assistance from the Egyptian *waqf* administration for the building and maintenance of mosques. A mosque in Tokar was fully financed by the Egyptian *waqf*. Only in 1912 were instructions issued by Wingate to stop Egyptian payments immediately.[52] An even greater departure from government policy was the case of the central mosque of Khartoum, which had been built almost entirely with Egyptian *waqf* funds.[53] In 1907 Slatin approached the Egyptian *waqf* administration on behalf of the Sudan authorities, for a grant

---

[47] Holt, *Holy Families*, 6.
[48] Trimingham, *Islam*, 200–1.
[49] *Sudan Gazette*, no. 19 (Jan. 1901); no. 35 (May 1902).
[50] Meinhof, *Kordofan*, 48–9; *GGR* – 1911, 141.
[51] Bonham Carter to Wingate, 13 July 1907, SAD/281/1.
[52] Wingate to Stack (private), 16 May 1912, SAD/181/2/2.
[53] *GGR* – 1904, 81.

of £E20,000 to complete the central mosque of Khartoum. The request reached Khedive 'Abbas Hilmi II, in whose jurisdiction the *waqf*s lay and he made a proposition to Sir Eldon Gorst, the British Consul-General, to the effect that in exchange for the funds granted to Sudan the Egyptian *waqf* administration be given land in Khartoum.[54] Gorst who had replaced Lord Cromer in Cairo in 1907, was inclined to accept the proposal but Wingate's reaction to it was unequivocally negative. Wingate withdrew the request for financial assistance from the Egyptian *waqf* administration explaining his policy to Gorst as follows:

I know of no subject (except perhaps the slavery question) which is of so thorny a nature as this, owing principally to the racial hatred between Egyptians and Sudanese. Egyptian maladministration, especially in wakfs [*sic*] matters, had a great deal to do with the original [Mahdi] revolt and it has been an essential part in our reorganisation of the Sudan to keep out of the country any interference on the part of the Egyptian Wakfs administration.[55]

This was undoubtedly a storm in a teacup, since the *waqf* had never been a major problem in the Turco-Egyptian administration of Sudan, nor had it been one of the factors leading to the Mahdi's revolt. The detailed report submitted in 1883 by Colonel Stewart, in which he specified all the defects of Egyptian rule in the Sudan, did not even mention the *waqf*.[56] The reason was that during the sixty years of their rule, the Egyptians had failed to introduce this institution into Sudan in any notable measure.

The pilgrimage

During the Mahdiyya the pilgrimage (*hajj*) to the holy places in Mecca and Medina had been stopped, and after the Mahdi's death believers were ordered to make the pilgrimage to his tomb, which had been erected in Omdurman, instead of to the tomb of the Prophet in Mecca. Wingate, who at that time had headed the Intelligence Branch of the Egyptian Army, knew that the abolition of the *hajj* had given rise to much bitterness among both the Sudanese Muslims and the *fallata* pilgrims from West Africa, who customarily passed through Sudan on their way to the holy places in the Hijaz.[57] Therefore, immediately after the reconquest the authorities made every effort to revive the *hajj* and make matters as easy as possible for the pilgrims. After a protracted struggle with the institutions of the International Quarantine Board in Venice the latter agreed to open a special quarantine

[54] Slatin to Khalil Pasha Hamdi, June 1907, SAD/284/12/3; Gorst to Wingate, 12 Dec. 1908, SAD/284/15.

[55] Wingate to Gorst (private), 22 Dec. 1908, SAD/284/12/3. Wingate failed to mention that the request for Egyptian *waqf* assistance was made by Slatin, acting for the Sudan government.

[56] Lieutenant-Colonel Stewart, 'Report on the Soudan', London 1883, C. 3670.

[57] Ohrwalder, *Ten Years*, 278–9.

station for pilgrims in Sawakin, the pilgrims' port of departure.[58] Special
villages were built for pilgrims in which they could stay both on their way
to the Hijaz and on their way back. They were organized in accordance with
tribal units and were placed under the authority of their own shaykhs. The
government helped to defray the expenses of maintaining the pilgrims in
the villages, and of the quarantine station. In 1911-12 the authorities allocated over £E3,000 annually to the *hajj*, while the pilgrims themselves
contributed only about £E500 towards their expenses.[59] This positive attitude towards the *hajj* was particularly remarkable during the First World
War; in spite of the danger of infiltration by enemy agents from the Hijaz,
the pilgrimage was suspended only for the first few months of the war and
was revived as early as July 1915.[60]

There can be no doubt that the authorities' positive policy regarding the
hajj caused satisfaction among Sudanese and raised the prestige of the
'ulama', who organized and headed the *hajj*. But there was a further reason
for encouraging the pilgrimage, namely, the shortage of manpower that had
made itself felt in Sudan during these years. The pilgrims from West Africa
who passed through Sudan when the *hajj* was revived used to spend a
number of years in Sudan, either on their way to the Hijaz or on their return
to their own countries. Many of them even settled permanently in Sudan
and, as a result made an important contribution to the economy of the country by serving as a cheap and efficient labour force. This phenomenon was
remarked upon in a conversation that took place between Wingate and one
of the religious notables of Omdurman, who said to him: 'Allah took away
our slaves, but sent us the Fallata.'[61] Finally, in promoting the pilgrimage
and granting financial aid to the pilgrims, Britain also enhanced its prestige
amongst Muslims from other regions who made the pilgrimage through
Sudan.

Fears of Mahdist 'revival', 1899–1914

The danger of a revival of Mahdism guided policy-makers in Sudan in
every field of administration, especially that of religion. The decisive factor
in the religious policy adopted by Wingate and Slatin was that they realized
that while Mahdism had been defeated on the battlefields, it had retained
its popularity among significant segments of the population. They therefore
employed a strong-arm policy against any movement of a religious nature
that deviated from orthodox Islam, with its suppression without mercy
when it resorted to an uprising. Up to the First World War hardly a year passed without a religious uprising or the imprisonment of *fikis* who declared

[58] *GGR* – 1904, 38; *Sudan Gazette*, 104 (Jan. 1907).
[59] 'Note by Said Shoucair on cost of pilgrimage', n.d., SAD/493/3.
[60] *SIR*, no. 252, July 1915.
[61] *GGR* – 1904, 38; *Sudan Gazette*, 104 (Jan. 1907); also Warburg, *Social and Economic Aspects*, 785–91.

themselves to be *nabi 'isa*s or *mahdi*s. Of these numerous Mahdist risings only two were significant: the Wad Habuba revolt, which broke out in the Gezira in 1908, and the Nyala revolt in Dar Fur in 1921.[62] The *nabi 'isa* and *mahdi*-style revolts of these early years occurred mostly in areas that had been traditional Mahdist strongholds, namely in the Gezira and in western Sudan, and were supported primarily by West African *fallata*, who had emigrated to the Nile Valley in considerable numbers and most of whom believed in the second coming of a *mahdi*. The most important of these uprisings took place, as mentioned, in 1908 when 'Abd al-Qadir Imam wad Habuba, a minor Mahdist *amir*, raised the flag of revolt in Masallamiyya on the Blue Nile and killed the British inspector and the Egyptian *ma'mur* who had come to persuade him to lay down his arms. Wad Habuba then attacked a military unit that came to arrest him and caused several casualties. But two days after this battle and without any further military action, Wad Habuba and his men were handed over to the authorities by the local inhabitants in the region.[63] All other uprisings, with the exception of the one at Nyala in Dar Fur, were suppressed even more easily than this one and sometimes without resort to arms. It would seem, therefore, that the authorities' fears regarding a revival of militant Mahdism, as opposed to the belief in non-violent Mahdism, were highly exaggerated. The claim made by Wingate, Slatin and other British officials that it was only the government's military superiority in Sudan that had prevented a general Mahdist revolt seems to have had no basis in reality. The Egyptian army units, composed of Egyptian and Sudanese units under British command, were scattered throughout Sudan, without adequate means of communication and lacking the strength to prevent a revolt on a broad scale, should one have occurred. In the whole of Sudan, there were no more than 600 British officers and men and even these were concentrated largely in Khartoum. It would seem, therefore, that the main reason why the religious uprisings never involved more than a few score of participants was the fact that the Sudanese still remembered the horrors of the Anglo-Egyptian conquest and the hunger, epidemics and other evils that had afflicted them during the last few years of the Khalifa 'Abdullahi's rule. As against this, the new authorities had afforded them the possibility of cultivating their lands in peace, introduced a wise land policy, eased the burden of taxation and granted a number of other benefits of an economic nature to the population. It was chiefly due to these circumstances that there was no revival of Mahdism as a militant movement and not the severe measures taken against *nabi 'isa*s or *mahdi*s who began to preach in the Nuba mountains or the villages of the Gezira. There is no doubt that the vast majority of Sudanese Muslims would have preferred to see their country ruled by Muslims rather than by

[62] See for instance Wingate to Maxwell (private), 12 May 1908, SAD/110/8; full details in Hassan, *Mahdist Risings*, 440–82.
[63] *GGR* – 1908, 49–52.

British infidels or even Egyptians of their own faith. But their attitude was realistic and cautious and they probably preferred the order that existed to the anarchy that could have resulted from a general uprising against the conquerors. Finally, the fact that Islam was recognized by the government and its functions were conducted by Muslim *'ulama* and *qadis*, with only minor interference by the authorities, was welcomed by most of the inhabitants.[64]

The First World War and the revision of policy

The outbreak of First World War in August 1914 found Wingate and the majority of British provincial governors spending their summer vacations in the more tolerable weather of the British Isles, whence they were forced to hurry back to Sudan. The time between the outbreak of hostilities in August and the entry of Turkey into the war on the side of Germany in November 1914 was used by Wingate and his colleagues for the purpose of conducting a well-orchestrated propaganda campaign among the religious and tribal leaders in Sudan. Wingate, who was the moving spirit in this activity, travelled to all the main centres in Sudan and met with *'ulama'*, heads of *sufi* orders and tribal chiefs. In his talks with them he stressed that the war would have no affect on the inhabitants of Sudan. He prepared them for the possibility of war between Britain and Turkey and maintained that Turkey could no longer be regarded as a truly Muslim state. Since the Young Turks' revolution in 1908, Turkey had, according to Wingate, been ruled by a gang of irresponsible hooligans who were working against the Ottoman Caliph and against the Muslims of other nations, chief among these being the Arabs, who were now being helped by Britain. Wingate reported to his superiors in Egypt and London on his efforts and on the extent of his success. In one of his letters Wingate described the enthusiasm with which he had been received by the local leaders in all regions of Sudan and concluded by saying that the Muslims of Sudan would not support Turkey, since the horrors of Turkish rule were still engraved in their memories and their hatred of the Turks had remained unchanged.[65]

The climax of Wingate's work among the religious leaders was his speech to the *'ulama'* of Sudan on 8 November 1914, three days after Britain declared war on Turkey. In his speech he stressed the material benefits the Sudanese had received as a result of the Condominium. He drew attention to the help given by the government to the building of mosques and

---

[64] For details see Warburg, *Wingate*, 100–6; see also Hassan, *Mahdist Risings*, further details below.

[65] Wingate to Cromer (private), 27 Nov. 1914, SAD/192/2. In a note attached to the letter Wingate stated that having received no recognition from British authorities in Egypt, he hoped that Lord Cromer would draw the attention of the Home Government and of the British public to the loyalty of the Sudanese Muslims, which was largely due to the wisdom of British administration.

Muslim schools throughout Sudan, and reminded his listeners that with the aid of the authorities they could now reach Mecca and Medina to perform the *hajj* within a few days and in greater comfort than ever before. His speech was devoted mainly to the war Turkey was waging against Britain and her allies. Wingate blamed the Young Turks and their adventurist policy for the fact that Turkey had lost its provinces in Europe and other regions. The Turkish rulers were characterized by Wingate as a 'Syndicate of Jews, financiers and low-born intriguers', while he portrayed Britain as the defender of Islam, whose true interests it was serving.[66] Wingate decided at this stage to mobilize all possible support for the war against Germany and Turkey. First and foremost he sought to prevent the Muslims from being 'led astray' by the Ottoman Caliph's call for *jihad*. Alongside Sayyid Sir 'Ali al-Mirghani, whom he viewed as a loyal supporter of Britain, Wingate decided to recruit the services of the Mahdi's son, Sayyid 'Abd al-Rahman and his followers, the Ansar. The historic hatred of the nineteenth-century Mahdiyya for both the Turks and the Egyptians, who were corrupting Islam, remained central in the movement's ideology. To gain their support Wingate first had to change his attitude towards Sayyid 'Abd al-Rahman. Up to 1914 the latter had lived in Omdurman and, after 1908, also on Aba Island in near obscurity and under the constant supervision of the Intelligence Department headed by Slatin, who suspected him of being dangerous to the regime.[67] Already in those years he exerted considerable influence in the region of the White Nile, and many admirers visited him to receive his blessing. When Wingate visited the White Nile province early in 1911, Sayyid 'Abd al-Rahman openly represented himself as the spokesman of the inhabitants of the province, a claim of which Wingate disapproved.[68] After war had broken out, Wingate decided to exploit this popularity and called upon the Sayyid to mobilize his supporters in the Gezira on the side of the British and to assist the authorities in preventing Turkish pan-Islamic propaganda from penetrating into Sudan. Sayyid 'Abd al-Rahman, together with some 500 religious leaders, shaykhs of *sufi* orders and tribes, also signed the 'Sudan Book of Loyalty', in compliance with the policy of the British administrators, in which they declared their full support for Britain and her allies in the war against Turkey, Germany and their associates.[69] When a rebellion led by a Mahdist *fiki* broke out in Jabal Qadir in the Nuba mountains in 1915, at the same spot to which the Mahdi and the Ansar had made their *hijra* in 1881, Sayyid 'Abd al-Rahman denounced them as pretenders and proved his loyalty to the authorities by

---

[66] H.E. the Governor-General's Speech to the Ulemas at Khartoum, 8 Nov. 1914, *SIR*, no. 244, Nov. 1914. On Wingate's views regarding British policy towards Islam and Arab nationalism during the world war, see Kedourie, *Cairo and Khartoum*; also Warburg, *Sharif*.

[67] Butler's diary, 13 Oct. 1911, SAD/400/10.

[68] Wingate to Gorst, 1 Jan. 1911, SAD/300/1.

[69] 'The Sudan Book of Loyalty', *Sudan Times*, 14 Aug. 1915; Juredini (editor of the *Sudan Times*) to Wingate, 20 Aug. 1915, SAD/196/3.

passing on to Wingate exact information about the *fiki* who had headed the rebellion.[70] This was in effect a turning-point in British policy towards the neo-Mahdiyya, which led to a major controversy after the war ended.

Declarations of loyalty to Britain signed by religious and tribal leaders in Sudan and addressed to Wingate poured in from all parts of the country. The letter-writers revealed a decided apathy towards the Ottoman Caliph's call for *jihad* and stressed the economic prosperity and religious freedom the inhabitants of Sudan enjoyed.[71] On 9 November 1914 the *Sudan Times* published an article, signed by 'a Muslim Notable', accusing Germany of having misled the inexperienced rulers of Turkey; the proof was that Turkey had declared a holy war (*jihad*) on Britain, 'the only country in the world which had proved her unreserved sympathy for Islam'. The article was devoted mainly to an analysis of the difference between *jihad* and a war caused by political factors. The writer explained that the present war was being fought between Christian countries and had no religious implications for Muslims. He therefore addressed himself to the religious leaders of Sudan, urging them to explain to Sudanese Muslims, most of whom were ignorant, that the war was not a holy war and therefore had no significance for the Muslims.[72]

In 1916 Wingate and his Private Secretary Stewart Symes prepared a memorandum on the political situation in Sudan. After a brief historical survey of the Turco-Egyptian regime and the Mahdist state, there followed a detailed description of the principles that guided the Anglo-Egyptian government and their implementation since the establishment of the Condominium in 1899. The authors stressed that the government of Sudan was decidedly British, since the Egyptians carried out only minor functions within it. As proof of the success of this policy they drew attention to the peaceful atmosphere that had reigned in Sudan since the outbreak of the war, emphasizing that this calm would continue 'so long as the population knows that their religious interests are being preserved intact and that the present Government is permanent'.[73] In an address in the House of Lords in June 1916 Lord Cromer, with whom Wingate was corresponding regularly, described the efforts of Wingate and his colleagues and insisted that the peace that prevailed in Sudan was the result of their religious policy and 'one of the greatest indirect compliments that had ever been paid to the wisdom and beneficence of English administration'.[74]

It is an open question whether it was indeed the religious policy of the Condominium rulers that had induced the inhabitants to remain loyal and

---

[70] Wingate to Clayton (private), 24 Apr. 1915, SAD/469/9.

[71] These letters, which were written in November 1914 and signed by hundreds of '*ulama*', *sufi* shaykhs and tribal leaders, were not spontaneous. They were invited by Wingate and his subordinates to write these letters, which are stored in SAD/192/2.

[72] *Sudan Times*, 9 Nov. 1914 (official translation of article in SAD/192/2).

[73] 'Note on the political state of the Sudan', SAD/199/1.

[74] *The Times*, 28 June 1916.

to disregard the Ottoman Caliph's call for a *jihad*. It is a fact that except for the revolt of 'Ali Dinar, the last Sultan of Dar Fur, and a revolt led by an insignificant *fiki* in the Nuba Mountains mentioned above, calm prevailed in Sudan from the beginning of the war until its end.[75] But the impression gained from reading between the lines of the letters written by Wingate and his colleagues is that in the main the inhabitants of Sudan were, not surprisingly, serving their own interests rather than those of their foreign rulers. They were enjoying peace and relative economic prosperity such as they had not known either under Mahdist rule or during the Turkiyya that preceded it. In 1914 there was a drought in Sudan, and Britain supplied the population with large quantities of subsidized *dhura*, specially imported from India at a very low price. In the letters in which the tribal chiefs and other leaders declared their loyalty to Great Britain, the supply of cheap *dhura* to the affected regions was praised as one of the most important actions of the British authorities, obliging the inhabitants to repay one good deed with another.[76]

Another circumstance that helped the British was the traditional hatred of the Sudanese for the Turks, a condition that the Mahdi too had skilfully exploited, as already mentioned. Wingate knew that among Sudanese the Condominium was nicknamed 'al-Turkiyya al-thaniya' (the second Turkish regime), which was distinguished from the previous Turkiyya by its incorruptibility and its generous economic policy. Both the first and the second Turkish regimes were alien to the Sudanese. But the older generation, which still wielded considerable influence in that period, preferred British rule to that of the Ottoman Sultan and the Egyptian Khedive. It is therefore not surprising that with the aid of Sayyid 'Abd al-Rahman al-Mahdi and Sayyid 'Ali al-Mirghani, together with other leaders of *sufi* orders and tribal shaykhs, Wingate succeeded in mobilizing on the side of Britain all those who were moved primarily by economic considerations, on the one hand, and by their hatred for Egypt and Turkey, on the other. This unexpected shift which entailed the flattering of traditional leaders of popular Islam in Sudan and especially the Mahdi's followers, who up to the outbreak of the war had no official standing, was in effect an indirect admission of the failure of the previous religious policy of relying solely on the 'orthodox' Islamic leadership. Side by side with the Board of Ulemas, which continued to head the official Muslim institutions, the leaders of popular Islam rapidly came to occupy a central place in the religious–political hierarchy of Sudan. The First World War therefore constitutes a turning point in Britain's religious policy in Sudan the results of which were felt even more strongly after the war. In 1919 a Sudanese delegation went

---

[75] For the uprising of 'Ali Dinar, which was instigated by Turkish and Sannusi propaganda, see Theobald, *'Ali Dinar*, 137–61.

[76] The Private Secretary [S.S. Symes] to H.E. the Governor-General, 23 Nov. 1914, SAD/192/2.

to London to explain its objections to the demands of the Egyptian Wafd regarding Sudan and to seek the protection of Britain. The delegation was headed by those whom Britain had named the 'Three Sayyids': Sayyid 'Ali al-Mirghani, Sayyid al-Sharif Yusuf al-Hindi and Sayyid 'Abd al-Rahman al-Mahdi. They were not representatives of the orthodox Islam that the British had tried to foster. However, they had greater influence on their followers and had taken up a bold stand against Egypt, thus serving the interests of Britain in Sudan.[77]

---

[77] Stack to Wingate, 3 July 1919, SAD/237/11; also Muddathir, *Imperialism*, 94–101; for details see below.

10

THE EMERGENCE OF NEO-MAHDISM

Sayyid 'Abd al-Rahman al-Mahdi, 1885–1959

'Abd al-Rahman al-Mahdi was born in Omdurman on 15 July 1885, three weeks after his father's death. His mother, Maqbula, was the granddaughter of Muhammad al-Fadl, a past Sultan of Dar Fur. Following the battle of Karari in September 1898 the family left for Talodi, probably hoping to join the Khalifa 'Abdullahi al-Ta'aishi at Jabal Qadir. However, they were prevented by the authorities from reaching their destination and were forced to return to the family homes on Aba Island. While they were crossing the Nile, a government force arrested the group and sent them to Shakaba under government surveillance. Following an unverified rumour that they were engaged in Mahdist propaganda, the government sent a military force which fired on the group at random, killing the Khalifa Muhammad Sharif as well as the Mahdi's two elder sons al-Fadil and al-Bushra. 'Abd al-Rahman himself was seriously wounded but recovered and was later allowed to settle in al-Shakaba on the Blue Nile.[78] It was Slatin Pasha's advice that led to the poor treatment of 'Abd al-Rahman and his family during the following years, when he was kept under constant intelligence surveillance receiving a monthly allowance of £S5. After the reconquest the Mahdiyya was not recognized as a religious movement and all the Mahdi's and the Khalifa's property as well as their writings, was confiscated, while the movement's prayer book (al-ratib) was banned. Hence 'Abd al-Rahman al-Mahdi was not allowed to use the title imam or the name al-mahdi, but was known as Shaykh 'Abd al-Rahman Muhammad Ahmad.

From 1908 'Abd al-Rahman's surveillance was relaxed to a certain extent. This enabled him unofficially to start to regroup the Ansar, the erstwhile followers of his father the Mahdi, and to lay the foundations of neo-Mahdism in a form similar to those of a sufi order. Being aware of the limitations imposed by the government he limited his actions so as not to clash with the authorities. During that year he built the family's mosque in Omdurman with a loan from the government. He was also permitted to cultivate part of the Mahdi's lands on Aba Island – which, beside its economic benefits enabled him to assert his position as imam of the Ansar. A second aim of the Sayyid was to overcome Slatin's enmity towards the

[78] Hassan, Al-Imam, 67.

movement. To do so he emphasized the peaceful aims of himself and his followers and denounced every Mahdist anti-government action or uprising. He even succeeded in convincing Edgar Bonham Carter, the Sudan's first Legal Secretary, following the latter's consultation with the 'Board of Ulemas' in 1908, that the Mahdist movement and its message were not opposed to the government and had no illegal intentions. During that period he also started to undertake frequent visits to the numerous mosques in Omdurman in order to meet his followers, covering his face so as to avoid government detection.[79]

As noted above, the outbreak of the First World War changed the fortunes of Sayyid 'Abd al-Rahman al-Mahdi and his followers. In 1915 Wingate sent him to Aba Island in order to gain the support of his followers against Turkey, but warned him, against attempting to exploit this opportunity for Mahdist propaganda. Sayyid 'Abd al-Rahman's tour of the island demonstrated the depth of Mahdist loyalties. Thousands of Ansar, armed with their swords as in the old days, greeted their Mahdi's son whereve↓ he appeared, praying that 'the day had arrived' (*al-yawm ata*). In order to avoid a Mahdist revival, which the British authorities viewed as undesirable, the Sayyid was ordered in 1916 to return to Omdurman forthwith.[80] Although he was explicitly forbidden from organizing the Ansar, this in effect took place. He appointed deputies and agents in many regions ostensibly in order to comply with the government's wishes and report on any illegal activity. They also represented him in front of the people and the local authorities. However, the Sayyid did not report on his agents' religious or economic duties, which were crucial for the future of the Ansar. Thus, while the agents encouraged the payment of government taxes, the payment of *zakat* to the Sayyid was their main concern. Also the Mahdist prayer-book, *ratib al-mahdi*, which had been declared illegal by the Anglo-Egyptian authorities since 1898, was once again used freely by the Ansar without being harassed. Consequently, the Sayyid appointed agents to act on his behalf first in the Blue Nile and Funj provinces in 1916 and from 1917 also in Kordofan and Dar Fur. The Sayyid informed the government as to who his agents were, in order to legitimize their roles. He also made an offfer to the government to use their good offices whenever required. He reported to the Governor of Kassala informing him of some false claimants to Mahdism in his province and suggested sending his agent in order to ensure their loyalty to the government. Thus the government, which had always viewed the Ansar as illegal and potentially dangerous, in fact employed agents from within the Ansar and thereby granted them de facto recognition.

In 1921 Sayyid 'Abd al-Rahman presented to the government a list of twenty-four provincial agents. They were at that time distributed throughout Sudan as follows: six in the White Nile, four in Kordofan, two in the

[79] Sadiq, *Istiqlal*, 1-15; see also Hassan, *Sayyid 'Abd al-Rahman*, 193–202.
[80] Hassan, *op. cit.*, 196–7.

Funj, four in the Blue Nile, three in Dar Fur and one each in five other provinces, making a total of twenty-four agents. A close look at the list shows that many of the agents were merchants and tribal shaykhs, rather than religious leaders.[81] Shaykh Babikr Bedri, a well-known educator who enjoyed the confidence of the British authorities as well as that of Sayyid 'Abd al-Rahman participated in a meeting called by the Sayyid at his home in 1921. Those present at the meeting signed two documents containing statements of the Sayyid's aims. The first stated the desire of the Sudanese to be ruled by Britain rather than Egypt. The second emphasized that Britain was only a trustee that would lead Sudan to self-government. Among those who signed these documents were the Hashim brothers whose followers were according to Bedri, 'uneducated masses' who would not have understood why their shaykh preferred the British 'apostate' to true Egyptian believers. Bedri tried to convince his British friends that the followers of Sayyid 'Abd al-Rahman were their most reliable allies, since they, as Mahdists, would reject any future pretenders to the title of Mahdi.[82] However, the Sayyid realized that religious and political power also required financial assets. He therefore expanded his agricultural enterprises during the war when both needs and prices ran high, and brought hundreds of Ansar, especially from the west, to cultivate his fields on Aba Island and on the banks of the Blue and White Niles.[83] In 1923 the Sayyid encouraged his followers to reprint the Mahdist *ratib* and an edition of 5,000 copies was published. Its full title was *al-ratib al-sharif li-sayyidina wa-muladhina al-imam al-Mahdi ibn 'Abdallah*, and it was officially distributed by his agents throughout Sudan.[84] By the 1920s Sayyid 'Abd al-Rahman had become an important Sudanese leader and by local standards a rich man.

Following the end of the war and the dismemberment of the Ottoman Empire, Anglo-Sudanese attention focused on the renewed menace of Egyptian nationalism and its repercussions in Sudan. By December 1918 Sir Lee Stack, then Governor-General of Sudan, had already warned the British authorities of the widespread negative effects of Egyptian nationalism in Sudan.[85] The Egyptian national revolt led by Sa'd Zaghlul and the Wafd, which started in March 1919, brought matters to a head. There was considerable unrest in various towns in Sudan and rumours were spread that following Egyptian independence Egypt would assume full control of

[81] *Ibid.*, 197–8; see also Hassan, *Al-Imam*, 89–90. Hassan emphasizes the Sayyid's shrewdness whereby he avoided clashes with the government whilst exploiting the latter's ignorance regarding his real aims.

[82] Bedri, *Memoirs*, vol. 2, 66–7, 236–8, 247–9.

[83] Sadiq, *Istiqlal*, 19–20.

[84] Hassan, *'Abd al-Rahman*, 198–9. The ban on the *ratib* was effectively rescinded in 1925 following an order by the British director of intelligence, who stated that it is unreasonable and impossible to stop its sale; quoted from National Records Office Intelligence, 7/1/3, by O'Fahey, *Sufism in Suspense*, 17.

[85] Stack to Wingate, 12 Dec. 1918, FO 371/3711. For a summary of Egypt's propaganda in the Sudan see Memorandum by Stack, 25 May 1924, FO 371/10049.

Sudan.[86] Egyptian claims and propaganda centred on several different issues. First, the unity of the Nile valley and the continued sovereignty of Egypt over Sudan were propagated and reiterated by Sa'd Zaghlul and other political and religious Egyptian leaders. Secondly, the British authorities were accused of assuming control of Sudan, contrary to the 1899 Condominium Agreement, and of turning Sudan into a Lancashire-dominated cotton farm. The Gezira development project was the focus of these attacks. Finally, they accused the British administration of encouraging 'an artificial Sudanese separatist movement' and of 'violently suppressing the manifestations of loyal attachment to Egypt'.[87] In a manifesto published by the Wafd in the *Egyptian Gazette* on 6 June 1924, Britain was warned that its suppression of pro-Egyptian nationalist feelings in Sudan would result in trouble. It further promised the Sudanese 'that the day of their emancipation is not far distant.' The British authorities in Sudan reacted vehemently against what they regarded as unlawful interference in Sudan's internal affairs. They not only accused the Egyptians of spreading propaganda but also claimed that Egypt supplied both the brains and the money for anti-British movements in Sudan. Although no conclusive evidence was ever produced to prove these allegations, which were repeatedly denied by Egypt, British policy-makers in Sudan had no doubt in their own minds that Cairo was a hot-bed of movements such as the 'White Flag League' and that the necessary funds for the operations of these movements were smuggled in from Egyptian sources.[88]

How were the British authorities to fight against what they viewed as 'annoying interference'? The most obvious solution was to get rid as fast as possible of all Egyptian officers serving in Sudan. The setting up of an independent Sudan Defence Force (SDF) and the evacuation of the Egyptian army units from Sudan were suggested by Keown-Boyd as early as March 1920.[89] By August 1924 details for the execution of this plan had been submitted by the Sudanese authorities to Lord Allenby in Cairo.[90] As for the replacement of Egyptian officials by Sudanese, the British proposed to do this at an accelerated rate 'even at a cost of administrative efficiency.'[91] The

---

[86] Allenby to Foreign Office, 20 Apr. 1919, FO 371/3715; see also *SIR*, no. 298, May 1919.

[87] Izzet Pasha to MacDonald, 27 June 1924, transmitting a personal message from Zaghlul, FO 371/10050. J. Murray of the FO minuted: 'if Zaghlul really believed . . . his message, his ignorance of the Sudan is colossal; if he did not, his message is an impertinence,' *ibid*.

[88] Allenby to MacDonald, 6 July 1924, FO 371/10050; see also Record of Conference held in Foreign Office on 13 Aug. 1924, FO 371/10051; details on the White Flag League in Muddathir, *Imperialism*, 102–8.

[89] Keown-Boyd to Allenby, 14 Mar. 1920, forwarded by Allenby to Curzon on 24 Mar. 1920, FO 371/4981. Alexander Keown-Boyd joined the Sudan Political Service in 1907 and was Wingate's Assistant Private Secretary in 1914–16; he moved to Egypt with Wingate in 1916 and became the High Commissioner's Private Secretary. In 1919 he was appointed Oriental Secretary and it was in that capacity that he wrote to Lord Allenby in 1920.

[90] Stack to Allenby (Confidential), 18 Aug. 1924, FO 371/10052.

[91] Allenby to MacDonald, 26 July 1924, FO 371/10051.

Wafd's claim that the evacuation of the Egyptians from Sudan was planned and decided upon before Sir Lee Stack's assassination in November 1924 was right. Stack's murder only provided Allenby with the pretext for executing the plan agreed upon.[92]

However, there was yet another way to combat Egyptian propaganda which could be effected immediately, namely, to recruit all Sudanese leaders who were regarded as loyal to British aims in order to prove that Egyptian propaganda affected only a small and insignificant part of the Sudanese. As noted above, this plan was initiated as early as 1919, when the national uprising led by the Wafd indicated to British authorities that Egyptian nationalism might undermine the loyalty of the Sudanese. Letters of loyalty from religious and tribal notables were once again encouraged by the British authorities and poured in from all the provinces. In April 1919 the Governor-General decided to take matters a step further and sent a delegation of Sudanese leaders to London to express their loyalty to the British throne and to the government and to dissociate themselves from Egyptian nationalist claims.[93] The delegation, headed by Sayyid 'Ali al-Mirghani, consisted of religious and tribal leaders, but was first and foremost a delegation of the leaders of the most popular Islamic movements, the Khatmiyya and the Ansar. In addition to Sayyid 'Ali, they included Sayyid 'Abd al-Rahman al-Mahdi and al-Sharif Yusuf al-Hindi, head of the Hindiyya *tariqa* and one of the most outspoken critics of Egypt in Sudan.[94] However, Sayyid 'Abd al-Rahman derived the greatest political advantage from this delegation. Describing the reasons for his anti-Egyptian stand and for his cooperation with the British authorities, the Sayyid wrote that he regarded the White Flag League and other pro-Egyptian elements as offshoots of Egyptian nationalism that had nothing to do with the true national aspirations of the vast majority of Sudanese, which was independence. He further claimed that cooperation with the British was dictated by political realities since an armed uprising, as advocated by some religious fanatics, could only have

[92] Lloyd to Maffey, 20 Mar. 1927, FO 141/669. Lloyd asked whether the Wafd's claim as to its possession of documents proving that the Egyptian evacuation was decided upon before Sir Lee Stack's assassination, could be substantiated. Maffey replied that the evacuation plans were completed on 10 Sept. 1924, more than two months before Stack's assassination. But as this 'highly secret' document was undated, the Wafd could not use it as evidence; Maffey to Lloyd, 11 Apr. 1927, *ibid.*

[93] Allenby to Curzon, 27 Apr. 1919, FO 371/3725. For the 'Letters of loyalty' see also Allenby to FO, 6 June 1919, *ibid.*; Scott to Curzon, 12 Oct. 1921, FO 371/6306; *SIR*, no. 358, May 1924. The authenticity of these letters was questioned not only by the Egyptian press, but even by certain British MPs, who suggested that the letters were orchestrated by British authorities; see Parliamentary Question by Mr Swan, 11 May 1922, FO 371/7759.

[94] The Hindiyya was founded in the Jazira, by Yusuf al-Hindi at the turn of the twentieth century. It never became a big *tariqa* and its adherents usually joined forces with the Ansar. However, after independence leading Hindiyya members were active in the Khatmiyya supported DUP. After Yusuf al-Hindi's death in Dec. 1942 the *tariqa* declined; see Barclay, *Hindiya*, 127–37; also *SPIS*, no. 27, Dec. 1942, FO 371/35580.

led to destruction. By collaborating with the authorities, the Sayyid and his followers hoped to reap both political and financial advantages and to advance gradually towards Sudanese independence.[95] His inclusion in the 'Delegation of Loyalty' presented him with a unique opportunity to further this aim. While in London, 'Abd al-Rahman presented the Mahdi's sword to King George V, thereby assuming the position of the true leader of the Sudanese and implying the emergence of a newly forged bond between the one-time enemies, Britain and the Ansar. Thereby the Ansar, who had hitherto been considered dangerous and illegal, assumed the position of important allies of Britain. Instead of relying on secret circulars, which he had sent to the Ansar beseeching them to keep their allegiance (*bay'a*) with *al-imam* al-Mahdi, 'Abd al-Rahman now preached openly to gatherings of the Ansar and the Mahdi's prayer-book (*ratib*) was used without fear of repercussions.[96] In addition to his traditional supporters, his emergence as a 'national leader' in the wake of the war enabled 'Abd al-Rahman to forge an alliance with certain sections of the young Sudanese intelligentsia which was beginning to emerge. To counteract followers of the White Flag League and other pro-Egyptian groups, the Sayyid helped to found the first graduates' club in Sudan in 1919 and was instrumental in establishing the first political newspaper, *Hadarat al-Sudan*, in 1920. The paper, edited by the Sayyid's nephew Muhammad al-Khalifa Sharif, became the most outspoken organ of the 'Sudan for the Sudanese' movement and succeeded in recruiting several of the ablest spokesmen of the younger generation to Sayyid 'Abd al-Rahman's camp. Among these was 'Abdallah Khalil, who was then an officer in the Egyptian army and was later to become General Secretary of the Umma party and prime minister of Sudan after independence. Others included Hammad Salih and Ahmad 'Uthman al-Qadi, who became editor of *al-Hadara* following Sharif's death. More surprisingly, the Sayyid also succeeded in establishing close relations with the Egyptian Wafd, despite his outspoken opposition to the 'Unity of the Nile Valley'.[97]

By the end of 1924, following the removal of the Egyptian army and most Egyptian officials from Sudan and the drastic decline of pro-Egyptian sympathies among Sudanese officers and educated classes, Sayyid 'Abd al-Rahman had a clear advantage over Sayyid 'Ali al-Mirghani. He had a well-organized body of followers in the Ansar, enjoyed the respect and

[95] Sadiq, *Istiqlal*, 24–6.

[96] *Ibid.*, 21–31. The use of the *ratib* was allowed following the advice of Shaykh Mustafa al-Maraghi, then Grand *Qadi* of the Sudan, who stated that it contained only orthodox prayers and quotations from the Qur'an: *ibid.*, 28.

[97] Sadiq, *Istiqlal*, 25–7; see also 'The political situation' by C.A. Willis, Director of Intelligence, Khartoum, 16 June 1924, FO 371/10050. On 6 June 1924 a meeting of White Flag League leaders and Egyptian officers decided that they needed the support of at least one of the two Sayyids in order to succeed. But as 'Sayed Abdel Rahman El Mahdi was simply English, Sherif Yusef El Hindi was too cunning and double faced to be relied upon . . . Their only hope was Sayed Ali El Mirghani.' *SIR*, 359, June 1924, FO 371/10039.

adherence of leading members of the young intelligentsia and had the financial means to further his political ambitions. In September 1924 Sayyid 'Ali al-Mirghani who became increasingly concerned with his rival's political ambitions, declared that he would prefer to see the Sudan under the Egyptian Crown rather than be subject to an independent Sudanese monarchy headed by Sayyid 'Abd al-Rahman.[98] Thus by the mid-1920s, while the smaller *sufi* orders continued to flourish at the local village level, the Khatmiyya and the Ansar had emerged as the largest and most popular Islamic movements contending for power. The die was cast for sectarian politics in Sudan.

The years of ambivalence, 1925–38

Following the expulsion of the Egyptian army and of Egyptian personnel from Sudan in 1924, the political importance of the two Sayyids, in so far as the Sudan Political Service (SPS) was concerned, became an embarrassment rather than an advantage. While the Sayyids' support had been crucial ever since the war started, it became evident that their political ambitions, especially those of Sayyid 'Abd al-Rahman, were in contrast with government policy to keep religion and politics apart. Moreover, through native administration and indirect rule, the SPS hoped to establish direct links with the tribal population and its leadership, thereby bypassing the religious leaders as intermediaries.[99] The adverse effects of this policy were felt by both Sayyids, but while Sayyid 'Ali could cope with the new situation, it created major difficulties for Sayyid 'Abd al-Rahman and the Ansar. Sayyid 'Ali's advantage lay both in his personality and in the organization and distribution of his supporters. The British regarded him as the most trustworthy leader in Sudan, due to the anti-Mahdist and anti-Egyptian inclinations he had shown in the past, as well as to the loyal support he had given the British after the reconquest. Moreover, the authorities viewed Sayyid 'Ali as a man without political ambitions who would be glad to resume his role as a purely religious leader. As for the Khatmiyya, its support was derived primarily from the more sophisticated population of the so-called 'three towns' (Khartoum, Khartoum North and Omdurman) and from the northern province, and therefore the effect of native administration on its membership was minimal. Native administration was aimed primarily at the more primitive-tribal regions and hence the Ansar were directly effected. An official biographical note on Sayyid 'Ali illustrates this view:

Sayed Ali . . . is by tradition and upbringing a conservative. A man of great personal charm and, through his followers, of great influence, he has loyally and consistently supported the Sudan government for the last forty years, though as an onlooker rather than a man of action.[100]

Hence, Sayyid 'Ali and the Khatmiyya were never regarded as a political threat and even his interest in Egypt did not seem to worry the SPS since they assumed that it did not have political implications.[101]

Sayyid 'Abd al-Rahman and the Ansar were in an altogether different category. Although the Sayyid had performed important political services for the British both during the war and during the years of Egyptian agitation that followed it, his political ambitions clashed with government policy. Now that his services were no longer required, he was expected to reassume the role of religious leader and to forgo his political ambitions. But, even as a religious leader, Sayyid 'Abd al-Rahman's position was far from secure. While the British regarded neo-Mahdism as a legitimate religious 'sect', fear of fanatical Mahdism was still acute and they therefore continued to view the Sayyid and his followers with suspicion.

The Nyala revolt, which broke out in Dar Fur in 1921, indicated that their fear of neo-Mahdism was not unwarranted. It was the worst millenarian uprising since the reconquest and brought about a change in British policy towards Mahdism. The Director of Intelligence at the time, Charles Armine Willis, who continued to believe and preach that neo-Mahdism and Sayyid 'Abd al-Rahman could be of great assistance to British rule, was overruled and dismissed from his post in 1926. Under his successor Reginald Davies the policy towards the Ansar was reversed and became one of suspicion bordering on hostility. Davies, who had served in Dar Fur during the Nyala revolt in 1921, saw no difference between the Mahdism of Sayyid 'Abd al-Rahman and that of the 'fanatic' *nabi* 'Isas who flourished especially in Dar Fur and the western Sudan and whom the Sayyid had consistently denounced. Explaining the background of the Nyala uprising Davies wrote:

It was therefore inevitable that the Mahdists of the Sudan should live in the expectation of the Second Coming; quite natural that the more impatient spirits should hope that this event lay in the near future . . . For such people the identification of the Sudan Government with Anti-Christ would present no difficulty.[102]

In 1926 Davies wrote a 'Note on Mahdism' stating: 'It is to be noted that the scene of the [Nyala] rising had been visited, within the year preceding its outbreak, by fikis newly returning from Aba island.' Although Davies admitted that this did not prove Sayyid 'Abd al-Rahman's complicity, his

---

[100] *Political Intelligence Paper*, no. 66, 'Biographical note on Sayed Sir Ali el Marchani (*sic* [Mirghani]) Pasha, KCMG, KCVO', Oct. 1944, FO 371/41363.

[101] Interview with Sir Angus Gillan, KBE, CMG, London, 6 Oct. 1970. Sir Angus was Civil Secretary of Sudan in 1934–9.

[102] Davies, *Camel's Back*, 149; for details on the Nyala revolt see *ibid.*, 148–57. Reginald Davies, CMG, served in the SPS in 1911–35; he served in Kordofan and Dar Fur in 1911–24 and in the Intelligence Department 1924–8. Charles Armine Willis, CBE, served in the Intelligence Department in 1915–26, when he was transferred to the Upper Nile as Governor.

suspicion of the Sayyid and his supporters became a dominant factor in formulating government policy – so much so that Sir Lee Stack, the Governor-General, wrote to Lord Allenby, the British High Commissioner in Egypt, that Sayyid 'Abd al-Rahman 'undoubtedly' played a role in propagating the Nyala uprising. However, although he might have sympathized with the Nyala revolt, the Sayyid continued to dissociate himself and his followers from all Mahdist uprisings and pledged his loyalty to the government in numerous letters.[103]

The result was growing ambivalence. On the one hand, some members of the SPS regarded neo-Mahdism as a legitimate religious sect not dissimilar to a *sufi* order. Others feared the fanatic manifestations of neo-Mahdism and therefore viewed the Sayyid and his followers with ever-growing suspicion.[104] As early as 1923 the authorities were concerned about the great number of Mahdist pilgrims who came to celebrate Ramadan on Aba Island. Of the 5,000–15,000 pilgrims who gathered on the island annually, many identified Sayyid 'Abd al-Rahman with *nabi* 'Isa (the prophet Jesus) and expected him, with the aid of the Ansar, to drive the Christian colonialist power, identified as *al-dajjal* (anti-Christ), out of Sudan. At that time suspicions with regard to the Sayyid's activities in northern Nigeria were also rampant. In 1923 the Nigerian authorities uncovered an ongoing correspondence between *al-Mu'allim* Sa'id b. Hayatu, an offspring of the ruling family in the Sultanate of Sokoto, an agent of the Ansar and Sayyid 'Abd al-Rahman. In one of these letters the Sayyid wrote to Hayatu about the revival of the Mahdist movement in Sudan and predicted that when 'the day would arrive' the rifles of the Christians would stop shooting. G.B. Lethem and H.R. Palmer, the British officials who uncovered the Sayyid's connections in Nigeria and Cameroon claimed that he was responsible for the unrest in their regions as well as in Dar Fur and Kordofan.[105] Following mass demonstrations of Ansar from West Africa on Aba Island in 1924, the authorities decided 'to stop these displays which were beginning to disturb the public.' The Sayyid was ordered to discontinue the pilgrimage and to command his adherents both from within Sudan and from West Africa to disperse.[106] A year later, when plans for the establishment of the SDF were discussed, the possibility of a Mahdist uprising was seriously considered,[107] the authorities therefore did their utmost to keep the Ansar out of the SDF.

---

[103] Davies, *Mahdism 1926*; Stack to Allenby 20 May 1924, FO 371/11613. Compare with Hassan, *Mahdist Risings*, 459–65, who clearly proves that even if the Sayyid sympathized with the Nyala revolt he explicitly denounced fanaticism and believed that the 'Mahdist cause . . . would be better served by cooperating with the government'(*ibid.*, 465).

[104] On this dispute see Warburg, *Historical Controversy*, 675–92.

[105] Hassan, *Al-Imam*, 90–3.

[106] *SIR*, annual report 1923, FO 371/10039. See also Hodgkin, *Mahdism*, 117, who wrote: 'Mahdist propaganda was thought of at this time as associated with Bolshevism, the Third International, Egyptian nationalism, pan-Islamism, and ideas of 'world revolution' in general.'

[107] Stack to MacDonald, 8 Aug. 1924, enclosing memorandum on the 'Possibility of another Mahadia [*sic*] or General Religious Rising of a similar type', FO 371/10052.

The *Sudan Secret Intelligence Reports (SSIR)*, which had been compiled on a monthly basis since the beginning of 1926, reported on the relative strength of the Ansar in the different units of the SDF. A special recruiting policy was therefore adopted in order to keep their numbers in the SDF down.[108]

Government fears of fanatical Mahdism were bound to have repercussions on Sayyid 'Abd al-Rahman's position. Although the authorities did not regard the Sayyid himself as a fanatic, they feared his ambitions and were suspicious of his growing wealth and influence. The forced resignation of Sir Geoffrey Archer, Governor-General of Sudan in 1925-6, is probably the best illustration of the Sayyid's growing strength on the one hand, and of British ambivalence on the other. When at the beginning of 1926 Sayyid 'Abd al-Rahman was awarded the KBE, senior British officials in Sudan regarded this as an ample reward for his services. They commented that 'from an insignificant Sheikh at £E15 a month he had been elevated by Government to a KBE at £E20,000 a year.'[109] Any further encouragement of the Sayyid's ambitions was viewed as detrimental to the political–religious balance of Sudan and to its security. Archer's visit to Aba Island in March 1926 was thus viewed by senior members of the SPS with the utmost suspicion. They had advised him to play down, the visit, but instead he arrived in Aba in full uniform accompanied by troops and a host of officials. What had been intended by the SPS as a courtesy visit became an official meeting between two leaders. To make matters worse, Archer made a speech extolling Sayyid 'Abd al-Rahman's loyalty and the ever growing bond between him and the British administration. This speech had two important results: first, Archer was forced by the senior members of the SPS to resign, to be replaced by Sir John Maffey; and, secondly, the political ambitions of Sayyid 'Abd al-Rahman, were drastically curtailed.[110] The Sayyid was ordered to instruct his supporters on Aba Island and elsewhere to disband their organizations and refrain from all religious and political activities. His own movements were restricted and he was directed not to leave Khartoum or Omdurman without government permission.[111]

[108] *SSIR*, no. 3, May 1926; *SSIR*, no. 8, Nov. 1926; *SSIR*, no. 9, Dec. 1926, FO 371/11614. Consequently, the relative strength of the Khatmiyya in the SDF and the police grew out of all proportions; *Political Intelligence Paper*, no. 66, Oct. 1944, FO 371/41363.

[109] Davies, *Mahdism 1926*.

[110] Archer to Lloyd, 2 Apr. 1926, forwarding his letter of resignation and twelve enclosures, FO 371/11609; Lloyd to Chamberlain, 10 Apr. 1926, *ibid.*; Chamberlain to Lloyd, 11 May 1926 (private), FO 800/259. In a reply to a query from Lord Stamfordham whether a command of Arabic were not essential for a Governor-General of the Sudan and hence Maffey's unsuitability, Chamberlain wrote: 'Lord Cromer's . . . record in Egypt in effect proves the contrary.' Chamberlain to Stamfordham, 21 Oct. 1926, *ibid.*; details in Daly, *Empire*, 335–9; see also Hassan, *Al-Imam*, 93–9, 100–5, according to Hassan Archer's appointment was resented by his senior staff even before his arrival, primarily out of resentment against an 'outsider' who gains the most senior position at their expense.

[111] Note on meeting at the palace, enclosed in Archer to Lloyd, 2 Apr. 1926, FO 371/11609.

The new policy was in fact intended to return the Sayyid's position to that of the pre-First World War *status quo*. This, however, could no longer be achieved. Although 'Abd al-Rahman complained constantly of his mistreatment by the government, he was shrewd enough to overcome most of the restrictions imposed on him in subsequent years, aided in no small measure by his growing wealth and by the strength of the Ansar. Among senior British officials in Sudan, M.J. Reid, Governor of White Nile province, was probably an exception in continuing to view the Sayyid and his followers as 'normal people' and insisting that the Sayyid was 'vainglorious' rather than politically 'ambitious'. Reid believed in Sayyid 'Abd al-Rahman's loyalty to the British and admired his character.[112] Describing his character and his ability to flourish despite adverse conditions in a rather more critical manner, Sir Stewart Symes, the Governor-General of Sudan in 1934–40, wrote in April 1935:

He has the defects of a Sudanese of his type, the liking of intrigue, vanity, irrelevance and opportunism. On the other hand, he has quick perceptions, panache and subtle tenacity of purpose . . . He has used (or misused) the opportunities . . . of laying the foundations of his Mahdist organization in the provinces . . . One moment's relaxation of Government's vigilance and he presents it with some *fait accompli* either in the shape of a new acquisition of land in a forbidden area, or of a large size advertisement of his pretensions to be a national figurehead. His favourite role is that of the loyal supporter of Government who is maliciously misunderstood.[113]

His ultimate ambition, according to Symes, was to rule the Sudan as his father had done. But as the future of Sudan had not yet been decided, Symes felt that 'it is impossible to decide whether Sayed 'Abd al-Rahman's ultimate ambitions are reconcilable or irreconcilable with the scheme. The Government, therefore, can only allow him to pursue limited ambitions.'[114]

Two years later, with the Second World War already threatening, the government's policy towards the Ansar was still ambivalent. Symes viewed the Ansar as a 'cancerous growth' and a potential 'rather than an imminent danger'. He insisted that the Khatmiyya and its leader Sayyid 'Ali, were 'politically more desirable' but declared that the government would not show its preference openly, since only by observing 'a kind of neutrality' would it be possible not to antagonize the Ansar and to justify the government's treatment 'of Mahdist ebullitions in different parts of the country and

[112] Hassan, '*Abd al-Rahman*, 1, quoting Reid's 'Note on Mahdism', dated 24 Nov. 1934; J.A. Reid was appointed to the SPS in 1914 and was Governor of the White Nile from 1931 to 1937.

[113] Symes, *Mahdism 1935*. Symes's sarcastic definition of Sayyid 'Abd al-Rahman's shortcomings in fact illustrate the Sayyid's leadership qualities demonstrated in adverse conditions. Sir Stewart Symes served in Sudan under Wingate in 1906–16; he then served in Egypt, Palestine, Aden and Tanganyika and returned to Sudan as Governor-General in 1934–40.

[114] Symes, *Mahdism 1935*.

especially wherever recalcitrant tendencies have been shewn in recent years.' Consequently Symes ordered that the ban on Mahdist agents operating within the tribes of Dar Fur, Kordofan and the Funj region be maintained and declared that Aba Island would not become 'a sanctuary for outlaws'. He also insisted that Sayyid 'Abd al-Rahman refuted his 'pretentious of temporal leadership'.[115] The policy Symes decided to pursue was to gradually turn the Sayyid once again into 'an ordinary, though distinguished citizen' and to stop him from exploiting religion for advancing his ambitions.[116] The Sayyid and the Ansar were thus confronted with a concerted effort to limit their activities not only by forbidding their expansion in the vast territories of the west, but also by trying to mould them into a purely religious *tariqa*-like movement, contrary to the basic concept of Mahdism, which saw in politics a major aspect of its religious mission. How was Sayyid 'Abd al-Rahman to overcome this predicament without antagonizing the authorities whose goodwill was essential for his future success? The key to the puzzle lay in the economic sphere and especially in the expansion of the Sayyid's agricultural ventures. Since land was the most easily accessible source of income for impoverished Sudan and since Sudanese entrepreneurs were scarce, the government viewed increased cultivation as imperative, even if it was undertaken by Sayyid 'Abd al-Rahman. Moreover, the authorities regarded cultivation as an antidote to involvement in politics and especially to fanaticism. A cultivator, according to this view, would be more interested in his crops and his profits than in fermenting religious or political trouble. Accordingly, already in February 1928 Sir John Maffey, the Governor-General who had replaced Archer, introduced the following policy: 'I consider that as the Sayed is behaving reasonably in the religious and political field we ought, as a measure of political expediency to bind him to us by economic fetters.'[117]

The result of this policy was spectacular. In 1928 Sayyid 'Abd al-Rahman started a pump-irrigation scheme extending over 200 acres on Aba Island. By 1930 he had expanded this scheme to 2,900 acres and a year later an additional 1,800 acres were added. When Symes wrote his report on Mahdism in 1935 the Sayyid was cultivating 'a gross area of some 15,000 acres (i.e. between 4,000 and 5,000 available for cotton each year)', from which he could derive an annual profit of between £E20,000 and £E30,000. Moreover, government laxity enabled the Sayyid to expand into the restricted areas of the Blue and White Niles. He owned a pump-irrigation scheme at Gondar, between Wad-Madani and Sinnar, which had been financed by

[115] Symes, *Mahdism 1937*.

[116] Hassan, '*Abd al-Rahman*, 3.

[117] Quoted in Symes, *Mahdism 1937*. In 1926 the Sayyid had been on the verge of bankruptcy and the government had decided not to come to his aid due to the political controversy surrounding him at the time.

the government at a cost of £E28,000. On the White Nile, between Aba Island and Geteina, Sayyid 'Abd al Rahman had acquired four large plots for cotton cultivation, using a relative in order to overcome government restrictions and acquire the leases. Even in the Gezira, where the government had done its utmost to keep the Sayyid out, he had managed by 1931 to lay his hands on 9,600 acres of cultivable land. To the considerable profits from cultivation one should add the *zakat*, which since 1919 had been collected annually from the Ansar, and the presents brought to the Sayyid by his richer adherents on the occasion of *al-'id al-kabir* or during their pilgrimage to Aba. Thus by 1935 Sayyid 'Abd al-Rahman was a large landowner and an affluent man by even the most conservative standards.[118]

While the authorities realized quite early that thousands of pilgrims from the west were cultivating Sayyid 'Abd al-Rahman's lands, they probably failed to grasp the political implications of this activity. The Sayyid's motives for acquiring new lands and cultivating them were viewed as quite legitimate. His 'cultivation colonies', where thousands of *fallata* toiled for a daily ration of grain and some clothing, were commented upon in many intelligence reports in the 1920s. But the main references were to his exploitation of cheap labour, and occasionally to the religious fanaticism, which was regarded as an inevitable by-product of West Africa migrants. Although leading members of the SPS tried to limit the pilgrims' stay on the Sayyid's lands and gave repeated orders that *fallata* immigration be ended, the authorities were in fact witnessing the growth and enrichment of the Ansar as a result of their own policy.[119] In binding the Sayyid to the government by so-called 'economic fetters', Maffey and his colleagues had enabled him to strengthen and enrich the Ansar and thereby increase his political power. Sayyid 'Abd al-Rahman himself admitted many years later that without his vast cultivation he could never have provided for the Ansar. However, he denied that either he or his followers regarded their relationship as motivated by financial considerations. The Ansar, he insisted, left their homes and their families thousands of miles away in order to seek spiritual guidance, while the Sayyid imbued them with the Mahdist mission and at the same time provided for all their material needs.[120] When the authorities realized in 1935 that Sayyid 'Abd al-Rahman's agricultural exploits were 'actuated by political rather than by commercial motives', they again tried to restrict his movements, especially in the *fallata*-popu-

---

[118] Symes, *Mahdism 1935*; also Sadiq, *Istiqlal*, 38–41. The Sayyid stated that he used his relatives in order to acquire new lands in restricted areas, which later became part of the Mahdist *da'ira* (domain); details in Hassan, *Al-Imam*, 115–23.

[119] Davies, *Memorandum*; see also *SSIR*, no. 10, Dec. 1926, FO 371/12374.

[120] Sadiq, *Istiqlal*, 38-41. In denying British charges of the exploitation of cheap labour, Sayyid 'Abd al-Rahman insisted that it would have been cheaper for him to use hired labour than to provide for the poorer Ansar.

lated areas of Kosti, Sinnar, Singa and al-Qadarif.[121] But it was too late since by then the Ansar were strong enough both in spirit and in wealth to withstand the half-hearted measures of the alien government.

Muhammad Ahmad Mahjub (Mahgoub), a political supporter of Sayyid 'Abd al-Rahman and one of the most prominent leaders of the Umma party in the post-independence period, wrote in his introduction to *Jihad fi sabil al-istiqlal* that the creation of the Ansar was the Sayyid's greatest achievement. But when it came to defining the Ansar, even Mahgoub found himself in difficulties. He limited himself to stating that the twentieth-century Ansar were not similar to their Mahdist forerunners of the previous century, nor were they a *tariqa*, a political party or a military organization. Indeed, their uniqueness lay in that they combined the features of all of these and in addition were an economic enterprise.[122]

The recruitment of the Ansar

The Ansar were composed of three main groups. The first and most numerous consisted of tribal supporters, whose adherence to the Sayyid was based on their belief in the second coming of a *mahdi* and in certain instances tended to border on fanaticism. This group was largely composed of West African fallata migrants (*muhajirun*), who flocked to the Sayyid *en masse* despite government measures, since for them 'there was little or no distinction . . . between Mahdism and their profession of Islam'.[123] By 1935 the number of buildings on Aba Island housing western immigrants had increased from 1,000 to 4,500, while the number of pilgrims continued to increase by approximately 15,000 per year. Thereby the Sayyid was able to penetrate Dar Fur and Kordofan, which the government had declared 'forbidden provinces'. He also succeeded in establishing there strong branches of the Ansar, under loyal deputies (*khulafa*). The fallata *muhajirun* were utilized in yet another way. In addition to supplying him with the necessary cheap labour on Aba Island they settled, on the Sayyid's orders, in villages in the four provinces of Kassala, Funj, the Blue Nile and the White Nile, thereby opening them to Ansar influence. The authorities became concerned with this infiltration in the 1930s and ordered all immigrants to be concentrated into one or two villages in each province. The Sayyid's agents were consequently allowed to visit only those villages inhabited by Ansar with government approval. But by then Mahdism had already taken root in other villages and government restrictions were of little

[121] Symes, *Mahdism 1935*.
[122] Sadiq, *Istiqlal*, b–d.
[123] The following information was derived, unless otherwise noted, from Symes, *Mahdism 1935*, Symes, *Mahdism 1937*; Davies, *Mahdism 1926*, Davies, *Memorandum*, and the *SIR* series for the years 1926–31.

avail. Geographically this group of supporters was by 1939 spread throughout the western provinces as well as in the regions to the south and east of Khartoum.

The second group consisted of more sophisticated elements within the tribal population, including many shaykhs of riverain tribes, for whom the Sayyid's wealth and temporal influence were probably of greater significance than his religious message. In this sector the Sayyid was hit by native administration as it aimed at establishing a direct link between government and tribal leaders thus making the Sayyid's political role superfluous. 'He was frankly hostile to tribal authorities, whose opposition to the spread of his influence he attempted to counter by obstructive criticism and interference.' After 1931 the Sayyid changed his tactics and instead of hampering the work of the shaykhs he came to their aid and tried to win their confidence by siding with them in their disputes with the authorities over taxation and other matters. He also entertained them lavishly both in Omdurman and on Aba Island. Having realized that tribal leadership was too weak to constitute a threat to his political ambitions, Sayyid 'Abd al-Rahman became an avid supporter of native administration which, in his words, brought the mass of tribal leaders to the 'Sudan for the Sudanese' camp as allies of the Ansar.[124]

The Sayyid adopted a similar posture with regard to *sufi* orders. Realizing that the only *sufi* order that could compete with the Ansar was the Khatmiyya, the Sayyid understood that other *tariqas*, while continuing to fulfill their religious and social functions at the village or tribal level, would not become involved in national politics. He therefore assumed the role of mediator in their internal disputes, solved a leadership dispute within the Sammaniyya order and gave presents and financial aid to the head of the Isma'iliyya in Kordofan in order to draw its members away from the Khatmiyya. He also sent special agents to Dongola to win the support of Idrisiyya members and helped the head of the Ahmadiyya order in the same province to win a land dispute. By 1945 the Sayyid's efforts to win the support of the smaller *tariqas* had produced results. He therefore invited them to the Ansar's annual marriage festival and allowed them, in contrast to Mahdist beliefs, to perform their own *sufi* rituals including the *dhikr* while enjoying his hospitality. The same *sufi* orders that had been denounced by his father the Mahdi in 1884 were now invited to participate in the Ansar's religious festivities with their flags and *dhikrs* and were treated as equal partners.[125] This mass recruitment of members of various *sufi* orders to the Mahdist flag was a clear indication of the Sayyid's political acumen and his willingness to compromise in order to win support. In this manner the Ansar established themselves throughout the rural areas of Sudan and gained

[124] Sadiq, *Istiqlal*, 29–30.
[125] *SPIS*, no. 51 July 1945, FO 371/45972, quoted in Dhaher, *Al-Mirghani*, 262.

adherents even in the Northern province whose inhabitants had traditionally been Khatmiyya supporters.

The third group from which the Sayyid attempted to draw his supporters consisted of the urban population especially in Khartoum, Khartoum North and Omdurman. Many of these kept their traditional links with their tribes and *tariqas* and could be won over by methods similar to those implemented in rural Sudan. However, there was, an increasingly influential body of educated Sudanese, mostly government officials, whose confidence the Sayyid sought to gain, and in order to do so he had to devise new methods. The members of this young intelligentsia were Muslim both in their heritage and in their education. However, their Islam was of a more sophisticated brand and they regarded the traditional village *fiki* and the *tariqa* as relics of Sudan's backward past. Moreover, due to their Western education, ideas such as secularism and the separation of religion and politics were not alien to them. Therefore, although he attempted to deepen their knowledge of Islam and their bond to its heritage, the Sayyid realized that the only way to gain their confidence and support was at the political level.[126] It was with this mind that he helped to found the first graduates' club in 1919 and became involved in the graduates' political debates through his co-ownership of *al-Hadara* in the 1920s. Until 1924, the government viewed the Sayyid's influence over the intelligentsia favourably, since it helped it to curb Egyptian nationalist influence. However, after Allenby's ultimatum in 1924 and the expulsion of the Egyptians, the Sayyid's efforts became superfluous and he could no longer rely on government support in his dealings with the younger generation. In fact, the government tried its utmost to stop his political interference with the intelligentsia. In 1925, a special committee consisting of senior members of the SPS, warned the authorities that the young Sudanese intelligentsia was potentially dangerous. They stated:

It would be entirely misleading to suppose that with the removal of the . . . opportunity for Egyptian instigation, the Sudan will revert to complete political apathy . . . There is now in the Sudan a class, small but vocal, which has ideas and aspirations.[127]

Talking to the Director of Intelligence about the young graduate class most of whom were government officials, Sayyid 'Ali al-Mirghani stated bluntly: 'The Government's best friends are the taxpayers, and its worst enemies those who receive pay from it.'[128] To avoid further expansion of this class the government decided to limit higher education to technical fields, such as agriculture. Justifying this policy Allenby wrote: 'I can conceive much harm and no utility from higher education among a people so profoundly

---

[126] Sadiq, *Istiqlal*, 177.

[127] 'A Review of the situation in the spring of 1925', by Davies, Baily and Ewart; encl. in Ewart to Private Secretary, 21 Apr. 1925, FO 371/10905.

[128] *SIR* – 359, June 1924, FO 371/10039.

backward as the Sudanese.'[129] Native administration seemed to provide an answer, since it sought to transfer both judicial and administrative functions to tribal leaders, thereby diminishing the need for higher education. The young graduates aspiring to become effendis were being persuaded by British officials to 'cast off their shoddy European clothes and tarbush and revert to national dress'.[130]

The pros and cons of this policy are outside the scope of this study, but for a better understanding of the position of the young intelligentsia, the following might be illuminating. In 1935, commenting on a very critical article by Sir James Currie on education in Sudan, Sir Miles Lampson, then British High Commissioner in Egypt, wrote:

With regard to indirect rule and the fostering of the tribal system, I believe with Sir J. Currie that we are working against the stream of natural forces at play in colonial and eastern lands today . . . Unfortunately a Sudanese intelligentsia already exists, and it regards this system as directed against its own future development which is bound up with the progress of the Sudan on modern state lines. Again we have adopted this policy and it must be allowed to run its course. Its effects on education must of course be retarding - not altogether a bad thing in the circumstances.[131]

A year later during a special meeting held in London by the Foreign Office on education in Sudan, Sir Lancelot Oliphant accused the British authorities in Sudan of repeating in Sudan Lord Cromer's erroneous educational policy in Egypt. He warned them that they would have to face the following criticism:

. . . namely that they had neglected the education of the natives and, instead, had concentrated solely on efficient government, a policy which might lead to the criticism that His Majesty's Government were actuated by self-interest and did not intend to relax their hold on the Sudan.

In responding Sir Stewart Symes, then Governor-General, admitted that since 1924, partly due to the world economic crisis 'education had been rather forgotten' but he maintained that efforts were now being made to remedy this.[132]

---

[129] Allenby to Chamberlain, 9 May 1925, FO 371/10879. For details on the government's educational policy during that period, see Beshir, *Education*, 88–90.

[130] Archer to Allenby, 27 Apr. 1925, FO 371/10880.

[131] Lampson to Campbell, 15 June 1935, FO 371/19095. James Currie's article 'The educational experiment in the Anglo-Egyptian Sudan' was published in the *Journal of the African Society*, vols 33–4 (1934–5). Currie was the first Director of Education in Sudan under Wingate, in 1900–14.

[132] 'Record of Meeting held in the Foreign Office on 13 Oct. [1936], to discuss Educational Policy in the Sudan', FO 407/219. Symes himself had admitted a year earlier that 'a lacuna of our present administrative system – perhaps an aftermath of the disturbances in 1924–5 – was that it did not afford sufficient opportunities for Sudanese in higher branches of the public service'. Political Memorandum on the Anglo-Egyptian Sudan by G.S. Symes, June 1935, FO 371/19095.

It is therefore irrelevant whether native administration and the educational policy which followed it were specifically designed to retard the development of a Sudanese intelligentsia or were the result of 'plain facts and circumstances', as claimed by Symes.[133] It is sufficient to note that even high-ranking British officials like Lampson or Oliphant stated explicitly that progress in education was retarded as a result of this policy. It is therefore no wonder that it was bitterly resented by the educated Sudanese themselves. In 1926 the government noted the hostile criticism of this policy by native officials and described the attitude of the graduates as 'despairing rather than militant. They feel themselves to be poor, weak and unorganised . . . The increase of British officials in the Government is one of the chief sources of discontent.'[134] Even the graduates' club, which had been founded with so many hopes in 1919 and was defined by one of its leaders as 'the focus of modern political ideas in the Sudan', was disbanded in June 1926.[135] With Egypt out of the way the club, which had originally been encouraged by the authorities as a political expression of 'the Sudan for the Sudanese' camp and hence as opposed to Egyptian plans for unity, had become more of an embarrassment than an asset as far as the authorities were concerned.

But Sayyid 'Abd al-Rahman, being aware that the graduates were even harder hit by native administration than he was, was ready to step in and to supply 'the roots of the graduates tree'.[136] The Sayyid found a common platform with the frustrated intelligentsia who, following the events of 1924, had become disillusioned with Egypt, which they felt had betrayed them. Consequently they were drawn to the Sayyid's politics 'of a genuinely Sudanese national movement. For such a movement a leader and figurehead was essential and it was in this capacity the Sayed now offered his services.'[137]

Sayyid 'Abd al-Rahman's real opportunity came in 1931. As part of its retrenchment policy following the world economic crisis the Governor-General's Council decided to lower the starting rates of pay for newly appointed Sudanese government officials.[138] Protests and demonstrations by students and young government officials asking that the new measures be reconsidered were of no avail and on 24 November 1931 a general strike was declared at Gordon College.[139]

[133] G.S. Symes, 'A Note on Local Government Policy', May 1939, FO 407/223.
[134] *SSIR*, no. 8, Nov. 1926, FO 371/11614.
[135] *SSIR*, no. 3, May 1926; *SSIR*, no. 4, June 1926, FO 371/11613.
[136] Sadiq, *Istiqlal*, 177–8.
[137] Symes, *Mahdism 1935*, reporting on the situation in 1927–8.
[138] Minutes of Governor-General's Council, 344th Meeting, 19 Feb. 1931; and 352nd meeting, 18–20 May 1931, FO 867/17.
[139] Maffey to Loraine, 27 Jan. 1932, FO 407/215.

An Intelligentsia Committee set up by the Omdurman Graduates' Club having failed to deal with the situation (and Sayyid Ali having locked himself up in his house at Sinka), the field was clear for Sayed Abdel Rahman.

The latter offered his mediation, which brought the strike to an end. This gave him a hold over the graduates that he has never lost. 'Since then the Sayed has associated himself with every movement sponsored by the Intelligentsia.'[140] A special committee was set up by the Ansar to deal with all matters concerning the educated class. Moreover, *da'irat al-mahdi* (the Mahdi's domain) purchased a printing house to assume overall responsibility for the Ansar's publications. This of course further enhanced the Sayyid's position *vis-a-vis* the intelligentsia as they could now publish their literary and political writings in the Ansar's publishing house.[141] In 1935 Sayyid 'Abd al-Rahman founded *al-Nil*, the first daily Arabic newspaper in Sudan, as an organ of the Ansar. The educated class thus became the natural consumers of the Ansar's political thinking and the Sayyid assumed his desired role of their spiritual guide and leader. By the end of 1935 'he had more adherents amongst the educated and politically minded young men than any other prominent native'.[142] His house in the 'Abbasiyya quarter of Omdurman became the meeting place of politically minded government officials and of graduates in general. Many of them joined the Ansar and remained ardent supporters of the Sayyid throughout their political careers. Others, such as Isma'il al-Azhari, 'Abdallah al-Fadil and Yahya al-Fadli, who later founded their own political party in opposition to Sayyid 'Abd al-Rahman, were among the Sayyid's staunchest supporters until 1942 and became regular participants in his political *salon*.[143]

Neo-Mahdist ideology

What ideology could hold together such a complex variety of supporters consisting of primitive *fallata* and Baqqara from western Sudan, settled tribes of the Nile Valley and the young educated class? If one adds to these the wide variety of Khatmiyya supporters and those believing in unity with Egypt, whom the Sayyid attempted to lure to his side, the problem seemed insurmountable. In studying a sample of Sayyid 'Abd al-Rahman's religious and political writings and talks, one is struck by its similarity with nineteenth century Sudanese Mahdism, with minor adjustments dictated by modern circumstances.[144] The Mahdi's *ratib* and his collected *manshurat*

[140] Symes, *Mahdism 1935*. Symes's view that the Sayyid 'never' lost his hold is exaggerated.
[141] Sadiq, *Istiqlal*, 178.
[142] Symes, *Mahdism 1935*; see also Salih, *Sudanese Press*, 6.
[143] Interview with Mr K.D.D. Henderson, CMG, Sept. 1972. Henderson served in the SPS from 1927 to 1953 and was in the Civil Secretary's Office from 1938–44 and Assistant Civil-Secretary from 1946 to 1949; see also *SPIS*, no. 22, Dec. 1942, FO 371/35580.
[144] Details in Warburg, *Mahdist Ideology*, 88–111.

(proclamations) continued to form the basis of the ideology of the twentieth-century Ansar. Modifications and reinterpretations were introduced whenever necessary in order to reconcile Mahdist principles with twentieth-century social and political realities. This also seemed to be the case, although on a modest scale, in other Islamic movements such as the Khatmiyya, which continued to propagate its nineteenth-century *da'wa* during the twentieth century with minor modifications.[145]

In his article entitled 'The Sudanese Mahdi: Frontier Fundamentalist', John Voll placed the Sudanese Mahdi within the fundamentalist tradition of Islam and his messianism as closely associated with *tajdid* (renewal). Though his *sufi* background and training were clearly demonstrated in his mystical revelations and in his teachings, the Mahdi also asserted the transcendence of God. This dual role of Mahdi and fundamentalist, closely affiliated with *sufi* traditions may also explain the movement's ability to adjust to twentieth-century realities.[146] A good example of this internal conflict and of the way in which it was resolved by Sayyid 'Abd al-Rahman, is afforded by his interpretation of the Mahdi's *bay'a* (oath of allegiance). The nineteenth century Mahdist *bay'a* was at first based to a large extent on *sufi* traditions. However, a later and more elaborate version indicated a return to early traditions linked with the Prophet's biography (*sirat al-nabi*). It resembled the *bay'a* given by the *ansar* of Yathrib (Medina) to the Prophet following his *hijra* from Mecca in AD 622. This version contains a summary of the principal aspects of the Mahdiyya, including opposition to *shirk* (polytheism), a call for the unity of God and an undertaking not to steal, not to commit adultery and not to make false accusations. An undertaking always to obey the ruler and to refrain from accumulating worldly goods follows it. At the same time, the Mahdi, according to Shaykh al-Husayn Ibrahim Wad al-Zahra, emphasized that his attack against those who were obsessed with their comforts in this world did not imply that they should neglect their maintenance since it was the duty of Muslims to ensure their livelihood. However, money in private hands was only in trust since it belonged to *bayt al-mal* – the Muslim treasury. The Mahdi warned against whoever boasted of their riches and overspent on weddings and other festivities. He advised those engaged in trade to avoid corruption, exploitation or exaggerated profits. Every person should subsist on the bare minimum. If he owned land, he should only cultivate as much as he himself was able to and leave the rest for others without seeking a profit. This rule was based on the belief that all Muslims were one community and the fruits of the land belonged to whoever cultivated it. All enterprises, such as banks,

---

[145] John Voll in his study of the Khatmiyya emphasized that there has been no real ideological development in that *tariqa* during the twentieth century, and that the great variety of Khatmi organizations made the formulation of a well-defined and generally accepted ideology impossible. Voll, *Khatmiyya*, 641–5.

[146] Voll, *Sudanese Mahdi*, 153–65.

shops or agencies, which involved large profits should belong to the public domain. They should be handed over to *bayt al-mal*, which was ultimately responsible for the well-being of all believers. Money was needed only for essentials and hence should never occupy the heart of the true believer.[147] The *bay'a* ended with the oath not to flee from the *jihad* – which, as the events of Aba Island proved, became an inseparable part of the Mahdiyya.[148]

When Sayyid 'Abd al-Rahman sought to adjust the *bay'a* to twentieth-century realities he stated that 'the *bay'a* is subordinate to the command of religion and to amendments of the *imam*, in accordance with the circumstances of time'. The *imam* who supervised the *bay'a* was according to the Sayyid, not allowed to change its wording. However, in certain cases 'satisfaction of God's will (*murad*) compels (the *imam*) to deviate from it'.[149] Such a case, according to the Sayyid, was the accumulation of wealth. While at the time of the Mahdi's *jihad* a renunciation of worldly goods was dictated by the war with the enemy 'now, lawful earning is an obligation especially if the acquisition of such earnings is [undertaken] for the cause of God'.[150] Moreover, the Mahdi's *da'ira* (domain) and its wealth was according to Sayyid 'Abd al-Rahman, a national (*watani*) necessity that would help to pave the path to Sudan's independence. Ways had to be found in which the Ansar could accumulate sufficient wealth with which to enable their movement to finance its religious and political activities. The reintroduction of *sadaqa*, both as a token of support and as a political commitment was therefore crucial. In fact the British authorities, who realized the political implications of this voluntary tax, attempted to outlaw it but had to give in since *sadaqa* was also collected from the supporters of the Khatmiyya and other *sufi* orders.[151] It should be stressed that financially the contributions to *da'irat al-mahdi* made by the pilgrims from West Africa who supplied the Sayyid with cheap labour for his vast estates in the fertile lands of the White and Blue Nile provinces, were far more significant than *sadaqa*.[152]

As noted above, *jihad*, was central in Mahdist ideology since its foundation and was effectively practiced until the conquest of Khartoum in 1885. Muhammad Ahmad pronounced the *jihad* as more important than the *hajj*

---

[147] Sadiq, *Yas'alunaka*, 193–7. Shaykh Husayn Ibrahim Wad al-Zahra was a well known *'alim* and poet from the Gezira and an early adherent of the Mahdi. He was appointed by the Khalifa *qadi al-qudat* in 1894 and imprisoned a year later. He died in prison in 1895; according to Abu Salim, *Haraka*, 62, Wad al-Zahra was appointed in 1892 and died in prison in 1894.

[148] An earlier version of the *bay'a* did not mention *jihad* (quoted from *Manshurat* II, 45–6, letter dated 18 Oct. 1882); for details see Holt, *Mahdist State*, 103–18, 170.

[149] Sadiq, *Istiqlal*, 183; see also 190, where the Sayyid is quoted with regard to the need to adapt Mahdist dictates to present circumstances.

[150] Sadiq, *Istiqlal*, 184, 189.

[151] In British sources this 'voluntary tax' is often referred to as 'Zakat'. However, since it is clearly stated that this 'tax' was also collected from the followers of Sayyid 'Ali al-Mirghani, it seems that it was *sadaqa* rather than *zakat*.

[152] Details in Warburg, *Islam and Communism*, 29–33.

(pilgrimage), though the latter was one of the five pillars of Islam. There are several *manshurat* dealing with various aspect of the *jihad* in which the Mahdi emphasized its centrality in his teachings. In a letter written in 1883 he wrote: 'know that a sword which has penetrated for the sake of God is preferable to seventy years of worship'. He warned his followers against plundering and ordered them instead to forsake all their comforts and luxuries and invest in the preparation of the *jihad* all that they have. Simple life, asceticism (*al-zuhd fi al-dunya*) and *jihad* were the things that really matter since life in the present world is of little consequence.[153] *Jihad* was continued under the Khalifa and led to the Abyssinian campaigns in 1888–9, which ended in Mahdist victory. However, in the more important encounter with the Anglo-Egyptian forces commanded by Field-Marshal Francis Grenfell, the Mahdist army suffered its most crushing defeat at the battle of Tushki in August 1889. While *jihad* continued to be preached even after this debacle, the Mahdist state was generally on the defensive and was attempting to consolidate within its borders rather than getting involved in hopeless battles. Once again Sayyid 'Abd al-Rahman had to offer a modified interpretation of *jihad*. He claimed that a correct understanding of the Mahdi's intentions would clarify that *jihad* did not necessarily imply holy war, but might just as correctly be interpreted as *jihad al-nafs*.[154] Muhammad Ahmad Mahgoub, a staunch non-Mahdist Umma party leader, wrote that Sayyid 'Abd al-Rahman had realized that Mahdist military power had been crushed and hence his movement's path to survival lay in cooperating with Great Britain against their common enemies Egypt and Turkey.[155]

Sayyid 'Abd al-Rahman emphasized the dual spiritual and temporal roles of his mission. In this too he followed in his father's footsteps stressing the continuity between his own mission and those of the Mahdi and the Prophet. Spiritually his task was to purify Islam and to unite the true believers, the Ansar, in order to restore the debased religion to its former glory. But there was also a political mission inherent in the Mahdiyya: its fight for independence. This would be accomplished by a continuation of the Mahdi's *jihad*, but only by peaceful means.[156] A conciliatory attitude towards the country's foreign rulers was, according to the Sayyid, dictated by circumstances and had been part of his policy ever since he had handed the Mahdi's sword to King George V in 1919. This policy, he noted, has 'enabled me to achieve the Sudan's independence without revolution and bloodshed'.[157] Al-Sadiq al-Mahdi, in a paper dealing with Islam's response to social change, defined the role of *jihad* as follows:

[153] Sadiq, *Yas'alunaka*, 175; see also Abu Salim, *Haraka*, 46–7.

[154] Sadiq, *Istiqlal* 183–4. Talking of the accusations made by the British authorities – that the more fanatical western Ansar were planning a holy war against the government – the Sayyid stated that this was a misinterpretation. A peaceful *jihad* could accomplish similar results and was a greater *jihad*, *ibid.*, 186.

[155] Cited from his introduction to Sadiq, *Istiqlal*, b–c.

[156] *Ibid.*, 184–6.

[157] *Ibid.*, 188–9.

Jihad does not mean enforced Islamization. *Jihad* refers to the supreme effort expected of all Muslims to promote the cause of righteousness within themselves and in their social environment. It means going to war to protect the freedom of Muslims to promote that cause or to deter aggression.

Even pagans were, according to al-Sadiq, protected as a rule by Islam, unless they were treacherous and initiated violence. Therefore, in its relations with the outside world, the Muslim community is bound to honour all agreements and contracts, whoever the other party may be.[158]

But overriding all arguments was the unifying aspect of the Ansar's mission. By employing elements of *sufi* symbolism, as his father had, Sayyid 'Abd al-Rahman emphasized that the Ansar were neither a religious order (*tariqa*) nor a sect (*ta'ifa*) but embraced all those whom God had chosen from among His believers. Anyone, therefore, who assisted the Ansar's adversaries or disagreed with them on matters of religion or politics 'has been employed by the enemy for the destruction of truth'.[159] This of course included the youth, whose upbringing and education were the guarantee of Sudan's future. Unlike the older Ansar who had fully shared the Mahdi's vision, the young generation had 'only seen a glimpse of that light' and therefore had to be educated by true believers who could convey to them the full significance and glory of the Mahdist mission, through wisdom and preaching.[160]

Neo-Mahdist ideology emphasized the inseparability of the religious and political aspects of its message. It also stressed the importance of the Mahdi's *baraka*, which had been passed on to his son. Thereby Sayyid 'Abd al-Rahman had also inherited his father's leadership qualities which, together with the eternal Islamic mission, enabled him to turn the Ansar into the only movement in Sudan before the Second World War which enjoyed mass support. They could therefore appeal, with equal authority, to ignorant tribesmen and to the sophisticated intelligentsia, while each of these groups gave its allegiance to the Ansar for different ideological, economic and political reasons.

---

[158] Sadiq, *Islam and Change*, 236–7. The reference to 'pagans' is especially significant in the realities of Sudan, although, while prime minister in 1986–9, al-Sadiq himself failed to reach a compromise on this very issue.

[159] Sadiq, *Istiqlal*, 185–6.

[160] *Ibid.*, 190–1. Throughout the book the Sayyid's own role in educating the young generation is repeatedly emphasized.

11

THE PATH TO INDEPENDENCE, 1939–55

The years between the outbreak of the Second World War and Sudan's independence were crucial for a number of reasons. First, Britain had viewed the continuation of the Condominium as axiomatic and had not planned for Sudan's transition to independence in the foreseeable future. However, the repercussions of the war and the Labour Party's victory in the 1945 elections had created new conditions that led to the adoption of new policies by Whitehall. Secondly, the emergence of political parties in Sudan during the war forced both Egypt and Britain to choose their allies among the antagonists. Once again the SPS made the wrong decision. Basing its views on principles applicable in the West, it continued to view the separation of religion and politics as imperative and rejected the involvement of the Ansar and the Khatmiyya in the political process. Thirdly, the southern non-Muslim provinces which had been practically cut off from northern Sudan and declared closed provinces since 1910, were reunited with the north following the Juba Conference in 1947, and it became clear that they would become part of an independent Sudan. This should have implied a radical change in government policy *vis-à-vis* the south; unfortunately this did not happen and the southern regions remained as backward as they had been throughout the Condominium. Finally, the collapse of the monarchy in Egypt, following the Free Officers' revolution in July 1952, and the subsequent emergence of President Nasser as the unchallenged and most charismatic leader in the Middle East created a completely new situation, for which Britain was not prepared. With King Faruq out of the way, the Free Officers believed that a united Nile Valley was at last within reach, whereas Britain was determined to stick to the status quo. As we now know, they were both wrong, for they had reached their conclusion without taking into account Sudanese views, which by and large corresponded with those of the Ansar and the Khatmiyya and clearly indicated that Sudan was heading for independence.

The 1936 Anglo-Egyptian Treaty and its impact on Sudan

The political situation had already begun to change in 1936 when Britain and Egypt signed the Anglo-Egyptian Treaty, which included a chapter

104

regarding Sudan. For the Sudanese the treaty was a slap in the face: first, because their future had been decided upon once again without consulting them; and, secondly, the phrasing of the Sudanese clause in the treaty was regarded as humiliating. In its formulation the signatories avoided the controversial issue of sovereignty. They undertook instead to pursue the administration of Sudan for 'the welfare of the Sudanese', implying that the latter were too backward and too ignorant even to be consulted. In reporting on the '[t]reaty reactions of the Intelligentsia in the Sudan', the British Controller of Public Security in Khartoum had to admit that there was a marked intensification of nationalist feelings and a strong demand that the intelligentsia should have a voice in determining Sudan's future. 'The Treaty, in short, had one notable result. It has put Sudanese nationalism on the political map.'[161]

The reappearance of Egyptians in Sudan, following the treaty, was of little practical consequence. An Egyptian battalion that was allowed to return to Sudan and a few Egyptian officials who were appointed to government posts were a symbol of goodwill rather than a threat to the continuation of British supremacy. However, the presence of Egypt as a political alternative created a new situation, which had similarities to the pre-1924 period. It meant in effect that in the forthcoming struggle over sovereignty Egypt could serve as a potential partner for Sudanese nationalists. It enabled those who opposed the Ansar dominated 'Sudan for the Sudanese' school of thought to re-emerge on the political scene after fifteen years of virtual absence and to preach their ideology and politics under the slogan of the 'Unity of the Nile Valley'.[162] Towards the end of the war, Arab unity also made its appearance on the Sudanese political scene as a possible alternative to union with Egypt. This was no doubt prompted by the events in the Arab world leading to the founding of the Arab League, early in 1945. As elsewhere in the Middle East, Arab unity enjoyed British approval, especially in Sudan, where it provided a possible solution to the Anglo-Egyptian puzzle.[163]

By 1938-9 the Sudan government had already become aware of evidence suggesting that a concerted effort was being undertaken by Egypt to gain a foothold in Sudan and to assume, in the eyes of the Sudanese, the role of their liberators. In a note on 'Post-Treaty Egyptian Relations', the Civil Secretary, Sir Angus Gillan,[164] enumerated the new dangers, which

[161] Enclosed in Kelly to Eden, 7 Nov. 1936, FO 407/219.

[162] For a more general analysis of this problem see Muddathir, *Arabism*, 228–38. The 'unity of the Nile Valley' was more of an anti-British slogan than a pro-Egyptian one; details below.

[163] *SPIS*, no. 46, Jan. 1945, FO 371/45972. According to the author of the report the support for an independent Sudan participating in some form of Arab unity 'received much stimulus from the visit to the Sudan during January of M. Albert Hourani', who had served under Toynbee in the Foreign Office International Research Department; see also Clayton to Burrows, 6 Apr. 1945, FO 371/45972.

[164] Sir A. Gillan, 'Post-Treaty Egyptian relations', 27 May 1938 (Sir A. Gillan's private

were mainly in the spheres of education, culture and religion. He referred specifically to the proposed opening, in Sudan, of an Egyptian secondary school, an Egyptian *ma'had* (seminar) and an Egyptian library, in which King Faruq and Shaykh Mustafa al-Maraghi were deeply involved.[165] But even more important was the change in attitude of the Egyptian government towards Sudanese nationalism. Gillan pointed out that the Egyptians propagated 'the theory of the sister countries joined by ties of blood, water and religion, with the inference of virtual independence except in the matter of sovereignty'. This line was infinitely more appealing to the Sudanese, since, by tying their future to that of Egypt they could now hope for a more rapid advance towards complete independence, with some loose bonds to the Egyptian Crown. Gillan's statement that 'Egyptian Government senior personnel, civil and military, have all been on their best behavior and would appear at present to be genuinely anxious to cooperate in a treaty spirit', tends to confirm the impression that Egypt was trying to win over Sudanese nationalists by adopting a more realistic attitude.[166]

It is interesting to note that Egyptian efforts in Sudan tended to ignore the intelligentsia, at least until 1943, and concentrated instead on the more traditional sectors of Sudanese society and leadership. Of special significance was the Egyptian attempt to win over the two Sayyids, both by granting them the title of Pasha and by publicizing their high standing and political importance in the Egyptian press.[167] However, both Sayyids, while pleased with the publicity, declined to take a pronounced pro-Egyptian stand and in fact remained very critical of Egyptian motives and intentions. In 1937 Sayyid 'Abd al-Rahman went on a visit to England and Egypt in order to present in person the Sudanese criticism of the Anglo-Egyptian treaty. Although he commented favourably on his talks with Butler and other high-ranking British officials, he continued to view his Egyptian hosts as unrealistic and openly criticized their plans for unity of the Nile Valley.[168] Yet the very fact that he agreed to visit Egypt seemed to disturb Sudan's

---

papers). Sir Angus, whom I met and interviewed in London on 6 Oct. 1970, kindly provided me with copies of this and other relevant papers.

[165] On al-Maraghi's dealing with the *ma'had* see Lampson to Oliphant, 12 Feb. 1937, FO 371/20870; Symes to Lampson, 23 Mar. 1938, FO 371/21998. King Faruq attempted to persuade Symes to agree to the appointment of an Egyptian Deputy Governor-General in Sudan: see Symes to Lampson, 16 May 1939, FO 371/23323.

[166] Sir A. Gillan, 'Post-Treaty Egyptian relations', 27 May 1938; see also Minute by C.S. [Civil Secretary] to D.P.S. [Director Public Security], 20 July 1939 (Sir A. Gillan's private papers). During my interview with Sir Angus he emphasized that the three southern provinces were excluded stating: 'I always hoped . . . that we should be able to carry on ourselves in the three southern provinces for a bit longer.'

[167] See, for instance, Lampson to Simon, 2 Mar. 1935; Symes to Lampson, 3 Mar. 1935, FO 407/218; Lampson to Eden, 7 July 1937, FO 407/221. Lampson wrote of the publicity given to Sayyid Siddiq al-Mahdi, Sayyid 'Abd al-Rahman's son, during his visit to Egypt.

[168] Sadiq, *Istiqlal*, 36.

British rulers. Egypt had always regarded the Sayyid as a British stooge and yet it granted his son, al-Siddiq al-Mahdi, a royal welcome when he came to Cairo in May 1937. Sayyid 'Abd al-Rahman therefore decided, that a well-publicized visit to Egypt and royal receptions by King Faruq and the Egyptian political leadership, could bring him valuable benefits with the suspicious Symes and his colleagues. He was not wrong since Lampson commented that the Mahdist sought to turn Cairo into a centre of their propaganda and Gillan warned of a Mahdist alliance with Egypt.[169] In reality it was a rather brief and superficial honeymoon, probably no more than yet another manipulation, aimed at softening British opposition.

The Sayyid constantly urged the British authorities to encourage 'Sudanese nationalism as a bulwark against this danger', of Egyptian ambitions to rule Sudan.[170] Sayyid 'Ali al-Mirghani's position was rather more complex and ambivalent. First, because of his role as a religious leader he tended to avoid politics whenever possible and had consistently done so since 1924. Secondly, British observers stated that he was 'suffering from an illusion that the Government has written him off and is advancing Sayed 'Abdel Rahman to the foremost position in the country'.[171] Therefore, although he viewed the ever increasing political impact of Sayyid 'Abd al-Rahman with dismay, Sayyid 'Ali consistently refrained from coming into the open. As late as 1944, when asked to comment on the Sudan's future, Sayyid 'Ali usually 'confined his conversation . . . to general observations on the weather in the Sudan, Egypt and England, dealing with the subject pretty thoroughly', but refused to be drawn into politics.[172] It is therefore almost impossible to define Sayyid 'Ali's political views during that period. His only consistent stand was to express total opposition to any proposal made by Sayyid 'Abd al-Rahman, let alone his political ambitions. Thus he opposed the reform of the Omdurman Islamic College (*al-ma'had al-Islami*), supported by Sayyid 'Abd al-Rahman, stating that under its present leadership it enjoyed a 'golden age'. Sayyid 'Ali hoped, through his support of the college's present leadership, 'to capture an institution of considerable social and religious importance' and therefore ignored the attacks in the Ansar's daily, *al-Nil*, which accused him of acting 'against the consensus of enlightened opinion in the country'.[173] An open conflict had already broken out, in 1936, when Abu Diqn, Shaykh al-'ulama' and president of the *ma'had* at the time, had announced that he had joined the Ansar.

[169] Hassan, *'Abd al-Rahman*, 12–13.

[170] *SMIS*, no. 69, Jan. 1940, FO 371/24633.

[171] *SPIS*, no. 1, Oct.–Nov. 1940, FO 371/27382.

[172] *SPIS*, no. 35, Feb. 1944, FO 371/41348, reporting on Mr Scrivener's interview with S.A.R. and S.A.M. [SAR and SAM were the abbreviations used by British authorities for the two Sayyids], 27 Feb. 1944. Scrivener was at that time Head of the Egyptian Department at the Foreign Office in London.

[173] *SPIS*, no. 6, Apr.–May 1941, FO 371/27382.

This was a blow both to the government and to Sayyid 'Ali, since Abu Diqn's posts were the most senior religious positions held by a Sudanese and his joining the Ansar seemed to be a betrayal of his supposed neutrality between the two sects.[174] When a few years later an even closer associate of Sayyid 'Abd al-Rahman was appointed president of the *ma'had*, Sayyid 'Ali refused to support the institute in any way thereby enabling the Ansar to accuse him of 'sacrificing public interest to partisan considerations'.[175]

Another development in the post-treaty years was the government's support of Sayyid 'Ali's attempts to recruit new followers in Ansar-dominated regions. He was encouraged to tour the White Nile and Kordofan in order to recruit new members to the Khatmiyya, while at the same time the government banned the pilgrimage of Ansar to Aba Island. The 'even-handedness' on which the government prided itself had thus been unceremoniously ignored in this case. Furthermore, a government that had always advocated the separation of 'Church and State' was in effect, exploiting a religious conflict to further its own political ends.[176]

The Italian conquest of the Kassala region in 1940, which included the Khatmiyya spiritual centre, became an issue in sectarian politics and seemed, for a while, to be detrimental to Sayyid 'Ali's fortunes. Due to the Mirghani family's close ties with Eritrea and the fact that Sayyid 'Ali's cousin and his mother's half-sister, al-Sharifa 'Alawiyya, were well-known supporters of Italian Fascism, he felt that he was suspected by the government. His misgivings were strengthened when Sayyid 'Abd al-Rahman was repeatedly publicized in BBC overseas broadcasts as the religious leader of Sudan, while his own name was not even mentioned. Next came a bitter attack on Sufism, made by Shaykh Ahmad 'Uthman al-Qadi and published in *al-Nil*. As the author was both a supporter of Sayyid 'Abd al-Rahman and a member of the central government Political Department, Sayyid 'Ali felt certain that the attack was inspired by the government.[177] In January 1941, following the expulsion of the Italians from Kassala, tension was somewhat relieved. An intelligence report stated that 'the Sayed's relations with the government have returned to normal and roses from his garden again grace the political breakfast tables of Khartoum.'[178]

Another of Sayyid 'Ali's activities that clouded his relations with the government was his attempt to organize a paramilitary youth section of the Khatmiyya. This so-called 'Mirghanist shirt movement' (*shabab al-Khatmiyya*), was first organized in February 1940, under the Sayyid's auspices.

[174] Dhaher, *Al-Mirghani*, 185–6.

[175] *SPIS*, no. 25, Mar. 1943, FO 371/35580.

[176] Dhaher, *Al-Mirghani*, 184, 190–1.

[177] *SMIS*, no. 73, Aug.–Sept. 1940, FO 371/24633. Following an Italian bombardment of Omdurman, the Khatmiyya leaders spread a rumour that the attack 'was directed against Sayed Abdel Rahman personally, since all the bombs fell in the Abbasia district. The Italians, it was pointed out, would never attack Sayed Ali's quarters.' See also *SPIS*, no. 1, Oct.-Nov. 1940, FO 371/27382; see also Hassan, '*Abd al-Rahman*, 5 (fn. 1).

[178] *SPIS*, no. 3, Jan. 1941, FO 371/27382.

It paraded 'the streets of Khartoum and Omdurman, in drilled formation, chanting slogans in praise of the Sayed and against all his enemies . . . mainly directed against Sayed 'Abdel Rahman'.[179] An important aim was to attract new members into the Khatmiyya ranks. Every Sudanese who wanted to join and was between ten and fifty years old was freely admitted as a member in the Mirghanist youth movement. It was a paramilitary movement, trained by retired army sergeants, under the direction of Muhammad Hasan Diyab and the supervision of Sayyid 'Ali al-Mirghani himself. Its centre was in the *bayt al-mal* district of Omdurman. It sought to educate the youth in accordance with the religious, cultural and social values of the Khatmiyya. Its appeal far exceeded the expectations of its founders and drove the Ansar to found their rival youth organization, *shabab al-ansar*. The government was in no mood to tolerate such movements, especially during the war, even if it belonged to the Khatmiyya, which they fully trusted. It was assumed that Sayyid 'Ali, having failed to capture the intelligentsia organized in the Graduates' Congress, had decided to concentrate on the less sophisticated youth of the three towns. The authorities, fearing the reaction of the Ansar, demanded the immediate disbanding of these youth movements and ordered both Sayyids to refrain from such activities in the future. The Sayyids promised to comply but in fact only forbade the youth to wear their uniforms and continued to exploit them for demonstrations whenever the need arose. Sayyid 'Ali also created the *ittihadat al-Khatmiyya*, during the early 1940s, and founded the Khatmiyya's daily newspaper *Sawt al-Sudan*. They were destined to serve as the political arm of the Khatmiyya in order to strengthen its position *vis-à-vis* the Ansar. After 1956 they performed the same role for the People's Democratic Party (PDP), which was founded as the political arm of the Khatmiyya.[180] This enabled Sayyid 'Ali to maintain his non-committal ambivalent stand towards the Sudan government and the Egyptian authorities. In 1944 he openly strengthened his ties with Egyptian officers and officials in Sudan, as well with Egyptian leaders and the Egyptian press.[181] However, he continued at the same time to express his support for Sudan's self-government under British guidance. The description of Sayyid 'Ali and his supporters by the British authorities as being constantly 'in a state of indecision and perplexity' is therefore probably the most accurate assessment of Khatmiyya politics until the end of the Second World War.[182]

[179] *SMIS*, no. 70, Feb.–Mar. 1940, FO 371/24633. The so-called 'shirt movements' were probably influenced by their namesakes in Egypt, organized by the Wafd and by Misr al-Fatat; it was rumoured that a Green Shirt movement had been founded in Wad Madani by Misr al-Fatat in 1939; see Hassan, '*Abd al-Rahman*, 9 (fn. 1).

[180] Dhaher, *Al-Mirghani*, 289–92; see also *SMIS*, no. 72, May–July 1940; *SMIS*, no. 73, Aug.–Sep. 1940, FO 371/24633.

[181] *SPIS*, no. 41, Aug. 1944; *SPIS*, no. 42, Sept. 1944, FO 371/41348.

[182] *Political Intelligence Centre Paper*, no. 66, 'The Sudan and the future', compiled by G.E.R. Sandars, Sudan Agent in Cairo, by K.D.D. Henderson, and by Samuel Atiyah of the Civil Secretary's Office, Khartoum (n.d. [Oct. 1944?]), FO 371/41363.

The Graduates' General Congress

The establishment of the Graduates' General Congress in 1938 was facilitated by a number of factors. First, central government authorities had realized that tribal organization in Sudan was weakened beyond repair and therefore the possibility of evolving a system of genuine local self-government was no longer realistic.[183] This did not imply a complete dismissal of tribal leadership, but rather an attempt to look for a possible alternative among the educated class. Secondly, the threat of war created a situation in Sudan in which the support of every segment of the population was essential to the government, not least the intelligentsia, which was by definition more open to hostile anticolonialist propaganda. Thirdly, the emergence of Sayyid 'Abd al-Rahman al-Mahdi and the Ansar as a political force and his growing influence on the intelligentsia suggested that an attempt to create an alternative, non-sectarian, basis for the latter's loyalty could be useful. Fourthly, the Anglo-Egyptian Treaty of 1936 had stirred public opinion in Sudan to such an extent that the politically minded intelligentsia could in any case no longer be relied upon to remain passive. Finally, the appointment of Sir Douglas Newbold as Deputy Civil Secretary in 1938 and as Civil Secretary in the following year was of great significance. For the first time since the establishment of the Condominium the man who stood at the helm of government was sympathetic to the educated class and tried to understand its aspirations. Newbold's predecessors in office were influenced by Wingate's and Stack's views about Sudan, which were largely formed before the First World War and influenced by the Anglo-Indian school. They carried their preference for the honest and primitive tribal population over the townie or effendi into the 1930s. Thus Angus Gillan and Reginald Davies, both senior members of the SPS, insisted that tribal shaykhs were more loyal and of much higher standing in Sudanese society than Gordon College graduates and that they had more character and intelligence.[184] Newbold had arrived in Sudan after the First World War and thus belonged to a generation with new ideas and perceptions. In addition he was also an extraordinarily bright, humane and capable man. Margery Perham, a close observer of British colonialism and of the Sudanese scene over a long period wrote of him: 'Newbold showed to me the highest standards I have

[183] Kelly to Oliphant, 18 Feb. 1938, FO 371/22003. The following will deal primarily with the penetration of sectarianism into the Graduates' General Congress. Further details in Henderson, *Modern Sudan*, 536–53; Muddathir, *Imperialism*, 124–32.

[184] Based on my interviews with Sir Angus Gillan, KBE, CMG, and Mr Reginald Davies, CMG, in 1970. I was impressed by their sincere belief in native administration and by their insistence that it was not intended as a measure to keep the intelligentsia down. See also 'Some notes about the Erkowit Study Camp' by Gaitskell (n.d. [May 1944?]), FO 371/41363; Gaitskell related that he and most of his British colleagues at the Erkowit Study Camp' had preferred the tribesmen, 'whom they judged as something foreign', to the *effendis* whom they looked down upon.

ever seen in colonial administration.'[185] Mekki Abbas, who as a Sudanese graduate and administrator had many political disagreements with Newbold, wrote of him after his sudden death in March 1945: 'we know that his motive, when he worked himself to death, was not just the discharging of a debt, but he had a more sublime motive for working so hard. That was his love for the Sudan.'[186]

Sayyid 'Abd al-Rahman, as noted, had emerged since 1931 as the most powerful political leader in Sudan, among both the Ansar and the graduates. The government therefore hoped that by encouraging the intelligentsia to found its own organization, it would deal a deathblow to the Sayyid's political aspirations within the intelligentsia. The British regarded these ambitions, based on Mahdist ideology, as impairing Sudan's progress.[187] When the government recognized the Graduates' General Congress in 1938, it was part of a well-devised plan which, though initiated by the intelligentsia, enjoyed the full backing of the authorities. Even the details of the congress constitution were hammered out 'in friendly collaboration, between the future scourge of the 'imperialist oppressors', Isma'il al-Azhari, and J.C. Penny, who, as Controller of Public Security, was immediately responsible for the detection and surveillance of 'subversive' political activity'.[188]

To hope that the weak and politically immature educated class could challenge the authority of the Sayyids and their well-organized supporters without succumbing to sectarianism in the process was, in hindsight, rather naïve. In 1938, there were about 3,000 graduates in Sudan who, in a total population of 6 million, accounted for less than one-tenth of 1 per cent. Moreover, the term 'graduate' was rather misleading since it included both graduates of Gordon College, which was the only secondary school in Sudan, and graduates of intermediate schools. It is therefore no wonder that the government itself, despite its interest in the emergence of a non-sectarian intelligentsia viewed it with certain misgivings. In explaining this new venture in Sudanese politics, Gillan, then Civil Secretary, wrote:

> It must not be inferred from the use of this rather grandiloquent title ('Graduates'), that we have already reached a stage in this country at which the intelligentsia are beginning to agitate collectively for political rights and political representation. It is possible that the Graduates' Congress may emerge at some future date as a nationalist organization with a political programme . . . [At present] it neither seeks formal recognition, nor does it claim to represent the views of any but its own members.[189]

Once again the government's attitude was both ambivalent and unrealistic.

[185] Henderson, *Modern Sudan*, xxvii.
[186] *Ibid.*, xxix, quoted from the *Arabic and English Newsletter*, Khartoum, 28 Mar. 1945.
[187] Kelly to Oliphant, 2 Feb. 1938, FO 371/22003.
[188] Sanderson, *Sudanese Nationalism.*
[189] Gillan to Lampson, 5 July 1938, FO 371/21999.

On the one hand it sponsored the intelligentsia as an antidote to sectarianism, and yet at the same time viewed them as too immature to play a significant role in the immediate future. Furthermore, by hoping – as the government did – that so-called self-imposed limitations would stop the graduates from moving into the political arena, it ignored both the natural aspirations of the intelligentsia and the political designs of Sayyid 'Abd al-Rahman. But even more detrimental was the government's failure to come to grips with the time element. In 1938, just as ten or twenty years earlier, the authorities simply did not foresee a future Sudan that would be administered by its own people without British supervision. Sir Stewart Symes, then Governor-General, wrote:

> The welfare of the Sudanese people is likely to be promoted neither by a spectacular process of development nor too rapid innovations. To the Sudan may truly be applied an Arab adage that 'haste is of the devil, slow deliberation is of God'.[190]

On 12 February 1938 some 1,180 graduates took part in founding the General Graduates' Congress. They constituted themselves into a permanent body with a supervisory committee of sixty and an executive committee of fifteen, to be elected annually. The committees were 'charged with laying down and executing a programme of social reform and bringing to the notice of the Government the views of the intelligentsia on legitimate matters of public interest'.[191] This vague definition, which had been insisted upon by the government, clearly invited trouble. Health, education and welfare were clearly within the definition. Yet from the outset the British regarded the Congress also as an expression 'of an indigenous Sudanese identity, implying rejection of the idea of national absorption by Egypt' and consequently a revival of 'The Sudan for the Sudanese' movement. Before long this controversial political issue was bound to bring about a split among the graduates and thereby enable the two Sayyids to move in. It was also bound to arouse conflict and to involve the graduates themselves in politics, as suspected by Egypt. The Egyptian government, sensing in the Congress a threat to its claim for Egyptian–Sudanese unity, dismissed it as a 'British invention' that 'had been created . . . with the object of resisting Egyptian penetration' into Sudan.[192] To overcome this suspicion, members of the Congress committee of fifteen tried to convince the Egyptians, through both private talks and articles in the press, that they represented an independent expression of Sudanese nationalism and maintained

---

[190] 'Monograph on some outstanding features and general purposes in the administration of the Sudan', by G.S.S. [Symes], May 1938, FO 371/22005. Symes's views in the 1940s were not dissimilar to those of Wingate or Slatin nearly half a century earlier.

[191] Notes on the Graduates' Congress, enclosed in Gillan to Lampson, 5 July 1938, FO 371/21999.

[192] *SMIS*, no. 64, June 1939, FO 407/224.

complete impartiality in the Anglo-Egyptian conflict. Congress leaders saw their chance when 'Ali Mahir, the Egyptian Prime Minister, visited Sudan at Symes's invitation in February 1940. A tea party was arranged by Congress for 'Ali Mahir and his mission in which 800 graduates took part. Congress speakers addressing the party stressed that theirs was the only independent and representative Sudanese organization and was not British-inspired. They also emphasized that Sudanese nationalism did not contradict their brotherly feelings for Egypt, since Sudan and Egypt were two distinct national entities.[193] The second and more significant step was taken by Congress when it decided to present a memorandum to 'Ali Mahir to be submitted by him to the Egyptian people. The government viewed this as unconstitutional, since it implied ignoring the Governor-General as the sole intermediary between Sudan and Egypt. Yet, despite a stern warning by the authorities, the committee of sixty decided to present the memorandum to 'Ali Mahir.[194] The memorandum itself was unimportant because as a result of the government's warning it had been watered down to such an extent 'that the requests embodied in it . . . became in themselves innocuous and largely meaningless'. Even 'Ali Mahir expressed disappointment at the fact that all the points raised in the memorandum, such as the Islamic College in Omdurman or the admission of Muslim 'missionaries' into the southern provinces, had already been settled between him and Symes before the submission of the Congress memorandum. However, the meeting between Congress and the Egyptian delegation was important since it convinced the Egyptian government 'that Congress was the genuine embryo of a nationalist movement and not . . . a British anti-Egyptian invention'.[195]

The memorandum became significant in yet another context. In debating the pros and cons of submitting the memorandum, the committee of sixty had split into two camps. 'The defeat of the more responsible and moderate elements', led by Mirghani Hamza and 'Abd al-Majid, both supporters of Sayyid 'Ali al-Mirghani, led the authorities to the conclusion that 'the composition and the functioning of the committee of sixty are

[193] Intelligence Summary no. 6 (for period ending 28th Feb. 1940), FO 371/24620. The author of the summary noted that some of the graduates were wearing felt hats, which he regarded as a 'significant sign of independence vis a vis Egypt . . . They are at least original in expressing their political views by the hats they wear and not by the shirts.'

[194] *SMIS*, no. 70, Feb.–Mar. 1940, FO 371/24633. Mahir's visit was described in detail by Muhammad Hassanayn Makhluf, who, in a book entitled *Two weeks with Ali Mahir in the Sudan* (in Arabic), claimed that the visit was a turning point in Egyptian–Sudanese relations. The book was, according to British interpretation, probably intended as 'personal propaganda pure and simple', for 'Ali Mahir had by that time (Mar. 1941) been dismissed from his post as PM on Lampson's insistence, due to his pro-Fascist sympathies: *SPIS*, no. 5, Mar. 1941, FO 371/27382.

[195] *SMIS*, no. 70, Feb.–Mar. 1940, FO 371/24633.

extremely unsatisfactory' and hence government intervention was warranted. In a meeting with Congress leaders, Newbold warned them that the
government might 'compel the withdrawal of officials from Congress membership, and if need be . . . dissolve the Congress itself'.[196] Congress, however, was threatened from yet another direction as the split within its ranks
made it easy prey for the two Sayyids. In January 1940 it had seemed to the
authorities that the various groups within Congress were 'tending to lose all
sectarian colour derived from connection with the Holy Men and to assume
an independent existence'. Moreover, the fact that from 1,180 graduates
attending the first annual meeting in February 1938 the number dropped
to 400 in 1939 and to only 250 in January 1940 suggested that this was due
to the graduates' feeling 'that the Congress has failed, through extreme
passivity and moderation, to achieve any results worth while'.[197] 'Ali
Mahir's visit was therefore a turning-point, as it gave the Congress a new
lease of life. The attendance of 800 graduates at the Congress reception held
for 'Ali Mahir and the subsequent publicity it received through the
submission of its memorandum enabled the graduates at last to appear on
the political scene. This, as noted, implied the involvement of the two
Sayyids: first, because the graduates were numerically and financially too
weak to make a real impact on a continuous basis without the Sayyids' aid;
secondly, the Sayyids owned the only non-governmental daily newspapers
and the sole Arabic publishing house belonged to Sayyid 'Abd al-Rahman;
and, finally, many of the graduates, especially the older ones, owed their
allegiance to the Sayyids and their sects long before Congress was founded.
While their initial attempt to keep sectarian politics out of Congress was
probably quite sincere, it became evident during the first two years of
Congress's existence that this was unrealistic. If Congress was to become
a political factor despite government opposition, the goodwill and support
of either one or both Sayyids were essential.

The first opportunity for Congress to become politically involved was
offered ironically by Symes himself when, on 11 June 1940 he invited
Congress leaders, along with the Sayyids and other notables, to a meeting
to acquaint them with Italy's declaration of war and to win their support for
his own proclamation to the people of Sudan. Congress seized this chance
to advertise its political role. Its secretary suggested to Newbold that Congress leaders should be permitted to broadcast to 'the people of the Sudan
with the object of giving them such advice and guidance as might be required'. This was refused on the grounds that a broadcast to 'the Sudanese
people was definitely presumptuous and implied an arrogation of status
and influence to which Congress was not entitled'. Instead, Congress leaders were advised to publish their proclamation in *al-Nil* and *Sawt al-Sudan*,

---

[196] *Ibid.*.
[197] *SMIS*, no. 69, Jan. 1940, *ibid.*

owned by Sayyid 'Abd al-Rahman and Sayyid 'Ali al-Mirghani, respectively.[198]

The split within Congress, between Khatmiyya and Ansar supporters, occurred during August–September 1940. It started with the decision of the committee of sixty to boycott government broadcasts on Sudanese culture. Members of Congress had been invited to participate individually in preparing these broadcasts but the committee of sixty decided to forbid participation unless Congress was also allowed to broadcast in its own name. This caused the resignation of the committee of fifteen, which had opposed the boycott and whose members were mostly Khatmiyya supporters. Next came an attempt by the Mahdist-dominated Congress to 'convert it openly into a political assembly'. Using the Ansar's *al-Nil* for their propaganda they advocated the establishment of a National Front. 'The object . . . was to bring the two Sayeds - or Sayed 'Abd El Rahman alone - and other elements (such as tribal leaders and urban notables) into open relationship with the Congress' and thereby provide it with adequate political backing.[199] Finally, an attempt was made both through the local press and by circular letters to attract some 3,000 new members into Congress. The tone of the articles and letters implied that the orientation of the pro-Mahdist leadership of Congress was now primarily political. 'Following these disquieting manifestations the Director of Public Security saw the Congress President and warned him off the political trend.' Moreover, the government was already so disappointed that it stated bluntly that 'Congress, as it stands now [September 1940], cannot live for long'. Officially Isma'il al-Azhari, the new president of Congress, agreed to cooperate with the government and to refrain from politics, and even wrote an article to that effect in *al-Mu'tamar*, the new Congress journal.[200] In reality *al-Nil* and *Sawt al-Sudan* provided the platforms from which the rival parties within Congress could attack each other so that the Ansar-Khatmiyya feud was once again in full swing.[201]

Not surprisingly the elections to the Congress committees held at the

[198] *SMIS*, no. 72, May–July 1940, *ibid*. It is noteworthy that during the war Sudan, unlike Egypt, Iraq and other Middle Eastern countries, was practically free of Nazi propaganda. The only occasion mentioned in the intelligence reports was 'The Nazi Bill-Posting Incident' in Khartoum, in which an Egyptian teacher and three schoolboys were involved; *SPIS*, no. 9, Aug. 1941, FO 371/27382.

[199] *SMIS*, no. 73, Aug.–Sept. 1940, FO 371/24633. According to this report Sayyid 'Ali, who was asked by Congress members to join the National Front, declined the offer. Instead, an article inspired by the Sayyid and published in his *Sawt al Sudan* stated that there were no 'political leaders' in Sudan and that 'religious leaders' should have nothing to do with Congress or the National Front: *ibid*.

[200] *SMIS*, no. 73, Aug.–Sept. 1940, FO 371/24633. Al-Azhari was at that time still a supporter of Sayyid 'Abd al-Rahman and hence it is probable that *al-Mu'tamar* received financial backing from Mahdist sources.

[201] The chief protagonists were Mirghani Hamza (under an assumed name) for the Khatmiyya and 'Abdallah al-Fadil and Ahmad Yusuf Hashim for the Ansar. The government's

annual meeting in January 1941 were contested on a purely sectarian basis with the Ansar winning an absolute majority in both. The Director of Public Security noted that the latter 'may well show themselves to be an able and irreproachable body, but the Mahdist label will be tied firmly to all their activities'.[202] For the first six months after the elections, the Mahdist-dominated Congress seemed to function well. In February 1941 it organized an 'Education Day', in which funds were raised to assist Sudanese non-government schools. The scheme was boycotted by Sayyid 'Ali al-Mirghani due to the Ansar's domination of Congress. But its success and popularity among all sectors of Sudanese society proved, as was the intention of the organizers, 'that a Mahdist Congress could do better social work than the mixed assembly of the past years'. At the same time, public opinion turned against Sayyid 'Ali and blamed him for 'his narrowly partisan and obstructive attitude'.[203] Another achievement of the new executive of Congress was its decision to cooperate with the government in broadcasts on cultural affairs, which they had previously boycotted. This again became a cause for internal strife as it brought about the resignation of the few remaining Khatmiyya members from the committee of sixty.[204] It should be noted that the Ansar had been the original advocates of this boycott, which the Khatmiyya had at first opposed. Hence it was a purely sectarian dispute which had no real political or ideological basis. In addition it should be noted that many members of Congress joined forces with one or the other of the two Sayyids on a purely pragmatic basis and changed sides whenever it seemed opportune. It therefore should not have come as a surprise that the Ansar, who had been in full control of Congress since January 1941, lost their dominant position before the end of 1942. This development had two major causes. First, many of the supporters of Sayyid 'Abd al-Rahman within Congress were not really Ansar. They were attracted to the Sayyid as the pillar of an independent Sudan and a source of financial backing, rather than to his religious credo and thus were quite willing to change sides when the opportunity arose. Secondly, Sayyid 'Ali decided to break away from his many years of political apathy, as a result of the Ansar's victory in the 1941 elections. He thereby provided the intelligentsia with a political alternative.

The first signs of an internal Mahdist conflict and of its repercussions in Congress came in August 1941. An attempt was made by several leading Ansar to oust 'Abdallah al-Fadil from his post as Sayyid 'Abd al-Rahman's *khalifa* in Omdurman and to replace him with al-Siddiq, the Sayyid's eldest

---

censor spent half his time 'trying to rub the poison off the shafts'. *SMIS*, no. 73, Aug.–Sept. 1940, FO 371/24633.

[202] *SPIS*, no. 3, Jan. 1941, FO 371/27382.

[203] *SPIS*, no. 4, Feb. 1941, FO 371/27382.

[204] *SPIS*, no. 7, June 1941, FO 371/27382.

son. The conflict was not resolved until 1943, probably because Sayyid 'Abd al-Rahman did not want to commit himself openly in a conflict involving his own son. But during the following two years the Ansar were considerably weakened as a result of this dispute, and their supporters in Congress were divided into two camps. Those backing al-Fadil were headed by Isma'il al-Azhari and Yahya al-Fadli, while their rivals included Ibrahim Ahmad, then President of Congress, who had the backing of Ahmad Yusuf Hashim, editor of *al-Nil*, and of the very strong Hashimab clan.[205] Matters came to a head in the Congress elections of December 1942, when the Azhari-Fadli faction emerged victorious. To the outsider it appeared that the internal rift between the two Mahdist blocs in Congress and the appearance of two additional groups, the *Abu ruf* and *al-Mu'tamirin al-Ahrar*, 'completely superseded the old sectarian division'. Moreover, the attendance of some 1,250 members at the Congress's annual meeting, many of whom were artisans, merchants and even illiterates, seemed to imply 'a great deterioration and a fundamental change in the character of Congress'. The Director of Public Security even suggested that this interplay of animosities would soon bring about the collapse of Congress.[206] In reality, however, it soon transpired that the bloc headed by al-Azhari which had gained control of Congress, enjoyed the backing of Sayyid 'Ali al-Mirghani and the Khatmiyya.

By the end of 1942 the government had written off the Graduates' Congress as a potential political organization of any significance. The events that brought about the final verdict against Congress started, as had been noted, in 1940 and came to a head in April–May 1942. At the beginning of April 1942 the committee of sixty under the presidency of Ibrahim Ahmad, formulated a memorandum containing twelve demands, ostensibly in the name of the Sudanese people, and submitted it to the government. Many of these demands dealt with political matters such as the right of self-determination, immediate steps toward self-government and the revision of Southern policy. From a government point of view this was clearly unacceptable both in content and in form. On 24 April, Newbold returned the memorandum to Ibrahim Ahmad together with a curt letter stating the government's reasons for refusing to accept or discuss its contents.[207] Newbold also instructed all Provincial Governors and Heads of Departments to refuse to discuss the memorandum, since the Graduates'

---

[205] *SPIS*, no. 9, Aug. 1941, FO 372/27382; *SPIS*, no. 21, Nov. 1942, FO 371/35580. Of those involved in the conflict, Yahya al-Fadli served as Minister for Social Affairs in al-Azhari's first government in 1953–6 and Ibrahim Ahmad became Minister of Finance under 'Abdallah Khalil after independence.

[206] *SPIS*, no. 21, Nov. 1942; *SPIS*, no. 22, Dec. 1942, FO 371/35580.

[207] Henderson, *Modern Sudan*, 540–2, gives all the details as well as the verbatim text of all the communications exchanged between Newbold and Ibrahim Ahmad; see also Muddathir *Imperialism*, 127-30.

Congress had, in his words, 'deliberately and after due warning forfeited its confidence'.[208]

What had prompted Congress, under the moderate leadership of Ibrahim Ahmad, to venture into the forbidden sphere of politics? According to Newbold and Huddleston, then Governor-General, the memorandum was inspired by several factors: first, the promises made by the Atlantic Charter with regard to self-determination; secondly, the part played by the SDF against Italy on the East African front; and, finally, the passage through Sudan of Sir Stafford Cripps a leading Labour Party member, who on his return trip from India gave an interview to the Arabic press, on 4 April 1942, in which he stated that Sudan's participation in the war effort 'will gain it a place in the new era which we all hope to see in the world when we have finished with the evil forces'.[209] But the government was still disturbed by the fact that the moderate committee of sixty, under an 'enlightened president, should have been stampeded into addressing to the Governor-General a letter containing extravagant and illconsidered claims'.[210] The answer to this may also be sought in the internal conflict in Congress between the Ibrahim Ahmad camp and the followers of Isma'il al-Azhari. A hint, suggesting this, can be found in Sayyid 'Abd al-Rahman's memoirs in which he stated that the memorandum was prompted by an article inspired by him and published in *al-Nil* at the beginning of 1942. By refusing to accept the memorandum or to discuss its 'moderate and legitimate' demands, the government, according to the Sayyid, was trying to humiliate and discredit the leadership of Congress and thus played into the hands of the extremists.[211] Ibrahim Ahmad's conduct during May–September 1942 provides further proof to that effect. Following a private meeting with Newbold, in which an understanding was reached, Ibrahim Ahmad tried to persuade the committee of sixty to accept the compromise. He failed, however, due to the opposition of al-Azhari and his supporters and had to retreat from his previously suggested compromise.[212] Ibrahim Ahmad's reluctance to force the issue may also have been prompted by the preparations for Congress elections, which were already in full swing, and his realization that a conciliatory line might play into the hands of his rivals. As noted above, both he and his followers were defeated and, to quote the Director of Public Security, the 'notoriously unstable Azhari' was elected once again to become President of the Graduates' Congress, backed by a

[208] Newbold to all Governors and Heads of Departments, 2 May 1942, FO 371/31587.

[209] 'Note on further association of Sudanese with local and central government in the Sudan' by D.N. Newbold; see also Huddleston to Lampson, 12 May 1942, FO 371/31587.

[210] 'Memorandum on Sudanese nationalism and the Graduates' Congress', enclosure 4 in Lampson to Eden, 22 May 1942 (secret), FO 371/31587.

[211] Sadiq, *Istiqlal*, 42–3.

[212] Newbold to Ibrahim Ahmed, 17 July 1942; Ibrahim Ahmed to Newbold, 23 July 1942; Newbold to Ibrahim Ahmed, 19 Sept. 1942, FO 371/31587; see also Henderson, *Modern Sudan*, 548–50.

committee of sixty, which, with few exceptions, consisted of his supporters, who were a 'very poor lot'.[213] The unrealistic hopes that Newbold had when he encouraged the intelligentsia to become active and play a non-political role in Sudanese society through cultural, educational and social activities had been finally dashed by the involvement of the two Sayyids which turned Congress into yet another sectarian political arena.

The emergence of al-Ashiqa' and al-Umma

By the end of 1942, the government entertained no further hopes from Congress. Plans for establishing Advisory Councils both in the provinces and in Khartoum were well under way. They were intended not only as a first step toward self-government, but also as a framework in which the 'more responsible' graduates, alongside tribal and religious leaders, could be associated with their own government. However, the authorities realized that it would take a year or two before an effective central Advisory Council could be established. If Congress should attempt during that period to step into the vacuum, the government decided to act firmly on the principle that 'trespassers will be prosecuted'.[214] Under al-Azhari's leadership, Congress tried in the meantime to assert itself as an independent political force. In July 1943, al-Azhari visited Egypt with two leading members of Congress. In a series of interviews with leading Egyptians, including Prime Minister Mustafa Nahhas, he tried to convey the impression that they were the legitimate spokesmen of Sudanese nationalism.[215] In November 1943, following long deliberations with the defeated group of graduates under Ibrahim Ahmad and Ahmad Yusuf Hashim, Sayyid 'Abd al-Rahman finally decided to sever his connections with the Azhari–Fadli group. He had been reluctant to withdraw his support earlier because of al-Azhari's success. But now the combination of several factors made an immediate decision imperative. First, the resignation of Ibrahim Ahmad and his supporters from the committee of fifteen made the feud between the two camps so intense that it became impossible to support both. Secondly, the government's plan for an Advisory Council, which had the Sayyid's full support, was boycotted by the al-Azhari-dominated Congress. Thirdly, the Sayyid disapproved of al-Azhari's flirtations with the Egyptian leadership. Finally, it became apparent to Sayyid 'Abd al-Rahman by the end of 1943 that 'Abdallah al-Fadil, his *khalifa* in Omdurman, was exploiting his connections

---

[213] *SPIS*, no. 22, Dec. 1942, FO 371/35580.

[214] Huddleston to Lampson, 18 Nov. 1942, FO 371/31587; see also 'Note on further association of Sudanese with local and central government in the Sudan', signed D.N. Newbold, 10 Sept. 1942, *ibid*. For details on the Advisory Council see Muddathir, *Imperialism*, 135–58.

[215] *SPIS*, no. 28, July 1943, FO 371/35580. Ansar tried during that period to discredit the Congress in Egypt and claimed that it did not represent even the educated class: *ibid*.

in Congress in order to secure his position as the Sayyid's successor within the Ansar. Sayyid 'Abd al-Rahman was therefore compelled to overcome his previous reluctance to intervene and severed his relations with the Azhari–Fadil faction, so as to secure the position of *khalifa* for his son, al-Siddiq. At first he ordered al-Fadil to resign from both committees of Congress and to devote himself fully to his duties within the Ansar. This in turn prompted Sayyid 'Ali al-Mirghani to promise his full support to Isma'il al-Azhari and the latter immediately deserted Sayyid 'Abd al-Rahman and changed sides.[216]

The story of Congress during the following two years is one of continuous internal strife, directed and manipulated by the two sectarian leaders. Al-Azhari's 1943 election victory was turned into defeat when Muhammad Khalifa Sharif, Sayyid 'Abd al-Rahman's nephew, stepped in and persuaded several of al-Azhari's supporters to desert him, thus securing the re-election to the presidency of Ibrahim Ahmad. But Ahmad's position was extremely shaky and his policy was largely dictated by al-Azhari and his supporters who continued to hold the majority in the committee of sixty.[217] Moreover, Ibrahim Ahmad himself was critical of Sayyid 'Abd al-Rahman's political line, as well as of his open intervention in Congress. He realized that the Sayyid's 'separatist attitude towards Egypt gave the impression that he hoped to become King of an independent Sudan'. This in turn played into the hands of al-Azhari and his Khatmiyya supporters and inadvertently helped them to found their own political party, al-Ashiqqa'.[218] Anglo-Egyptian rivalry over Sudan's future therefore helped to further the sectarian feud within Congress:

> The neo-Mahdists and the Khatmiyya were rivals for the ear of the government and, increasingly, for the growing number of Western-educated Sudanese. The British attempt to balance neo-Mahdism with the Khatmiyya further helped encourage the rivalry.[219]

In the 1944 Congress elections the newly-formed al-Ashiqqa' party, led by al-Azhari and supported both morally and financially by Sayyid 'Ali al-Mirghani won an overwhelming victory.[220] For Isma'il al-Azhari it was a

[216] *SPIS*, no. 32, Nov. 1943, FO 371/41348. In a way this conflict was the forerunner of the disagreement regarding the Advisory Council, details below.

[217] *SPIS*, no. 33, Dec. 1943, FO 371/41348. According to the report, out of 966 graduates who participated in the elections, only 200–300 were 'intelligentsia', while 'the rest were from the artisan and suk class': *SPIS*, no. 37, Apr. 1944, *ibid.*

[218] 'Extracts from a conversation between Ibrahim Eff. Ahmed, President of Graduates' Congress, and Mr E.S. Atiyah, Public Relations Officer', 7 Jan. 1944, FO 371/41363. Edward Atiyah was a Lebanese, educated in Cairo and Oxford, who had served in Sudan since the early 1920s, first as a master at Gordon College and later in the intelligence department and the civil secretary's office; see his account in Atiyah, *An Arab*.

[219] Woodward, *Islam in Sudan*, 97.

[220] The choice of the name *al-ashiqqa'* – brothers on both the paternal and the maternal sides – was politically significant. It described the relationship between Sudan and Egypt as propagated by the party's founders.

personal triumph since he beat Ibrahim Ahmad, his rival for the presidency, by nearly 1,500 votes. What were the reasons for the overwhelming Khatmiyya-Ashiqqa' victory? The British Director of Public Security mentioned the following reasons: the Mirghanists constitute a majority in the Three Towns; the Ansar had not entered the field in earnest until a short time before the elections, whereas the Khatmiyya had solidly supported the Ashiqqa' throughout the year; and, quite apart from sectarian support, the Ashiqqa' were a better-organised and more united party and had behind them the bulk of the younger graduates.[221] However, this was not an entirely satisfactory explanation, since it tended to ignore Sayyid 'Abd al-Rahman's predominance within the intelligentsia in the preceding years.

The following reasons for the decline in the Ansar's popularity among the graduates should also be considered. First, many of the intelligentsia feared and opposed the renewed emphasis on tribal leaders, which they felt was implied by the creation of the central Advisory Council in May 1944. While the council enjoyed the full backing of Sayyid 'Abd al-Rahman, Sayyid 'Ali viewed it with a suspicion similar to that of the bulk of the Graduates, because the Ansar and the tribal leaders enjoyed a majority among its members.[222] Hence, many graduates who were not necessarily Khatmiyya followers found themselves on the latter's side in the 1944 elections. In doing so they expressed their disapproval of the government and their anti-Ansar feelings. Secondly, the intelligentsia had by and large, favoured some connection with Egypt, primarily as an ally against prolonged British domination. In many cases, fear of an Ansar-dominated monarchy under Sayyid 'Abd al-Rahman gave an added impetus to some form of alli-ance with Egypt and hence to the support of al-Ashiqqa'.[223] Finally, the death of Sayyid 'Abd al-Rahman's brother, whose funeral coincided with the Congress elections, kept many of the leading Ansar fully occupied, thus indirectly helping the Ashiqqa'-Khatmiyya coalition.[224] The collaboration between an important section of the intelligentsia and Sayyid 'Ali al-Mirghani can therefore be described as a marriage of convenience, from which both partners benefited. Sayyid 'Ali stated quite openly, in a private conversation with the Commissioner of Police, that he had no

[221] *SPIS*, no. 44, Nov. 1944, FO 371/45972. The number of registered Congress members had risen from 1,300 in 1943 to 9,400, out of whom 4,667 attended the annual meeting. Most of them were defined in the report as: 'ignorant Tariqa members'.

[222] *SPIS*, no. 36, Mar. 1944, FO 371/41348. In Oct. 1943, al-Azhari demanded in the committee of sixty that any member of Congress who accepted nomination to the advisory council be expelled from Congress. He referred specifically to Ibrahim Ahmad and Ahmad Yusuf Hashim, whom he called 'kalb al-hukuma' (government dog); *SPIS*, no. 31, Oct. 1943, FO 371/35580.

[223] During the Ansar annual 'Marriage Festival' in July 1944 a poem was recited extolling Sayyid 'Abd al-Rahman's services to Sudan and declaring British intention to reward him with its crown. *SPIS*, no. 40, July 1944, FO 371/41348; Killearn to Huddleston, 5 June 1944, FO 371/41363; Sadiq, *Istiqlal*, 43–4.

[224] Bedri, *Hayati*, III, 66; see also *SPIS*, no. 44, Nov. 1944, FO 371/45972.

interest in or political affinity with al-Ashiqqa' and that his sole motive was 'to prevent Sayed Sir 'Abdel Rahman from capturing the Congress as he had already captured the Advisory Council'.[225]

To the internal strife that had already torn Congress apart two elements were now added: pressure from the British authorities to confine Congress membership to the educated classes only; and a demand by Egyptian politicians that Congress declare itself openly in favour of union with Egypt. Early in 1945, the British Governor of Khartoum alerted al-Azhari to the fact that the Congress elections of November 1944 had been unconstitutional, since many of the new members 'did not possess the prescribed or any educational qualifications'.[226] This was followed by an even more explicit statement to the effect that the government had decided to withdraw its recognition of Congress as it was no longer a true representative of the educated classes.[227] Although an attempt was made by al-Azhari to renew the government's confidence, the latter tended to ignore Congress and apart from occasional rebukes, it paid little attention to the Congress's political ventures.[228]

The problem of Sudan's sovereignty and its relations with Egypt assumed increasing importance as the Allies' victory in the war became apparent. The Sudanese assumed that, as soon as the war was over, a new Anglo-Egyptian treaty was likely to be negotiated. They wanted to assure their own participation in any forthcoming negotiations and if possible present both Egypt and Britain with a united Sudanese front. To achieve this al-Azhari had to compromise, since neither of the Sayyids was likely to support his previously propagated policy of complete unity with Egypt. In December 1944, despite mounting pressure from Egypt, al-Azhari made a public statement to the effect 'that the aim of the Ashigga [sic] is not fusion with Egypt but Dominion status under the Egyptian Crown and flag'. He put forward two arguments in support of this aim: '(a) that alignment with Egypt is a necessary safeguard against incorporation in an African system; (b) that Egypt is the Sudan's only link with the Arab world'.[229] Early in April 1945 a resolution was passed by the Congress committee of sixty stating that 'Sudan shall be ruled by a Sudanese democratic government within a union with Egypt under the Egyptian Crown.' While most of the Egyptian press

[225] *SPIS*, no. 45, Dec. 1944, FO 371/45972. In Apr. 1945, Sayyid 'Ali was already regretting the close link with al-Ashiqqa' and was 'contemplating a withdrawal into the obscurity of his favourite religious background, where he could merely let things slide, leaving himself free to deny complicity or even knowledge if they slid too fast'; *SPIS*, no. 48, Mar.–Apr. 1945, *ibid.*

[226] Mackintosh to Azhari, 7 Feb. 1945, FO 371/45984.

[227] *SPIS*, no. 48, Mar.–Apr. 1945, FO 371/45972.

[228] *SPIS*, no. 52, July, FO 371/45972. Al-Azhari in effect admitted the government's accusations when he promised that Congress would attempt 'to enforce the educational qualifications at the next elections': *ibid.*

[229] *SPIS*, no. 45, Dec. 1944, FO 371/45972.

greeted this resolution favourably, reactions in Sudan varied between indignation and a certain amount of ridicule.[230] The indignation within certain sections of the graduates, especially those aligned with the Ansar, was so great that al-Azhari feared that both he and al-Ashiqqa', who in fact had formulated the pro-Egyptian resolution, would be defeated in the forthcoming elections if he did not compromise.[231] He therefore decided to establish a 'United Parties Committee', composed of three representatives from each of the six factions represented in Congress, to try to work out a formula that would be acceptable to all concerned. On 25 August a compromise was reached, calling for 'the establishment of a free, democratic Sudanese Government in union with Egypt and in alliance with Britain'.[232] Although the British authorities viewed the resolution as ambiguous and vague, they regarded it as moderate enough to be accepted by the Sudan government. However, they expressed doubts on Egyptian reactions to the words 'a free democratic Sudan', which in fact denoted independence and ignored the Egyptian Crown.[233] Yet, on the very same day that the 'United Parties' Agreement' was adopted by Congress, a secret session of the committee of fifteen passed a resolution calling for 'the formation of a democratic Sudanese Government in a union with Egypt, under the Egyptian Crown'. Al-Azhari communicated this resolution to the Prime Ministers of both Britain and Egypt, ignoring the compromise reached by the United Parties Committee.[234] This gave the authorities the opportunity to discredit Congress completely. First, by leaking al-Azhari's letter to the opposition within Congress, they helped to create an uproar against al-Ashiqqa' in the Ansar-dominated press. Secondly, in its response to al-Azhari, the government was able to ignore the resolution and to state quite bluntly that it was unconstitutional and did 'not appear to enjoy the confidence of more than a section of the Graduates' Congress itself'.[235] Al-Azhari's apologetic and belated response was unconvincing, since he claimed that 'union with

[230] *SPIS*, no. 48, Mar.–Apr. 1944, FO 371/45972; see also Killearn to F.O. 16 Apr. 1945, FO 371/45984. Apparently al-Azhari had advocated a more moderate resolution by inserting the word 'independent', but was overruled by his more extremist colleagues.

[231] Report of Cairo Police on interview with Azhari, enclosed in Killearn to Eden, 11 July 1945, FO 371/45984.

[232] The parties represented on the Committee were: al-Ashiqqa', al-Umma, Ittihadiyyin, Ittihadiyyin Ahrar, Ahrar and Qawmiyyun. Apart from al-Ashiqqa' and al-Umma, these were in effect factions that had broken away from the two main parties mainly because of the latter's subservience to the two Sayyids. 'The Agreement (Covenant) of the United Parties' (n.d. [25 Aug. 1945?]), FO 371/45986: for details on these parties see below.

[233] Robertson to Haseldene, 28 Aug. 1945, FO 371/45986. The word *hurr*, which was used in the original resolution and translated by the authorities as free, might just as well have been employed to denote independence.

[234] Farquhar (acting British Ambassador in Cairo), to Bevin, 17 Sep. 1945, FO 371/45986; see also *SPIS*, no. 52, Aug. 1945, FO 371/45972.

[235] Robertson to Azhari, 1 Sept. 1945, FO 371/45972.

Egypt under the Egyptian Crown' was just a 'more accurate definition of the word union' used by the 'United Parties Committee' in its resolution.[236] However, the government was in no mood to pursue the argument. Congress elections were due in November and, with strife within Congress at its peak, it was quite uncertain whether the organization would survive until the end of 1945. The pro-Ansar elements within Congress realized that they would be defeated in the elections and therefore tried to cancel them and come to an agreement with al-Ashiqqa' regarding the allocation of seats on Congress committees. Failing to achieve this, they decided to boycott the elections in order 'to make it clear to the world that the Congress of 1946 . . . was a single party organisation and that it could no longer rightfully call itself the Graduates' Congress'.[237] In fact Congress, though formally still in existence, ceased to play any role in Sudanese society or politics from 1946 onward. Al-Umma and al-Ashiqqa' became the dominant organizations in the political arena, with the two Sayyids continuing to pull the strings.

The founding of the Advisory Council and the decline in the stature of the Congress intensified the political activity of the two Sayyids. While the intelligentsia continued to dominate the political press, the religious–political centre tended to shift to the rural region. This came about partly as a result of the founding of the Advisory Council, in which tribal and other rural leaders were predominant. In addition, the two Sayyids considered the intelligentsia both unreliable and inconsistent, a fact that also contributed to the rapid decline of the Graduates' Congress. Both Sayyids thus congratulated the Sudan government on its decision to set up an Advisory Council. But whereas Sayyid 'Abd al-Rahman did so wholeheartedly Sayyid 'Ali expressed certain reservations. He was aware of the Ansar's strength in the countryside and therefore emphasized that the council's success would depend 'on the quality of those chosen to be members'.[238] Moreover, having initially agreed to accept the government's invitation to become an honorary member of the Advisory Council alongside Sayyid 'Abd al-Rahman, Sayyid 'Ali later withdrew, due to the preponderance of Ansar on the council. It was only after much prompting that he finally attended the opening session of the Advisory Council, 'though it was evident that he viewed the whole affair with extreme distaste.'[239]

The weakness of the Khatmiyya in the countryside, and hence on the Advisory Council, where tribal leaders predominated, persuaded Sayyid 'Ali to try to strengthen his standing in rural Sudan. An uprising on Tuti Island in April 1944 was exploited by Sayyid 'Ali for Khatmiyya propaganda. He tried to give this local incident 'a national colour and lift it from

[236] Azhari to Governor-General, 15 Oct. 1945, enclosed in Robertson to Mayall, 29 Oct. 1945, FO 371/45986.
[237] Penney to Haseldene, 26 Nov. 1945, FO 371/45986. Out of 10,000 Congress members, only 5,470 paid their dues for 1945 and only 3,512 actually took part in the elections.
[238] *SPIS*, no. 30, Sept. 1943, FO 371/35580.
[239] *SPIS*, no. 38, May 1944, FO 371/41348; *SPIS*, no. 36, Mar. 1944, *ibid*.

the administrative to the political plane'.[240] In June Sayyid 'Ali undertook a propaganda campaign in the Northern province to prove his political supremacy among the members of the Idrisiyya *sufi* order. The campaign was intended to counter a visit by Sayyid 'Abd al-Rahman to 'Atbara, al-Damir and Berber, all of which were regarded by Sayyid 'Ali as his own 'special reserve'.[241] By August Sayyid 'Ali was considering the severance of his connections with al-Ashiqqa', and plans for a new Khatmiyya party, called *al-Sha'ab*, were well under way. His aim, according to government sources, was to rid himself of the 'unreliable Azhari clique' and of its pro-Egyptian programme. At the same time he hoped to formulate a policy that would enable him to win over certain sections of the rural population and to mend his fences with the government.[242]

Sayyid 'Abd al-Rahman, though disappointed with his political setback in the Graduates' Congress, had regarded the political scene since 1944 with growing optimism: first, because the Advisory Council was dominated by Ansar supporters; and, secondly, because the opening statement of the Governor-General in the first session of the council coincided with his own views. Huddleston emphasized in his speech 'that the aim of the Government is to create a self-governing Sudanese nation', thereby implying clear support for Sudanese independence.[243] However, the split within the Ansar supporters in Congress made it clear to the Sayyid that an organizational reform of the 'Sudan for the Sudanese' camp was urgently required. The close link between the Ansar apparatus and leading members of Congress had been resented even by staunch supporters of Sayyid 'Abd al-Rahman such as Ibrahim Ahmad. This link had been partly responsible for the emergence of al-Qawmiyyun and al-Ahrar, two small parties that appeared on the political scene in 1944. Both supported Sudanese independence but resented the close connection between their political camp and the Ansar.[244] The solution seemed to be the founding of a political party that would unite pro-independence groups without being identified with Sayyid 'Abd al-Rahman's religious mission. In August 1944 the Sayyid therefore invited a number of senior Congress members and tribal leaders to discuss this proposal. The gathering came to the conclusion that the first step should

[240] *SPIS*, no. 37, Apr. 1944, FO 371/41348. The riots in Tuti, according to the government, resulted from a misunderstanding of a government development plan. In the clash with the police one of the inhabitants was killed and several were wounded. As most of the island's population were Khatmiyya supporters, Sayyid 'Ali assumed his favourite role of intermediary with the government.

[241] *SPIS*, no. 39, June 1944, FO 371/41348.

[242] *SPIS*, no. 52, Aug. 1945, FO 371/45972; *SPIS*, no. 53, Sept. 1945, *ibid*.

[243] *SPIS*, no. 38, May 1944, FO 371/41348.

[244] Al-Qawmiyyun's importance lay in their leader, Ahmad Yusuf Hashim, who as editor and owner of *al-Sudan al-Jadid* was in a position to publicize his party's line; al-Ahrar were a small group, composed mainly of teachers; see 'The Programmes and personalities of the Congress group contesting this year's elections', Appendix in *SPIS*, no. 43, Oct. 1944, FO 371/41348.

be the publication of a new independent daily newspaper, quite separate from Sayyid 'Abd al-Rahman and the Ansar's daily *al-Nil*. This daily newspaper would express the views of 'responsible graduates' and tribal leaders who supported an independent Sudan but did not necessarily belong to the Ansar. By December most of the provincial members of the Advisory Council had agreed to join the new venture. They declared their willingness to contribute the necessary funds for the publication of *al-Umma*, a daily propagating the 'Sudan for the Sudanese' ideology, which thereafter became known as the Umma party.[245] The choice of the name al-Umma is significant as it implied a link with the nineteenth-century Mahdist state and its belief in the establishment of an Islamic community (*umma*) both in Sudan and in other Muslim countries. It was also significant in the political sense, as it implied adherence to the concept of Islamic unity and to anti-sectarianism, while advocating a separate Sudanese national entity.[246] By February 1945 preparations for the foundation of al-Umma were completed and 'Abdallah Khalil, the party's First Secretary, applied in writing for the required government licence for its establishment. Al-Umma's constitution, which was also submitted to the government, defined the party's aims as follows:

The principle of the Party: The Sudan for the Sudanese. *Object of the Party*: To work for the independence of the Sudan within it's recognized geographical frontiers, while preserving friendly relations with Britain and Egypt.[247]

Membership of al-Umma was open to 'all adult Sudanese who believe in the principle and object of the party'. The party's control and management were to be vested in a central committee. There was no mention of Sayyid 'Abd al-Rahman, the Ansar or sectarian divisions in Sudan in the party's constitution. The party's founders, probably intending to emphasize its non-sectarian composition, even asked Sayyid 'Ali al-Mirghani to join its ranks. 'The Sayed received them well, expressed, in his usual platitudes, his sympathy with the project and concluded by saying that he would reserve his judgement until their words and intentions had been translated into actions.'[248] The only indication of the Umma's apparent dependence

---

[245] *SPIS*, no. 41, Aug. 1944, FO 371/41348; *SPIS*, no. 45, Dec. 1944, FO 371/45972; *SPIS*, no. 46, Jan. 1945, *ibid*.

[246] Sadiq, *Istiqlal*, 46-50. Muhammad Sulayman claimed that the Umma took its name and its ideology from the Egyptian Umma party which was founded by Ahmad Lutfi al-Sayyid in 1907. Both were supported by the British rulers and advocated cooperation with them. Both were led by members of the local aristocracy and the big landowners but enjoyed the support of certain sections of the intelligentsia too, see Sulayman, *Al-Yasar*, XIX–XX; four of the founders of the Umma party were among those requesting a full discussion on Sudanese nationality in the Advisory Council: see *SPIS*, no. 43, Oct. 1944, FO 371/41348.

[247] 'Constitution of the Nation [Umma] Party', submitted by Abdallah Khalil for approval, 20 Feb. 1945, FO 371/45984; also *SPIS*, no. 47, Feb. 1945, FO 371/45972.

[248] *SPIS*, no. 47, Feb. 1945, FO 371/45972.

on Sayyid 'Abd al-Rahman was, significantly, in the financial sphere. The party's funds, as stated in its constitution, were to be derived from: '(a) Membership fees amounting to 5 P.T. (piastres) to be paid once in life; (b) Subscriptions; (c) Donations.'[249] A political party run by an independent apparatus throughout Sudan and possessing a daily newspaper could hardly hope to be financially independent if it relied only on membership fees and on anonymous donations. Al-Umma must have been assured by Sayyid 'Abd al-Rahman of massive and continuous financial support, even though it claimed to depend neither on the Ansar nor on *dai'rat al-mahdi*. Already in April 1945 the Sayyid realized that 'the Umma Party is seriously embarrassed by its close connection with the Mahdist Daira'. He therefore stated that he would support any other movement working for the well-being of Sudan and instructed leading Ansar not to become openly involved in al-Umma's politics.[250] However, the Ansar–Umma connection could not be hidden. Moreover, many regarded the Umma party as a government creation aiming at the establishment of a Sudanese monarchy under Sayyid 'Abd al-Rahman. Rumours to that effect circulated freely without being denied either by al-Umma or by the Sayyid himself. Consequently, many moderate supporters of an independent Sudan were driven into al-Ashiqqa' out of fear of a Mahdist revival. By June 1945, the government decided to intervene and to deny publicly its intentions to support a Mahdist monarchy.[251] At the same time the authorities warned both Sayyids to cease their involvement in party politics in order to avoid an upheaval inspired by religion. On 30 June 1947 Sayyid 'Abd al-Rahman called a meeting in his house – to which he invited Shaykh Babikr Bedri – in which the advantages of the al-Ashiqqa' in any forthcoming elections, were discussed. This forecast was based on two reasons: first, the election law limited the right to vote to 'men of means', which excluded most of the poor Umma supporters; and, secondly, since Egypt financed al-Ashiqqa' in a big way, only British financial support could save al-Umma.[252] However, the government feared that

. . . the adherence to two rival political parties of thousands of illiterate and semi-illiterate tribesmen and provincials, to whom politics are meaningless, and by whom the jargon of the party canvasser can only be interpreted as a 'call' to support their own particular Holy Man, must lead eventually to a wavering in the state of public security.[253]

[249] *SPIS*, no. 47, Feb. 1945, FO 371/45972.

[250] *SPIS*, no. 48, Mar.–Apr. 1945, FO 371/45972. The financial connection between *da'irat al-mahdi* and the Umma was later openly admitted by Sayyid 'Abd al-Rahman; see Sadiq, *Istiqlal*, 49-50.

[251] *SPIS*, no. 50, June 1945, FO 371/45972; see also *GGR*, 1945 (Sudan no. 1, 1948, CMD 7316).

[252] Bedri, *Hayati*, III, 71–2.

[253] *SPIS*, no. 49, May 1945, FO 371/45972.

The ambivalent attitude of the authorities towards the Umma was reminiscent of their attitude towards Sudanese nationalism in the 1920s. The government viewed the emergence of a political party propagating independence favourably and even regarded the attempt to unite tribal leaders and graduates in one party as an encouraging development. However, they feared and disliked the Mahdist link, which, as they should have known, was the only one that could hold the party together. In a lengthy letter tracing the history of Sudanese politics to the 1924 mutiny, Sir James Robertson, Sudan's Civil Secretary, described the Ansar–Umma connection as a natural reaction to the Khatmiyya's support for al-Ashiqqa'. But he complained that the main political issue, namely, 'separatism' versus some form of union with Egypt, is 'hopelessly obscured by the old Mahdist/Mirghanist rivalry'. Furthermore Robertson admitted that the government's support for the Graduates' Congress and the Advisory Council was meant to 'damp down the Sayeds' rivalries and to form some sort of a united front which would devote its immediate energies to the practical realisation of our internal self-government programme . . . These hopes were defeated by the intransigence of the Sayeds.'[254]

At the end of the Second World War the Sudan government therefore faced a grave dilemma in its internal policies. Its attempt to form a non-sectarian political leadership had failed. Egypt was demanding a new treaty and was openly supporting al-Ashiqqa', and other pro-unity groups in Sudan. The Muslim Brothers were attempting to organize a Sudanese branch, of their movement, while labour unrest, especially among railway workers, seemed to signify Communist infiltration. The Umma party thus remained the only political force of any consequence that advocated policies similar to those of the government. Hence, despite their distrust of Sayyid 'Abd al-Rahman and his personal ambitions, the authorities regarded their support of al-Umma as inevitable, since it was their main ally against the 'Egyptian invasion'.[255]

The two Sayyids on the eve of independence

Sayyid 'Ali al-Mirghani's decision to renew his support for al-Ashiqqa' was made in January 1948 following the first appearance of the so-called 'Mahdist Tents' during the *mawlid* festivities, aimed at luring the smaller *sufi* orders to the Mahdist camp. Fearing a Mahdist majority, Sayyid 'Ali attempted to counter this move by uniting pro-independence *sufi* orders against the Ansar–Umma block. This move brought about internal splits within certain *sufi* orders, such as the Isma'iliyya, the majority of whose

[254] Robertson to Fouracres, 8 Apr. 1945, FO 371/45984.

[255] Sudan Agent (Cairo) to Civil Secretary (Khartoum), 13 June 1945 and 9 July 1945, FO 371/45984; Robertson to Mayall, 25 Oct. 1945, FO 371/45986.

adherents under Mirghani al-Makki joined the Ansar, while his rival, al-Bashir, succeeded in persuading a minority to side with the Khatmiyya.[256]

On 19 July 1949 the Government promulgated an ordinance that paved the way for the founding of Sudan's Legislative Assembly. Since Egypt failed to respond, the ordinance was passed without opposition, but it was boycotted by al-Ashiqqa' and other pro-unionist parties, who viewed it as British inspired and anti-Egyptian. The Khatmiyya was split between those who favoured participation in the forthcoming elections to the Legislative Assembly and those who sided with the unionists. Sayyid 'Ali al-Mirghani refused to state his views openly, but, judging by the results of the elections to the assembly, in which only 18 per cent of those eligible to vote took part, it is clear that the majority boycotted the elections and thus paved the way for an Umma-dominated Legislative Assembly.[257] However, al-Umma and the Ansar were far from docile collaboration with the British administration, as later events proved. They demanded immediate self-government and even flirted with the newly elected Egyptian Wafd government in 1950, to prove that Britain was not their only potential ally. On 13 December 1950 the Umma faction passed a motion in the Legislative Assembly calling for self-government by the end of 1951. It was endorsed by a slim majority of 39 to 38 in the assembly. Although the Governor-General overruled the motion, it enabled the SPS to claim later that despite British pressures the assembly had voted in favour of independence. Leading members within the SPS hoped that this might persuade Sayyid 'Ali al-Mirghani and the Khatmiyya to enter the assembly, since they would realize that the government had opposed the Umma in earnest. Consequently, some historians claim that the Legislative Assembly and the executive council 'were less schools for parliamentary democracy than simply markers in sectarian competition'.[258] However, whatever the truth behind this allegation, the assembly was an important venture in Sudanese politics, since it was the only experience Sudanese politicians had in parliamentary procedures or in running government offices prior to the 1953 elections. This experience was therefore crucial for the relatively smooth operation of the first elected Sudanese Parliament in 1953. In addition, we know that sectarianism continued to dominate Sudanese politics throughout the second half of the twentieth century. Therefore, the quest for real 'parliamentary democracy', in the conditions prevailing in Sudan during the early 1950s, seemed rather unrealistic. Educated Sudanese, most of whom were themselves members of one of the two sects, were even less representative than the sects or the tribes whose leaders dominated both the Legislative Assembly and the political parties.

---

[256] Dhaher, *Al-Mirghani*, 308–10. As noted, the Isma'iliyya had been the first *sufi* order to support the Mahdi in 1881.
[257] Daly, *Imperial Sudan*, 267–9.
[258] *Ibid.*, 277–8.

Egypt's unilateral abrogation in October 1951 of the Anglo-Egyptian Treaty of 1936 and of the 1899 Condominium Agreement created a new situation. As the result, it could no longer participate even in the marginal role it had hitherto played in Sudan's administration, since such participation would imply Egyptian recognition of a regime that it had declared illegitimate. It thereby enabled Sudanese politicians of all political shades to act in near unison and demand Sudan's right of self-determination not later than December 1953. Al-Dardiri Muhammad 'Uthman, a leading Khatmiyya, politician, promised Sir James Robertson full Khatmiyya support against the Egyptian step which moved the two Sayyids towards agreement.[259] A draft resolution for the transition to self-government was passed by the Legislative Assembly in April 1952 and was sent to London and Cairo for ratification or amendments. This so-called 'Self Government Statute' was to be implemented as it stood, unless the Co-Domini submitted their counter-proposals within six months.

It was at this time that the SPS initiated the founding of the Socialist Republican Party (SRP) in a last and rather naïve attempt to overcome sectarianism. Though proof of SPS implication in its founding was not conclusive it was quite clear that this was the non-sectarian pro-independence party for which Robertson and his colleagues had prayed for so long.[260] It consisted of tribal leaders, whom the SPS viewed as the 'real Sudan', and was led by Ibrahim Bedri, son of Shaykh Babikr Bedri, the well-known educator. Robertson believed that the SRP would win over the pro-independence Khatmiyya as well as others who feared Mahdist domination, and he concluded: 'Egypt has lost the Sudan'. As we now know he was wrong on all counts. In Sudan the SRP was viewed by a vast majority as a British puppet and many of its would-be supporters shied away from collaborating with it. Sayyid 'Abd al-Rahman and the Umma party resented the SRP as an attempt to undermine their own constituency. Al-Umma's refusal to collaborate with the SRP in the 1953 elections is one of the reasons leading to the sweeping victory of the NUP–Khatmiyya bloc. It was in effect yet another SPS blunder that was brought about by the false British belief in the invincibility of tribal leaders and *nazirs*. 'Although by simple calculation the shaykhs could be said to "represent" a large majority of the Sudanese, they had no party apparatus and no real programme. Nor were they still the authoritative figures some believed.'[261] According to Henderson, who for many years served in Khartoum and thus knew Sayyid 'Abd al-Rahman well, the Sayyid's reaction towards the SRP was hostile:

---

[259] Dhaher, *Al-Mirghani*, 313–18, 331.

[260] According to Daly, *Imperial Sudan*, 287–8, 'evidence points to two officials, H.A. Nicholson and K.D.D. Henderson, as instigators'.

[261] Daly, *Imperial Sudan*, 288. Dr 'Ali Bedri, Ibrahim Bedris brother and an Umma party member, viewed the SRP as a 'set up under the influence of a few misguided British officials', *ibid.*

SAR was so furious over the Socialist Republican Party, which he thought had been invented by Desmond Hawkesworth. He simply would not listen to any reason on the subject. I remember going to see him on one of my rare visits to Khartoum, and SAR said: 'On this occasion the government really has let me down right, left and centre. You have deliberately concocted this party in order to cause me damage.' I said: 'We haven't concocted it; this is really the same lot of chaps who in 1944 wanted to found a newspaper in order to combat press propaganda on behalf of the landed gentry. You took them over then, although a lot of them were in fact Khatmiyya who drifted away and left you, didn't they?' and he said: 'Yes'. And I said: 'What do you want? An independent Sudan? You don't want to go under Egypt. Here is a party which is also in favour of an independent Sudan and which has got Sam's [Sayyid 'Ali al-Mirghani] backing. And in fact, you have got two parties on your side instead of one.' But he would not listen and I don't think he ever spoke to me again. He was very angry indeed. I don't think he trusted any of the British after that.[262]

In hindsight it seems rather strange that senior members of the SPS of such calibre, who knew the two Sayyids reasonably well and whose experience in Sudanese politics was considerable, failed to realize, even at such a late juncture, that sectarian politics were so deeply entrenched in Sudan that any attempt to separate politics from Khatmiyya and Ansar domination was futile.

Matters changed after the Free Officers' revolution in Egypt in July 1952. While the Free Officers were as committed to the unity of the Nile Valley as their predecessors in power, the dethronement of King Faruq removed an important obstacle, thereby making a compromise possible. Furthermore, General Muhammad Najib (Nagib), Egypt's new President, had been born in Sudan in 1901 and was of mixed Egyptian–Sudanese ancestry. He had been educated in Sudan, and many of its political and religious leaders had been his contemporaries. It was therefore no wonder that Sudanese leaders, many of whom knew him personally from his early years in Khartoum, flocked to Cairo in order to seek interviews with him and express their views regarding Sudan's future relations with Egypt.[263] It seemed that the stage was set for a rapid solution of this cumbersome problem that had bedevilled the triangular relations between Britain, Egypt and Sudan since the 1919 revolt. In Cairo, where the young and politically inexperienced Free Officers were deliberating the future of their country, the assumption that unity between Egypt and Sudan would soon be realized seemed a foregone conclusion. As we know, this did not happen since this

---

[262] Interview with Mr K.D.D. Henderson, CMG, Aug. 1972. Henderson had served in the Civil Secretary's office in Khartoum from 1938–44 and from 1946–9, hence his acquaintance with the two Sayyids. Desmond Hawkesworth had served as the Political Assistant Civil Secretary in 1949–52 and had been involved with the new SRP in this capacity. See also 'Record of meeting between Secretary of State and Mr R. Allen, with SAR, Sayyid Ali Taha and Siddik el-Mahdi', 11 Oct. 1952, FO 371/96910.

[263] 'Ali Taha, *Al-Haraka al-Siyasiyya*, 555–61.

assumption was based on an Egyptian misreading of Sudan's political aspirations. Egyptian politicians of all shades had wrongly assumed that the pro-unity forces in Sudan included both the Khatmiyya and the majority of the educated class and thus enjoyed massive popular support. However, they underestimated the role and the strength of the Ansar-dominated Umma party and misinterpreted Sayyid 'Ali al-Mirghani's political ambivalence as pro-Egyptian. In fact, the two Sayyids pulled the political strings of all parties and, when the moment of truth arrived, only a handful of pro-unity politicians continued to support Egypt. The British authorities in Sudan made the same mistake. The Governor-General, Sir Robert Howe, reported to London that he did not believe that he and his colleagues in the SPS were in a position to counter Egyptian influence in Sudan, which employed religion, language, race and bribes in order to seduce the Sudanese into some form of unity with Egypt. 'The issue will ultimately lie with the Sudanese political parties or possibly even with SAR and/or SAM, as one or both of these holy men may well hold the key.' Thus it was not surprising that when Selwyn Lloyd, then Minister of State for Foreign Affairs, visited Sudan in March 1953 he met the Sayyids and openly discussed with them the forthcoming general elections as well as the future of their country. Sir Winston Churchill, then Prime Minister, even promised Sayyid 'Abd al-Rahman the Crown of Sudan's monarchy, so that he – like his father the Mahdi – could help Britain keep the Egyptians out of Sudan. The irony of Churchill's suggestion was that it was made just after the Umma party had openly declared that Sayyid 'Abd al-Rahman had renounced his desire to become Sudan's ruler and had announced his full support for a democratic republic.[264]

One of the few members of the Free Officers who later claimed to have realized the truth was Husayn Dhu al-Faqar Sabri (Sabry), who had served in the Egyptian army stationed in Sudan since 1949 and was asked to represent the Free Officers in Khartoum. He had come to realize that the Egyptians had been deceived by Sudanese pro-unionist politicians and that future relations between Egypt and Sudan would have to be negotiated through a process of self-determination, which he knew would probably lead to an independent Sudan.[265] Since the RCC in Cairo was engaged in endless discussions on matters that it regarded as more urgent than Sudan, Sabry was granted a free hand and assured by his superiors that the RCC would support whatever conclusions he reached. His first move was to seek

[264] Howe to Eden, 18 Mar. 1953, FO 371/102752; 'Report on Min. of State's visit in the Sudan, Mar. 1953, FO 371/102754. Sir Winston Churchill's promise was made when he met Sayyid 'Abd al-Rahman in June 1953; report by Minister of State, 10 June 1953, FO 371/102773; also *al-Sudan al-Jadid*, 28 June 1953, in *ibid*. SAM and SAR were the abbreviations used by the British as nicknames for the two Sayyids.

[265] For details see Sabry, *Sovereignty*. The author was 'Ali Sabri's half brother and later served as a senior Egyptian diplomat in several countries.

interviews with the two Sayyids, who, as was well known to him, though not to the RCC, with the exception of President Nagib, held the keys to Sudan's political future. Sayyid 'Ali al-Mirghani had always resented Egyptian unilateral assertions regarding the indisputable unity of the Nile Valley and it was therefore hardly surprising that he refused to be interviewed by such a relatively junior officer as Sabry. Sayyid 'Abd al-Rahman al-Mahdi, on the other hand, was as keen as always to assert his political supremacy and to express the views of the 'Sudan for the Sudanese' camp. His position was quite simple: if the new Egyptian regime would give its full and unreserved support to an independent Sudan, the two countries could establish a close and cordial relationship. If, however, Egypt were to seek formal unity, even now that the Egyptian Crown had been removed, nothing would be achieved.[266] Consequently, most of Sabry's contacts in the period leading to the agreement signed between Egypt and Sudan's political parties, on 10 January 1953, were with pro-independence Sudanese rather than with the so-called unionists who had hitherto dominated Sudanese–Egyptian relations. The latter included leaders of the Khatmiyya, who, while in favour of some link with Egypt, advocated full autonomy for Sudan as the first essential step. Among those who spoke frequently with Sabry were al-Dardiri Muhammad 'Uthman, Mirghani Hamza and Khalafallah Khalid, the so-called 'triumvirate' of the National Front. As for the Ansar–Umma contingent, most of Sabry's negotiations were held with al-Siddiq al-Mahdi, Sayyid 'Abd al-Rahman's son, and with 'Abdallah Khalil and Ibrahim Ahmad, two of the Umma's most respected leaders. The neglected unionists, including Isma'il al-Azhari, travelled to Cairo to seek appointments with President Nagib. Sabry dismissed them as ineffective and viewed al-Azhari's deputy, Muhammad Nur al-Din, as 'a cunning, though bungling schemer'.[267]

What Sabry proposed, in the name of the RCC, was immediate self-determination for Sudan, provided that the elections to its Constituent Assembly could be held in a 'free and neutral atmosphere' conducive to self-determination. He did so with the full knowledge that this was the desire of the two Sayyids as well as the vast majority of Sudanese, that it would lead to an independent Sudan and that it was the only way in which cordial relations could later be established between Egypt and Sudan. He stuck to this view even after the NUP under al-Azhari's leadership gained the majority in the 1953 elections, stating that the NUP never really backed full unity with Egypt and would ultimately support an independent Sudan. However,

---

[266] Sabry, *Sovereignty*, 28–33.

[267] *Ibid.*, 38–42; see also Muhammad Anis, 'al-'alaqat al-Misriyya al-Sudaniyya, al-madi wa'l-mustaqbal', *al-Musawwar*, 1 and 8 Aug., 12 Sept. 1986. Muhammad Anis, a respected Egyptian historian, who had previously been a staunch supporter of unity, seemed to have changed his mind following the publication of Sabry's book in Arabic. Muhammad Anis died before the final instalment of this article was published.

Sabry realized that his position was rather weak since it lacked credibility. As he himself admitted, 'any man in his senses could have only considered my proposals to be wishful thinking . . . My propositions were so extravagant that they could not be made to fit into traditional Egyptian policy.' In fact, most of the decision-makers in Nasser's Egypt were brought up in the firm belief that once Britain evacuated the Nile Valley, Egyptian–Sudanese unity would be the natural outcome.[268] As it transpired, Sabry was far better informed than his superiors in Cairo were. Moreover, the removal of President Nagib and the manipulations of Colonel Salah Salim, who was acting for the RCC in Sudan and was thus Sabry's superior, convinced practically all Sudanese politicians that their future lay in an independent Sudan and not in unity. In July 1953 *al-Nil* reported that Nagib had expressed his support for an independent Sudan. At the same time Sayyid 'Ali asked for a meeting with the Governor-General's Constitutional Adviser, Sir William Luce, in which he stated that he and all his followers would openly declare their support for an independent Sudanese republic provided Sayyid 'Abd al-Rahman would do likewise, namely give up his monarchical ambitions. The desired announcement was made by Sayyid 'Abd al-Rahman during the *'id al-fitr* celebrations, on 21 August 1953, when he openly denied the rumours about his monarchical ambitions and declared his unwavering support for a democratic republic. In fact, a few weeks earlier, the Umma party, represented by al-Siddiq al-Mahdi, had reached an agreement with British government representatives on the promotion of Sudanese independence. The terms of this agreement were as follows. First, if Egypt broke its undertakings to the Umma, the latter would launch and sustain a vigorous campaign against Egyptian influence in the Sudan. Second, the Umma would conduct the strongest possible pro-independence campaign against Egypt and the NUP. Third, the Umma would try to reach an understanding with the Socialist Republicans so that the NUP would not benefit from the conflict. And finally, if the majority of Southern parliamentarians asked for continued British administration in the South after independence, the Umma will support them. The agreement was initialled by the President of the Umma, Sayyid al-Siddiq al-Mahdi and by senior members of the SPS. It seemed rather ironic that the SPS, which had always opposed sectarianism, was now seeking sectarian Mahdist support against the common Egyptian enemy just as it did during the First World War.[269]

The victory of the NUP in the 1953 general elections was largely the result of Sayyid 'Ali's decision to activate the Khatmiyya leadership in the

[268] Sabry, *Sovereignty*, 50–3; for details see Warburg, *Sudan's Path*, 309–24. The NUP was founded by al-Ashiqqa', with Khatmiyya support, so as to form a united anti-Umma party.

[269] 'Conditions for cooperation between HMG and the Umma party . . . to promote the cause of Sudanese independence', n.d., minutes dated 31 July 1953, FO 371/102758; Luce to Boothby, 24 Oct. 1953, FO 371/102713.

election campaign in order to gain control of the NUP from within. Thus even the first Sudanese elections were run on a sectarian basis with the intelligentsia led by al-Azhari being manipulated by the Khatmiyya leadership. Consequently the Khatmiyya contingent within the government made it clear to Prime Minister al-Azhari that since he owed his electoral victory to them, they expected him to follow their advice.[270] It is incomprehensible that even at this stage senior members of the SPS failed to comprehend the overwhelming power of sectarianism. This is demonstrated in the following conversation held by Mr Kenrick, a senior British official, with Sayyid 'Abd al-Rahman and his son Siddiq al-Mahdi, after the 1953 elections:

I thought it best to be brutal . . . and said that in my opinion their defeat was primarily due to the fact that against all our advice they had insisted on fighting the elections on sectarian lines. Instead of pressing the contrast between Sudanese independence and Egyptian control . . . they had chosen to presume that the idea of independence was the monopoly of the Ansar.[271]

Furthermore, in order to prove their point regarding the evils of sectarianism SPS members quoted Muhammad Ahmad Mahgoub, Mirghani Hamza and other respected members of the intelligentsia. They all seemed to agree that sectarian politics were deplorable and believed that they would vanish as soon as the 'two old Sayyids died'. Based on this ill-founded assumption, senior members of the SPS concluded that the vast majority of those who voted for the NUP did so only out of their fear of a new Mahdist state.[272]

The event that had a lasting effect on Sudan's politics, including its ties with Egypt, was the mass demonstration of the Ansar on 1 March 1954, which turned into a violent bloodbath. On that day thousands of armed Ansar from all over Sudan gathered in Khartoum for the festive opening of the first Sudanese Parliament (*majlis al-sha'ab*). Since their number was nearly double that of Sudan's security forces, the latter's commander Babikr al-Dib, decided to play it safe and to avoid a direct confrontation. He therefore diverted the guests of honour, who included President Nagib and the delegation accompanying him, to an alternative route, unoccupied by the Ansar. The reason for the Ansar's presence was abundantly clear since they roamed the streets of Khartoum and Omdurman chanting: '*al-Sudan li'l-Sudaniyyin*', implying that Sudan was to be ruled by the Sudanese and not by Egypt. Al-Azhari realized that Mahdist supporters were in a position to endanger Sudan's peaceful path to independence. Instead of acting harshly and arresting 'Abdallah Khalil and Sayyid Siddiq al-Mahdi,

[270] Dhaher, *Al-Mirghani*, 342–3; quoting *al-Nil*, 24 Aug. 1953; and *al-Umma*, 25 Aug. 1953; also Daly, *Imperial Sudan*, 358.

[271] Minute by J.W. Kenrick, 2 Dec. 1953, FO 371/102760.

[272] 'Analysis of the Sudan General Election', November 1953, FO 371/108336.

as demanded by some of his close colleagues, he treated the Ansar and their leaders rather prudently probably realizing that the latter would go to any length in order to oppose even a symbolic union between Sudan and Egypt. Moreover, he feared that a breakdown in public security might undermine the progress towards self-determination. While there seems to be general agreement with regard to the repercussions of this event, politicians and historians alike remain divided both with regard to the circumstances leading to it and as to who was to blame for the outcome.[273] Whether or not these events had a significant impact on al-Azhari's subsequent decisions is unclear. However, it is a fact that his first public proclamation rejecting unity with Egypt was made later in that year. It was issued on 13 October 1954 on the eve of his first trip to England as his country's Prime Minister, when he begged Britain and its people not to prejudge Sudan:

> Many foreign political observers have been convinced by our party's name [National Unionist] into thinking that the aim of the administration of the Sudan is that the Sudan's personality will be lost in that of Egypt . . . It is absolutely not our aim to lose our identity in Egypt, nor to entrust her with [managing] our affairs. The Sudan Agreement specifies that the Sudanese will choose, when determining their future, [either] complete independence or a connection with Egypt, and the phrase 'connection [*irtibat*] with' has many meanings.[274]

Al-Azhari committed himself and the NUP to an early decision regarding the future of Sudan and its relationship with Egypt, hinting that he favoured close relations, 'as between two brothers'.[275] The deposal of President Nagib and his subsequent house arrest occurred while al-Azhari and his colleagues were in London. Though wisely avoiding actual involvement in what was clearly an internal Egyptian affair, al-Azhari and his fellow NUP members could not deny where their sympathies lay. He was therefore upset when he realized that his deputy, Muhammad Nur al-Din, had in his absence published a declaration in the name of the NUP, pronouncing Nagib's guilt and supporting the RCC, who had acted against him. Most of the members of the NUP, as well as its leadership, were up in arms against this announcement and al-Azhari tried his best to restore peace within the party. In addition there was an internal crisis in the NUP that ended with Mirghani Hamza and two other Khatmiyya members leaving both the party and the government and accusing al-Azhari of submission to the RCC and to Salah Salim. They demanded an immediate public declaration defining

[273] Quoted from al-Azhari's memoirs, *al-Ayyam*, 12 and 21 Aug. 1957; and Sa'id, *Azhari*, 189–92. Gawain Bell, who was Permanent Under-Secretary at the Ministry of Interior under al-Azhari, credits the latter with acting wisely under the circumstances and for not blaming the British for what had been the result of his mistake: Bell, *Shadows*, 212–13. President Nagib discarded this version and blamed the British Governor-General for turning a peaceful demonstration into a bloodbath in order to postpone the completion of the Anglo-Egyptian agreement: Najib, *Kalimati*, 119–21.
[274] Sa'id, *Azhari*, 216–17.
[275] *Al-Ayyam*, 6 June 1954, see Sa'id, *Azhari*, 217–18.

future relations between Sudan and Egypt. But although al-Azhari complied, Sayyid 'Ali and his supporters decided to leave the NUP and to found their own independent People's Democratic Party (PDP). In March 1955, the 'Higher Khatmiyya Union' in Khartoum, which had been founded by Sayyid 'Ali in December 1954, started to recruit members for the new *hizb al-sha'ab al-dimuqrati* (PDP).[276] It is interesting to note that a suggestion to add 'Islamic' to the party's name was rejected, probably for pragmatic reasons. This was the first time that the Khatmiyya, with Sayyid 'Ali's active backing was openly venturing into politics. All Khatmiyya members were instructed to join the new party, which was officially inaugurated on 26 June 1956, with Sayyid 'Ali as its patron. The Sayyid called upon all sufis, regardless of their *tariqa*, to join the new party. The party's President, 'Ali 'Abd al-Rahman al-Amin, unofficially had to gain the approval of Sayyid 'Ali for all political appointments and important decisions.[277]

These were the events which – according to Bashir Muhammad Sa'id, the editor of *al-Ayyam* and Azhari's biographer – brought about al-Azhari's decision to take the plunge and to declare openly that he did not favour union with Egypt but an independent Sudan. On 26 December 1954 he made this announcement to *al-Ayyam's* editor who published it in a special issue of his paper. Basically al-Azhari stated that Sudan would become an independent presidential republic. A Supreme Council would govern its relations with Egypt, consisting of the governments of the two countries, which would discuss all matters of mutual interest such as defence, foreign policy or the Nile waters. Its recommendations would then be brought before the respective Parliaments of the two independent states for amendment and ratification. As expected, al-Azhari's open declaration was received with blessings by the pro-independent front and by most of the unionists. But the Egyptians regarded it as an act of betrayal and Salah Salim even accused al-Azhari of collaborating with Britain against the unionists and Egypt.[278]

It was the growing antagonism between the Khatmiyya and the NUP and the suspicion with which Sayyid 'Ali viewed al-Azhari that had driven the two Sayyids into closer cooperation and led to several meetings between them and their representatives. In July 1955 Sayyid 'Ali started to propagate actively for a referendum that would decide Sudan's future, which he knew would lead to independence. He was supported by Sayyid 'Abd al-Rahman, who believed that Egypt, who had, according to him, manipulated the 1953 election results, would find it harder to manipulate the results of a

---

[276] On 22 Dec. 1954 a large group of Khatmiyya leaders met in Sayyid 'Ali's house and decided to form a 'Higher Khatmiyya Union' in order to coordinate their policy under Sayyid 'Ali's guidance; see Dhaher, *Al-Mirghani*, 370.

[277] Dhaher, *Al-Mirghani*, 386–93.

[278] Sa'id, *Azhari*, 224–8. Azhari's declaration was ratified by his party, following lengthy deliberations, and led to Muhammad Nur al-Din's departure from the *NUP* with a few of his supporters; see *ibid.*, 233–4, 237–8, quoting *al-Ayyam*, 2 and 11 Apr. 1955.

referendum. Al-Azhari, who had advocated a straight vote in Parliament, was forced by the two Sayyids to bring a motion requesting a referendum to Parliament and ask the Co-Domini to amend their agreement to that effect. Although ultimately al-Azhari succeeded in outmanoeuvring the two Sayyids and led Sudan to independence as he had proposed, in effect it was a victory for sectarian politics. On 30 November 1955 the two Sayyids met and agreed on full Sudanese sovereignty under a national government. The reason for this sudden 'meeting of hearts' is not difficult to discern. Al-Azhari's 'secular' political independence was a threat to both Sayyids and to the supreme position of the Khatmiyya and the Ansar in Sudan's politics. Hence he had to be stopped and a Khatmiyya–Ansar coalition seemed to be the only viable alternative.[279]

The Southern question

The Southern mutiny at Torit, which started on 18 August 1955, was the most crucial event that occurred during the year before independence. This violent expression of opposition to al-Azhari's government and to what Southerners regarded as its discriminatory policies in the South was a clear indication that security in Sudan would break down if its Muslim majority failed to take the southern problem into account. Southern education, as noted above, had suffered from complete stagnation during the Condominium. It had been entrusted to missionary societies and had been limited to a small number of sons of prominent tribal leaders. Plans for expanding education in the South, presented in 1944 and 1946 by C.W. Williams the new Director of Education, suggested an increase in expenditure for elementary education but practically none for intermediate or secondary education during the next five years. According to his five-year plan, only thirty Southern boys were to be enrolled in Ugandan secondary schools and twenty at Makerere by 1950. The agreement to grant Sudan self-government as early as 1953 was not taken into account even at that late stage. The dominant feature guiding educators and administrators alike continued to be that the tribes would remain the most stable part of society and the strongest anti-Muslim barrier. Hence the aim they executed was: 'Do not detribalize: make each boy a better member of his tribe.' Teaching agriculture, animal husbandry or tribal folklore, was therefore preferred to more general subjects such as mathematics, history or literature. Although most British officials blamed the missionaries for the neglect, it was at least partly due to half a century of government negligence.[280]

Government disregard, especially in the fields of education and economic development, presents the key to an understanding of the outcome

---

[279] Dhaher, *Al-Mirghani*, 362–7.
[280] Daly, *Imperial Sudan*, 201–5.

of the Juba Conference in 1947, in which Southern and Northern representatives studied their future for the first time, under British guidance. The conference deliberated two main questions: first, whether southern Sudanese wanted to participate in the future Sudan's Legislative Assembly or would rather have their own separate advisory council and; secondly, what southern views were regarding Sudan's unity following self-determination.[281] However, according to Abel Alier, one of the most qualified Southern leaders, Sir James Robertson, the Civil Secretary, 'took his case to the South, not to ask the Southerners to determine their future, but rather to inform them of the decision the government had already taken'.[282] It simply implied that when Britain moved out of the region the Southerners would be left to fend for themselves. Southerners failed to comprehend that the guarantees required for equality in a united Sudan, which had been promised by British representatives at Juba, were in effect meaningless. This transpired during the deliberations of the Constitution Amendment Commission, appointed in 1951, which refused to accept a southern request that constitutional guarantees for the South would be granted, whether it opted for separation or unity. In addition, a provision that had been included in the draft constitution, which vested powers in the Governor-General 'to ensure fair and equitable treatment to all the inhabitants of the various provinces of the Sudan', thereby safeguarding the interests of the south, was watered down to an unrecognizable generality as a result of northern Sudanese and Egyptian pressures.[283] One consequence was that although in the 1953 general elections the Southern Liberal Party won 22 out the total 97 seats, not a single northern party was willing to support the idea of a federation, which was a southern request supported by nearly all southern Members of Parliament. Moreover, the so-called 'Sudanization Commission' appointed as a result of the Anglo-Egyptian agreement, filled 800 administrative posts with northern Sudanese Muslims, but only four minor posts were assigned to southerners, with the excuse that they lacked education and practice. Consequently, in October 1954 Southerners of all shades of opinion held their own conference at Juba, in which they decided 'that the South could remain united to the North only under a federal government'.[284]

With backward economic and educational systems and a lack of political organization and qualified manpower, the South was soon overrun by Northern politicians and officials, many of whom were quite ignorant of conditions in the South and were not of the highest quality or of the purest intentions. Southerners were therefore not surprised when, on 18 August

[281] Oduho and Deng, *Southern Sudan*, 16–17; Alier, *Southern Sudan*, 20–3
[282] Alier, *Southern Sudan*, 21.
[283] *Ibid.*, 22–3; Oduho and Deng, *Southern Sudan*, 21. The Southern member of the committee handed in his resignation in protest; see Daly, *Imperial Sudan*, 234–42.
[284] Oduho and Deng, *Southern Sudan*, 22–4, 27; Alier, *Southern Sudan*, 23.

1955, a revolt started among the Equatorial corps at Torit. This mutiny, which ended only after 261 Northerners and seventy-five Southerners had lost their lives, signified the beginning of the Sudanese civil war, which has tormented that country since independence.[285]

In order to overcome Southern suspicions, Northern politicians had promised to consider a federal solution for Sudan, whereby some form of autonomy would safeguard the interests of the backward South. It was with this understanding in mind that Southern politicians consented to vote for an independent and united Sudan. Once independence was achieved, promises were, however, soon forgotten. Political power was subjugated to the dictates of the traditional Muslim leaders of the Khatmiyya and the Ansar. With the exception of the Communists and some other well-wishing but marginal parts of the intelligentsia, all political parties in Sudan agreed on an Islamic constitution and regarded the rapid Arabization and Islamization of the South as one of their most significant missions, leading to a united Sudan. Consequently, the ensuing conflict assumed both religious and ethnic dimensions. In addition, government economic policy continued to discriminate against the South, even after the 1947 Juba conference, which had decided to reverse this trend. By the end of the Condominium over three-quarters of all government expenditure went into the northern Gezira cotton-growing scheme, since it served colonial interests. What happened in Sudan were the emergence of a landed aristocracy, on the one hand, and the creation of urban élites, on the other. All of these were concentrated in the three towns, of which Khartoum was the centre, and in their immediate hinterland. Thereby Greater Khartoum, with only 6 per cent of the population, contained 85 per cent of all commercial companies; 80 per cent of all banks; seventy three percent of all industrial establishments and 70 per cent of all industrial labour. This so-called 'growth pole' strategy, which advocated the concentration of investments in a favoured region in order to create centres of growth, was implemented in Sudan to the advantage of the ruling élite, comprised of the leadership of the Ansar and the Khatmiyya, as well as certain other sections within the urban élite. Its uninterrupted continuation after independence was in no small measure responsible for the growing suspicions of southern leaders regarding the good intentions of their new 'colonizers'.[286]

Summing up the main causes and misconceived policies, leading to the Southern tragedy, Daly wrote as follows:

The fate of the South was that common to peripheral regions, determined in part by geography, reinforced by colonial economic priorities and mismanagement,

---

[285] It is interesting to note that it was the disgraced Egyptian Colonel Salah Salim who demanded the redeployment of British and Egyptian troops in the South following the massacre, to the dismay of both al-Azhari's government and the British Governor-General.
[286] Hale, *Sudan Civil War* in Joseph and Pillsbury, *Muslim–Christian Conflicts*, 173–8.

overlain by a legacy of slavery and consequent spectre of exploitation, and enforced by religious and racial aspects of Northern Sudanese nationalism. Stirring this witch's brew was Egypt's last act in the drama of Condominium.[287]

Egypt was of course not the only culprit, not even the main one, and yet the South, as a result of mistaken policies and mismanagement, had definitely become a major source of conflict, threatening Sudan's unity right from independence onwards.

---

[287] Daly, *Imperial Sudan*, 381.

Part IV

INDEPENDENT SUDAN, 1956–89

On 1 January 1956 the Republic of Sudan was born as an independent state within the territorial boundaries that had existed under the Condominium. From its very first days it had to face numerous problems, most of which it had inherited from preceding regimes. Many of these problems have become even more severe over the years and have remained part and parcel of Sudan's precarious existence as an independent and united state. This discussion will be limited primarily to those problems that are directly concerned with the role of religion in independent Sudan. However, as will be noted, some of the other developments had repercussions for this topic. Thus, for instance, the Islamic resurgence that started in the 1960s, albeit a phenomenon of international dimensions, had direct implications for the role of Islam in Sudanese society and politics. Similarly, though Sudan had opted for independence, its relations with Egypt have remained on its national agenda due to geopolitical reasons connected with Egypt's central role in the region, on the one hand, and to its total dependence on the Nile waters, on the other.[1] Sudan's ethnic diversity and the ensuing conflicts which spread into other parts of the Nile Valley, burdened Sudan's relations with most of its neighbours, including Ethiopia, Eritrea and the Horn of Africa and at times with Uganda, Kenya and the Congo. Our discussion will none the less deal primarily with the following questions. First, was independent Sudan going to become a secular or an Islamic state? Secondly, how would it incorporate the religious and ethnic minorities within the state? Finally, would it remain a democratic state, as promised by its founders, or would it opt for an autocratic form of government in order to overcome the diverse and often conflicting interests of its religious and ethnic minorities?

Between the destruction of the Mahdist state in September 1898 and the emergence of the independent Republic of the Sudan in January 1956, several factors intervened that made the creation of an Islamic state problematic. First, historically there were those in Sudan who, for a variety of reasons, had viewed the Mahdi as an impostor (*mutamahdi*) and his movement

---

[1] For details see Collins, *Waters of the Nile*, 1–25; Warburg, *Nile*, 73–90.

as un-Islamic and had consequently opposed neo-Mahdism when it emerged in the twentieth century. They included, first and foremost, the followers of the Khatmiyya *sufi* order, for whom any regime, even a secular one, was preferable to a Mahdist-led Islamic state. Secondly, during the first half of the twentieth century, Sudan was ruled by a colonial administration, and the separation of religion and state was one of its most cherished goals. Many of the young Sudanese intelligentsia who were educated during the first half of the twentieth century in accordance with these Western-inspired principles were willing to respect the traditional religious leaders of the Khatmiyya, the Ansar and other *sufi* orders, to whom most of them belonged through family ties, but not to be ruled by sectarian parties, which were run according to norms that they were taught to regard as old-fashioned and undemocratic.[2] Thirdly, in the mid-1950s, when Sudan was taking its first hesitant steps towards independence, President Nasser of Egypt was reigning supreme in the Arab world, with Arab unity, Arab socialism and positive neutralism being far more popular than an Islamic state ruled in accordance with the shari'a. Finally, Sudan had always been a country of ethnic and religious diversity and contradictions. The complex relationship between the Muslim north and the non-Muslim south, inherited from previous regimes, as well as regional and ethnic conflicts, thus continued to be major obstacles faced by the newly born state following independence.

A brief examination of Sudan's political and social history since 1956 proves beyond doubt that none of the main problems it had to face had been solved by the end of the millennium. The fact that military coups have interrupted democratic rule on numerous occasions, was a direct result of the above. Three military regimes have ruled Sudan, in 1958–64, 1969–85, and from 1989 to the present, namely (at the time of writing) for three-quarters of the period since independence. This seems to suggest that for as long as the religious–ethnic divide, dominated by sectarianism and led by a northern Muslim élite, continues to play a central political role, there is little hope for stability.

---

[2] The term 'sectarianism' was used during colonial times in order to express the power base of the two main religio-political groups. In modern Sudanese historiography it has become identified with the Ansar–Khatmiyya conflict.

12

STATEHOOD AND CONSTITUTION-MAKING

The Temporary Constitution of 1956, which was intended to be a *laissez-passer* leading Sudan to independence and enabling it to promulgate its Permanent Constitution later on, has proved to be the most resilient constitution in Africa. It has withstood three military coups and has been resurrected with certain modifications whenever the military lost power. Even the Permanent Constitution of May 1973, promulgated by President Ja'far Numayri, lasted for only thirteen years before it was replaced, once again, by the temporary constitution of 1956. The reasons for the apparent unattainability of a permanent constitution are partly due to the irreconcilable conflict of interests of the social forces in Sudan. Representing the northern and central Muslim élite, these forces were organized in the two sectarian parties: the Umma, backed by the Ansar and the Khatmiyya, backed by the NUP (later the DUP). The third Islamic party consisted of modern Islamists, organized in the small but radical Muslim Brotherhood (after 1985, reconstituted as the NIF and, since 1998, as the National Congress). The latter was determined to enforce an Islamic constitution but was too weak to do so without collaboration with more popular traditional Muslim parties. These political–social forces, which included a substantial number of the officer's corps, also had economic and social interests in common and were seeking to consolidate their privileged positions. In concrete terms their vision entailed the adoption of Islam as the religion of state, the shari'a as the main source of public laws and Arabic as the official language. The exponents of this view probably preferred to impose this platform democratically, by majority vote. However, many of them did not refrain from coercion whenever the military were in power. Although those advocating this vision never agreed on all its details, they were united in their desire to keep the hegemony in the hands of the Muslim Arabic-speaking, riverain élite and to exclude the peripheral regions, whether Muslims, Christians or animists, from the centres of political and economic power.[3] Conversely, those in the marginalized regions, who had received a raw deal both under colonial rule and since independence, have advocated the redistribution of

[3] The main sources used for writing this section are Kok, *Governance*; Na'im, *Islamic Constitution*.

wealth in order to compensate their historically neglected regions. They demanded the creation of a federal or confederate secular state in which power was shared and which would enable other cultures and languages to flourish alongside Islam and Arabic. These two contradictory visions have remained at the centre of Sudan's constitutional conflict since 1956. However, until 1986, all northern political parties, except the Communists, have rejected a federal solution and have insisted that Sudan's Permanent Constitution would be Islamic and should be determined by a democratic majority. They promised the non-Muslim and non-Arab minorities to preserve their rights and to allow them to use their languages and develop their cultures. Provided however that the predominance of Arabic was preserved in all educational institutions and state offices, while Islam remained unchallenged as the religion of state.

The search for a nationally acceptable constitution started as early as September 1956, with the establishment of a committee for drafting a Permanent Constitution. It argued about the nature of this constitution and for the first time the possibility of an Islamic constitution was raised, though with little effect. By early 1957 the Constitutional Committee had committed itself to the principle that Islam was to be the official religion of the state and the shari'a one of its main sources of legislation. To eliminate any doubt about where they stood in this regard, the sectarian leaders Sayyid 'Abd al-Rahman al-Mahdi and Sayyid 'Ali al-Mirghani, both of whom had never really reconciled themselves to the secular–liberal model of the Transitional Constitution, demanded jointly that Sudan be declared an Islamic parliamentary republic with the shari'a as the main source of legislation. In this they were strongly supported by the Muslim Brotherhood, who had campaigned for the adoption of a permanent constitution based on the Qur'an and the *Sunna* since 1954. Their views were largely patterned on the ideas of the Jama'at Islami in Pakistan. They sought the establishment of an Islamic republic, under a Muslim head of state, with a parliamentary democracy based on Islamic law and legislating in accordance with shari'a. Muslims would thus be able to shape their lives according to the dictates of their religion and to uproot social evils and corruption as required by Islam. A period of five years was set for the state to be fully Islamized and for all its laws to comply with shari'a. However, there would be no discrimination on the basis of race or religion, and non-Muslim citizens would enjoy all rights granted under Muslim law.[4] This draft constitution, which had been agreed upon by the Constitutional Committee was never promulgated. By April 1958, when it was finally presented to the Constituent Assembly, the latter was otherwise engaged and failed to ratify it before the military coup of November 1958, which was led by General Ibrahim 'Abbud.

The arguments presented at the time by the Islamist thinker Ahmad Safi

---

[4] Affendi, *Turabi's Revolution*, 156–7; see also Cudsi, *Islam and Politics*, 38.

al-Din 'Awad, who was propagating an Islamic constitution, were also relevant in Sudanese politics. He stated that unlike other religions, which do not require comprehensive legislation of society, 'Muslims cannot observe and abide by any legislation unless under the rule of Islam . . . Accordingly, the issue of an Islamic Constitution for Muslims is part and parcel of their basic human rights.'[5] However, non-Muslim and non-Arab minorities did not accept the claim that an Islamic constitution would allow them to practise their religions freely and that they would be granted full citizenship and equal rights under Islamic law. Consequently, the future of a united Sudan was threatened. As stated above, the two Sayyids expressed sympathy for the idea of an Islamic constitution, but showed no enthusiasm for enforcing it, knowing that it did not really affect their adherents. Furthermore, they realized that an Islamic constitution, as demanded by the Muslim Brothers, might undermine Sudan's unity.

It is interesting to note the views of Muhammad Ahmad Mahjub (Mahgoub) on sectarianism and especially on the role of the two Sayyids in politics, on the eve of General 'Abbud's coup. Mahgoub was at the time one of the most important leaders of the Umma party and was to become Prime Minister in 1965. His anti-sectarian views may therefore sound somewhat surprising:

The alliance between Al-Mahdi and Al-Mirghani was the most catastrophic in the history of Sudanese politics. The two life-long foes, prompted by their greed for power, their vanity and personal vested interests, sought to dominate the field of politics. I had the greatest respect for the two men as religious leaders. But they should have kept out of politics.[6]

One should, however, take into account that Mahgoub was not a member of the Ansar and that he had joined the Umma party only after independence. In fact, according to a report made to the British Foreign Office, many Ansar and Umma party members did not trust him and viewed his joining the party as the lesser of two evils, since he could have caused greater harm in opposition.[7]

The 1956 Transitional Constitution survived the military regime of General 'Abbud and was resurrected when Sudan started its second democracy in 1965. The Constitution was slightly amended, in the wake of the civilian uprising of October 1964, but in essence remained unchanged. The demand of the Southern Front for the right of self-determination for the southern Sudan and for a referendum that would enable its inhabitants to decide on the nature of its relations with the Muslim North had therefore no chance of being accepted even by moderate northern parties. Although

---

[5] Sidahmed, *Politics and Islam*, 65; quoting from Ahmad Safy al-Din Awad, *Ma'alim al-dustur al-Islami* (n.p.; n.d.).

[6] Mahgoub, *Democracy*, 176.

[7] Enclosure in letter from Khartoum (1011), 25 Jan. 1958, FO 371/31707.

it was agreed that the Constituent Assembly that was to be elected in 1965 would approve a permanent constitution, it was in reality a return to the status quo ante, which had proved ungovernable and had led to the November 1958 military coup. Thus after the first caretaker government was dismissed, in February 1965, and even before general elections, the traditional parties were back in power propagating similar views and programmes to those they had proposed in 1956–8. The 'Round Table Conference', which discussed this problem for about ten days, in March 1965, consequently failed to reach an agreed compromise.[8]

The Muslim Brothers, now under Hasan al-Turabi's leadership, had reorganized themselves and some minor *sufi* orders within the Islamic Charter Front (ICF), which sought to implement an Islamic order. Since it constituted an insignificant minority, it was only natural that the ICF should attempt to align itself with sectarian forces which, though traditionalist, relied on grassroots Muslim adherents and were thus possible partners in the quest for an Islamic constitution. This was not dissimilar to the 'marriage of convenience' between the pre-independence intelligentsia within the Graduates' Congress and the two Sayyids. Now it was the ICF that needed the sectarian umbrella to achieve its goals. The Ansar, under al-Sadiq al-Mahdi's leadership, provided this in 1966–7, when he actively supported Hasan al-Turabi in his quest for an Islamic constitution. For the first time in his career, which had hitherto been primarily academic, al-Turabi was actively involved in a Constitution Committee alongside several members of the ICF. The three options discussed were: an Islamic constitution proposed by the ICF; a secular constitution proposed by southerners and a few members of the northern intelligentsia; or a 'constitution with an Islamic orientation', as proposed by the NUP. The latter, which was rather similar to the Transitional constitution, was finally adopted and its draft was presented to the Constituent Assembly on 15 January 1968. Al-Turabi's memorandum to the committee listed the following advantages of the Islamic constitution:

1. The constitution should represent the will of the people and since the majority are Muslims their will should prevail.
2. Unlike other religions, Islam is a *religion and state* and it instructs (the believers) to govern in accordance with Allah's Revelation.
3. The adoption of a non-Islamic political system in the Sudan had not been in response to popular demand, but rather a work of despotic rulers with Western culture and orientation.
4. The ostensibly Islamic states that ruled Muslims were bad models whose knowledge of Islam was very poor.
5. An Islamic constitution would be a rule of sacred *law* and not a rule of *men* because in Islam there is no place for *theocracy* or 'clergy men'.
6. Islam opposes dictatorship.

[8] Beshir, *Southern Sudan*, 88–97; for details see below.

7. Islam protects private freedoms and guarantees freedom of opinion and parti-
    cipation in public affairs.
8. Islam encourages *ijtihad*, because the final opinion is the public's and every
    individual, group of individuals or political party had the right to advocate their
    views and to work for the assumption of power through *shura*.
9. Islam recognized freedom of religion before Europe had ever thought about
    it and calls for the protection of citizens with other religious beliefs.
10. Islam calls for equality before the law and in public rights.[9]

This document demonstrated al-Turabi's political–ideological pragmatism
and flexibility, since it claimed that Islam protected private freedoms and
guaranteed freedom of opinion, while at the very same time he was actively
propagating the outlawing of Communist Ideology and the expulsion of the
democratically elected Communist members from Parliament. Al-Turabi's
interpretation of *ijtihad* even raised opposition among the more conservative of his fellow Muslim Brothers, who opposed his unprincipled opportunism. But his main opponents on the Constitution Committee were the
southerners and Muslim leaders from Dar Fur, the Nuba Mountains and
the Red Sea hills. Although Muslims, they regarded an Islamic constitution
as a ploy for consolidating the hegemony of northern central Sudan under
the umbrella of an Arabic Islamic culture, which would thus consolidate the
marginalization of Sudan's southern, western and eastern populations.[10]

The split within the Ansar and the Umma party, between *al-imam* al-
Hadi al-Mahdi and his nephew al-Sadiq, had strengthened the bargaining
power of al-Turabi and the ICF. But, following the reconciliation between
the two factions of the Mahdi's family, in April 1969, al-Hadi al-Mahdi, as
imam of the Ansar, and al-Sadiq al-Mahdi, as leader of the Umma, had
agreed that, in the forthcoming elections, the first would run for the presidency of Sudan and the second would become Prime Minister. The problem of the Permanent Constitution thus stopped being the main issue.
Muhammad Ahmad Mahgoub commented rather cynically: 'They thus
seemed to consider the rule of the state a booty to be inherited and divided
between them, to the exclusion of the other members of the [Umma] Party
who did not belong to the Mahdi family.'[11]

On 23 May 1969 all the political parties in the Constituent Assembly accepted the principle that Sudan should have an Islamic presidential constitution, and general elections were scheduled for January 1970. Less than
forty-eight hours later, the army assumed power once again, under Colonel
Ja'far Numayri.[12] Mahgoub commented in hindsight: 'After Independence,

---

[9] Sidahmed, *Politics and Islam*, 103–10; quotation from *Technical Committee Reports*
(Khartoum: Government Press, 1968), *ibid*. 105.

[10] Details in Alier, *Southern Sudan*, 36–40.

[11] Mahgoub, *Democracy*, 224; for details on the internal conflicts within the Ansar-Umma,
see below.

[12] Cudsi, *Islam and Politics*, 39–41.

Government and Parliament set about looking for a permanent constitution – as if a constitution was a magic wand with which a country could be ruled and everything turned to gold.'[13] He concluded as follows: 'There should have been no quarrel on whether the constitution should be Islamic or secular. The Sudanese could have had a constitution without calling it Islamic, thereby practising their Islamic faith and using the tolerance embodied in its tenets.[14] Whether or not Mahgoub, who was then Prime Minister, was involved in enabling the army to move into Khartoum remained unclear and is not really relevant. What matters is that 'the major parties had wasted enormous amounts of time jockeying for positions of individual advantage in their reconciliation meetings, while national crisis kept mounting.'[15]

Sudan's first permanent constitution was thus promulgated by the military regime under Numayri on 8 May 1973, nearly seventeen years after independence. It tackled the two thorniest issues that had frustrated constitutional efforts in the past: the status of the South and the question of religion and politics. In many ways, it was the first and only time since independence that Sudan was governed by a regime that was secular by design. It established a presidential system and proclaimed the SSU as the only legally recognized political organization in Sudan. In Part One of the Constitution Sudan was proclaimed a 'unitary, democratic, socialist and sovereign republic'. Article 9 stated: 'Islamic laws and customs shall be the main sources of legislation. Personal matters of non-Muslims shall be governed by their laws.' But Article 16 was even more significant, since it tackled the issue of the place of Islam in the state, while attempting to accommodate all other religions on an equal basis, in the following manner:

(a) In the Democratic Republic of the Sudan, Islam is the religion and society shall be guided by Islam, being the religion of the majority of its people and the state shall endeavour to express its values.

(b) Christianity is the religion in the Democratic Republic of the Sudan, which is professed by a large number of its citizens who are guided by Christianity, and the state shall endeavour to express its values.

(c) Heavenly religions and the noble aspects of spiritual beliefs shall not be abused or held in contempt.

(d) The State shall treat followers of religions and noble spiritual beliefs without discrimination as to the rights and freedoms guaranteed to them as citizens by this constitution.

(e) The abuse of religious and noble beliefs for political exploitation is forbidden. Any act which is intended or is likely to promote hatred, enmity or discord among religious communities shall be contrary to this constitution and punishable by law.[16]

[13] Mahgoub, *Democracy*, 177.

[14] *Ibid.*, 181.

[15] Bechtold, *Politics in Sudan*, 257.

[16] Quoted from *The Permanent Constitution of the Sudan* (Khartoum: Democratic Republic

The significance of this constitution was that it attempted, for the first time since independence, to accommodate all religions on the basis of equality and openly to promote secularism. This attempt failed, and the 1973 Constitution remained in force only for a brief moment in history. Already in 1975, a constitutional amendment drastically curtailed basic human rights. It was followed by National Reconciliation in July 1977, which readmitted the conservative political forces, both sectarian and Islamist into the decision-making process, thereby undermining both the Addis Ababa Agreement of 1972 and the secular basis of the 1973 Constitution. Finally, once Numayri embraced the Islamic path (*al-nahj al-islami*), in 1983, it was in direct contradiction with the secular intentions of the constitution, which were consequently overruled by presidential decrees pronounced by Numayri. Peter Nyot Kok addressed the question as to whether a constitution imposed by a military regime, supported by a centrist northern minority can survive. He defined it as: 'secular, presidential, one-party state, quasi-federal, pseudo-constitutionalist, mixed economy oriented'. Since it was based solely on a majority of members of the ruling élite represented in the 1972–3 Peoples' Assembly, it could not, according to Kok, rely on a national consensus.[17]

Under the third democratic government, in the years 1986–9, a somewhat different approach was adopted, which advocated a national consensus as a precondition for the formulation of a Permanent Constitution and its subsequent ratification by Parliament. A National Constitutional Conference (NCC) was appointed to undertake this task. However, it was not even convened during the three years of the regime's existence, due to the opposition of the NIF. The latter was 'surprised and dismayed by the pro-NCC stance of the army'. It was also aware of its own weakness should a constitution advocating multicultural rights and the freedom of religions be promulgated. Without the hereditary popular support enjoyed by the Umma and the DUP, the NIF needed time in order to consolidate its grip on state power. This was one of the reasons leading to the NIF-inspired military coup in June 1989. According to Kok,

The search for a permanent constitution under liberal democratic regimes has been fundamentally flawed by the assumption . . . that such a constitution could be imposed by a special parliamentary majority. Such an assumption is the very antithesis of a constitution by consensus.[18]

However, the assumption that a consensus was possible in a country like Sudan, 'characterised by marked dysfunctional ethno-cultural heterogeneity', is questionable.

---

of the Sudan Printer, 1973). See also Sidahmed, *Politics & Islam*, 115–16; Warburg, *Islam & State*, 403–5.

[17] Kok, *Governance*, 121–3.
[18] *Ibid.*

The 'elusive Islamic constitution' has therefore failed to materialize, despite the overwhelming majority of Muslims in Sudan and the repeated commitment of its two main political parties, the Umma and the DUP, and the even more extreme support of the Muslim Brothers and later the NIF to promulgate such a constitution. This failure was especially apparent in 1986–9, when the NCC, as mentioned, failed to convene and could not even agree on its agenda. The answer to the puzzle why Sudan, dominated by three Islamist parties, failed to agree on an Islamic constitution until 1998 seems to lie in the nature of Sudanese Islam. Its origin, as stated, was in popular Islam in which Sufism played a predominant role. The political power wielded by the two most powerful groups, the neo-Mahdist Ansar and the Khatmiyya, was the result of the hereditary loyalty of their adherents rather than their ideological commitment to an Islamic state. Although the leaders of these sects continuously declared their support for an Islamic constitution and an Islamic state, being astute politicians they moderated this quest whenever in power in order to safeguard the unity of a multireligious, multicultural and ethnically diverse Sudan. According to Abdel Salam Sidahmed's study on *Politics and Islam in Contemporary Sudan*, the sectarian alliance between the Ansar and the Khatmiyya was the result of their quest for power, their rejection of the NIF and its allies and, last but not least, their class interests as landlords. The author does not even mention Islam as a factor in this regard and states that, although the two Muslim sects owed their influence to their loyal adherents, 'the conduct of their politics and government was virtually secular.' He explains this phenomenon by stating that secular Sudanese politicians also owed their power to the same sectarian influences in the countryside and hence the gap between the 'liberal intelligentsia' and the supporters of the Ansar and Khatmiyya was rather narrow. This was also due to another reason, namely that the sectarian leaders were 'neither fanatics nor advocators of vigorous Islamic-isation of Sudanese politics'.[19] Finally, the popular Islamic belief system, as practised by the Ansar and the Khatmiyya, was traditionally more relaxed and relied on the goodwill and loyalty of their adherents rather than on a rigorous set of orthodox rules as propagated and implemented by force by the modern Islamists. The Islamic constitution therefore had to wait until it was imposed by an alliance between President 'Umar Hasan al-Bashir's military regime and the NIF in 1998.[20]

[19] Sidahmed, *Politics & Islam*, 58–61.
[20] Details in Ch. 17.

13

THE ISLAMIC PATH, 1977–85

Details of Numayri's Islamic beliefs and policies were published in three books, two of which were ascribed to his authorship. The first, *Al-nahj al-islami limadha?* (The Islamic path why?), was published in Cairo in 1980. It described the reasons for Numayri's shift from secularist, nationalist and leftist tendencies in the early years following the May 1969 coup to a strict observance of Islam since the mid-1970s. The second book was entitled *Al-nahj al-islami kayfa?* (The Islamic path how?) and was scheduled to be published in August 1983, but by an irony of fate it appeared only in April 1985, the month of Numayri's removal.[21] It attempted to explain and illustrate how the Islamic path was to be implemented. A third book contained the proceedings of an international Islamic conference which was convened in Khartoum in September 1984 to celebrate the first anniversary of the implementation of the shari'a. It was published by Sudan's Parliament under the title: '*Am 'ala tatbiq al-shari'a al-islamiyya fi al-Sudan* ('One year following the implementation of Islamic laws in the Sudan'). In the first book, Numayri ascribed the beginning of his shift to an Islamic path to the abortive Communist coup of July 1971, which opened his eyes to the truth. He glorified the nineteenth-century Mahdiyya and its founder, Muhammad Ahmad al-Mahdi. Even more revealing was his attitude towards the Ansar, the present-day followers of Mahdism, and their acting *imam*, al-Sadiq al-Mahdi. If we bear in mind that the Ansar under al-Sadiq al-Mahdi's leadership, had been in open opposition to Numayri's regime since the very beginning and had tried to overthrow it as late as July 1976, Numayri's praise could be viewed either as part of a major ideological shift or as a political manoeuvre.[22] The connection between Islamic revival and reconciliation with the sectarian enemies of the May 1969 revolution was no coincidence. It occurred at a time when secular Nasserist-style nationalism and leftist ideologies, which had accompanied Numayri's regime in its early stages had been discredited in Sudan as in Egypt and elsewhere, whilst political and at times militant Islam was forging ahead in Iran, Algeria and

---

[21] It is irrelevant whether the two books were indeed written by President Numayri. However, many Sudanese attributed them to 'Awn al-Sharif Qasim, a leading Sudanese scholar and the author of several books on Islamic issues, who was closely associated with Numayri. Others ascribed them to Muhammad Mahjub, his Egyptian adviser and speech writer.

[22] Numayri, *Al-nahj al-islami*, 218–23.

other Muslim states, including Egypt. Under President Anwar al-Sadat, the Muslim Brothers and the Islamic student organizations (*al-Jama'at al-islamiyya*) had risen to new prominence. Finally, poverty-stricken Sudan had an ever-growing need for economic aid from its oil-rich Arab neighbours, in particular Saudi Arabia. The Islamic path and reconciliation with the Ansar and the Muslim Brothers could therefore have been viewed by Numayri as politically wise and potentially profitable.[23]

Numayri's Islamic path was ascribed by some observers to his close association with *sufi* leaders such as the Abu Qurun *sufi* family, a branch of the Qadiriyya, which regarded the fifteenth century of the *hijra* as a turning-point in the history of Islam. They believed in a 'second coming' of a great *mahdi*, who would be one of their adherents. This *sufi* trend in Numayri's spiritual thinking started, according to him, following the abortive communist coup in July 1971, when he renounced his previous secularist–leftist allies. In his book on *Nemeiri and the Turuq*, Idris El-Hassan examined this change as related to the Badrab Khalifa in Umm Dubban in some detail. In the early 1970s Numayri started to invite *sufis* belonging to various brotherhoods, to the presidential palace during the month of Ramadan. He also introduced an annual 'Qur'an Contest' under his auspices, which thereafter became a major annual event. He established a Ministry of Endowments (*awqaf*) and Religious Affairs, in order to lure the smaller *sufi* orders to his side. In 1974, Numayri started to invite members of the Sammaniyya, the Isma'iliyya, the Qadiriyya and other *sufi* orders to go on the pilgrimage to Mecca at government expense, including free medical services while abroad. Members of these orders were also assisted in participating in Islamic festivities, such as *mawlid al-nabi*, by supplying free transport for their followers from their homes to the capital and setting up special tents for their accommodation whilst away from home. The building of mosques and *zawiyas* by *sufi* orders was subsidized by the government from 1975, and from 1976 these orders were formally organized within the SSU. All *sufi* orders except the Khatmiyya and the Ansar were invited to attend special events in the capital and to demonstrate thereby their approval of the regime's policies. It was during these years that Numayri often visited the Khalifa Yusuf wad Badur of Umm Dubban and his close relations with the Badrab Islamic centre was viewed as an additional sign of his religiosity.[24] A natural outcome of this policy was an impressive growth in the wealth and influence of the Badrab *Khulafa'*. For example, the Umm Dubban Rural Council, consisting of twenty-two members, did not make any important decisions that were not approved by the Badrab Khalifa.

[23] Details in Warburg, *Islam in Egypt*, 131–57; also *idem*, *Shari'a*, 624–37.

[24] Idris, *Nemeiri and the Turuq*, 85–6; also Hofheinz, *Idrisi*, 179–82. The Badrab school of Umm Dubban, situated east of the Blue Nile, is a famous centre of Islamic learning in Sudan. It was founded by Muhammad wad Ahmad Badr (*c*. 1810–84) and has been run by his descendants, the Badrab, ever since.

Consequently, nothing could happen in the region without the latter's knowledge and approval. He was believed to possess superior spiritual powers, which could cause harm to whoever disagreed with him. 'Thus, although the Khalifa did not control significant economic enterprises in Um Dubban, he nevertheless had enough wealth to oust any potential competitor.' Consequently, the Khalifa possessed considerable political power, which was enhanced as a result of his special relationship with Numayri and the latter's support of the *sufi* orders.[25]

By the time Numayri was overthrown, in April 1985, practically all the smaller *sufi* orders had become supporters of the regime. Some of their shaykhs were appointed to government posts, including minor ministries, while others were active within the SSU. In addition, they benefited from new opportunities at secondary schools and universities. This, in turn, enabled them to appeal to the rich Arab states in the Arabian Peninsula and the Gulf for donations, thereby alleviating their position even further. In this way, the anti-sectarian policy of Numayri helped the smaller *sufi* orders to enhance their position. On the other hand their dependence on Numayri alienated some of their most devout adherents who abandoned Sufism and joined instead the non-sectarian brotherhoods such as the Muslim Brothers, the Republican Brothers or the Ansar al-Sunna, an offshoot of the Wahhabiyya, which had started penetrating Sudan as early as the 1930s.[26]

In his political novel *Seed of Redemption* Francis Deng portrayed the President's 'encounter' with God, in which he was ordered to reform his ways and to return to the path of a true believer. Following this encounter the President sent for his 'local spiritual leader' in order to receive his guidance, and the latter addressed him as follows: 'Mr President, said the mystic, by revealing Himself, it is clear that God has chosen you to be the leader of this country. You are President, but you are also the Imam of God. He will change you as he desires. I am but a tool of His will. The power to transform you has already descended from God.'[27]

Numayri's association with Shaykh 'Abd al-Qadir Abu Qurun, mentioned above, led to his subsequent cooperation with his son, al-Nayil 'Abd al-Qadir Abu Qurun, and his fellow student, 'Awad al-Jid Muhammad Ahmad, both of whom had graduated from the Faculty of Law in 1971. Al-Nayil began to show ambitions of religious leadership towards the end of his studies and, instead of applying himself to the pursuit of a career in the judiciary, he developed his own notions of strict adherence to the *Sunna* of

[25] Idris, *Nemeiri and the Turuq*, 89–95; quotation from 92.

[26] Karsani, *Beyond Sufism*, 144–7.

[27] Deng, *Seed*, 205–7. Although all characters in this novel are, according to the author, purely imaginary, their identity seems indisputable. Ambassador Francis Deng was previously minister of state for foreign affairs in Khartoum and Ambassador of Sudan to several countries including Canada and the United States. He is the author of numerous anthropological studies and a Senior Fellow for Foreign Policy Studies at the Brookings Institution in Washington, DC.

the Prophet.[28] Following Numayri's initiation into their *sufi* order, he appointed al-Nayil and 'Awad al-Jid, first as Judicial Assistants in the presidential palace, and in 1983 he promoted 'Awad al-Jid Minister for Judicial Affairs and Attorney-General, a post he held during the crucial period when the Islamic laws were proclaimed.[29]

While Numayri's spiritual inclinations towards Sufism were well known, it is none the less difficult to assess the extent of its impact on his policies. Was it a genuine mystical tendency towards Sufism, so dominant in Sudanese Islam, or a pragmatic step based on his reading of the political map? It is also possible that his change of heart was the result of a combination of political pragmatism, based on the predominance of Islam both in Sudan and in other parts of the Muslim world, mixed with his inclination to Islamic mysticism. But, whatever the reasons leading to this policy, it is of greater significance to assess and analyse the outcome of this shift and its subsequent repercussions on Sudan.

The implementation of the Shari'a

In 1977, soon after Numayri pronounced National Reconciliation with the opposition in exile, he appointed a special committee for the 'return of the laws to compatibility with the shari'a' (*lajnat muraja't al-qawanin li'tatamasha ma'a al-shari'a*), with Dr Hasan al-Turabi as its chairman. It was entrusted, as its title suggests, with bringing Sudan's legislation into full harmony with the Shari'a. It drafted seven bills on matters such as the prohibition of alcoholic beverages and the banning of usury (*riba*) and gambling. Other draft bills were concerned with the implementation of the *hudud* – penalties prescribed in the shari'a for murder, theft, adultery and the like. But most important was the draft bill on the sources of judicial decisions (*usul al-ahkam al-qadiyya*), since it provided for the application of the Shari'a in all matters not covered in other legislation. But Numayri was in no hurry to implement these new bills, and in the first five years of the committee's work, only the bill regulating the payment of *zakat* was approved, probably because it was less controversial.[30]

Only in July 1983 was the 'Islamic path' (*al-nahj al-islami*) endorsed by the SSU's national congress. Following its approval actual legislation started in earnest in July–August 1983, when Numayri appointed a new committee, consisting of three lawyers, which was entrusted with the task of converting Sudan's legal system into an Islamic one.[31] The acts drafted by this

[28] Duran, *Centrifugal Forces*, 572–600; for details, see 577. Shaykh 'Abd al-Qadir Abu Qurun was arrested following the removal of Numayri, in Apr. 1985.
[29] Shamuq, *Shakhsiyyat*, 320; see also Khalid, *Nimeiri*, 277. Mansour Khalid dismissed 'Awad al-Jid and Nayal Abu Qurun as 'legal upstarts'. For his assessment of Numayri's Islamic path, see *ibid.*, 254–71.
[30] Na'im, *Apostasy*, 197–224; also Warburg, *Shari'a*, 90–107.
[31] Al-Turabi was at that time Attorney-General and not a member of this committee.

committee, largely based on the drafts of al-Turabi's committee, were enacted into 'Provisional Republican Orders' and confirmed by the People's Assembly in its November 1983 session during two brief sittings without any debate. The most significant of these was the Sources of Judicial Decisions Act, mentioned above, which paved the way for the implementation of the shari'a. In addition, a full new Penal Code, a Code of Criminal Procedure, the Civil Procedures Act and the Civil Transactions Act were enacted to facilitate the 'just and fast execution' of the *hudud*. Numayri described the process by which these 'foundations of the Islamic state' were laid down in his speech to the International Islamic Conference in Khartoum, on 22 September 1984. In justifying the new measures Numayri also alluded to practical reasons. The crime-rate in Sudan was singled out as an example. In the year before the implementation of the *hudud* nearly 12,500 murders or attempted murders were committed, while the number of thefts had risen to nearly 130,000. According to Numayri, following the implementation of *hudud*, the crime-rate dropped by over 40 per cent in one year. He claimed that the deterrent effect of the *hudud* had been proved beyond reasonable doubt and it was more than likely that Sudan would soon be free of crime. The essence of the implementation of the shari'a was, according to Numayri, the creation of a righteous individual who would ultimately lead to a just society as prescribed by Islam.[32] Numayri's claim was disputed by al-Sadiq al-Mahdi, who opposed implementing the *hudud* in an unjust society, whereas al-Turabi supported it claiming that it was part of an educational process.

Moving to the economic sphere, Numayri proudly ascribed Sudan's success to the implementation of the Zakat and Taxation Act. The *zakat* had, according to Numayri, become the 'heart of Sudan's economy', since it was one of the pillars of Islam, enabling the poor to receive their rightful share of the national income. As for non-Muslims, a similar tax was imposed on them. According to this act, taxes on individual income would in no case exceed 2.5 per cent, while tax on capital gains would not exceed 10 per cent. As a result of these benevolent taxes, Sudan, according to Numayri, had been able to attract massive investments both from foreign markets and from local private entrepreneurs. Finally, Numayri devoted part of his speech to the Southern conflict – which, he stated, was, an imperialist plot. It was not a matter of religious rivalry, since the number of Muslims in the south exceeded that of Christians, while the majority of the population were neither Muslims nor Christians but adhered to their own indigenous religions. The shari'a had, according to Numayri, no implications for the south, where everybody could freely practise his religion without interference.[33]

Al-Nayil Abu Qurun and 'Awad al-Jid, the two judicial assistants mentioned above, were instrumental in drafting these laws; see Khalid, *Nimeiri*, 277–9.

[32] Quoted from 'Am 'ala tatbiq al-shari'a; also Warburg, *Shari'a*, 94–5.

[33] '*Am 'ala tatbiq al-shari'a*, 17–32; in Numayri, *Al-nahj*. He also dealt with these issues;

In one of his last interviews as President Numayri claimed that as the *imam* to whom total obedience was dictated by Islam, he alone could interpret laws and decide whether they were compatible with the shari'a. In assuming the title of *imam,* uncommon in Sunni Islam, he seemed to have been tempted by the all-embracing powers of the *shi'i imam* prevailing in Iran since the Islamic revolution in 1979. But this idea of leadership, embraced by Numayri, can also be traced to Mahdist ideology.[34] First, Numayri's 'appointment' as *imam* by Shaykh 'Abd al-Qadir Abu Qurun was probably an attempt to follow in the Mahdi's footsteps and thereby enhance his following among the Mahdi's supporters. Secondly, al-Sadiq al-Mahdi had stated on several occasions that Mahdism – in both the nineteenth and twentieth centuries – had acted as a bridge between the *shi'a* and the *sunna.* He thereby inadvertently helped Numayri to legitimize his claim to an all-embracing *shi'i* concept of leadership.[35]

Under these circumstances it is hardly surprising that Numayri was not greatly concerned by the fact that certain elements within the Islamic legislation were inconsistent with the 1973 Constitution. Though he attempted in June 1984 to have his constitutional amendments endorsed by *majlis al-sha'ab,* he withdrew his request once he realized that it did not enjoy the required two-thirds majority within Parliament. Since Numayri had declared a state of emergency already in April that year, it enabled him to act without parliamentary approval and do away with all the freedoms and rights guaranteed by the 1973 Constitution.[36] Discrepancies between the constitution and the Islamic laws could be overcome by the special powers granted to the President under the State of Emergency Regulations. These special powers enabled Numayri to amend 123 out of a total of 225 articles in the constitution. One of the articles involved was article 8, which granted southern Sudan constitutional status. Another involved article 16, in which Numayri proposed replacing the reference to 'Christianity and noble aspects of spiritual beliefs . . . by an unequivocal reference to "religious freedoms".' Other amendments involved the articles dealing with the President's titles, powers and duties. In addition to becoming the *imam* and head of state, for life, to whom all citizens had to give an oath of allegiance (*bay'a*), he also assumed the title of *qa'id al-mu'minin* (Commander of the Faithful).

---

see Khalid, *Nimeiri,* 270–6. Numayri failed to mention that about 2 million non-Muslim Sudanese were living in northern Sudan and were thus affected by these laws; on this, see Warburg, *Shari'a,* 99–101.

[34] Shuqayr, *Ta'rikh,* 642–3. There is a similarity to the manifestation of Muhammad Ahmad as Mahdi in June 1881. Shaykh al-Qurashi wad al-Zayn, one of the spiritual leaders of the Sammaniyya order, to which Muhammad Ahmad belonged, allegedly appointed him as his successor and told his followers that the expected *mahdi* would be one of his adherents, namely, Muhammad Ahmad b. 'Abdallah.

[35] Zein, *Religion and State,* 73–5. For al-Sadiq's views see interview in *The Middle East,* 64 (Feb. 1980): 40.

[36] Na'im, *Islamic Constitution,* 202.

Finally, *majlis al-sha'ab* was to become *majlis al-shura* (Consultative Council), whose selected members were to swear total loyalty to the President.[37]

The achievements of the newly implemented laws as claimed by Numayri are questionable. It is hardly possible to examine the truth regarding Numayri's claim about the decline in the number of crimes committed in Sudan in 1984. The statistics presented by him seem irrelevant for several reasons. First, an argument based on the crimes committed during one year can hardly be regarded as conclusive. Secondly, there seems to be no independent statistical evidence to corroborate Numayri's claim. The conditions prevailing in Sudan at the time in which the *hudud* were implemented were a state of emergency which did away with all civil rights, including freedom of expression. The President and his assistants therefore enjoyed unchallengeable powers in all spheres. Under these conditions the statistical proof regarding the decline in crimes cannot be accepted as conclusive. Thirdly, we should bear in mind that the Islamic laws were executed arbitrarily by specially constituted 'Prompt Courts'. According to independent reports certain social habits, such as the drinking of alcoholic beverages or the relations between the sexes, were certainly affected. But the same sources claim that the implementation of *hudud* did not bring about 'a significant decrease in crime nor improved ethical standards. On the contrary, due to the rampant economic and social hardships and the release of seasoned criminals . . . armed robbery became more widespread than ever before.'[38] This increase in the number of thefts and armed robberies, despite the severe punishments specified in the new Islamic laws, seems to suggest that President Numayri's claims in this regard are questionable. Furthermore, the Islamic laws executed in Sudan were regarded as illegal and un-Islamic by some Muslim leaders and scholars, though most of them were reluctant to declare their views in public. On the other hand, Numayri had the active support of most of the Muslim Brothers' leadership as well as that of his *sufi* mentors and other shaykhs incorporated within the Islamic Revival Committee. He also enjoyed the support of most of the leaders of the more militant Muslim groups.

In the economic sphere Numayri's claims are easier to refute since the attempt to enforce an Islamic economy was a total failure with disastrous and well-documented repercussions. In 1983 Sudan was beginning to recover economically as a result of massive foreign aid and careful economic planning. The Islamic economy interrupted this process and brought it to a halt. The Civil Transactions Act of February 1984 abolished limited liability and interest charges on all transactions not involving foreign interests. Confidence in the already shaky economy was thereby undermined even further. Even more disastrous was the Zakat and Taxation Act of

[37] Sidahmed, *Politics & Islam*, 136–7.
[38] *Ibid.*, 139.

March 1984, whereby revenue from previous taxation was virtually stopped, while the new act proposed by Abu Bakr, a close associate of Numayri, was so obscure that it could not be fully executed. The only revenue collected was the flat rate of 2.5 per cent on personal incomes exceeding 200 Sudanese pounds (at that time US$154) per month. *Zakat* on agricultural production and livestock was not even implemented because of the act's obscurity. A further loss in government revenue, of several hundred million dollars annually, was the result of the ban on alcoholic beverages. The final blow to the ailing economy was dealt by the Islamization of the banking system, in December 1984, which was undertaken despite repeated warnings from some of Numayri's closest financial advisers. The Islamic bank was run primarily by the Muslim Brothers and was of great benefit to the future NIF, but not to the population at large. The constant rise in the cost of living and a devalued currency, accompanied by rapid inflation and related hardships, proved that Numayri's claims regarding success were a far cry from reality. On the eve of Numayri being deposed Sudan was on the brink of bankruptcy. By April 1985 its accumulated arrears to the International Monetary Fund alone amounted to US$130–50 million, while its national debt stood at about $13 billion. The severe economic crisis, which was the final blow to Numayri's regime, was at least partly brought about by the new Islamic economic policy.[39]

Numayri and his colleagues, in the sixteen years that they were in power, had brought Sudan full circle back to its sectarian starting-point. When the Sudanese Free Officers came to power in May 1969, there were very few issues on which they were in full agreement. One of these was their conviction that sectarian politics had to be brought to an end. This led to the massacre of the Ansar on Aba Island in March 1970, and the subsequent confiscation of Mahdist property in the months that followed. The Ansar were the largest sect in Sudan, and Numayri and his colleagues believed that they had to be destroyed both politically and economically if the new regime wanted to endure. Although lands belonging to the Khatmiyya were also appropriated in July 1970, the latter were treated less harshly than the Ansar, for the simple reason that they were not as affluent and, even more important, they presented no political threat. According to Numayri, this so-called secular, radical phase came to an end already following the abortive Communist coup of July 1971. Although Numayri was neither a Communist nor an Arab nationalist he had exploited their support in the early stages of his regime. Following his return to power after the abortive coup, he performed the *hajj* to Mecca and in Jedda met leaders of the Sudanese Muslim Brothers who had escaped from Sudan. While in the Saudi capital Numayri also had long discussions with King Faysal about the new Islamic

[39] *African Economic Development*, 21 Dec. 1984, estimates that the loss in revenue resulting from the ban on alcohol ran as high as $300 million; see also Sidahmed, *Politics & Islam*, 238, en. 1.

phase which he now envisaged, probably hoping that this would lead to massive financial help. Although there was no immediate follow-up with regard to the return of the Muslim Brothers to active politics, these meetings paved the way for the new constitution of May 1973. According to one report Numayri had promised King Faysal that this constitution would turn Sudan into an Islamic state, but he was opposed by some of his closest advisers, who objected to his proposed pact with the Muslim Brothers. The amended version of the constitution, which was finally approved, did not satisfy the Saudis, and bankrupt Sudan had to manage without the aid that had previously been promised by King Faysal. The ideological gap between Ja'far Numayri, the secular military leader of the May Revolution and the *imam* Muhammad Ja'far Numayri, implementing the shari'a laws in September 1983, seemed remarkable.[40] Mansur Khalid who was an associate of Numayri in the early years and played a leading role in forging the Addis Ababa Agreement in February 1972, became one of his harshest opponents following the adoption of the Islamic path. He defined Numayri's ideology as 'a hotchpotch of Islam, superstition and witchcraft'. According to Khalid,

All Nimeiri's public utterances on Islam oscillate on the irrational and the superstitious, albeit always interspersed with verses from the Qur'an, misread, misunderstood and misconstrued . . . Nimeiri's ignorance of Islam is matched only by his ignorance of economic management.[41]

The trial and execution of Mahmud Muhammad Taha[42]

On 18 January 1985 Mahmud Muhammad Taha, founder and leader of the Republican Brothers, was publicly hanged in Khartoum in the presence of some 3000 onlookers shouting: 'Death to the enemy of God'. The trial and subsequent execution of this highly respected person, aged seventy-six, was probably the most controversial act undertaken in accordance with the September 1983 laws. Who was Mahmud Muhammad Taha and why was he executed?[43] Taha first appeared on Sudan's political scene in 1945, when he and several of his colleagues founded the Republican Party. A civil

---

[40] The account of Numayri's Islamic shift following the July 1971 coup is told by Ghandur, *Qissat al-Jaysh*. Muzamil Salman Ghandur, was a close associate of Numayri during that period.

[41] Khalid, *Nimeiri*, 259–61.

[42] The following, unless otherwise stated, is based on Rogalski, *Republikanischen Brüder*; Stevens, *Republican Brothers*; Mangarella, *Republican Brothers*. See also Haydar, *Mahmud Muhammad Taha*: the book consists of six studies, five by Sudanese scholars and one by Rogalski, examining Taha's ideology and deeds.

[43] Taha was born in Rufa'a on the Blue Nile in 1909, to an old and well-established *sufi* family. He graduated from Gordon College's School of Engineering in 1936, one of its first graduates, and was employed on the Sudan Railways. Following his founding of the Republican Party in 1945, he resigned from his post; see Haydar, *Mahmud Muhammad Taha*, 10–11.

engineer employed by the Anglo-Egyptian administration, Taha and his colleagues were opposed both to the sectarian-dominated parties, headed by the Ansar and the Khatmiyya, and to the more secular pro-Egyptian Sudanese Graduates led by Isma'il al-Azhari. They advocated a fully independent Sudanese republic, free from both British and Egyptian tutelage and guided by the teachings of Islam. Though politically rather insignificant, the Republicans were from the outset intellectually visible primarily due to their leader. Twice the British authorities arrested Taha in the late 1940s because of his outright opposition to their interference in what he viewed as internal Sudanese affairs. On his release from prison on 30 November 1951 Taha resumed his fight for an Islamic, non-sectarian, independent republic. The Republicans did not view themselves as a political party but rather as an Islamic *da'wa* movement. They did not participate in elections or in other party-political activities. Yet they expressed their views on all internal or external political matters of public interest, though the level of their influence was rather narrow except in limited intellectual circles.[44] The Republicans supported an independent nation-state in Sudan, embracing the Condominium borders. They advocated a presidential federal socialist republic with freedom of religion and equality before the law for all inhabitants. Taha opposed the implementation of shari'a claiming that the Islamic principles of state would be preserved through adherence to individual freedom and justice for all.

During the 'Abbud years, when party politics were outlawed, the Republicans met in private homes for discussions and their prime activity was at the university. Here the Communists and the Muslim Brothers were competing for student support, with the latter advocating an Islamic state with the shari'a as its law. The Republicans succeeded in gaining student support for their humane non-legalistic view of Islam and statehood. Despite their anti-communist views they supported the leftist-dominated transitional government after the October 1964 civilian revolution, hoping that it would overcome sectarianism. However, it was a short-lived episode and the sectarian parties were back in power by 1965. As has been noted, one part of the Umma party, led by al-Sadiq al-Mahdi, advocated an Islamic state based on shari'a and collaborated with al-Turabi's ICF. The Republicans therefore found themselves compelled to attack the Umma both because of their opposition to sectarianism and because ideologically they opposed the discriminatory aspects of an Islamic state, especially in so far as women and non-Muslim minorities were concerned.

It was therefore not surprising that Taha published his major works on this topic in 1966–7, attacking the political–legalistic Islam that al-Sadiq and al-Turabi were attempting to enforce in Sudan. First he wrote *Tariq Muhammad* (Muhammad's Path), in 1966, to be followed by his most important

[44] *Ibid.*, 12–13.

book, *Al-risala al-thaniya min al-Islam* (The second message of Islam), in 1967. A year later Taha was accused of apostasy and found guilty by the supreme shari'a court in Khartoum. He was sentenced *in absentia*, since he refused to acknowledge the court's right to decide on matters of personal belief. The sentence remained on paper because the shari'a courts at that time were limited to jurisdiction on matters of personal status. The court consisted of two judges, propagating ideas similar to those of the Muslim Brothers. One of the two, Husayn Muhammad Zaki, continued to demand Taha's execution for apostasy, following Numayri's assumption of power in May 1969. His reason was that Taha persisted in spreading his anti-Islamic message and thus had to be stopped.[45] However, after the May 1969 military coup, when all political parties were outlawed, the Republican Brothers were in a somewhat easier position than others since they were not a political party but rather an ex-parliamentary pressure group. Moreover, the Republicans viewed Numayri's early years with approval and were among his closest allies. He fought against sectarianism, eliminated Communism and promulgated a relatively liberal constitution, based on religious, ethnic and cultural diversity. Furthermore, the Republicans regarded the 1972 Addis Ababa Agreement as a vindication of the federal solution for southern Sudan, which they had propagated since 1951. In his study of *Politics and Islam*, Sidahmed, pays attention to the curious alliance between Numayri, the 'born-again' *sufi* with a superficial understanding of Islam, and the Republican Brothers. The latter supported him in return for his allowing them to preach freely their 'scholastic neo-Islamic views', which enabled them, for the first time since the 1950s, to reach wider circles of the intelligentsia, at the expense of the Muslim Brothers and the Communists.

Taha offered a formulation of a socio-political blueprint for a neo-Islamist alternative based on his interpretation of Islam as consisting of two kinds of messages: a universal message, which is embodied in the Meccan Quranic texts, and a limited message for the circumstances of the 7th century.[46]

The alliance between Numayri and Taha came to an end in 1977 as a result of Numayri's Islamic policy and his reconciliation with the Muslim Brothers and the Ansar, both of whom regarded Taha's views as heresy. The Republicans, along with various secular groups, regarded the new trend as endangering Sudan's unity. However, they avoided an open clash with the regime and preferred instead to attack the Muslim Brothers and their leader, Hasan al-Turabi, whom they regarded as being the power behind Numayri. In March–April 1983 Muhammad Najib al-Muti'i, an Egyptian Muslim preacher who had been involved in anti-Coptic agitation

---

[45] Rogalski, *Republikanischen Brüder*, 35–6; the above is largely based on Zaki, *Al-Qawl*; also Haydar, *Mahmud Muhammad Taha*, 19–20.

[46] Sidahmed, *Politics and Islam*, 122–4; quotation from 123 from Taha, *Second Message of Islam*.

at the al-Hamra Mosque near Cairo, was exiled from Egypt to Sudan where he was allowed to air his radical Islamic views on Sudanese television. He used this privilege in order to arouse his audience against the Christians in the South, whom he accused of oppressing Muslims. In his preaching at the Kobar Mosque in Khartoum and in his television broadcasts, he called for the immediate arrest of the heretical Republican Brothers.[47] The Republicans retaliated and called upon General 'Umar al-Tayyib, Numayri's first Vice-President and Chief of Security, to put an end to the fanatical hatred preached by Shaykh al-Muti'i. The result, as might have been expected, was the arrest of Taha and some fifty of his adherents in June 1983. They were kept in prison without being charged until December 1984. On their release from prison the Republicans published their denunciation of the shari'a laws, under the title: *'hadha...aw al-tufan'* (this . . . or the flood). They claimed that the Islamist laws, which had been enacted while they were in prison, violated shari'a, distorted Islam and jeopardized Sudan's unity and therefore should be repealed immediately. Islamic enlightenment should, in their view, come through the *sunna* and not the shari'a. They openly expressed their views in one of the leaflets they published upon their release from prison:

The September 1983 Laws have distorted Islam in the eyes of intelligent members of our people and in the eyes of the world . . . These laws violate the Shari'a and violate religion itself. They permit, for example, the amputation of the hand of one who steals public property, although according to Shari'a the appropriate penalty is the discretionary punishment [*ta'zir*] and not the specific [*hadd*] penalty for theft . . . Moreover, the enforcement of the specified penalties [*hudud* and *qisas*] presupposes a degree of individual education and social justice which are lacking today. These laws have jeopardized the unity of the country and divided the people in the north and south by provoking religious sensitivity, which is one of the fundamental factors that has aggravated the southern problem. It is futile for anyone to claim that a Christian person is not adversely affected by the implementation of the Shari'a.[48]

Following his open denunciation of the 1983 Islamic laws Taha was rearrested, together with four of his colleagues and sentenced to death for apostasy *(ridda)*. They were accused of stating that women had equal rights with men in the Islamic law of inheritance. They were also charged with renouncing the Muslim duties of *jihad* and the daily prayers. Another charge was that Taha had rejected the dictates of the *'ulama'* and the *fuqaha'* and declared them unbinding. According to Judge al-Mikashfi

---

[47] *Neue Züricher Zeitung*, 21 Oct. 1983, quoted in Duran, *Islam*, 75.
[48] The translation is quoted from Taha, *Second Message*, 10–11; also Rogalski, *Republikanischen Brüder*, 44–5; for a detailed examination of this issue see Na'im, *Apostasy*. 'Abdullahi Ahmad An-Na'im is an internationally recognized scholar of Islamic law who taught at the Faculty of Law in Khartoum University until 1985. He is a member of the School of Law at Emory University in Atlanta.

Taha al-Kabbashi, who presided over the court, Taha asserted that he had bridged the gap between God and the Prophet and had thereby brought about the personification of God. Al-Kabbashi therefore claimed that in sentencing Taha to death he and his fellow-judges had fully abided by the jurisdiction of Sunni Islam.[49] According to some scholars this may be viewed also as part of the ongoing conflict between the jurist and the mystic within Islam, a conflict that has re-emerged with neo-Sufism. Ahmad Ibn Idris's rejection of political Islam and his insistence that every Muslim had the right to define Islam according to his own faith and to redefine the shari'a were articulated by Mahmud Taha and his followers and were among the factors that led to their being charged with apostasy.[50] In the context of Sudanese politics Taha's execution may be viewed as a pragmatic move to rid the regime of one of its most outspoken critics without endangering itself. The defenders of the Islamic laws were thereby warning other prospective antagonists with much greater political support, such as al-Sadiq al-Mahdi, that they too might suffer severe punishment should they continue to criticize the September laws. According to Mansur Khalid, Numayri deliberately chose Taha as an example to others with more popular support who also opposed him. But Khalid claimed: 'The tragedy is greater than the loss of one man. Taha's death symbolizes the end of hope for Nimeiry's May Revolution which only ten years ago was seen by the world to have peace, unity and development within its grasp.'[51]

On the Islamic international front Numayri received the blessing of the Islamic World League, based in Mecca, whose most prominent *faqih*, Shaykh Ibn al-Baz congratulated Numayri on ridding the Muslim world of Mahmud Muhammad Taha, an atheist and enemy of God. There were others, both in Egypt and Sudan, who rejoiced at Taha's execution and regarded it as a great victory for Islam against a dangerous heretic. In an article published in *al-Nur* on 6 February 1985, the paper's editor celebrated the fact that the four Republican Brothers who had been sentenced to death together with Mahmud Muhammad Taha had renounced their previous erroneous beliefs and returned to the fold as true believers.[52] Others reacted less favourably and accused Numayri of misusing the shari'a to commit murder. Following Taha's public execution on 18 January 1985, his body was hurriedly, removed by the security forces, probably in order to avoid his funeral turning into a mass demonstration against Numayri and his regime.[53] Some sources claim that it was Taha's execution that convinced President Mubarak of Egypt that Numayri no longer warranted

[49] Kabbashi, *Tatbiq al-Shari'a*, 80–96.

[50] For instance Rogalski, *Republikanischen Brüder*, 46–7.

[51] See Mansur Khalid's letter to *The Times* (London), 9 Feb. 1985; also *al-Watan al-'Arabi*, 13 Apr. 1985.

[52] According to Sudanese sources this was the result of a deal made by Judge al-Mikashfi Taha al-Kabbashi with the Republican Brothers.

[53] This is somewhat reminiscent of Kitchener's act, after the battle of Omdurman in 1898,

Egypt's support. President Mubarak, as well as other prominent leaders, had explicitly asked Numayri for clemency prior to Taha's execution, but his request like those of others, was ignored by Numayri.

The Shari'a laws and the South

President Numayri's Republican Order Number 1 of 5 June 1983 divided the South into three regions. In fact, it abrogated the Addis Ababa Agreement, in which it had been stipulated that a majority consisting of three-quarters of all members of the National Assembly was required in order to amend this agreement. Although the hostilities that broke out in the South following that act preceded the September 1983 Islamic laws by several months, the implementation of the shari'a caused further deterioration. Up till 1983 the Addis Ababa Agreement of 27 February 1972 had rightly been regarded as the most important achievement of Numayri's regime. It had put an end to seventeen years of internecine strife and had courageously granted recognition to the pluralistic nature of Sudanese society, which had hitherto been ignored. In awarding the South regional autonomy, the Muslim-dominated regime acknowledged that culture, race, religion and economics dictated a new approach to the internal structure of Sudan and to its constitution. This was in fact part of a plan to decentralize Sudan, especially in the sphere of economic development, which had been aired by Numayri since 1971. The size of Sudan, the immense differences between its regions and the concentration of economic and political power in the hands of a minority Northern élite had brought about demands for decentralization. Criticism of the preferential treatment granted to central Northern Sudan at the expense of so-called marginalized regions was repeatedly expressed. The latter included not only the South but also Dar Fur, Kordofan and especially the Nuba tribes in southern Kordofan and the Beja tribes of the Red Sea Hills in the east. Since independence this neglect had caused several attempts by ethnic groups in these outlying regions to gain at least partial autonomy.[54]

The Addis Ababa Agreement had provided for the equality of all citizens regardless of race, colour, or religion. It recognized southern cultural identity and hence proclaimed its right to legislate in accordance with its tribal customs. Free elections to the Southern Regional Assembly were decreed and the assembly was empowered to elect its own president. While, as Numayri later announced on more than one occasion, the Addis Ababa

---

when he whisked away the Mahdi's skull from his grave. The ostensible reason was to stop *qubbat al-mahdi*, which had been destroyed on purpose during the fighting, from becoming a centre for Mahdist pilgrims and renewed fanaticism. Taha was not, of course, as popular as the Mahdi, nor could he be accused of fanaticism. The similarity is limited to the fear of the ruler that the funeral or place of burial would become a centre of opposition to his regime.

[54] Rondinelli, *Administrative Decentralization*, 595–624; for details on Numayri's southern policy, see Khalid, *Nimeiri*, 41–62.

Agreement was neither a Qur'an nor a Bible and hence was admissible to amendments, the proviso stating that a majority consisting of three-quarters of all members of the National Assembly was required in order to amend this agreement seemed sufficient to reconcile even the most suspicious southern leaders. The unalterable foundation of this concept was expressed in the Permanent Constitution of the Sudan promulgated in May 1973. Articles 6 and 7 of that constitution specified the principles of decentralization and promised that the details of this new system of government would be issued in the near future. Article 8 established regional self-government in the South on a permanent basis, which could only be amended in accordance with the provisions of the Self-Government Act of 1972. No less significant was the provision that non-Muslims would be governed by their own personal laws. Moreover, unlike the constitutions of other Muslim states, Sudan's constitution did not declare Islam as the religion of the state. The pluralism of Sudanese society, including its multireligious composition, was dealt with in the constitution, as elaborated above. This was also emphasized in article 38 of the constitution, which stated that all Sudanese were equal in rights and duties 'irrespective of origin, race, locality, sex, language or religion'. Many southern politicians were none the less opposed to the constitution since it specified that 'Islamic Law and Custom shall be main sources of legislation' (Article 9) and that Arabic would be the 'official language' of Sudan.[55] Yet if we take into account both the realities prevailing in Sudan and the radicalization of Islam in surrounding countries, including Egypt, the 1973 Constitution could be viewed as a step towards liberalization and coexistence in a multiethnic society.

The end of the Addis Ababa Agreement was already in sight following Numayri's unconstitutional act of dissolving the Southern Regional Assembly and its government in February 1980. This was not purely arbitrary, since interethnic tensions in the South, especially between the Dinka and the Nuer, led to animosity and intertribal warfare as time went on.[56] Next came the Decentralization Act, which divided the South into three separate regions and the Regional Government Act of 1980, which divided the Sudan, excluding the South, into five regions.[57] This Act was also caused by unrest in the outlying regions, especially Dar Fur, and by Numayri's desire to shift certain responsibilities to regional governments. However, in the South it was interpreted as an outright assault on its newly discovered

---

[55] All quotations are from the English text of *The Permanent Constitution of the Sudan*, published by the Sudan government in Khartoum on 8 May 1973; for details, see above.

[56] Jok and Hutchinson, *Militarization of Nuer and Dinka Ethnic Identities*, 125–45. This tragedy was raised by the Comboni missionaries in an open declaration made in Jan. 2001, in which they denounced the intertribal and interethnic fighting in the South which had further intensified.

[57] The Regional Government Bill 1980 sought to establish five regional governments in Sudan, each with its own governor and minister; see Khalid, *Nimeiri*, 205–10.

wealth, since it coincided with the discovery of oil in the South, which the Southerners believed should be used for the benefit of its inhabitants.[58]

It is noteworthy that al-Turabi, then Sudan's Attorney-General, was the one who advised and helped President Numayri in all these actions. According to Bona Malwal, al-Turabi viewed the weakening of the South as an essential step towards applying the shari'a and hence supported its partition. Many southern leaders and intellectuals therefore viewed al-Turabi as their major antagonist during the last few years of Numayri's rule. If there were justice in Sudan, claimed Malwal, al-Turabi should not only have lost his post as Attorney-General, but should have been 'charged with plotting to overthrow the legally constituted government of the state' since he openly advocated an Islamic coup. Southern leaders had equal fears of a renewed Umma-Ansar government since the latter's record in the 1960s had convinced many of them that the traditional sectarian leadership was no better than its so-called modern Islamist followers. According to Malwal, al-Sadiq al-Mahdi had stated as early as 1966 that 'the failure of Islam in the southern Sudan would be the failure of Sudanese Muslims to the international Islamic cause. Islam has a holy mission in Africa and southern Sudan is the beginning of that mission'.[59]

The anti-Numayri coup in April 1985 did not alleviate matters with regard to the South since the transitional government that followed it refused to become involved in the conflict about the shari'a laws. The Muslim Brothers who founded the NIF following Numayri's removal, were the first to present their views with regard to the South. The NIF published its platform on the southern Sudan question in May 1985 at a conference attended by some 100 of its southern supporters.[60] All ills prevailing in the South were blamed by the NIF on the West and primarily on Britain, who ruled the region both under the Turks, in the nineteenth century, and during the Condominium. It was they who introduced the slave trade, which became the most significant trade in the South. Mahdist neglect was according to the NIF, responsible for opening the door for 'neo-colonialism where the Belgians invaded the region'. In other words the NIF did not recognize any

---

[58] Attached to the Regional Government Bill was a map in which, so it was claimed, the boundary between Kordofan and Bahr al-Ghazal had been shifted to the north so as to include the newly discovered oilfields in Kordofan; Alier, *Southern Sudan*, 215–24. It was only in Aug. 1999 that the export of crude oil, to the tune of 185,000 barrels, started: *Reuters*, 10 Jan. 2000.

[59] Malwal, *Second Challenge*, 30–7; *idem*, 'Has the Sudan eliminated Secularism'? *Africa*, 98 (Oct. 1979), quoted in Duran, *Islam*, 73–4; also Malwal, *People*, 41–2. Bona Malwal was at one time Minister of Culture and Information under Numayri, and resigned from the government in protest against the President's shift to Islamist policy. He currently lives in England where he publishes and edits the monthly *Sudan Democratic Gazette* (*SDG*); see also Alier, *Southern Sudan*, 235–7.

[60] The following, unless otherwise stated, is from the brochure, National Islamic Front, *Southern Sudan*, 1–34.

faults that should be blamed on Northern Sudanese or on other Muslims in their dealings with Southerners before 1956. It was British southern policy that isolated the South and made it feel ethnically and culturally distinctive. 'It instilled in their minds the idea that the northerners are slave-traders and aroused hatred and fued [*sic*] between them.' However, the NIF claimed that there were no objective reasons leading to hatred before independence. It admitted that there were shortcomings in Sudan's government policies since independence. General 'Abbud's Southern policy was singled out for severe criticism, whereas the Muslim Brothers were the most significant force in Sudan that consistently endeavoured to find a just solution. It was, according to the authors of this document, the Muslim Brothers' ideas that prevailed at the Round Table Conference in 1965 and provided the blueprint for future negotiations. The Addis Ababa Agreement of February 1972 is described as a 'provisional peace', since it failed to tackle Sudan's 'national dimensions'. The renewal of hostilities in 1983 is blamed by the NIF on a wide range of factors, from corruption to budgetary difficulties and culminating in internal ethnic strife among the Southern tribes. The discovery of crude oil in the South is not mentioned in this brochure while the redivision of the South into three regions is listed as one of the factors that helped John Garang to overcome southern opposition to his leadership of the rebellion. The NIF analysis described the religious composition of the South stating, that 65 per cent of its population, composed of 5,371,296 people, were 'non-religious', which implied that tribal religions and laws were not recognized by the NIF. Only 17 per cent of southern Christians, exceeded slightly by 18 per cent Muslims, were viewed by the NIF as religious. Stating that Arabic and Dinka were the most widely spoken languages in the South, English none the less maintained its predominant position in government institutions, as well as in schools and universities. This of course led to one of the main difficulties, namely lack of communication. As for the future, the NIF insisted that Southern Muslims, who had suffered for so long from discrimination, should at last be granted their rightful share of power in the South. Secondly, it advocated the continued Islamization of the South, which was now taking place under the guidance of the Islamic Association of the Southern Sudan. Lastly, the NIF asserted that 'a general system based on the Islamic Shari'a is a religious and political necessity to every Muslim'. Since the shari'a is closer than any other legal system to the African cultural heritage and since it 'protects the entity and the culture of the non-Muslims', it should be maintained as the law of Sudan, which through its flexibility will guarantee the compromises required by non-Muslims. In addition al-Turabi quoted the precedent set by the Prophet during his migration to Medina as a possible solution for minorities such as the pagans of southern Sudan. '*Ahd al-umma* (pact of the Umma) enabled Muslims from Mecca, converts to Islam in Medina, non-Muslim Jews and others to lead their autonomous tribal-religious lives under the supremacy of the Prophet, with the latter acting as arbitrator, judge and leader in domestic, foreign and military affairs. Because of the size of the non-Muslim minority in Sudan and the fact that only a reasonable compromise can maintain unity within an Islamic state, al-Turabi suggested the Medina model of *'ahd al-umma* as a possible solution.[61]

These views were upheld by al-Turabi and his colleagues throughout Sudan's third democratic interlude, when they consistently opposed any meaningful change in Sudan's Islamic laws and in their implementation. Al-Turabi insisted that one of the reasons for the NIF's success in the 1986 elections was the massive support it received from Southern Muslims. He therefore dismissed the outcry against the shari'a laws emanating from the West, whose only aim was to separate Sudan from its Arab and Muslim brothers. He also asserted that John Garang's demand for the abolition of these laws had nothing to do with religion and was based on pure Marxist principles.[62] In the *Sudan Charter*, which was adopted and published in 1987 by the NIF, the principles guiding its southern policy were listed explicitly. It guaranteed the rights of all religious minorities, including African religions, to adhere to the laws and customs of their religion and to propagate them freely. In the 'Sphere of Law', the charter stated that 'Islamic jurisprudence shall be the general source of law: [since] it is the expression of the will of the democratic majority.' However, the charter 'recognizes the principles of religious freedom and equality . . . and allows for partial legal multiplicity in regard to religious affiliation of persons or to the predominance of non-Muslims in any particular area'.[63] In the sphere of education, the charter stated: 'Every parent is entitled to bring up his issue in the religious manner of his liking.' In order to determine Sudan's future constitution and government, a Constitutional Conference, open to all national political forces will prepare 'a national concord and the program for its implementation . . . The resolutions of the conference shall be adopted by unanimity, while recommendations may be adopted by majority.'[64]

---

[61] Furman, *Minorities*, 14–15.

[62] The above is also based on Hasan al-Turabi's interviews in: *al-Musawwar*, 1 July 1987; *Awraq 'Arabiyya*, 7 (1988): 62–76. The claim that Muslim tolerance is the best guarantee for minority rights was also used by other Islamist leaders, notably in Malaysia, to mollify non-Muslim minorities.

[63] National Islamic Front, *Sudan Charter*, 3.

[64] *Ibid.*, 10–11.

14

THE ANSAR–UMMA IN
POLITICS, 1956–86

The leadership of the twentieth century neo-Mahdist movement clearly demonstrates that, not unlike the leadership of a *sufi* order, it passed exclusively within one family, that of the nineteenth-century Mahdi. His son, Sayyid 'Abd al-Rahman al-Mahdi, became the *imam* of the Ansar in 1914 and from 1945 he was also the spiritual head of the newly-founded Umma party. This was not solely based on the fact that he was the Mahdi's son, it was also the result of his diplomacy, and of his control of the Mahdist *daira* (domain). He thus succeeded in controlling the movement and led it both religiously and politically. Furthermore, as noted above, he helped to oust Sayyid al-Fadil al-Mahdi from his position as the number two man in the Ansar, in order to make room for his own son, al-Siddiq al-Mahdi. Al-Sadiq al-Mahdi claimed that the only reason why his grandfather, Sayyid 'Abd al-Rahman al-Mahdi, assumed the imamate was that the three *khulafa'* of the Mahdi had perished in battles with the Anglo-Egyptian forces and hence the mantle of leadership reverted to the Mahdi's only surviving son.[65] Al-Sadiq argued that Sayyid 'Abd al-Rahman did not embrace the *shi'i* concept of the hidden *imam* or accept its insistence that the imamate had to be inherited within the Hashemite–Fatimid families. On the other hand, al-Sadiq admitted that the Mahdist *da'wa* incorporated moderate aspects of *shi'i* heritage.[66]

The centrality of the *imam*'s role within the Ansar was discussed at some length in a report written by a British diplomat in Khartoum in 1958. Following a brief historical survey of the Mahdiyya, elaborating the differences between it and *sufi* orders such as the Khatmiyya, he stated:

Their distinctive quality is not doctrinal but personal loyalty (which usually nowadays arises from family or tribal allegiance) to the Mahdi. Sayed Abdel Rahman el Mahdi is the Imam and the heir apparent is his son Sayed Siddiq el Mahdi . . . There are, however, other forces at work. Many of the Ansar regard Sayed Siddiq as too

---

[65] Sadiq, *Mustaqbal*, in Muddathir & al-Tayyib, *Islam*, 379. Al-Sadiq emphasized the difference between the Ansar and the *sufi* orders, wherein leadership and *baraka* were passed on within the founder's family.

[66] Sadiq, *Yas'alunaka*, 235. This may be of significance in examining Numayri's claims to the imamate and the text of his *bay'a*; according to Abu Salim, *Haraka*, 79, the concept of the Sudanese Mahdiyya was *sunni*, with strong *sufi* undertones but without any *shi'i* elements.

worldly to assume the religious mantle. The more fanatical prefer Sayed Hadi, his brother, who though educated at Gordon College has never adopted Western habits. The religious aspect of the Mahdiya is nationalistic, and therefore, in a sense, anti-Western, anti-foreign, even anti-Egyptian and anti-Arab.[67]

It is hard to determine whether this observation was accurate or not. However, following Sayyid 'Abd al-Rahman's death in 1959, his son, al-Sayyid al-Siddiq al-Mahdi, became the *imam* of the Ansar, a post he held for two crucial years, during which he led the opposition against Sudan's first military regime under General Ibrahim 'Abbud. One of the peaks of this struggle was an armed clash between the Ansar and the army during the mass celebrations of the Prophet's Birthday (*mawlid al-nabi*) in 1961. But following this incident, in which several lives were lost, al-Siddiq al-Mahdi vehemently opposed the suggestion made by Isma'il al-Azhari that the Ansar should launch an armed attack against the 'Abbud regime and assassinate its military leadership. This was based on Sayyid Siddiq's fear that once he ordered the Ansar to use violence against the present rulers of Sudan, it might have been impossible to stop them from assuming power and thereby harming the future prospects of democracy in Sudan.[68] Whereas we have evidence as to Sayyid Siddiq's political leadership qualities, we have none with regard to his functions as the *imam* of the Ansar.

After al-Siddiq's death in 1961 the first crack seemed to occur within the Mahdi's family. In line with the decision of the Ansar's *shura* council, Sayyid al-Hadi al-Mahdi, al-Siddiq's brother, became the *imam* of the Ansar, whereas al-Siddiq's Oxford-educated son al-Sadiq al-Mahdi became the leader of the Umma party. As long as the military were in power, this functional division seemed to work. Al-Sadiq devoted his efforts to the reform and modernization of the Umma party, while *al-imam* al-Hadi created his power base within the Ansar. They disagreed, however, with regard to the Ansar–Umma relations with the military. Al-Hadi suggested collaboration and a low profile, while al-Sadiq proposed outright opposition. Matters changed following the 1964 civilian coup and the return to democratic government. When the general elections were held in 1965, al-Sadiq was not yet thirty years old, the statutory age required for being elected to Parliament, and thus could not assume the role of Prime-Minister as he would have liked. But, a year later, having reached the required age, al-Sadiq outmanoeuvred al-Hadi and the then prime minister, Muhammad Ahmad Mahjub (Mahgoub), and with the help of the NUP he became prime minister in July 1966, thus splitting the Ansar and the Umma into two factions.

---

[67] Enclosure in Khartoum letter (1011), 25 Jan. 1958, FO 371/31707. The rift between the more conservative al-Hadi and his more westernized nephew erupted in 1966, as will be noted.

[68] Mukhtar, *Kharif*, 30–3, 164–5. There may be an additional explanation based on al-Siddiq's pragmatism and his realization that the Ansar might be decimated in further violent clashes.

Less than one year later, *al-imam* al-Hadi and Mahgoub ousted al-Sadiq from office with the help of the NUP. When the split was finally healed, in April 1969, following an agreement between the two factions, Mahgoub the Umma leader and ex-Prime Minister, commented that the Mahdi's family 'seemed to consider the rule of the state a booty to be inherited and divided between them to the exclusion of other members of the [Umma] party who did not belong to the Mahdi family'.[69]

Many observers of the Mahdiyya, both Sudanese and European, commented on the centrality of the *imam* of the Ansar. The following comment by a British official may be relevant:

> As for personal loyalty, the three Imams so far, the Grand Mahdi Sayed Mohamed Ahmed el Mahdi (died 1886 [*sic*]), Khalifa Abdullahi ('the Khalifa', killed 1899) and Sayed Abdel Rahman el Mahdi (the posthumous son of the Grand Mahdi) have all been men of tremendous strength of will, personality, and presence, who have known how to exact obedience. A weak Imam, or worse still, a divided succession, could mean the end of the mahdiyya. The man, and not the dogma maintains and rules it.[70]

It is true that the divided loyalty of the Ansar during the years 1965–9 weakened the Umma party considerably, but it caused no irreversible damage. Attempts made by al-Sadiq both then and later to broaden the party's power base by adding supporters from trade unions and other professional associations had only marginal results. None the less, the long-term effects of the split within the Ansar–Umma bloc seem to have been minimal judging by their political success after Numayri.

Under President Numayri the Mahdist family was once again split. Following the May 1969 coup al-Hadi al-Mahdi retreated to Aba Island, the spiritual center of the Ansar, with many of his close supporters. Numayri was well aware that the Ansar were a major threat to his regime and he therefore attempted to annihilate their political power base by ordering the bombardment of their center on Aba Island in March 1970. *Imam* al-Hadi al-Mahdi was killed with several of his followers when he tried escape across the border to Ethiopia in March 1970. Most of the other Mahdist leaders either were by then under arrest or stood aside following the massacre. Al-Sadiq al-Mahdi went into exile following his release from prison and led the National Front (NF) opposing Numayri together with al-Sharif Yusuf al-Hindi, one of the Awlad Hindi a leading *sufi* family. Al-Sadiq remained in

---

[69] Mahgoub, *Democracy*, 224. This is reminiscent of the power struggle between the *ashraf* and the Khalifa 'Abdullahi, when the Mahdi accused his kinsmen of exploiting their family ties. It is interesting to note that the Khalifa 'Abdullahi's sons were not even involved in this neo-Mahdist power struggle and that one of his sons, 'Umar al-Khalifa, was an active member of the Khatmiyya, the Ansar's main rival. It is also significant that the NIF promoted the Khalifa's family, during the 1990s, helping them refurbish their mosque, probably in order to undermine the prestige of al-Sadiq and the Ansar. Mahgoub was of course not a member of the Ansar and had joined the Umma for political rather than religious reasons.

[70] Enclosure to Khartoum letter (1011) 25 Jan. 1958, FO 371/31707.

exile, attempting several anti-Numayri coups, until he signed the National Reconciliation agreement with President Numayri in July 1977. Some members of the Mahdist family joined him in exile while others remained in Sudan and at times collaborated with the military regime and challenged al-Sadiq's leadership. Numayri was of course aware of the internal jealousy and animosities within the Mahdi's family and was probably not averse to exploiting them to his own advantage. Since the Ansar did not elect an *imam* following al-Hadi al-Mahdi's assassination, the office of the next *imam* of the Ansar remained in abeyance. Moreover, Numayri argued that in Mahdist ideology the imamate was open to all believers and should not be inherited. Hence his claim to become *imam*, following his shift to an Islamist regime in 1983, was legitimate even according to the Sudanese concept of Mahdism as defined by al-Sadiq. Once the *imama* was bestowed on him, Numayri had hoped to exploit Mahdist popularity while eliminating its leadership.[71]

How did al-Sadiq al-Mahdi, who was both a Muslim scholar and leader of Sudan's largest Islamist party, react to Numayri's Islamic path? Following al-Hadi al-Mahdi's death, in 1970, al-Sadiq al-Mahdi fulfilled the dual role of acting *imam* of the Ansar and leader of the Umma party and spent the next seven years in exile. Many Sudanese and foreign observers claimed that following the March 1970 bombardment of Aba and the subsequent assassination of *al-imam* al-Hadi al-Mahdi, the Ansar's political power base had been destroyed. However, al-Sadiq and his followers succeeded in re-building their movement, both in Sudan and in the refugee camps in Ethiopia and Libya. From there the NF launched its most daring revolt against Numayri, in July 1976. Numayri's survival was at least in part responsible for the National Reconciliation, which started exactly one year later. Both he and al-Sadiq probably realized that they could not defeat each other militarily and hence decided to join forces. Each of the antagonists believed that he could outmanoeuvre his foe politically. Indeed, al-Sadiq probably thought that it was possible to decide the matter at the ballot box. However, two years later it became quite clear that, as far as the Ansar were concerned, reconciliation had not produced the expected results. The gap between them and the regime became wider and, when Numayri announced his Islamic path in September 1983, al-Sadiq did not hesitate and denounced his policy as un-Islamic. What did the Ansar achieve as a result of reconciliation? First, according to al-Sadiq, they mended their fences with the Sudanese army which since the July 1976 uprising had been made to believe that the Ansar were its enemies. Secondly, between 1970 and 1977 the Ansar had been in disarray in Sudan, since most of their surviving

[71] Details in Zein, *Religion and State*, 196–7. Numayri was told by his *sufi* mentor, Shaykh Abu Qurun, that the 'second coming' of the *mahdi* would be from amongst his followers. This is reminiscent of the assertion made by the Sammaniyya adherents of al-Qurashi wad al-Zayn, following his death in July 1878, that the expected *mahdi* would be one of them, namely Muhammad Ahmad b. 'Abdallah, the future Mahdi.

leaders and active cadres were in exile. Having returned to Sudan, al-Sadiq was able to devote his time to rebuilding the movement and overcoming the internal rift, which had prevailed since he went into exile in 1970. He claimed that as a result of his return to the Sudan after reconciliation, the Ansar were more united and stronger than at any time in recent history.

Al-Sadiq openly criticized Numayri's policies from the time of his return. This criticism was practically all-embracing and included his rejection of Numayri's economic and internal policies as well as his opposition to the latter's support for President Sadat's peace initiative with Israel and his acceptance of the Camp David Accords. Al-Sadiq's rejection of Numayri's concept of an Islamic state, which was probably not foreseen by Numayri, was of even greater significance. As a great-grandson of the Sudanese Mahdi and the leader of the most popular Islamic movement in Sudan, one might have expected al-Sadiq al-Mahdi to advocate a rigid and uncompromising brand of Islam. However, in defining his concept of an Islamic state he first of all rejected *taqlid*, the uncritical acceptance of Islamic codified doctrines, which he thought had served a useful purpose historically but was now outdated and hence a source of rigidity within Muslim society. According to al-Sadiq, the basis of Islam was accommodation with change rather than its denial; he therefore propagated social change within the Islamic state even at the expense of introducing far-reaching reforms within traditionally accepted Islamic ways of thinking. These reforms should embrace the Islamic legislative system:

[T]he most specific injunctions, injunctions which have been explicitly specified by the holy texts, are contingent upon conditions which permit a high degree of flexibility, Thus the canonical punishments known as *hudud* . . . and the inheritance regulations known as *faraid* are associated with elaborate conditions which allow circumstantial considerations to qualify their application.[72]

Al-Sadiq argued that there had never been a single model for an Islamic state and that the ideal state had to be in tune with modernity without losing its Muslim identity. He insisted that the Islamization of the legal system in an Islamic state could not be fully entrusted to the *'ulama'*. Though well versed in Islamic law, they had little, if any, understanding of modern legal methods or of the needs of modern society. Hence this extensive reform should be entrusted to scholars trained in modern legal systems, familiar with contemporary social needs and assisted by economists, sociologists, political scientists and statesmen.

That workshop or think tank could base itself on the Quran and *Sunna* and proceed in the spirit of a new *ijtihad* interpretation of Islam to codify a civil criminal, personal and international law.[73]

---

[72] Sadiq, *Islam and Change*, 238.
[73] The above quotations are from *ibid.*, 238–9.

Al-Sadiq's concept of an Islamic state left the door wide open for the introduction of innovations. He insisted that democracy and human rights were among the most basic political principles of any Islamic state. The Ansar, under al-Sadiq, seemed to be moving towards far-reaching accommodation with modernity, viewing the inherent rigidity in contemporary Muslim thought and politics as a major threat to the future of Islam. This concept was expressed by al-Sadiq when he was asked to define the differences between the Ansar and the Muslim Brothers:

> The Muslim Brothers think of Islam in terms of the traditional pattern . . . We think in terms of constructing a new pattern on an Islamic basis. They conform to the Sunni school of thought and are bound by the four Sunni schools of law. We draw from all schools of Muslim thought and we are not bound by any school of law. We recognize the original texts and seek new formulation, conscious of changes in time and place. They are a branch of a movement which originated and developed outside Sudan. We have developed in Sudan and would give it a leading role in the revival of Islam.[74]

Al-Sadiq also alluded to the élitist nature of the Muslim Brothers, as opposed to the popular appeal of the Ansar. Finally, he emphasized the difference between the movements with regard to reconciliation: 'Their attitude to National Reconciliation is to accept what there is and work within it. Our attitude is that Reconciliation means the development of alternative institutions and policies.'[75]

Al-Sadiq's outspoken opposition to Numayri's September 1983 laws, imposing the *hudud* should therefore not have come as a surprise. In several public speeches held at the Mahdist mosques in Omdurman and on Aba Island, al-Sadiq specified the conditions that had to prevail in a Muslim society before the *hudud* could be applied. These included, first and foremost, social justice, individual liberty and civil rights, as well as an independent legislative authority. He argued that in a country based on tyranny, wherein the bulk of the population enjoyed neither civil rights nor the means to support itself, the implementation of the *hudud* was in contravention of the dictates of true Islam. To use al-Sadiq's words in a sermon preached at the Ansar's mosque in Omdurman: 'To cut the hand of a thief in a society based on tyranny and discrimination is like throwing a man into the water, with his hands tied, and saying to him: beware of wetting yourself.'[76] Al-Sadiq was willing to support the ban on alcoholic drinks and to put an end to prostitution, but he openly denounced Numayri's policy as an act

---

[74] 'Interview with Sudan's Sadeq Al-Mahdi', *The Middle East*, 64 (Feb. 1980): 38–41. The interview was conducted amidst rumours that al-Sadiq would be appointed Prime Minister of Sudan under President Numayri.

[75] *Ibid.*

[76] Quoted from 'Al-khutba al-lati alqaha al-Sayyid al-Sadiq al-Mahdi, fi Ummdurman', 17 Sept. 1983 (mimeographed); for details, see Umma, *Dimuqratiyya*, 97–107.

of desperation for which Sudan was not ready. In a pamphlet entitled *Al-nizam al-Sudani wa tajribatahu al-Islamiyya, 1983–85* (The Sudanese regime and its Islamic experiment, 1983–5), the Ansar assessed and condemned Numayri's Islamic experiment. Its author, probably al-Sadiq himself, denounced Numayri's experiment as un-Islamic and expressed his hope that its ultimate and inevitable failure would not be blamed on the 'modern Islamic revival movement', to which the Ansar belonged. Furthermore, al-Sadiq announced that while the Ansar viewed the implementation of the shari'a as a blessing, they condemned Numayri's attempt as a falsification of Islam and as opposed to the views of prominent *'ulama'*, such as Hasan al-Banna or Abu al-'Ala. The latter had explicitly rejected the application of the *hudud* as a first step in the implementation of the shari'a, stating that it led to the corruption of Islam and thereby harmed the very purpose of the Islamic laws.[77] Numayri's false Islamic policy was accordingly nothing but a desperate political attempt to suppress his opponents both in the North and the South in order to save his regime. Taking into account the vehemence with which leading Ansar attacked the September laws, it was therefore not surprising that al-Sadiq and several other Ansar leaders were periodically detained and were excluded from active participation in Numayri's new Islamic state.

Analysing the reasons behind the popular uprising against Numayri in April 1985 and the army's decision to step in and join the people, al-Sadiq offered the following as prime factors: first, the unimaginable economic crisis; secondly, the Islamic experiment, which had led to totally negative results; and, finally, the challenge of the Southern rebellion, which had reached dangerous dimensions. However, according to al-Sadiq the single most important factor that had enabled the popular uprising to succeed was the fact that the monopoly of the Muslim Brothers within the student movement had been broken. The students, who had played a leading role in previous popular uprisings, had been neutralized since 1977, following al-Turabi's decision to collaborate with Numayri unconditionally. Al-Sadiq accused al-Turabi of having joined forces with Numayri, although he knew that Numayri's Islamic order was nothing but a political ploy.[78] Al-Sadiq was rearrested on 5 April 1985, a few days before Numayri's downfall, for speaking out against the regime at Al-Hijra mosque in Wad Nubawi. He denounced Numayri's Islamic policy in strong terms and called upon the army to join the people and topple Numayri's regime. Once Numayri was removed, al-Sadiq was even more outspoken. He analysed Numayri's legal pronouncements regarding the Islamic system, proving to his audience that they constituted a total corruption of Islam. He also denounced the legal decisions reached on the basis of the shari'a laws as totally un-Islamic, both

[77] Umma, *Dimuqratiyya*, 100.
[78] Interview with al-Sadiq al-Mahdi, *Al-Majalla*, 20 Apr. 1985.

in their spirit and in their execution. Apart from his total rejection of the way in which the *hudud* were applied, he singled out Numayri's Islamic economy, which he criticized severely, explaining that it did not conform to a true understanding of Islam. However, not unlike Sayyid Muhammad 'Uthman al-Mirghani, the leader of the Khatmiyya, al-Sadiq supported the creation of an Islamic state provided it was based on the perfect application of the shari'a in all political issues and on social justice in its economic policy. The implementation of the shari'a would be based on new *ijtihad* (independent judgement), which would take into account present conditions and derive its judgement from the *Qur'an* and the *Sunna*.[79]

[79] The above is based on the mimeographed texts of al-Sadiq al-Mahdi's *khutbas* during 1984–5 and on his interview in *al-Musawwar*, 26 Apr. 1985; also Umma, *Dimuqratiyya*, 99–100.

15

THE MUSLIM BROTHERS
AND NUMAYRI

Who were the Muslim Brothers and why was their collaboration so important for Numayri when he set out on his Islamic path? In the political realities of Sudan, as seen by Numayri since he came to power in May 1969, the main dangers to its stability and unity were presented by the sectarian parties and primarily by the Ansar. His first allies following his coup were therefore the Communists, who had a considerable following among the graduates as well as within the Sudanese army's officer corps. They shared with Numayri the determination to annihilate sectarianism and also supported his search for an accommodation with the south however, this brief honeymoon ended in July 1971 when, following an abortive military coup, headed by pro-Communist officers, and with the tacit support of the Sudan Communist Party's (SCP) Central Committee, Numayri executed most of the party's leadership and started the second phase of his regime.[80]

Numayri stated in his introduction to *Al-nahj al-islami limadha?* that during his brief imprisonment after the Communist coup he decided to follow the Islamic path. This shift paved the way for the July 1977 National Reconciliation. The details of this reconciliation were hammered out between President Numayri and al-Sadiq al-Mahdi in Port Sudan. Meanwhile, Hasan al-Turabi, who had remained in Sudan since Numayri came to power and had spent nearly seven years in detention, held several meetings with Numayri. He came to the conclusion that, following Numayri's new political trend the Muslim Brothers would benefit from being incorporated within the regime, which would enable them to become active within the SDF.

Early years

The Muslim Brothers, not unlike the communists, were an élitist movement whose support came primarily from within the University of Khartoum and its graduates and from the urban intelligentsia in the towns of central northern Sudan.[81] Their first political success was in 1953 when they won a landslide victory in the elections to the Khartoum University Student Union

[80] Details in Warburg, *Islam and Communism*, 93–140; see also Khalid, *Nimeiri*, 21–5.

[81] Details in Osman, *Muslim Brotherhood*; also in Affendi, *Turabi's Revolution*, 46–103; Warburg, *Muslim Brothers*, in Esposito, *Modern Islam*, I, 92–3.

(KUSU), which since 1947 had been monopolized by Communists. Their then President, al-Rashid al-Tahir, soon became a prominent politician, who succeeded in establishing a close relationship with the Egyptian RCC and with the Muslim Brothers in Cairo. He also initiated strong relations with Colonel Salah Salim, who had been nominated by the RCC to handle Egyptian–Sudanese relations. However, when the Free Officers turned against the Egyptian Muslim Brothers in 1954, following the latter's abortive assassination attempt on President Nasser, Rashid al-Tahir and his supporters demonstrated against Egypt and changed their previous pro-Egyptian unionist tendencies to outspoken support for Sudan's independence. This in turn brought them into close association with the Ansar–Umma bloc, which, under Sayyid Siddiq al-Mahdi, opened its newspapers and its ranks to these new political allies. Al-Tahir's subsequent political career was indicative of the confusion reigning in the Muslim Brotherhood. He had made his entry into politics through KUSU and had propagated a radical line from the outset. He participated actively in an abortive anti-'Abbud coup in 1959, following which he was imprisoned and expelled from the Muslim Brothers' leadership. While in prison his views were further radicalized by encounters with Communist fellow-prisoners, and after his release he retired temporarily from active politics and opened a private legal practice in his hometown, al-Qadaref. But after the removal of the military regime by the October 1964 civilian uprising, al-Tahir's leadership qualities persuaded his colleagues to bring him back into politics and to appoint him as one of the Muslim Brothers ministers in Sirr al-Khatm al-Khalifa's transitional government. He won a seat for the ICF in the general elections of 1965 and became their spokesman in Parliament, where he soon shocked his colleagues once again by suggesting a common platform with all other opposition parties. Finally, in July 1965 he publicly disassociated himself from all ICF policies, resigned from the party and joined the NUP. Thus the last of the radicals, who had led the Muslim Brothers since the early 1950s, was finally removed and al-Turabi's position at the top was secure.[82]

Hasan 'Abdallah al-Turabi joined the Muslim Brothers' first front organization, the ILM, while an undergraduate at Khartoum University College in 1954. He then left for postgraduate studies in London, completing his MA thesis in 1957. While in London, Turabi was Secretary-General of the Sudanese Student Union in Britain and an active opponent of the 1956 Suez campaign against Egypt. He returned to Khartoum for a brief period, during which he taught in the Faculty of Law and was also elected to the ILM executive. Al-Turabi then carried on his studies in Paris where he submitted

---

[82] Affendi, *Turabi's Revolution*, 77–9; also Weissbrod, *Turabi*, 13–22. According to Bona Malwal, al-Tahir left the movement following a personal dispute with al-Turabi. Malwal, who served under al-Tahir while the latter was Prime Minister under Numayri, described him as a sincere and very religious Muslim, who was one of the most talented politicians among the Muslim Brothers. (Interview with Bona Malwal, Oxford, Jan. 1991)

his PhD dissertation on 'States of Emergency in Constitutional Jurisprudence' in 1964.[83] Dr Hasan al-Turabi returned to Khartoum University to take up his teaching position in the Faculty of Law shortly before the October 1964 civilian revolution in which he played an active role. The strategy he proposed for the ICF at the time was that it should become an élitist, non-partisan, pressure group, which would urge political parties of kindred views to form a broadly based non-violent opposition front in which the small élitist Muslim Brothers could play a leading role. This was also based on the fact that the Muslim Brothers had not succeeded in broadening their membership outside the university and a few secondary schools and therefore were too weak politically to act independently. Members of the Brotherhood drifted away following graduation and, in many cases, resumed their families' sectarian loyalties. Al-Turabi believed that a small élitist group, such as the ICF, seeking an Islamic state and the implementation of the shari'a, could pressure the Ansar and the Khatmiyya into supporting these aims which were openly supported by their leaders.

Al-Turabi's return to Sudan in 1964 also coincided with an upsurge of activity in the university caused primarily by the impasse the government was facing in the civil war in the south. His status as a Western-educated Professor of Law and later as Dean of the Faculty gave him the prestige that the Muslim Brothers had hitherto lacked. Following the discrediting of al-Rashid al-Tahir, the leadership of the movement had remained vacant and nobody seemed in a hurry to fill the gap. The supreme *shura* council of the Muslim Brothers also decided at that time on a policy of escalation, with the university as the focal point. In a number of speeches made by al-Turabi and other faculty members belonging to the Brothers, they accused the 'Abbud regime of being directly responsible for the southern débâcle and demanded an immediate return to civilian rule. The Brothers' militancy, as opposed to the Communists, who advocated caution, rallied many of the students around al-Turabi. It was he who led the crucial student debate at the university on 21 October 1964, in which one of the students was killed by the police. He also helped turn the assassinated student's funeral into a mass demonstration against the 'Abbud regime. Al-Turabi's entrance into national politics can thus be attributed to 'Abbud's downfall. The way in which the Muslim Brothers succeeded in outmanoeuvring the Communists and in undermining their predominance in the professional associations and in KUSU signified al-Turabi's future tactics and his long and bitter anti-Communist crusade.[84]

Following 'Abbud's removal al-Turabi played the central role in shaping the Muslim Brothers' future policy. He realized that general elections would lead once again to a sectarian majority in which the élitist Brothers could exert their influence only if they refrained from interfering in national

[83] Hamdi, *Turabi*, 1–2.
[84] Bechtold, *Politics in Sudan*, 211–13.

politics and concentrated on a limited Islamic agenda. He therefore persuaded his colleagues to set up the ICF, which was composed of the Muslim Brothers, *Ansar al-Sunna* and several *sufi* orders, such as the Tijaniyya, the Qadiriyya and sections of the Sammaniyya. On 2 November 1964 al-Turabi issued his first communiqué as the new Secretary-General of the Muslim Brotherhood, a post that had not previously existed, and persuaded his colleagues on the *shura* council to approve all his measures. Shortly thereafter, the ICF published the Islamic Charter, which proposed the establishment of an Islamic state ruled in accordance with an Islamic constitution. Under the banner of the ICF the Muslim Brothers, participated in the March 1965 general elections with some 100 candidates. These included the fifteen graduates constituencies, which had been set up before the first general elections in 1953 to allow the educated class to exert a greater impact on politics than warranted by its numerical strength. The ICF's election platform propagated the following aims: an Islamic orientation; a peaceful solution of the southern problem; and economic reforms. The eleven seats won by the ICF included two Graduates' Constituencies, of which one was won by al-Turabi and signalled his entry into national politics. However, despite this achievement, al-Turabi and his colleagues were shrugged off by the two sectarian leaders as politically insignificant stating that they had attained limited success only because of their role in the October 1964 revolution. Furthermore, since the PDP had been ordered by the Khatmiyya to boycott the 1965 elections, the ICF had gained many votes in traditional Khatmiyya strongholds. In other words, Sayyid 'Ali al-Mirghani and the Khatmiyya leadership viewed the Brothers' success as a temporary setback, which would be reversed in the next elections.[85] However, their entry into national politics enabled al-Turabi and the ICF to create a common front with the section of the Ansar–Umma bloc led by al-Sadiq al-Mahdi, with whom al-Turabi was in agreement on most central issues. Al-Sadiq had, as noted above, proclaimed his support for an Islamic constitution already in 1958 and, following his appointment as Prime Minister in 1966, he rewarded the ICF by appointing three of its members to the Constitutional Committee, which he established in January 1967. He also implemented several laws suggested by the ICF such as a ban on usury and outlawing of prostitution. Moreover, when the Constitutional Committee made its final recommendations in January 1968, it transpired that the three ICF members had succeeded in influencing its decisions.[86]

The ICF's collaboration with al-Sadiq was also prompted by their common opposition to Communism. In the 1965 elections, the SCP had gained eleven of the Graduates' constituencies, compared with only two won by

---

[85] On the elections and an analysis of the voting, see *ibid.*, 229–35.

[86] Affendi, *Turabi's Revolution*, 79–81. According to the author, one of the reasons for their success was their calibre and persistence as compared with the other forty-four committee members; see also Sidahmed, *Politics and Islam*, 101–9.

the Brothers. The communists thus continued to present the only challenge to the Brothers' supremacy among the intelligentsia and on the campus. To outlaw Communism, the ICF required allies and the Ansar were their natural choice. In the new draft constitution, they managed to insert a clause outlawing atheism, Communism and anti-religious propaganda. A statement denouncing Communism made by Shaykh al-Azhar at their request in August 1965 expedited the Muslim Brothers' anti-Communist crusade. But Parliament's decision to outlaw Communism created a crisis when the Sudanese Supreme Court declared it unconstitutional. Al-Sadiq, then Prime Minister, supported Parliament against the Supreme Court's ruling and brought about the resignation of the Chief Justice, Babikr 'Awadallah, whom he regarded as an Egyptian agent and an arch-enemy of the Ansar. For the Brothers this constituted one of their greatest victories, in which al-Turabi played a leading role. With the objective of 'unmasking the treacherous elements' of Communism, he and his followers had set out to outlaw the SCP and had gained overwhelming support in Parliament. The fact that the Supreme Court could overrule the Constituent Assembly was, according to al-Turabi, due to 'the existence of an imported constitution, formulated in rigid lifeless texts unrelated to the conditions surrounding it'. He claimed that these 'amputated limbs had created big gaps that now threaten the whole of our democratic system'.[87] Al-Turabi had stated on more than one occasion that he was opposed to both Western liberal democracy and to so-called people's democracies, established under Soviet guidance. Both these forms of democracy were governed by men and therefore led to suppression. Turabi argued that in the people's democracies people enjoyed economic equality but suffered from political suppression, while in liberal democracies free expression existed but only as a result of the market economy, which led to a monopoly on political power by the rich, while the mass of the people were helpless. Only *hakimiyyat Allah* (the sovereignty of God) would, according to al-Turabi, guarantee both the people's rights and their freedom.[88]

The ICF continued to collaborate with al-Sadiq after his defeat by a new coalition, headed by *al-imam* al-Hadi al-Mahdi and Muhammad Ahmad Mahgoub. However, the 1968 elections proved the disastrous effects of the split within the Umma. Although al-Sadiq's faction of the Umma party succeeded in gaining thirty-six seats in Parliament, as opposed to thirty won by *al-imam* al-Hadi, al-Sadiq was defeated in his own constituency. The ICF fared no better and, of their twenty-nine candidates, only three were elected to Parliament and al-Turabi, like al-Sadiq, failed in his bid and was not re-elected. The great winner was the DUP, which won 101 seats (out of a total

[87] Affendi, *Turabi's Revolution*, 83; on the Brothers' anti-Communist crusade, see *ibid.*, 81–4.
[88] Weissbrod, *Turabi*, 34–5.

of 218) in the new Parliament.[89] The prophecy of the Khatmiyya leadership regarding the marginal status of the Muslim Brothers, made in the wake of its failure in the 1965 elections, became true within less than four years. Even more significant was the overwhelming majority gained by the two sectarian parties, who held 167 of 218 seats in the new Parliament.

For al-Turabi's rivals within the Muslim Brotherhood, this was a clear indication of his failure and a vindication of their rejection of his policies. He had, in their view, neglected the true mission of the Muslim Brothers, namely, education and *da'wa*, and had wasted the movement's efforts in futile politicizing. The anti-Turabi struggle was undertaken by two prominent faculty members in the University of Khartoum, Ja'far Shaykh Idris and Muhammad Salah 'Umar, who demanded in the Muslim Brothers' Congress, convened in April 1969, that al-Turabi be dismissed and that the movement revert to its true educational role. They charged him with complete political failure, since his futile association with al-Sadiq had only backfired, while the right course would have been an alliance with *al-imam* al-Hadi al-Mahdi, the true supporter of an Islamic state. But Turabi's eloquence and charisma enabled him to defeat his rivals and, had it not been for the May 1969 coup, he would probably have succeeded in expelling them from the movement.[90]

From opposition to collaboration

The anti-secular and especially the anti-Communist bias of the Muslim Brothers was fundamental in their early opposition to Numayri whom they, like many others, regarded as pro-Communist when he first came to power in May 1969. But the Brothers were hardly in a position to act, since the students, their sole power base, were at their homes on summer vacation. Many of their leaders were arrested following the May 1969 coup, some fled to Aba Island and joined the Imam al-Hadi al-Mahdi and others left the country and joined al-Sharif Yusuf al-Hindi who was organizing the NF against Numayri's regime. Those who had escaped to Aba took part in the Ansar's attempt to stop Numayri's troops from landing on the Island in March 1970 and some of them, including Muhammad Salah 'Umar, were massacred. Others attempted to cross the border into Ethiopia with the *al-imam* al-Hadi, and Muhammad Sadiq al-Karuri was arrested while trying to escape.[91]

However, the mutual hostility between the Muslim Brothers and Numayri gradually subsided as a result of developments both in Sudan and in Egypt under President Sadat. First came Numayri's clash with the Communists in July 1971, which ended in the annihilation of the Communist

[89] Bechtold, *Politics in Sudan*, 246–53.
[90] Affendi, *Turabi's Revolution*, 85–8.
[91] *Ibid.*, 104–7.

leadership, much to the satisfaction of the Muslim Brothers. Secondly, Numayri's anti-sectarianism made the Muslim Brothers his natural allies, since their political future also depended on the end of sectarian supremacy. Under President Sadat, the Egyptian Muslim Brothers, once President Nasser's most outspoken opponents, had become important supporters of the regime. They gave their backing to Sadat's measures against the pro-Nasserist left and later helped him in fighting the radical Muslim student groups. Despite the different conditions prevailing in the two parts of the Nile Valley, a marriage of convenience with the Brothers made sense to Numayri in his attempt to neutralize the Ansar and to promote an Islamic state. Numayri's Islamic policy, which started to take shape in the mid-1970s, therefore encouraged al-Turabi and some of his colleagues to join him even before reconciliation was finally hammered out by al-Sadiq in July 1977. The appointment of al-Rashid al-Tahir as Deputy President and Prime Minister in 1976 was a clear indication of the changing policy. Since al-Tahir, though no longer a member of the Brothers, was identified ideologically as an Islamist adherent by the population, his inclusion in top government positions was a clear sign as to the regime's new policy. While, according to al-Turabi, there had been strong reservations among his colleagues who were opposed to cooperation with Numayri, they had later realized that it had worked out to their advantage. He viewed Numayri at that time as a tolerant leader whose conversion to Islam had helped to eliminate secularism.[92] The natural conclusion was that in March 1977, four months before National Reconciliation, al-Turabi decided that the Muslim Brothers would opt out of the NF and continue their struggle for Islam from within the regime. In the presence of the full quorum of the NF politburo members headed by al-Sadiq al-Mahdi and Yusuf al-Hindi, which was held in London, al-Turabi informed his colleagues that the Muslim Brothers had reviewed Numayri's second-term presidential programme, which was announced in January 1977, and had concluded that its new 'Islamic Orientations' fully satisfied them. He therefore announced the withdrawal of the Muslim Brothers from the NF and the resumption of its activities within Sudan.[93] Numayri's close association with the Muslim Brothers was, as already mentioned, initiated as early as 1971 when he met some of their exiled leaders in the Saudi capital. However, real cooperation started only in 1977 when al-Turabi and his colleagues returned to active politics. As both chairman of the committee entrusted to bring Sudan's laws into line

[92] Turabi, *Secularism*, 71–3; also Hamdi, *Turabi*, 3–5.

[93] Quoted from an unpublished paper written by Ustaz Abdelrahman Alamin for the Al-Sudan Center for Democracy, Peace, and Civil Rights, USA, 31 Dec. 1998; see also Hamdi, *Turabi*, 21. Al-Turabi stated in his interview with Hamdi that the Brothers' new strategy was drawn up before the anti-Numayri uprising of July 1976 but was only adopted later, following consultations with leaders of the Muslim Brothers who were released from prison.

with the shari'a and as Sudan's Attorney-General, al-Turabi could now influence government policy considerably. His leverage exceeded the political power of the Muslim Brothers, whose support was limited at that time to an important but relatively small section of the urban élite. However, al-Turabi was a pragmatist whose prime concern was political rather than ideological, hence the purist tendencies of some of his Islamic colleagues were of little concern to him. His pragmatism enabled the Muslim Brothers under his guidance to achieve two additional and crucial advantages during the Numayri era: first, their infiltration into the armed forces, which had important implications for the future; and secondly, the manipulation of the Islamic economy to their benefit, which Sidahmed called 'Islaminomics', enabled them to consolidate their political base and to achieve unexpected support during the 1986 elections.[94] Following the July 1977 National Reconciliation the Muslim Brothers were consequently fully integrated within the governing bodies of the SSU, the National Assembly and the government. For them National Reconciliation was a most welcome decision, since it coincided with their new strategy, based on disappointment with the other opposition groups and especially with the Ansar. But even more important was their belief that Numayri's Islamic policies worked to their advantage. Therefore, once reconciliation became the official policy of the regime the Brothers had no difficulty in rushing to grasp whatever positions the government offered. Their strategy required that they prepare themselves for their future role in the Islamic state, and the chances offered by Numayri seemed ideal.[95] While a minority within the Brothers' *shura* council constantly opposed al-Turabi's pragmatic approach, the vast majority, led by al-Turabi, became fully identified with the regime.

The internal rift within the Muslim Brothers was never really healed, since some of the more senior leaders, such as 'Abdallah 'Abd al-Majid and Ja'far Shaykh Idris, continued to attack al-Turabi's strategy and tactics from their exile in the Gulf States. They were closely associated with the Egyptian Muslim Brothers and, following the release from prison in 1973 of Hasan al-Hudaybi, Hasan al-Banna's successor and the leader (*al-murshid al-'am*) of the Muslim Brothers in pre-revolutionary Egypt, they suggested joining the world organization of Muslim Brothers under his leadership. Politically they objected to al-Turabi's un-Islamic views with regard to the role of women in society and criticized his intimacy with Numayri and his regime. However, all their suggestions were defeated in the Ikhwan's *shura* council, and although 'Abd al-Majid was offered the deputy leadership upon his return to Sudan in the late 1970s, as an act of conciliation, he refused the offer

---

[94] Sidahmed, *Politics & Islam*, 207–10; details below.
[95] According to Hamdi, *Turabi*, 4, Turabi and his colleagues 'did not show much interest in government posts, [they] needed a period of security and stability to stake out a broad-based presence in all sections of Sudanese society'.

and the rift remained unhealed. A number of opposition leaders, headed by Dr al-Hibr Yusuf Nur al-Da'im, a Professor of Arabic Literature at the University of Khartoum, were even expelled from the Muslim Brotherhood and any further association with them was forbidden. The expelled members, who were later joined by 'Abdallah 'Abd al-Majid, formed their own independent Muslim Brotherhood and also split the student organization. In 1986 they competed under their own banner in the general elections against al-Turabi and the NIF, but without success.[96] Al-Turabi's close collaboration with the regime did not appeal to the Ikhwan's student supporters, who had been the movement's backbone while in opposition and failed to comprehend the new turn of events. Al-Turabi wisely allowed the student leadership to remain in opposition, as before, notwithstanding their elders' collaboration with Numayri. But the illegal SCP and the Republican Brothers were quick to seize the opportunity and denounced the Brothers' duplicity. Consequently, in the 1980 elections to KUSU the Muslim Brothers lost their leading position.[97]

In an interview with *Sudanow* in March 1982 al-Turabi declared that reconciliation, as far as the Muslim Brothers were concerned, had been fully accomplished and it was now time to deal with such crucial issues as the constitution, within the existing political system, and the strengthening of the legislative institutions in particular. When asked about the relationship between his movement and the *sufis* or Mahdists, al-Turabi stated:

There is fortunately no conflict between the modern Islamic movement and the traditional-based on the ideologies of the Sufis or the Mahdists. Hence these will form a base, a form of Islamization which combines the modern and the traditional . . . Our program is religiously comprehensive excluding only nonreligious ideologies such as Marxism or secularist creeds and those opinionated movements which claim to hold direct mandates from God.[98]

However, al-Turabi warned, 'if Islam were to be repressed in the Sudan the possibility of a Khomeini-like revolt should not be excluded'. When asked about the chances of al-Sadiq al-Mahdi's becoming a political leader, al-Turabi stated that the latter should limit himself to the leadership of the Ansar and not strive for national leadership, since 'Numeiri knows that there is only one seat at the top.'[99]

The vehemence of al-Turabi's anti-Communist onslaught was criticized by some participants in a conference on 'Islam in the Sudan' held in Khartoum in November 1982, by the Society of Islamic Thought and Civilization

---

[96] Affendi, *Turabi's Revolution*, 118–19. According to El-Affendi, this splinter group did not exceed a few hundred members in 1987.

[97] *Ibid.*, 113–16.

[98] This is a reference to the Republican Brothers; see Turabi, *Sudanow*, Mar. 1982.

[99] Quotations from Turabi, *Secularism*, 71–3; see also Turabi, *Sudanow*, Mar. 1982; Turabi, *Sudanow*, Jan. 1983, 22–3.

(*Jama'at al-fikr wa'l-thaqafa al-islamiyya*). At that conference al-Turabi maintained that Islamization was the central issue in the Muslim Brothers' policy and he regarded the reform of Sudanese law, in accordance with the shari'a, as the most urgent task. The final communiqué of the conference was in general agreement with the ideas put forward by al-Turabi and the Muslim Brothers in the course of the previous few years. It advocated essential social reforms, which should precede the gradual implementation of the shari'a. However, al-Turabi's undertaking to act accordingly was broken less than a year later, when, in contradiction with the conference's decision that social reforms had to precede the gradual implementation of shari'a, he openly collaborated with Numayri's immediate implementation of the *hudud* in September 1983. According to al-Turabi, Numayri dismissed him from his post as Attorney-General earlier in 1983 so that he would not claim the credit for the Islamic laws.[100] However, there are indications that al-Turabi continued to wield considerable influence over Numayri throughout 1984. One indication is the role played by him as Presidential Adviser on Foreign Affairs, when he accompanied the President to the United States and played a leading role in advising the United States with regard to its anti-Libyan plans. Dr Muhammad Yusuf al-Maqrif, then leader of Libya's anti-Qadhafi opposition, accompanied al-Turabi to discuss with the CIA the situation in Libya and in the Libyan training camps in Sudan. Following this meeting, Numayri delegated the decisions as to details of future collaboration between Sudan and the Libyan opposition to Hasan al-Turabi. This meeting with al-Maqrif was naturally resented by the Libyan regime and, on 16 March 1984 a single Libyan aeroplane bombed several public and other buildings in Khartoum, so as to warn President Numayri against pursuing his anti-Qadhafi campaign in collaboration with the CIA any further.[101]

In his attempt to gain the full confidence of Numayri al-Turabi attempted in June 1984 to undermine the position of 'Umar Muhammad al-Tayyib, Numayri's Vice-President and head of the security apparatus. Through his right-hand man in Parliament, 'Ali 'Uthman Muhammad Taha, al-Turabi proposed a constitutional amendment, known as paragraph 80, which stated that in future the President would be the *imam* and the Commander of the Faithful and leader of the Sudanese *umma*. Paragraph 81 gave the President–*imam* absolute and irrevocable powers in all spheres. This proposed amendment was a constitutional revolution, since an *imam* had no deputy and the *bay'a* was given to him as *imam* and not to anyone else. Had

---

[100] Turabi, *Mustaqbal al-Islam*, 427–36; interview with Hasan al-Turabi in *al-Wasat*, 22–28 Feb. 1999; also Hamdi, *Turabi*, 25. Al-Turabi stated that, while he and the Brothers were not involved in the actual implementation of the sharia laws, it fitted into their strategy and they exploited it for its popular appeal.

[101] Haydar, *NIF & SDF*, 81–4. However, the Omdurman broadcasting building, which was the main target of the attack, was not hit.

the amendment been passed, Numayri would have been surrounded by councillors and men of learning, but without executive powers. In the event of his death a new President-*imam* would have had to be elected and 'Umar Muhammad al-Tayyib's leading position would have been undermined. Although this amendment failed to be passed by Parliament, it none the less proves how close al-Turabi was to President Numayri as late as 1984. 'Umar Muhammad al-Tayyib realized that al-Turabi had attempted to undermine his position but, knowing the extent of the latter's influence, he continued to support him. Consequently he helped the Brothers both politically and financially and appointed several of their members to the security forces. He also supported their case against the leader of the Republican Brothers, Mahmud Muhammad Taha, when they accused him of apostasy.[102]

Al-Turabi's collaboration with Numayri was regarded by many observers of the Sudanese political scene both as proof of his duplicity and of his being the power behind the Numayri's Islamic policy. When, in March 1985, al-Turabi and some of his followers were accused of treason and put behind bars, it therefore seemed to be an illogical step, since by discrediting one of his few remaining allies Numayri seemingly undermined his own credibility. Many of al-Turabi's critics, including those who had left the Muslim Brothers in protest against his collaboration with Numayri, did not express their sorrow following his imprisonment. Others, who had followed Numayri's relations with the Muslim Brothers closely, were not surprised since they had regarded this uneasy alliance as a temporary 'marriage of convenience'. According to Abdelwahab El-Affendi, the final blow against the Muslim Brothers was brought about by United States pressure following Vice-President George Bush's visit to Sudan in March 1985.[103]

One of the Muslim Brothers who had been closely associated with Numayri's Islamic experiment, al-Mikashfi Taha al-Kabbashi, wrote a full justification of the implementation of the Islamic laws.[104] Although he was briefly imprisoned in 1985 with other leading Muslim Brothers, he continued to regard the September 1983 Islamic laws as a correct step in the right direction. Moreover, he viewed Numayri's support of these laws as purely incidental since his support was needed, while the Muslim Brothers alone constituted the true Islamist movement in Sudan. The next step in that direction, according to al-Kabbashi, should have been the total Islamization of the political system, probably indicating the Iranian model. This of

---

[102] *Ibid.*, 87–92. For details on Taha's execution, see above.

[103] Affendi, *Turabi's Revolution*, 126–30. Affendi describes this 'crackdown' as a gradual process brought about by the growing animosity between some of Numayri's corrupt aides and the Muslim Brothers, who in many cases sentenced them in the shari'a courts.

[104] Kabbashi, *Tatbiq al-shari'a*, details above. Al-Mikashfi Taha al-Kabbashi is an offspring of a prominent *sufi* family of the Qadiriyya order. He was first trained as a *qadi* and in 1987 he received his PhD from the University of Umm al-Qura in Mecca, details in Shamuq, *Shakhsiyyat*, 440–1.

course was unacceptable to Numayri since it would have meant a change of leadership. But, for al-Kabbashi and his colleagues there was never any doubt as to Sudan's Islamic identity which implied the *jahili* status of all non-Muslims. According to their view even the armed forces would become an Islamic army fighting the enemies of Islam, whether 'Communists, Crusaders, Zionists, Freemasons' or their Sudanese supporters, under the banner of Islam.[105] Al-Turabi also had no regrets and regarded the shari'a laws of September 1983 as a blessing for Sudan:

We can see that the efforts we put into the implementation of the shari'a laws has borne fruit, much more than we had ever expected . . . Islam today is the unquestionable choice of the Sudanese people; the secular alternative has been thrown out by the masses for good.[106]

The army and the economic system in Ikhwan politics

The Sudanese Muslim Brothers started to infiltrate into the SDF officer 'corps', in 1955. They first did so in the wake of the 1952 Egyptian Free Officers' coup, with the active help of a member of the secret organization (*al-nizam al-sirri*) of the Egyptian Muslim Brothers who had escaped to Sudan following the assassination attempt made on President Nasser in Alexandria in November 1954. However, it was the rather clumsy effort of a politically immature movement, and the attempt to infiltrate the Military College in 1955 had little success. The abortive anti-'Abbud coup of 9 November 1959, initiated by the Brothers' leader al-Rashid al-Tahir with the participation of both Muslim Brothers and other supporters within the army, was a clear indication as to their weakness at that time but indicated their willingness to use military power for the achievement of political goals in the future.

Following their reconciliation with Numayri in 1977 the Muslim Brothers, led by al-Turabi, undertook a concerted effort with a definite political goal and succeeded in gaining a more solid foothold within the military. Their better-educated membership, experience, superior organization and relative financial affluence, gained as a result of the new Islamic banking system introduced by Numayri with their active assistance, enabled the Brothers to achieve greater success in the army too. First, Muslim Brothers were put in charge of courses on Islamic ideology for senior army officers, thus enabling them to infiltrate into the officer corps. Four members of the military council that ruled Sudan after the June 1989 coup, including its leader 'Umar Hasan al-Bashir, attended these courses. Secondly, they urged their graduates to join the officer corps following the conclusion of their medical, engineering or accountancy studies. A third method entailed the

[105] Kabbashi, *Tatbiq al-shari'a*, 8.
[106] Hamdi, *Turabi*, 26, quoting from his interviews with al-Turabi in the 1990s.

search for ex-Muslim Brothers or their relatives serving in the SDF in order to lure them back into the movement. All these efforts were undertaken in 1977–85, when conditions within Sudan, including the SDF, were ripe for revolt due to the deteriorating economy, growing corruption and, since 1983, renewed civil war. Basically, the Brothers had two aims: first, the creation of conditions within the army that would enable them to impose an Islamic state by force of arms if other methods failed; and, secondly, to lay the foundations of an Islamic army so as to supersede the SDF. This second reason was central, since the Brothers viewed the existing armies in the Muslim world as supporters of the *status quo* and hence as the last refuge of secularism.[107] Following Numayri's removal from power the NIF succeeded in strengthening its support within the army even further, by openly supporting the army's demands for better pay and equipment, while the Umma and the DUP remained hesitant. In the post-Numayri military council, the NIF's main allies were Suwwar al-Dhahab and Taj al-Din 'Abdallah Fadl. In the provisional government their supporters included al-Jazuli Dafa'allah, the Prime Minister, and Dr Husayn Abu Salih. Thus the NIF, which was founded by al-Turabi in April 1985, became the most important ally of President Suwwar al-Dhahab and his colleagues, despite its relative weakness.[108] Finally, it was the 1989 military coup and the regime that followed it that proved beyond doubt that the NIF's infiltration into the army had paid the expected dividends.

The second and even more important aspect of al-Turabi's pragmatism was his ability to manipulate Islamic economics with the purpose of enabling the Ikhwan and later the NIF to gain financial affluence, which was essential if they sought to gain political power. Al-Turabi and the NIF leadership realized that in the past the Brothers had lost elections since they had no financial basis for party politics. They had therefore failed to gain a foothold in outlying regions, which was essential if they hoped to lure prospective supporters. One of the most remarkable ways in which the Brothers succeeded in achiving this goal under Numayri was their clever exploitation of the Sudanese diaspora. The phenomenon of emigration (*ightirab*) of male workers from Sudan to the Arab oil-producing countries had assumed large proportions in the 1970s and 1980s and it was estimated that in 1985, the year Numayri was removed from power, some two-thirds of the professional and skilled Sudanese male workers (*mughtaribin*) were employed for long periods outside the country.[109] This enabled the Muslim Brothers to exploit the *mughtaribin* in order to enhance their economic

---

[107] Haydar, *NIF & SDF*, 61–3; on the Egyptian connection see Vatikiotis, *Nasser*, 138–45. According to Thomas, *Sudan*, 108, al-Turabi had stated in an interview with him that the NIF had some fourteen cells in the army.

[108] Haydar, *NIF & SDF*, 116–22.

[109] For details on this remarkable phenomenon see Sidahmed, *Politics & Islam*, 195–210; the following is based on Sidahmed's account, unless otherwise stated.

viability. These emigrants included university graduates and others who had either belonged to the Brothers or had been active supporters. They were eager to find social and cultural ties in which they could overcome their loneliness while cut off from their families and friends in alien surroundings. If we take into account that these migrants earned good salaries and that their financial assets were partly smuggled back into Sudan to help their families, it is easy to comprehend their importance not only for the ailing economy of Sudan, but also for propagating the Islamist *da'wa* among the women and the poor urban population in Sudan, whom al-Turabi had targeted as the Brothers' future supporters. The remittances smuggled annually into Sudan, largely through informal channels, by means of this hidden economy amounted, according to a survey conducted in 1984–5, to some US$3 billion. These considerable fortunes, which were partly put at the disposal of the NIF in the years 1978–87, explain to a large extent their unexpected success in the 1986 elections and their impressive penetration into various sectors of civil society, including Sudan's female population. The NIF's alliance with the *mughtaribin* therefore enabled it to exploit the 'hidden economy' for furthering girls' education and for enhancing the position of families, especially those who had a *mughtarib* supporter. The role of women in these families assumed greater importance, since they took part in public life and in the absence of their husbands or fathers, became dominant within their families. The NIF played a major role within these new social classes, through its organizations of *shabab al-bina'* (youth for reconstructing) or *raidat al-nahda'* (scouts), whereby it succeeded in gaining their support. It also supported women's rights, in both education and work, and even endorsed their public activities. If we add the fact, from 1978, the Muslim Brothers partly controlled the Islamic banking system and many financial institutions and that the latter were exempt from income tax, the rapid extent of their growth may be easier to comprehend.[110]

As mentioned above, President Numayri's collaboration with al-Turabi was brought to an abrupt end when the latter's usefulness to the regime seemingly outlived itself. In his last volte-face in March 1985 Numayri, apparently relying on Iraqi intelligence sources, accused the Muslim Brothers of attempting to seize power with Iranian revolutionary aid, following which al-Turabi and about 100 of his colleagues were imprisoned. In retrospect, this probably helped the Muslim Brothers after Numayri's collapse, since it enabled al-Turabi to blame all the ills of the latter's policies squarely on the shoulders of his former benefactor.[111]

On 6 April 1985 Numayri was unseated while *en route* from Washington

---

[110] On the evolution of Islamic banks in Sudan, see *Islamic Banking*; on al-Turabi's views on women, see also Weissbrod, *Turabi*, 51–8.

[111] *The Horn of Africa*, 8/1 (1985) 7, 16.

to Cairo. Although there were many reasons for his downfall, as indicated by the mass demonstrations and the popular uprising the preceded it, the implementation of the shari'a seemed to loom large in the background. The Sudan's grave economic crisis was not brought about by the Islamic economy but was definitely exacerbated by it. Civil war in the South can also be attributed to numerous factors, but Southern fears of Islamization, especially since September 1983, led to further deterioration. Last but not least, the shari'a was used by Numayri to crush major groups that opposed his regime. By appealing to what he believed to be the popular sentiments and beliefs of the majority of Sudanese Muslims, Numayri first of all hoped to discredit all leftist or nationalist opposition groups, such as the Communists or the Ba'th. In applying the shari'a he also intended to 'nationalize' Islam and harness it to serve his interests. He hoped thereby that such popular Muslim movements as the Ansar or the Khatmiyya would become superfluous. Even the Muslim Brothers' leaders, who throughout this period had been his close collaborators, were arrested on charges of treason. Therefore, when Numayri set out on his last presidential trip to the United States in March 1985, he had run out of political allies. He depended for his survival on Western support, on the loyalty of the army and the security forces and on the fact, so he believed, that his political antagonists, in both the north and the South, were in such disarray that they would not be able to unite in a popular front against him. However, he underestimated the volume of popular opposition and erred in assuming that the army's high command would remain loyal. Numayri was forced to seek asylum in Egypt where he remained as a guest of the Egyptian government until 1999, when he returned to Sudan under the new law allowing politicians to establish political parties.

The question regarding religion and politics thus assumed centre stage after Numayri's fall, for three main reasons: legal, political and ideological. Legally, the majority supporting the post-Numayri regime, headed by al-Umma, had denounced the September 1983 laws as contravening Islam and wanted to replace them with new Islamist legislation. Even the NIF, which had supported the September laws at the time, sought to replace them with a new set of Islamic laws. However, there was no agreement with regard to an alternative. Thus the September laws remained on the statute books throughout Sudan's third democratic government, although the sentences passed according to the *hudud* were not executed. On the political level, the NIF succeeded in converting both the DUP and the Umma to its point of view, namely, that the Islamic laws promulgated by Numayri, could be replaced only by a modified set of shari'a laws. The DUP was the first convert and it had already forged an alliance with the NIF during the rule of the Transitional Military Council (TMC) in 1985–6. Al-Sadiq al-Mahdi, though committed to a revision of these laws, also failed to reach an agreed version. Thus 'the shari'a laws became a legitimizing cover for the DUP–NIF alliance during the transitional period'.[112] However, these laws also brought about the subsequent failure of the third democratic regime since they made a compromise with the SPLA practically impossible.

[112] Sidahmed, *Politics and Islam*, 177.

16

THE THIRD DEMOCRATIC INTERLUDE, 1986–9

Neither the transitional military government that was formed following Numayri's removal nor its civilian successors came out with any clear pronouncement with regard to the future of the shari'a laws. General 'Abd al-Rahman Suwwar al-Dhahab and his colleagues, who led Sudan during the year following Numayri's deposal, promised to deal with the ailing economy, to end civil war in the South, to reintroduce civil rights and democracy to Sudan and to re-establish cordial relations with all 'law-abiding nations', headed by Libya and Ethiopia. But when asked whether the new regime would re-examine the implementation of the shari'a, the response was either negative or evasive. According to Suwwar al-Dhahab and Prime Minister al-Jazuli Dafa'allah, the Islamic laws enjoyed the support of the vast majority of Sudanese and they required only minor revisions. But they shied away from intervening, since, as a non-elected transitional government, they did not want to become involved in what was bound to evolve into a major political controversy. The fact that the newly founded NIF was a well organized and financially affluent organization that enjoyed considerable influence within the military also prompted the TMC to avoid an unnecessary dispute. Both Suwwar al-Dhahab and al-Jazuli Dafa'allah not only were devout Muslims but had openly announced their support for the September 1983 laws when they were first promulgated, further explaining their vacillation.[113]

Hasan al-Turabi was released from prison on 6 April 1985 and was the first political leader to meet General Suwwar al-Dhahab, Sudan's temporary head of state. He was also the first to call upon his supporters to attend a mass rally in Khartoum University stadium, where some 25,000 people showed up. Whether these were indeed Muslim Brothers, as claimed by al-Turabi, or just ordinary people lured by their suddenly regained political freedom is not really crucial. What is more important is that the Muslim Brothers' leadership, having spent only one month behind bars, was far better funded, organized and equipped than its major political rivals, the Umma and the DUP. Unlike al-Sadiq al-Mahdi and Muhammad 'Uthman

---

[113] Suwwar al-Dhahab is mentioned as a Muslim Brother recruit within the SDF. According to one source Suwwar al-Dhahab, Bashir Muhammad 'Ali, 'Abdallah al-Tahir, and 'Abd al-Rahman Farah were members of a secret Muslim Brothers cell within the SDF in the late 1950s; see Haydar, *Azmat al-Islam*, 60–3.

al-Mirghani, Hasan al-Turabi had supported Numayri's pursuit of the Islamic path ever since reconciliation started. He had promoted the implementation of the shari'a in the past and advocated its application in the future. When asked about those who were punished or executed under these laws, he replied bluntly that such executions were prescribed by the Qur'an. He also justified the amputations of hands of thieves even if, as stated by his interviewer, they stole because they were hungry. He praised the economic measures such as the law of *zakat* and the advance it had made towards a just society. His only criticism regarding the implementation of the shari'a was that it had not been all embracing, since it did not include important issues such as constitutional law, especially regarding the *shura*. With regard to his own and the Muslim Brothers' record under Numayri, al-Turabi was quite proud. They had fought against the May 1969 regime in its early leftist stages, but since reconciliation started in 1977 and an Islamist policy was implemented the Brothers had consistently advocated an Islamic constitution and this had been partly achieved. With regard to the future, al-Turabi was convinced that the power of the NIF, especially among students and intellectuals, would remain dominant. Thus in coalition with the other traditional groups, namely the Khatmiyya and the Ansar, an absolute majority of those seeking to establish an Islamic state was assured. Al-Turabi was equally positive when asked about the Islamic state in Iran. Khomeini led a popular Muslim revolution against imperialism and oppression and this had a great appeal for African Muslims, who were equally oppressed. Al-Turabi insisted that the Islamic state in Sudan would pursue its own Islamist course based on the unique conditions prevailing there. Hence, he expressed his hope that the Islamic order started under Numayri would be pursued peacefully until the ideal Islamic state was established. However, he declared bluntly that the Muslim Brothers would be willing to raise arms against any outside interference. In al-Turabi's view the Islamic state in Sudan was a reality based on popular support and hence those opposing it could only be alien forces who would be fought in a *jihad*.[114]

In the general elections, which took place in April 1986, the Umma Party won 101 seats, followed by 64 for the DUP and 54 for the NIF.[115] Other seats in the new Parliament went to regional parties from the South, the Nuba Mountains, and the Red Sea Hills, while the Communists and other leftist groups received negligible support.[116] The elections proved that the two sectarian parties had retained their overwhelming majority despite sixteen years of military rule. The re-emergence of the Umma as the biggest political party is especially significant. Numayri had tried to eliminate it in his early years and had subsequently attempted to undermine al-Sadiq's leadership by encouraging rivalries within al-Mahdi's family. The DUP, though the second largest party, was none the less considerably weakened and won

---

[114] *Al-Majalla*, 20 Apr. 1985; *al-Watan al-'Arabi*, 26 Apr. 1985.
[115] The NIF won 23 seats in the Graduates' Constituencies; see Hamdi, *Turabi*, 6.
[116] Salih, *Fading Democracy*, 201–19; also Warburg, *Democracy*, 77–94.

only ten seats more than the NIF. The Khatmiyya had underestimated the potential power of the NIF in traditional Khatmi strongholds. The NIF had also received considerable support from some *sufi* orders, most of whom had previously supported the DUP. The Niassiyya, for example, from its center in Kaolack called on all its adherents in Dar Fur and Kordofan to vote for the NIF in the 1986 general elections. Cooperation between al-Turabi and the Niassiyya leaders facilitated a common election platform for the NIF and the Niassiyya, supporting the establishment of an Islamic state in preparation for the coming of the *mahdi*. This also partly explains the penetration of the NIF into certain strongholds of the Ansar.[117] The emergence of the NIF as a significant political power was thus the most important outcome of the 1986 elections. It partly explains the failure of the newly constituted government to agree on a revised version of the disputed Islamic laws or to reach an accommodation with the South.

Al-Sadiq al-Mahdi, Sudan's newly elected Prime Minister, had openly denounced the September 1983 Islamic laws, as mentioned above. Yet when elected to power in 1986 he was either unwilling or unable to deal with these laws as he had previously promised. Instead their implementation was temporarily halted while a revised version of shari'a laws was being hammered out by the various contenders for power.[118] Hasan al-Turabi claimed that the Islamic laws were instrumental in putting an end to crime and in healing other social and economic ills in Sudan. Although he consented to a possible revision of these laws after Numayri's deposal, he insisted that they should neither be abolished nor frozen as long as an agreed upon revised version was not introduced to replace them.[119] Since the Umma, the DUP and the NIF, all favoured Islamic laws in one form or another but could not agree on a revised version of such laws, it was no wonder that in the ensuing three years of democratic government the September laws though not implemented, remained on the statute books and provided Sudan with a major bone of contention.

Endless attempts at mediation between al-Sadiq al-Mahdi and the SPLM failed as a result of the unwillingness to compromise on the shari'a laws, especially as long as al-Sadiq sought the support of the NIF. The only leader who was willing to reach a compromise with John Garang and the SPLM and who was politically able to undertake it was Muhammad 'Uthman al-Mirghani, the head of the Khatmiyya. Al-Mirghani had assumed the Khatmiyya leadership in 1968, following the death of his father Sayyid 'Ali al-Mirghani. The Khatmiyya had traditionally avoided active involvement

[117] Karsani, *Beyond Sufism*, 139–44.

[118] According to Umma sources consultation regarding the new laws started as early as Sept. 1986 and a year later all proposals regarding these laws were submitted to a committee headed by Dr Khalid Farah in order to prepare the new law; see Umma, *Dimuqratiyya*, 101–3.

[119] *Al-Tadammun*, 17 May 1986; the Thames TV interview is quoted from *The Horn of Africa*, 8/1 (1985): 35.

in politics and had persisted in this line under Numayri. Unlike the leaders of the Umma party, the Muslim Brothers or the DUP, the religious leadership of the Khatmiyya, headed by Sayyid Muhammad 'Uthman al-Mirghani, did not get involved in active political opposition to Numayri. They had remained in Sudan while their partners in the DUP were in exile and were fighting Numayri's regime within the NF, under the leadership of al-Sharif Yusuf al-Hindi. Al-Hindi and his DUP supporters remained in opposition even after the National Reconciliation of July 1977 and al-Hindi remained in exile until his untimely death in Athens in 1984. Muhammad 'Uthman al-Mirghani, on the other hand, became head of the *sufi* Islamic Revival Committee, founded in 1978, and lent his full support to Numayri's Islamist policy. The DUP was therefore in complete disarray when Numayri was overthrown in April 1985. It also suffered from a leadership crisis, from which it did not recover until the 1986 elections. During these years Sayyid Muhammad 'Uthman al-Mirghani was playing an ever-increasing role in the internal politics of his country, thereby reversing previous Khatmiyya practices and moving closer to the *modus operandi* of his Ansar rivals. He regarded the Khatmiyya and the Ansar as the dominant popular forces in Sudan and dismissed all their rivals, including the Muslim Brothers, as temporary and irrelevant. He was convinced that even the young intelligentsia would lend its massive support to the Khatmiyya oriented DUP rather than to the Brothers or the Communists. After Numayri's removal, al-Mirghani changed his tune and denounced the implementation of the September 1983 Islamic laws as false, misleading and unjust and defined the Numayri regime as based on the law of the jungle. However, he expressed his conviction that under proper religious and spiritual guidance of trained *'ulama'* and *fuqaha'*, this could soon be remedied. The Islamic republic that would emerge in Sudan would, according to al-Mirghani, be based on consultation (*shura*) and on the true Islamic spirit of forgiveness, human kindness and mercy. The main concern of Islam was human dignity and the preservation of the individual's fate, his honour and his property.[120]

Following the April 1986 elections, in which the DUP, as expected, did badly, Sayyid 'Uthman al-Mirghani led his followers within the Khatmiyya and the DUP into al-Sadiq al-Mahdi's coalition government. Although al-Mirghani and the Khatmiyya had collaborated with al-Turabi under Numayri, they opposed al-Sadiq al-Mahdi's intention to bring the NIF into the coalition, as well as his terms for ending the conflict with the South. The conflict was caused by political–pragmatic concerns rather than ideologically motivated. The NIF had succeeded in capturing considerable support in Khatmiyya constituencies in the 1986 elections and al-Mirghani decided

---

[120] Al-Mirghani was interviewed in *al-Watan al-'Arabi*, 26 Apr. 1985; *al-Musawwar*, 26 Apr. 1985. Among traditional Khatmi supporters, there were many who opposed Muhammad 'Uthman al-Mirghani's involvement in active politics.

that this should not be repeated. Sudan's government of 'National Agreement' (*wifaq watani*), established in May 1988, which for the first time included the NIF, was therefore bound to bring about a rift between the Umma and the DUP. The NIF regarded an Islamic state and an Islamic constitution as its ultimate goal and al-Turabi viewed the NIF's inclusion in the new government as a personal triumph for himself and for al-Sadiq al-Mahdi and a setback for al-Mirghani. Al-Sadiq had, according to al-Turabi, wanted the NIF in his government ever since 1986 but had to overcome internal opposition both within the Umma party and in the Khatmiyya-DUP leadership. Al-Turabi and his fellow Muslim Brothers had viewed the Khatmiyya as its main political antagonist, since the latter controlled most constituencies in which the Brothers hoped to gain support. Thus the NIF emerged as the real winner in the new coalition, since it succeeded in controlling much of the agenda and policy direction of the new government. Al-Turabi became not only the Attorney-General but also the Minister of Justice and was responsible for introducing a new Islamic penal code.[121] Al-Sadiq al-Mahdi viewed the NIF's inclusion in his government as a way of broadening its popular support, on the one hand, and making the NIF bear part of the responsibility for enforcing difficult and at times unpopular policies, on the other. These included first and foremost, the controversial Islamic laws and the end of civil war. In fact, 'the question of the shari'a, like that of peace, had become a pawn in the struggle for power'.[122] Two sets of draft laws were presented to the Attorney-General to replace the September laws, one by the NIF and the second by an *ad hoc* Concord Committee which included members of all political and religious groups and was initiated by Khalid Farah the editor of the daily *al-Siyasa*. It reached a consensus, after prolonged discussions and decided to refer the controversial *hudud* to a Constitutional Conference. But instead of accepting this draft as a basis for discussion al-Sadiq al-Mahdi preferred the NIF draft since the latter had seemingly joined the coalition on condition that its draft would be implemented. This draft included application of all the *hudud*, *qisas* and *diyya*. However, 'it purported to exempt the Southern regions from the application of *hudud* penalties, unless the accused specifically request their application to him.'[123] According to Sidahmed, al-Sadiq al-Mahdi found himself more at home with the NIF proposed laws than with those of the Concord Committee, which he himself had encouraged. This was also in line with his claim that 'Islam protects the rights of non-Muslims because of its inherent values of justice and respect of human dignity.'[124]

[121] Salih, *Fading Democracy*, 206; quoted from *al-Siyasa*, 8 Apr. 1988; *al-Sudani*, 13 and 27 Apr., 1 and 15 May 1988; *al-Watan*, 4 and 11 May 1988; and *al-Ayyam and al-Jarida*, 15 May 1988.

[122] Sidahmed, *Politics and Islam*, 177–8, also 150–1.

[123] *Ibid.*, 180; the first to be sentenced to cross-amputation under the revised *hudud* was Michael Gassim, a Christian southerner caught in a robbery with three Muslim accomplices in Port Sudan; see 'First Victim of Islamic Punishments a Christian!', *SDG* (May 1991): 3.

[124] Sidahmed, *Politics and Islam*, 180–3.

The Khatmiyya had, as noted above, supported the implementation of the shari'a under Numayri but its approach was pragmatic and depended on politics rather than ideology. This was also the case with regard to the South and consequently effected the DUP's attitude towards the Islamic agenda. Al-Mirghani's pragmatism enabled him to offer the SPLM an agenda, which would enable it to come to the negotiating table on its conditions. Following continuous failures of al-Sadiq al-Mahdi and his emissaries to reach an agreement with Garang al-Mirghani surprised his colleagues when he took the initiative, in November 1988, and signed a draft agreement in Addis Ababa with the SPLA leadership that called for a cease-fire, the freezing of the shari'a laws, the lifting of the state of emergency, and the abolition of all political and military pacts with other countries. It stipulated that a constitutional conference would be convened in order to discuss the relationship between religion and politics, to decide how to share political power, and to work out a formula by which Sudan's natural resources would be evenly distributed between the different regions of Sudan. Al-Mirghani's major concession - one that al-Turabi had opposed vehemently and al-Sadiq had previously refused to offer – was that the Islamic laws would not be included in the government's platform when negotiations started. Over one million people welcomed al-Mirghani on his return to Khartoum with the signed agreement in November 1988, demonstrating their popular support for his peace initiative. The timing was also not accidental. The superior position of al-Turabi and the NIF in the new coalition government since May 1988 clearly indicated that the best route by which al-Mirghani could recapture the center of the political stage was by coming to an agreement with the SPLM, which was bound to be rejected by al-Turabi and the NIF. The NIF's condemnation of this agreement should thus have come as no surprise. Reiterating its previous positions, it stated that it would oppose any move to freeze or abolish the shari'a law. It organized a massive rally, attended by more than 100,000 supporters, in order to put pressure on the government. Al-Turabi stated that although the NIF was ready to negotiate a peaceful settlement it was against any dictated preconditions – a reference to the SPLA's demand that the shari'a laws be abolished prior to the convening of a constitutional conference. The NIF also stated that it would oppose any negotiations as long as the SPLA continued its armed struggle in the south.[125]

When the government refused to back the agreement the DUP retaliated by withdrawing its ministers and its support, thereby contributing two months later to the downfall of the third coalition. Its replacement by an all-party coalition led to yet another effort to end the civil war, bring about the endorsement of the agreement by the newly formed cabinet and later to its

[125] According to 'Ali 'Uthman Taha, the NIF's parliamentary spokesman, the reasons for his party's opposition to the initialled agreement were its unwillingness to sign an agreement with the SPLA before a cease-fire, as well as its rejection of southern demands to abrogate Sudan's agreements with Egypt and Libya; *al-Musawwar*, 15 Dec. 1988.

ratification by the Constituent Assembly.[126] It was this concession that led the NIF to leave the government and to conduct a personal smear campaign against Muhammad 'Uthman al-Mirghani, who had been hailed by public acclaim as the champion of peace and as Sudan's most popular leader. In the months that followed, Sudan lapsed into near anarchy, with the slogan 'Peace in the South' as a unifying factor of those opposing al-Sadiq's submissiveness to the NIF. Others condemned the SPLM for its adamant refusal to compromise and suggested that in this it was encouraged by Egypt.[127]

Al-Sadiq al-Mahdi's performance as Sudan's Prime Minister in the years 1986–9 cannot be reconciled with the more liberal views he had expressed previously. Even some of his closest associates from within the Ansar and the Umma were critical of his policies and resented his close association with Hasan al-Turabi and the NIF. This was especially true with regard to his adamant refusal to revoke the Islamic laws, which he had previously condemned as un-Islamic. When in March 1989, he was finally forced to compromise with the South, he had already lost the initiative. An alliance of trade unions, professional associations and sections within the army's high command submitted, on 22 February 1989, an ultimatum to the Council of State clearly indicating that both the army and the civilians were losing patience with al-Sadiq's politics. The final attempt to save democracy under the leadership of the 'National Salvation Government', brought about the only serious effort to deal with Sudan's problems. On 30 June 1989, a committee of senior lawyers, including former Chief Justices, an ex-Minister of Justice and several senior advocates, presented to the government a draft repealing law which, if accepted, would have brought about the abrogation of the September 1983 laws, thereby paving the way for peace talks with the SPLM. But it was already too late, since those in the army who, not unlike the NIF, opposed this conciliatory trend and demanded the uninterrupted implementation of the shari'a acted before the new policy could be implemented.[128] Al-Turabi's version was not surprisingly quite different. He claimed that the sole purpose of al-Umma and the DUP was to strike a deal with the SPLA that would exclude the NIF from the center of power. According to Turabi, they agreed 'with Garang that the shari'ah would not exist in the Sudan . . . Our position was quite clear; we argued that no law can be canceled just because two parties make a political deal.'[129] Al-Turabi

[126] Salih, *Fading Democracy*, 201–19; quoting from *al-Siyasa*, 15 July 1988, 29 Mar. 1989; *al-Watan al-'Arabi*, 2 Dec. 1988.

[127] *Al-Musawwar*, 15 Dec. 1988; 10 and 17 Mar. 1989; see also *October*, 12 Mar. 1989; 23 Apr. 1989.

[128] *October*, 12 Mar.; 9 & 16 Apr. 1989; I am grateful to Professor Mohamed Ibrahim Khalil, former Speaker of the Sudan's Parliament and Visiting Fellow at the Woodrow Wilson Center, Washington, DC, in 1989/90, for allowing me to quote from our very informative talk on this topic on 10 Jan. 1990.

in fact accused the Umma and the Khatmiyya of being disloyal to Islam just in order to make political gains. He claimed that 'they will not be loyal even to an agreement with the southerners, because if any other opportunity avails itself tomorrow, they will just forget their promises'.[130]

The Islamic laws promulgated by Numayri and advocated by the Muslim Brothers have thus outlived Sudan's third democratic episode. On 30 June 1989 the military, led by 'Umar Hasan al-Bashir, put an end to al-Sadiq al-Mahdi's government, arrested the political leaders of all parties, and assumed power. With a military dictatorship guided by radical Islamic principles, prospects for change seemed rather remote. The problems alluded to by al-Sadiq al-Mahdi as having led to Numayri's downfall not only remained unsolved under his own leadership but were actually exacerbated. On the eve of al-Bashir's coup, Sudan was bankrupt financially, politically and morally, largely as a result of its inability to overcome its eternal sectarian and regional struggle for power. The only viable non-sectarian political force, following the demise of the Communists in 1971, were the Muslim Brothers. However, they played a divisive role in Sudanese politics and have been one of the main forces preventing the end of civil war. Their insistence on the shari'a laws and on the creation of an Islamic state was one of the main causes that led to al-Sadiq al-Mahdi's downfall and to the end of yet another brief democratic interlude in Sudan's turbulent politics. The Secretary-General of the Umma, 'Umar Nur al-Da'im, stated in an interview in December 1994 that if the NIF had really believed in democracy, it could have forced the military after the June 1989 coup to hold new elections. But al-Turabi and his colleagues opted for the short cut proposed by their military allies. It may thus be concluded that Turabi's support for multiparty democracy in 1986 had no sound ideological base but was part of his pragmatic quest for an Islamist state. The achievement of an Islamic state justified, according to Turabi, the NIF's collaboration with the military.[131] When asked whether the NIF's assumption of power was part of the resurgence of political Islam, 'Umar Nur al-Da'im responded that the NIF had never really believed in democracy and had regarded armed intervention as both preferable and more effective.[132]

---

[129] Hamdi, *Turabi*, 101.

[130] *Ibid.*, 102.

[131] Woodward, *Islamic Radicalism*, 100. Woodward's claim that Turabi's 'support for multi-party liberal democracy was made eminently clear in the 1986 elections' seems to be open to question.

[132] 'Interview with Dr 'Umar Nur al-Da'im, General Secretary of the Umma party, *al-Ahali*, 7 Dec. 1994. Nur al-Da'im received his doctorate in agricultural engineering in Germany in 1965; he served twice as Minister of Agriculture, in 1967 and 1986, and was elected to the post of General Secretary of the Umma in 1986.

Part V. ISLAMISM AND DEMOCRACY

The final decade of the twentieth-century symbolizes the complexities with which Sudan is burdened in dealing with religion and politics, whilst attempting to solve its ethnic, cultural and economic problems and to preserve its unity. Whether or not these efforts will succeed and yield stability was as unclear at the dawn of the new millennium as it had been when independence was first declared in January 1956. A partial consolation was the fact that similar problems burdened many states and that the viability of statehood based on nationality, whether ethnic or religious, seemed to be in deep trouble not only in Africa and Asia, but also in the Balkans and other parts of the Western world. The concept of a nation-state did not seem to suit multiethnic or multireligious countries such as Sudan. However, even its territorial viability as a united state seemed rather questionable as the year 2000 drew to an end.

Civil war, sectarianism and the Islamist trend initiated by Numayri in 1983 remained the main issues that had to be faced by any regime assuming power, whether democratic or military. However, the growing gap between the riverain élite, consisting of Arabic-speaking Muslims settled along the Nile, and peoples of the marginalized, non-riverain regions of northern Sudan became an additional source of political unrest and armed conflict. These regions, which included sections of both western and eastern Sudan, consisted primarily of non-Arab Muslims such as the Nuba, the Fur and the Beja. Although most of them were Muslims, they resented the supremacy of the central riverain élite. Many of them also rejected the Islamist (Arabized) path, which had been introduced by Numayri and became even stricter during the Islamist regime of al-Bashir and al-Turabi. They viewed this trend as part of a plot to eternalize the supremacy of the Muslim–Arab élite at the expense of all others, and they gradually joined forces with the south in an effort to gain equal rights for their regions.[1] At present differences between these groups outweigh similarities, both because of ethnic solidarity and because they have been marginalized by central authority

[1] On ethnic and territorial nationalism, see Lesch, *Contested National Identities*, 6–8, 21–4; also Harir, *Racism*, 291–311. Harir relates the story of Dauod Bolad, a Fur born near Nyala in southern Dar Fur on the eve of Sudan's independence. Bolad was born into a tribe, a family and the Ansar sect and yet, like many of his generation, he opted for the modern Islamist Muslim Brothers. Once he realized that the NIF's Islam was racist, he joined the SPLA in order to fight for Fur rights. 'Bolad and his generation discovered that various forms of political Islam were being manipulated to galvanize Northern, alias riverain Central Sudanese nationalism' (*ibid.*, 307).

and by ruling élites. Consequently, while the ongoing civil war periodically embraced most of those in opposition to the Islamist regime, including Muslims in the outlying regions, they were in no way united. Since 'the regime declared that its war effort is a JIHAD war in which the warriors had only two options: to vanquish the infidel enemy or to die in martyrdom', those who opposed the regime were united by a common enemy and were driven to extremities, but they had no other common agenda.[2]

At the dawn of the new millennium, Sudan was therefore in a deep crisis. The opposition parties, 'united' within the NDA as an alternative to the military regime, were in no way in agreement and lacked a common platform. In addition, there evolved an ongoing controversy between President 'Umar al-Bashir and Hasan al-Turabi which had unfolded since the mid-1990s and led the two leaders into open conflict. Consequently the National Congress (NC), which had replaced the NIF as the ruling party, has split into two factions, with al-Turabi leading the Popular National Congress in opposition to Bashir. The outcome of this conflict is as yet unclear, nor is it clear whether Sudan will remain under the rule of the military or will witness yet another attempt to return to democracy. Sudan has been ruled by military regimes for about three-qarters of the time which has passed since independence. All of them came to power in collaboration with political parties. Democratically elected governments have never lasted longer than four or five years. However, there seems to be a strong and sincere desire among Sudanese to return once again to democratic rule. It is also significant that the two previous military regimes, led by 'Abbud and Numayri, were overthrown by civilian uprisings with the tacit support of parts of the military. This may happen again.

Numayri's regime, which was initially supported by the Communists and other leftist movements, was brought to an end by a coalition made up of trade unions, professionals, student organizations and political groups, with the support of the army's high command. It was in many respects not unlike the civilian uprising that had put an end to General Ibrahim 'Abbud's regime in October 1964. 'Abbud came to power in collaboration with 'Abdallah Khalil, then Secretary-General of the Umma party. His regime was brought to an end by a coalition that was led by students, especially those of Omdurman Islamic University, the professional associations and trade unions. Both in October 1964 and in April 1985 the army refused to intervene once it realized that the use of force would lead to a bloodbath. But here the similarity ended since in 1964 the army officers returned to their barracks and even 'Abbud himself was forced to abdicate on 14 November 1964, after a brief period as President.[3] In contrast, after the April 1985 uprising the army, which staged its own coup and assisted the

---

[2] Sadiq, *Second Birth*, 10–11; also Lesch, *Contested National Identities*, 210–11.
[3] Bechtold, *Politics in Sudan*, 211–13; also Sadiq, *Second Birth*, 30–7.

civilian uprising, remained in control of Sudanese politics for an entire year and paved the way for the third democratic episode. It did so with the support of the Alliance of National Salvation, which included students, professionals, trade unions and other groups who had marched against Numayri, including the Umma–Ansar and the DUP– Khatmiyya, the two most popular religious–political movements in Sudan.[4] It appears that Numayri himself never really grasped the magnitude of his failure nor did he understand the reasons for the vehement opposition of his antagonists. As late as December 1998 he insisted that his regime was far better than those that had been run by corrupt politicians who had only worked for themselves and did nothing for Sudan. His conclusion, not surprisingly, was that 'in places such as Africa and Asia, the soldiers are better than civilians at ruling the country'.[5] To this one should add the relative strength and apparent integrity of Sudan's professional associations, who have played a leading role in opposition whenever the military were in power. The fact that the most successful governments were those in which the professional associations participated, though only briefly, is also significant. Sirr al-Khatm al-Khalifa's transitional government in 1964–5 is the best example of such a historical episode, which was terminated, as expected, by Islamist, sectarian intervention. The 1972–82 Addis Ababa Accord under Numayri is yet another example of the anti-sectarian policy of a military regime leading to cooperation with professional associations and preparing the way for a peaceful settlement. The National Reconciliation of July 1977 and the Islamic path undertaken by the regime thereafter, in close cooperation with the Islamist movements, paved the way for the renewal of civil war. Since both civilian and military governments have so far failed to deal with Sudan's real problems, it was in a more hopeless situation at the end of the millennium than it had been when it first assumed independence in 1956.

---

[4] Details in Lesch, *Contested National Identities*, 61–2; Sadiq, *Second Birth*, 42–4.

[5] *Egypt's Insight* (Dec. 1998), 'Feature, Personal insight': Josh Mandel interviews ex-President Jaafar Nimeiri'. It thus seems quite understandable that Numayri decided to compete in the presidential elections in Dec. 2000.

17

THE ISLAMIST COUP AND THE
NIF–MILITARY COALITION

On 30 June 1989 a military coup headed by Lieutenant-General 'Umar Hasan al-Bashir took place and the military have ruled Sudan since then up till the time of writing. As in previous military coups there were numerous interpretations of the reasons leading to the coup and differing opinions as to whether the army acted on its own or was prompted and aided by civilian collaborators, as its predecessors had been. In a brochure purporting to include *Documents and Truths*, which was published one year after the Islamist regime assumed power and which seems to be an official publication endorsed by the regime, the reasons leading to the 1989 Islamist coup were listed. The authors emphasized the neglect of the army by al-Sadiq al-Mahdi's government, on the one hand, and his attempts to exploit the army politically, on the other, as the two main reasons leading to the coup. The Umma and the DUP were blamed by the writers as being responsible for the failure of the democratic regime. The NIF, on the other hand, was praised as the only party that consistently opposed the politicization of the army by the sectarian parties and by the political left. Furthermore, according to the brochure's authors, al-Sadiq had attempted to infiltrate militias loyal to the Umma into the SDF and was accused by the army's high command of undermining it. They claimed that many officers were forced into early retirement only because they did not agree politically with the two sectarian parties. Finally, al-Sadiq was accused of appointing his son as an officer in the army, in contrast to the laws and customs prevailing in the SDF. These did not allow any appointments of officers who had not graduated from the Military College in Khartoum.[6]

However, other documents at our disposal that were not included in the official brochure quoted above, as well as printed secondary sources blame the NIF and especially al-Turabi as being the main instigators of the Islamist military coup of 30 June 1989. Al-Sadiq al-Mahdi stated:

From the word go, the NIF coup d'état, and the regime it set up, used deception on a systematic basis. The coup makers exploited the briefing made by the

---

[6] *Thawrat al-inqadh al-watani*, 31–4. It was stated that al-Sadiq' son graduated from the Jordanian Military College by 'special arrangement'.

military . . . to assume that their coup was a take over by the high command of the armed forces.

Moreover, even the arrest of al-Turabi together with a few NIF leaders was, according to al-Sadiq, part of the deception undertaken in order 'to give the impression that it was a national and not partisan coup'.[7] Comparing Numayri's May Revolution with the Salvation Regime of 'Umar Hasan al-Bashir, al-Sadiq al-Mahdi lists the following differences:

The first was a One-Man rule, the second was a hydra-headed oligarchy. The first applied a more professional oppression; the second applied a vindictive oppression. The first was ambivalent about its ideology. The second more single-minded.[8]

It therefore seems that the Islamists led by al-Turabi, both in the NIF and in the army, realized that Muhammad 'Uthman al-Mirghani's draft agreement with the SPLM which he had signed in November 1988 and which was later endorsed by al-Sadiq al-Mahdi's government, would become a reality. This, they feared, would undermine the NIF's chances of gaining power and of enforcing its Islamist agenda in Sudan. According to al-Sadiq, the NIF-led Salvation Regime had, since 1989, left behind a catastrophic legacy with regard to the civil war. It had not only aborted the peace process, which had been almost brought to a successful end, but also 'injected a religious element in the civil-war and increased its bitterness and violence'. By declaring *jihad*, Sudanese society, not only in the South, was polarized to such an extent that the conflict 'boiled over regionally to Sudan's neighbors', who exploited religious differences to meet their own political needs.[9]

As already stated, al-Turabi, who together with other political leaders was briefly imprisoned by the new regime, has continuously denied any complicity in the 30 June 1989 coup. None the less, the NIF has reaped all the benefits from its collaboration with Bashir, which al-Turabi and his co-leaders of the NIF had rightly expected. The NIF's ideology and political programme were implemented by President Bashir and his fellow-officers, while al-Turabi and his colleagues soon became the power behind the throne and many of them assumed leading positions both in the Civil Service and in academia. According to Abdel Salam Sidahmed, 'the choice of the NIF of the military *coup* as a means of its transition to power is a legitimate offspring of the movement's pragmatism'. In fact, 'Hasan al-Turabi deliberately refrained from specifying the means of transition to his projected "Islamic" order.'[10] Thus a military take-over was quite legitimate.

Haydar Taha, in a study on the Muslim Brothers' penetration of the military, claims that the first steps in this direction had already been undertaken

[7] Sadiq, *Second Birth*, 51.
[8] *Ibid.*, 49.
[9] *Ibid.*, 52.
[10] Sidahmed, *Politics and Islam*, 212.

in the 1970s. 'Ali 'Uthman Muhammad Taha was the moving spirit within the Ikhwan's secret organization (*al-nizam al-sirri*), which was founded in 1972. It was Taha who organized its ranks and decided who would be entrusted to undertake underground tasks. The years of training and preparation started earnestly in camps hidden throughout Sudan. Members of the secret organization received military, security, propaganda, intelligence and other training within these camps, led by expert *mujahidin*, who had participated in the Iranian, Lebanese, Libyan, or Afghani *jihad*. Between 1978 and 1985 graduates of these camps were prepared for the next stage of *jihad*. According to Haydar Taha, the 1986 elections were, as far as the NIF was concerned, a period of transition only. For al-Turabi the exploitation of 'ballot box democracy', with its limited opportunities for the Islamist movement, was none the less an important stage towards the final goal. Whether in opposition or in government, the NIF exploited democracy in order to further its own goal – the seizure of power by whatever means available. However, already in 1987 al-Turabi was convinced that democracy had outlived its usefulness and was therefore an obstacle as far as the NIF was concerned.[11]

It was not the first time that al-Turabi had made alliances with military rulers, provided it served his Islamist agenda. His tactical alliance with Numayri in 1977–84 was based on a similar approach, namely, that such cooperation (*musharaka*) would enable the Islamists to gain useful footholds both in the economy and within the armed forces, once they were allowed to preach freely with the government's blessing. It made no difference to al-Turabi whether a tactical alliance (*tahaluf*) was made with the Ansar, the Khatmiyya or the military, as long as it served the Muslim Brothers' Islamist agenda. Al-Turabi's interpretation of Islamist ideology in a modern world enabled him to stretch pragmatism to its utmost limits, to the dismay of many of his fellow-Islamist allies. He advocated ideological flexibility or pragmatism, in order to reach alliances (*tahaluf*) with political forces such as al-Umma or the DUP, both in the 1960s and in the 1980s. He abandoned these alliances once he felt that they no longer served the political–Islamist agenda. It made little difference whether his temporary allies were political leaders such as al-Sadiq al-Mahdi, his brother-in-law, or military dictators, such as Numayri or al-Bashir. All that mattered was that these alliances enabled the Islamist programme to make rapid progress.[12]

Al-Sadiq al-Mahdi has blamed the relationships between the political leadership and the armed forces for many of Sudan's misfortunes since independence. Political leaders erred in taking the armed forces for granted and in expecting them to keep only to their military functions. This was

---

[11] Haydar, *NIF and SDF*, 192–4, 214; also Lesch, *Contested National Identities*, 113–14. Lesch rightly states that '[t]he coup d'etat enabled the NIF to implement its ideology without facing any constraints from traditional Islamic parties.' (*ibid.*, 113).

[12] Details in Weissbrod, *Turabi*, 121–4.

especially true in such troubled and complex situations as those existing in southern Sudan. Al-Sadiq mentioned several incidents to prove this point which occurred both during the 1960s when the Umma was in power, and during the 1980s while he himself was Prime Minister. These mistakes led to the politicization of the armed forces and its high command and to the army's increasing involvement in Sudanese politics. Not surprisingly, al-Sadiq claimed that this trend reached new heights following the Islamist coup of June 1989, when the 'National armed forces were manipulated to become party to the new ideology.'[13]

The complicity of the NIF in the 1989 coup and its dominant position within the regime thereafter become evident from a reading of the *Charter of the National Democratic Rally in Sudan*. It was adopted by eleven political parties and by fifty-one trade unions and professional associations on 21 October 1989, but the NIF not surprisingly refused to sign, thereby confirming its support for the regime. The first and main concern of the signatories of this document was the return to democracy and the active participation of the modern forces, such as professional associations, in the political process. Secondly, it demanded the preservation of human rights and the 'restoration of fundamental freedoms including the freedom of association, thought, creed, expression, printing, [and] movement'. Thirdly, it called for the peaceful solution of all conflicts dividing Sudanese society, thereby strengthening 'the basis of national unity . . . by solving the issues of identity, development and sharing of power and wealth; and by identifying the relations between religion and state and formulating a permanent constitution'. This in turn would lead to the 'abolition of all laws restricting freedom, and specifically the September laws of 1983'.[14]

The charter and other documents presented by the NDA to the military Islamist regime at a later stage and containing demands or suggestions were ignored by both the NIF and its military partners who did not even respond to them. 'Umar Hasan al-Bashir and his allies adamantly refused any compromise in their dealings with the SPLA and with the internal opposition. They simply provided the military umbrella for the NIF, which was acting as the ideological mentor of the new regime. They viewed Islam as the only solution to the crisis prevailing in Sudan, including the southern problem. As the Egyptian Islamic periodical *liwa' al-Islam* put it, American and Jewish aid to the 'leftist' or 'Communist' uprising of John Garang's SPLA

---

[13] Sadiq, *Second Birth*, 25–7, quotation from 48.

[14] *Mūhaq al-tajammu' al-watani al-dimuqrati fi al-Sudan* (Khartoum, 21 Oct. 1989). This charter was ratified with minor amendments at a joint meeting of its signatories with representatives of the SPLM, held in Cairo in Mar. 1990. I am grateful to Professor Mohamed Ibrahim Khalil, Speaker of Sudan's Parliament under al-Sadiq al-Mahdi, for giving me a copy of this document and of its English translation entitled *The Charter of the National Democratic Rally in Sudan*; quotations are from the English version. Dr Khalil later published his own assessment of these events entitled 'Sudan's Democratic Experiment: Present Crisis and Future Prospects' (Khalil, *Democratic Experiment*).

provided clear proof of the anti-Muslim aims of Sudan's enemies. Since Islam has had the upper hand even in southern Sudan, where the number of Muslims exceeded that of Christians, it was clear that the Islamic liberation movement would prevail in the current crisis too. It therefore made no sense to abolish or to freeze the shari'a laws, even temporarily, since they alone protected Sudan against the destructive forces of the South and its Western allies.[15]

The Islamist regime has therefore not only refused to abolish the Islamic laws but also implemented a new Islamic Penal Code, in March 1991. Executions, amputations and other punishments, prescribed by shari'a were restored. Moreover, public-order emergency courts, whose judges were officers, were empowered to arrest or flog illegal vendors, confiscate their goods and destroy their equipment.[16] On the international political front, the regime gradually moved nearer to Iran, whom many viewed as Sudan's Islamic regional mentor. During a visit to Iran in March 1993, al-Turabi proudly declared that: 'Islam is ruling in Sudan; Islamic values prevail in society and Islamic injunctions are being implemented in all fields.'[17] President Bashir also stated on more than one occasion that he and his fellow officers, who all belonged to the middle echelons of the officer corps, were in full agreement with the Islamist agenda. 'They maintained that Islam, the majority religion, and Arabic, the language of the Quran, represented the essential bases of the country's nationalism.' Consequently, 'adherents of traditional African faiths could be compelled to convert, since they were not monotheistic "People of the Book".' Even more explicitly, *'ulama'* issued a *fatwa* in 1992 ordering soldiers to kill apostates and heathens who oppose the *da'wa* and defy the Islamist regime. Finally, al-Bashir stated that he and his fellow-officers had recruited cadres from the NIF when they seized power in June 1989, in order to implement their Islamist programme in the Sudan.[18]

A Western observer stated that since 1989 'An Islamic state has been constructed by a degree of repression in the north and south unprecedented in Sudan's post-independence period . . . Instead of becoming a beacon for Islam, Sudan has become internationally isolated – as a reward for trying to attain the unattainable.'[19]

In contrast, al-Turabi, before his split with President Bashir, asserted that

[15] 'Al-Sudan min al-Mahdi ila al-Bashir', *Liwa' al-Islam* (3 Aug. 1989), 10–11, 23; also Lesch, *Khartoum Diary*, 36–7. The demonization of the SPLA was part of the government's propaganda as portrayed in its daily newspapers.

[16] Lesch, *Contested National Identities*, 129–30; these courts were also known as 'Prompt Courts'.

[17] Lesch, *Contested National Identities*, 130, quoting Turabi's declaration made in Tehran on 1 Mar. 1993, *FBIS-NES*, -93-044, 9 Mar. 1993; also *SDG* 19 (Dec. 1991): 6, & *SDG* 20 (Jan. 1992): 6; quoting Amnesty International Report, 6 Dec. 1991.

[18] Lesch, *Contested National Identities*, 130, 113; quoted from *Sawt al-Sha'ab*, 23 Feb. 1993.

[19] Woodward, *Islam in Sudan*, 113.

'the Sudanese people have now come back to Islam' and that 'Umar al-Bashir was the symbol of this phenomenon. Moreover, al-Turabi viewed this Islamist victory as a dream come true and stated that, in case he passed away, he would die contented, knowing 'that the cause I have worked for all my life has been fulfilled and that Islam will continue to be strong and well established in the Sudan.'[20] Furthermore the NIF legitimized its coming to power under a military umbrella as the only way to establish an Islamic state in Sudan. It was also the only way to put an end to sectarianism once and for all and to deal with Sudan's real problems. Carrying populism to the extreme, the NIF insisted that it was the only political group in Sudan that enjoyed genuine popular support and was therefore capable of eliminating sectarianism. According to al-Turabi, 'a multi-party system in the Sudan would not be democratic because political parties or a government governed by the House of *Khatmiyyah* and the House of the *Mahdi* was a dynastic thing'.[21] In addition, he claimed that when the coup occurred no one had rejected al-Bashir for his alleged dictatorial tendencies. When he first assumed power, he was welcomed by the Sudanese masses as well as by the rulers of Egypt, Saudi Arabia and even the United States. It was only when they realized that he was advocating an Islamist order that they turned against him since the West will never allow unacceptable views, namely Islam, to gain power.

One way of ascertaining the maintenance of power in NIF hands was by implementing al-Turabi's version of 'grass-roots democracy', which was embodied in a 'Congress' system, introduced in 1993. It embraced such populist policies as free education for all, focusing on rural populations, self-sufficiency and the setting up of popular institutions such as the Popular Defence Force (PDF), the Popular Police Corps and Popular Neighbourhood Committees. All these were intended to counter the popular support enjoyed by the Ansar and the Khatmiyya, which the NIF sought to eliminate and to replace. Of these, the PDF was the most significant, since its final aim was to replace the army and thereby eternalize Islamist rule as propagated by the NIF. First, al-Turabi and Bashir purged the army's command, dismissing nearly 40 per cent of the officer corps, and declared that in order to mobilize the Sudanese for the forthcoming *jihad*, the SDF should be dissolved and parts of it would be absorbed in the newly constituted PDF. Enlistment into the Islamic force, which was to number about 150,000, was made compulsory for all higher education candidates and for civil servants.[22] President Bashir defined it as 'the legitimate child of the armed forces' and viewed its role as a 'school for national and spiritual education'.[23] Apart from units from within the SDF the new army was to consist

[20] Hamdi, *Turabi*, 59–60.
[21] Lowrie, *Islam and the West*, 26.
[22] Woodward, *Islamic Radicalism*, 101.
[23] Lesch, *Contested National Identities*, 135, quoting Lowrie, *Islam and the West*, 94, and *FBIS-NES*, Oct. 1993, 197–9.

of the following components: Arab tribal militias (especially from Kordofan and Dar Fur); NIF volunteers including its youth movement *shabab al-watan*; students drafted from institutes of higher learning; civil servants; and forcibly enrolled teenagers. By 1994–5, every male between eighteen and thirty became liable for recruitment in the PDF, to replace the large number of casualties suffered in the *jihad* in the South.[24] This in turn induced popular opposition, led mainly by women, against the forcible conscription of Sudanese boys into the PDF and sending them to die in the *jihad*. Protesters included university professors and political activists, some over sixty years old, who were punished by lashing and other humiliating punishments.[25]

To observers of the Islamist regime it soon became clear that al-Turabi's liberal pronouncements regarding the treatment of women in Islamic society, as well as his insistence on Islamic tolerance towards minorities, had not been realized in the Islamist state in Sudan since the mid-1990s. There was a major drive towards Arabization and Islamization of education at all levels and among all ethnic groups. 'There was also a crackdown on women at work in the name of defending an Islamic conception of the family, and the numbers of women active in professions dropped sharply.'[26] An interesting and apparently typical incident regarding the treatment of women by the regime was studied in western Sudan and seems worth relating. The authors examined two conflicts in the village of Bireka during the years 1989–92. One concerned the administration of a women's grain bank and the second concerned the participation of women in market activity along a roadside. In both cases, local government became involved and ruled against the women despite the NIF's liberal ideology regarding women's equality.[27] The NIF had, as noted, declared that by treating women as equal partners in the Islamic state their status was no longer an issue. However, 'the result is an ambiguous government ideology encouraging the comparative luxury of political participation [of women], but discouraging the necessity of working outside the home, by promoting an image of the Sudanese woman devoted to home and family life.'[28] Sondra Hale also uncovered the ambiguity of the NIF's ideology regarding women:

In its drive to gain power the NIF has taken on a 'modern' look. Sudan's NIF projects a highly sophisticated articulation of Islam and commerce, especially banking and insurance. Women are important in building the infrastructure of this new class.[29]

[24] Lesch, *Contested National Identities*, 136.
[25] Souad T. Ali and Abdullahi A. Gallab, 'Sudanese Women's Humiliation: A Grave Insult to Human Civility', Al-Sudan Center for Democracy, Peace and Civil Rights, 2 Dec. 1997.
[26] Woodward, *Islamic Radicalism*, 102; also Weissbrod, *Turabi*, 87. It is noteworthy that following his break with President Bashir al-Turabi accused his erstwhile ally of being responsible for all the evils committed by the regime, especially those contravening Islam.
[27] Kevane and Gray, *Kordofan*, 273.
[28] *Ibid.*, 277.
[29] Hale, *Women & NIF*, 239.

What Hale asserts is that women became an important part of this new class not because of ideological reasons but rather as a result of the NIF's political–economic interests, in which they played an important role. Thus women were allowed to work only in 'appropriate' jobs, which were an extension of their domestic roles.

The NIF, on the other hand, accused al-Mahdi's and al-Mirghani's families of misusing Islam to deceive their unenlightened followers and to accept blindly their dynasties as leaders for eternity. The NIF claimed that the Ansar and the Khatmiyya misled the Sudanese into believing that the majority supported them, thereby legitimizing their political dominance. Al-Turabi and his followers denounced such dynastic ambitions because the Umma and the NUP–DUP had succeeded in maintaining power in all general elections since 1956. Al-Turabi stated that 'the ideal, of course, is democratic Islam. Islam shuns absolute government, absolute authority, dynastic authority and individual authority.'[30] He therefore condemned the Khatmiyya and the Ansar as undemocratic and hereditary dynasties, rather than as political parties, and asserted that they were to blame for the fact that real democracy, based on a multiparty system, could never flourish in Sudan.

People would vote for the *Mahdi*, because of his great-grandfather, because of his achievements in the 19th century. Likewise for *Mirghani*. His followers are indifferent to what he thinks today and what he would do and would never ask him questions about the way he conducts politics. They would vote for him whether he goes left or right or whether he makes a mess of politics.[31]

Consequently, al-Turabi claimed that the new Islamic democracy that had emerged under NIF guidance since 1989 was superior to the fake democracies led by sectarian parties since 1956.

To overcome sectarianism the NIF required a sound financial basis. As noted above this was partly achieved during the 1970s and 1980s and helped the NIF in the 1986 elections. By 1989 economic and financial companies under direct or indirect NIF control, both in Sudan and in other countries, had accumulated some US$800 million, an amount that could play an important role in both the social and the economic fields as well as politically. An example of this new development was the NIF's success in mobilizing merchants and other entrepreneurs to further its cause. Another outcome of this affluence was the setting up of propaganda organizations under NIF guidance such as the Islamic African Centre, which ostensibly sought to bring together all those concerned with research and studies of Islam in Africa. The Islamic *Da'wa* Organization was yet another example of the exploitation of financial affluence for the promotion of Islam, as propagated by the NIF.[32] In 1991 al-Turabi founded the Popular Islamic and

---

[30] Lowrie, *Islam and the West*, 19.

[31] *Ibid.*, 26; compare with Esposito and Voll, *Islam and Democracy*, 101.

[32] Haydar, *NIF and SDF*, 54–6.

Arabic Conference (PIAC) in Khartoum with himself as Secretary-General. Its foundation coincided with the Gulf War and its prime aim was to mobilize progressive Islamic movements against the Western imperialist plot, including the denunciation of states such as Egypt, Saudi Arabia and Syria for collaborating with the West. The PIAC was intended as a vehicle for promoting the Islamic revolution within reactionary Muslim states, using the Gulf War as an incentive for popular mass demonstrations against Muslim leaders who, according to al-Turabi and his fellow-Islamists, had betrayed the cause of true Islam. Not surprisingly, the revolutionary programme of al-Turabi and the PIAC was not popular among most of the leaders of Muslim states and the Islamic Conference Organization, centred in Saudi Arabia, boycotted its activities and cancelled a meeting of Muslim Foreign Ministers scheduled to be convened in Khartoum in 1992 by the PIAC.[33]

One result of the aggressive Islamist programme, executed by al-Turabi and the NIF was that relations between al-Bashir and al-Turabi and between the RCC and the NIF were not without conflicts. As early as 1991, when the Islamic legal codes were first promulgated, NIF cadres announced that the Islamic Republic would soon supersede the military-led regime. Two years later al-Turabi predicted that 'Sudan's military rulers will step down in the following weeks or months.' In fact, on 15 October 1993 the RCC was officially dissolved and the NIF's take-over seemed complete. Although al-Bashir maintained his position as head of state, NIF leaders seized all leading economic and social positions and had a hold on the security apparatus as well. By February 1995 they had seized the Foreign Ministry.[34]

The NIF has therefore managed to hold the reins of power due to its military and economic superiority. However, its claim to have established a more representative government than that of the Ansar-Khatmiyya coalitions and hence to be more democratic, seems rather questionable and cannot be validated. The NIF's claim rested on the following arguments: its 'grassroots democracy'; its victory in the 1996 elections; and the approval by referendum of the Islamic constitution promulgated in June 1998.[35] The first elections in Sudan since April 1986 took place on 6-17 March 1996. They were for both the 400-member National Assembly and for the presidency. Al-Bashir won the elections to the presidency with a majority of 75.7 per cent of the votes cast. Al-Turabi, who had never won a parliamentary election before except in the Graduates' Constituencies, won one of the capital's constituencies.[36] If one takes into account that the percentage of those taking part in the elections, according to Western reports, was less than 50 per cent and that in the South elections were cancelled due to continuous fighting, the 1996 elections cannot be regarded as signifying a real move towards democracy. Moreover, of the 400 members of the

---

[33] Woodward, *Islamic Radicalism*, 104; also Turabi, *Islam and the West*, 60.
[34] Lesch, *Contested National Identities*, 117–20.
[35] Kok, *Constitution*, 10–11.
[36] 'For all the pain: the election farce wins no points for the regime', *SDG* (Apr. 1996): 12.

National Assembly, 125 were chosen as early as January 1996 by the NIF-run National Congress. The NIF also nominated fifty of its own cadres to run unopposed in the other constituencies. It thus controlled 175 of the 400 Assembly's members before elections were held. With al-Turabi as its Speaker, the National Assembly in effect became a vehicle for implementing NIF policies in a seemingly democratic manner.[37]

The next step was taken in June 1998, when Sudan became an Islamic state ruled in accordance with its Islamic Constitution, which had been adopted by referendum.[38] In part I, article 1, of the constitution, under the heading 'Nature of the State', it offered the following formulation on the question of the diversity of religions and cultures:

The state of Sudan is an embracing homeland, wherein races and cultures coalesce and religions conciliate. Islam is the religion of the majority of the population. Christianity and customary creeds have considerable followers.

The question of languages was defined in part I, article 3:

Arabic is the official language in the Republic of the Sudan; and the state shall allow the development of other local and international languages.

Part I, article 4 concerned 'supremacy and sovereignty' and suggested the following definition regarding religion and state: 'Supremacy in the State is to God the creator of human beings.' According to al-Sadiq al-Mahdi, 'this concept is a conduit to theocracy, because it allows humans to speak on behalf of God, and exercise that sovereignty . . . However, sovereignty is a political concept which should be vested in the people.'[39] Part IV of the constitution dealt with 'The Legislative Power'. Article 65 defined sources of legislation as follows:

Islamic law and the consensus of the nation, by referendum, constitution and custom shall be the sources of legislation; and no legislation in contravention with these fundamentals shall be made.[40]

The Islamic constitution thus seemed to attempt a compromise that would enable non-Muslims to observe their respective religions without interference, speak their respective languages and be judged in accordance with their own religions and customs. However, the supremacy of Islamic law remained unchallengeable as a source of legislation. The Sudan federal system divided the country into twenty-six states. It thereby eliminated the

---

[37] Lesch, *Contested National Identities*, 124–5. The regime claimed that 72 per cent of those eligible participated in the elections, whereas the opposition claimed that 95% boycotted the polls. Independent observers concluded that between 7–15 per cent voted in Khartoum.

[38] *The Constitution of the Republic of the Sudan* (authorized English version), adopted June 1998 (London: The Sudan Foundation, 1998); the following quotations are from this source.

[39] Sadiq, *Second Birth*, 60.

[40] Al-Sadiq al-Mahdi stated that this article should have included not only shari'a and custom, but 'all revealed Truths, appropriate human developed jurisprudence, and custom, as sources of legislation'. Sadiq, *Second Birth*, 60.

South as a separate political entity which it had been under the Addis Ababa Agreement of 1972 and the July 1973 Constitution. However, most of the powers remained under the jurisdiction of central government thereby reducing the regional autonomy offered to the South under previous administrations even further.[41] In article 26, 'The Freedom of Association and Organisation' was described as follows: 'Citizens shall have the right of association and organization for cultural, social, economic, professional or trade union purposes without restriction save in accordance with the law.' It further stated explicitly: 'There shall be guaranteed for citizens the right to organize political associations', as long as they do not contravene the fundamentals of the constitution and their leadership is democratically elected.[42]

This brings us to the next step in the establishment of the Islamic state and its claim to strive for democracy. The Political Association Bill (*qanun al-tawali al-siyasi*) was first approved by the National Congress, consisting of over 6,000 delegates, supposedly representing all Sudan's regions and localities. In March 1998, Parliament was called upon to discuss and ratify the new bill. The main point of discussion was whether the opposition parties, illegal since June 1989 and active either in exile or underground, should be allowed to re-emerge legally in Sudan. Al-Turabi stated in an interview with the *Frankfurter Allgemeine Zeitung*: 'Let them only come and participate, whether Umma party or Communists.' He admitted that he was opposed to a multiparty system, since it disrupted unity, which is the cornerstone of the Muslim *umma*. But he expressed his confidence that the old feudal dynasties, namely the Umma and the DUP, had lost their base of support for good and that the days of sectarian politics were finally over. He concluded that corruption and mismanagement were the sole heritage the sectarian parties had left behind and therefore in the next general elections they would lose most of their electorate.[43] The Association Bill was finally approved by Parliament and was officially announced early in October 1998. It was to become effective on 1 January 1999, following its approval by President Bashir. It permitted a minimum of 100 eligible voters to form a 'political association' and to secure financing from any source inside Sudan. On 27 November 1998, al-Turabi announced his intention to resign from his post as Speaker of Parliament, once the new Association Bill was implemented, in order to devote all his time to the newly founded National Congress party, which was to replace the NIF.[44] Sudanese opposition

---

[41] For details regarding the federal system see Lesch, *Contested National Identities*, 125–8.

[42] See Sadiq, *Second Birth*, 61; al-Sadiq translated *tawali* as succession and quoted this article as requiring all associations to be based on *shura*. He concluded that 'the majority of the people of the Sudan have rejected the new constitution' (*ibid.*, 62).

[43] Interview with Dr Hasan al-Turabi, 'Die Falschen tun das Richtige', Thinkmar von Münchausen, *Frankfurter Allgemeine Zeitung*, 30 Mar., ch. 98.

[44] *Reuters*, Khartoum, 24 Nov. 1998; see also BBC news, 27 Nov. 1998; the fact that the new party was named National Congress is significant. It is reminiscent of the first attempt of the

leaders in exile were asked by *al-Musawwar* to express their views on the new Bill. Sayyid Muhammad 'Uthman al-Mirghani stated that he and his colleagues in the NDA leadership were opposed both to the Islamic constitution and to the new Association Bill. Sudan's only way out of its malaise was, according to al-Mirghani, to put an end to the present regime, set up an interim government, draft a new constitution by a constituent assembly and finally hold general elections under international supervision. Faruq Abu 'Isa', the spokesman of the NDA, explained that the Bill allowing political parties was nothing more than an exercise in public relations, since the NIF had no intention of letting its absolute power decline. All it wanted was to achieve legitimacy and improve its image as a supporter of democracy, both at home and abroad and especially in the United States and Europe. The NDA therefore rejected the offer and decided to continue to fight the regime until it was defeated and free general elections were held.[45] But the strongest opposition was expressed, on 29 December 1998, by the United Front of the opposition inside Sudan, representing all major political parties and professional associations. They rejected the democratization measures of the Islamist regime, including the Association Bill, as insufficient and called upon President Bashir to hand over the reigns of government to a national interim government. The memorandum, signed by nearly sixty prominent opposition leaders, all living inside Sudan, was handed to the President, who declined to accept it. The memorandum's signatories were condemned as 'part of a foreign plot against the successful Islamic experiment in Sudan'.[46]

However, there were some political leaders both in Sudan and in exile who decided to accept the Association Bill in good faith. They included al-Sharif Zein El-'Abdin El-Hindi, a prominent leader of the DUP, who applied for permission to reestablish his party under the new law. The party's leadership in exile rejected his initiative and Mohammad al-Azhari, one of its younger leaders, told the daily *al-Khalij* that the DUP demands 'the restoration of freedoms and the establishment of a democratic system in the country' as a precondition for its return to Sudan's political scene. Al-Azhari also stated that the DUP rejected Zein el-'Abdin el-Hindi's initiative for dialogue with the regime.[47] Father Philip 'Abbas Ghabush, a political leader from the Nuba Mountains who had played political roles during the democratic era, also decided to come to terms with the Islamic state and to found his own political association under the new Bill. Ex-President Ja'far Numayri announced in an interview in *al-Musawwar*: 'I return by public demand . . . and I am not seeking the Presidency.' He

---

Sudanese intelligentsia to move into politics, when they founded the Graduates' Congress in 1938, in line with its Indian namesake.

[45] *Al-Musawwar*, 5 Feb. 1999.

[46] *SDG*, 105 (Feb. 1999): 2–3.

[47] *Al-Khalij* news report, 4 Jan. 1999.

stated that he was determined to return to Khartoum on 25 May 1999, despite the warnings of many of his friends and supporters. He chose that date to commemorate the thirtieth anniversary of the May 1969 Revolution which had brought him to power.[48] Haydar Ibrahim Ali's Memorandum calling for 'Musawamah Tarikhiyyah' (Historical Compromise), published in the *al-Khartoum daily* on 24 November 1998, was probably the most serious attempt to argue in favour of bargaining with the present Sudanese regime in an attempt to reach a compromise. However, Haydar set down numerous conditions that the regime had to implement prior to such a compromise. He specified four areas as being fundamental for understanding Sudanese reality:[49]

1. The diversity of the Sudan makes it impossible for it to be ruled by one single political force, regardless of its ideology or its ability to rule. This holds true both for military dictatorships as well as for arbitrary majorities resulting from democratic elections.
2. The gravest mistake of the present regime is that it insisted that the multi-party system has been done away with and buried forever. In addition, the regime consistently confused between the failure of the multi-party system and the failure of democracy as a way of ruling. Therefore, they condemned democracy when they seemingly intended to condemn parties. But there must be an intellectual and political answer to the following question: has the current regime and the Islamic movement - after its experience in power - realized the fact that democracy in its multi-party system form, is the only 'true and correct' way to solve Sudan's problems?
3. We are in need of confidence building between the various parties which are at conflict. The Islamic movement and its allies, are at present in total control of all government and scientific institutions and it is inviting the other political forces to come back to Sudan and to participate in the political process based on the current conditions which make their return senseless. Obviously the opposition cannot accept a political suicide. A compromise has to be based on concessions made by both sides and guaranteed by the constitution. The regime has to dissolve all its non-governmental political security institutions, before the opposition can be asked to return to Sudan. This is based on the principle that Sudan is a country of all its citizens, which guarantees their right of movement, work and political organization and association.
4. It is in the interest of all Sudanese political movements and in the interest of the Islamic movement in particular, that there must be an agreed upon investigation into two areas: a) Torturing; b) Corruption. It is not an honour for the Islamic

---

[48] 'Al-usbu' al-siyyasi', *Al-Musawwar*, 7 May 1999, 28–9. Ja'far Numayri was interviewed by Hamdi Rizq; none the less, in Dec. 2000 Ja'far Numayri announced his candidacy in the presidential elections.

[49] All quotations are from the English summary of Dr Haydar Ibrahim 'Ali's letter to Dr 'Abd al-'Aziz Shidu, who was appointed by the government to deal with all requests regarding 'Political Associations'. The original letter in Arabic was sent to Dr Shidu by Dr Haydar, the Director of the Center of Sudanese Studies in Cairo, in Feb. 1999. It was also published under the title 'Musawama Tarikhiyya' (Historical Compromise) in *al-Khartoum*, 24 Nov. 1998.

movement that its reign has been characterized by the spread of these two phenomena. The Islamic movement must exonerate itself of these accusations even it has to sacrifice those of its members who violated its principles and conduced these practices. With regard to corruption, which did not start with the June 1989 regime, one of the conditions to make this Historical Compromise a success, is that the investigation of corruption must start with independence and continue until today. To do this Sudan should set up a national committee, based on the experience gained in South Africa and with the help of interpol to trace illegal foreign accounts.

Dr Haydar's memorandum had a considerable impact on political circles both in Sudan and in exile. While many of his observation had been previously discussed by Sudanese politicians, his all-embracing analysis seemed to suggest a possible breakthrough. However, this failed to materialize and the futile debate regarding the Association Bill (*qanun al-tawali al-siyasi*) continued both inside Sudan and among Sudanese in exile. The conclusions that can be drawn from the 1977 National Reconciliation undertaken by President Numayri and the opposition National Front have of course been exploited by both defenders and opponents of the newly proposed Historical Compromise. Many politicians and other exiles have returned to Sudan during 1999–2000, for a variety of reasons and regardless of the doubts raised by political leaders. At the same time, in Sudan itself strong opposition to the new Law of Association continued on both the political and the popular levels. On 1 January 1999 a crowd of over 30,000 gathered in and around the house of Isma'il al-Azhari, Sudan's first President, to celebrate Sudan's Independence Day. However, among the slogans chanted by the crowd, many expressed opposition to the regime and a rejection of its reconciliation attempts. The rally, which was organized by the DUP and the Umma, was addressed by leaders of the opposition, which included numerous messages from NDA leaders in exile. The main slogan chanted at the rally were '*la tawali ma'a al-Turabi*' (no association with al-Turabi) and '*ahfad al-Azhari fi al-midan*' (al-Azhari's grandchildren are in the square [front line]). The reference to Isma'il al-Azhari was significant.[50]

The government's initiative thus seemingly succeeded in splitting the opposition. According to a report published in the *Sudan Democratic Gazette* the disintegration of the NDA had become a fact and 'reconciliation, hitherto a word regarded by the NDA as sacrilegious, has suddenly

---

[50] *Al-Khartum*, 3 Jan. 1999, English translation by Al-Sudan Center for Democracy, Peace, and Civil Rights. This is reminiscent of the mass demonstration organized by supporters of the *Wafd*, which took place in Cairo in 1977 to commemorate the fifteeth anniversary of Sa'd Zaghlul's death in *Bayt al-Umma*. It took place against the background of political relaxation, announced by President Sadat, when he allowed in 1975–8 the formation of *manabir siyasiyya* (political platforms), some twenty-three years after all political parties had been banned in Egypt.

become the golden password'.[51] How did this happen? According to al-Sadiq al-Mahdi the possibility of the return to Sudan of the Umma leadership's was discussed as early as September 1999 and it actually took place on 6 April 2000. Al-Sadiq himself stayed behind in Cairo in order to assess the outcome of this step before he decided whether to return. Summarizing a three-hour interview with al-Sadiq al-Mahdi, *al-Musawwar* quoted al-Sadiq as stating that, following the return of his party's leadership to Sudan, other parties within the NDA were also discussing terms for their return to Khartoum.[52] With regard to the future policy of the Umma and to his own return to Sudan, al-Sadiq declared that this would be a gradual process and will be decided upon by the party's conference which will be convened in Khartoum in late 2000. When asked why the Umma took this decision without consulting other groups within the NDA, al-Sadiq responded that the NDA had failed to appreciate the new policy of the Sudanese regime and hence al-Umma decided to take the initiative. Responding to a question regarding the conflict between President al-Bashir and Hasan al-Turabi, which was reaching a new climax, al-Sadiq stated that this crisis was far from a solution but he regarded it as the concern of the Congress party (*hizb al-mu'tamar*) and not of the Umma party or the Sudanese people. The future, according to al-Sadiq, centred on the extent of al-Turabi's and Bashir's willingness to compromise. Since both the Islamic world and the international community were moving away from armed conflicts and towards political solutions based on moderation, al-Sadiq believed that Sudan, whoever led it, would soon follow suit. However, al-Sadiq declared that al-Bashir's promise to respect all cultures and religions, to achieve an equitable division of natural resources, to grant equal rights to the southerners and to guarantee a democratic Islam was insufficient since it continued to view the non-Muslims as second class citizens. To achieve unity, the 'religious [Islamic] constitution' (*dustur dini*), promulgated by the present regime had to be replaced. Once John Garang was convinced that a political solution was both possible and desired by the majority of southern Sudanese and by the African continent and had the backing of the international community, he would probably support it. Al-Sadiq reminded Bashir that before the June 1989 coup his government had reached such an agreement with the SPLA. It undertook to convene a national conference on the issues of religion and state, as well as on the division of Sudan's natural resources. However, the Islamist coup of June 1989 rejected the compromise and thus led to the present impasse. The fact

[51] 'Has the NDA lost control of the opposition politics against the NIF?', *SDG*, 115 (Dec. 1999): 7–8.

[52] Hamdi Rizq, interview with al-Sadiq al-Mahdi, *al-Musawwar*, 21 Apr. 2000, 52–6, on which the following is based; also Sadiq, *Second Birth*, 64–7. Al-Sadiq al-Mahdi returned to Sudan on 23 Nov. 2000 and was welcomed by a crowd estimated at over two million people. *SDG* (Dec. 2000): 5–6.

that both President Bashir and his military command had at last realized that they had failed and that only a political solution was possible had led to the present opportunity. In an earlier report *al-Musawwar* noted that John Garang's conditions for return were far more demanding than those of the Umma, the DUP and other members of the NDA. This was based on the fact that he was both the leader of the SPLM and the commander of the SPLA, an army consisting of 5000 armed men, which was in control of large sections of southern Sudan.[53]

But the situation in the South was further complicated as a result of ethnic conflicts in the region itself. These ethnic wars involved primarily the Nuer and the Dinka and since 1991, have led to increased violence and resulted in many casualties and massive kidnapping. Unfortunately the military leaders of this conflict, John Garang (Dinka) and Riek Machar (Nuer) have failed to reach a compromise and the initiative has, since 1998, passed into the hands of regional civilian chiefs. It led to the 'Dinka and Nuer Peace Conference', which was held at Wunlit in March 1999 and which concluded that these ethnic conflicts were primarily the outcome of the political and military ambitions of individuals and only led to massive suffering. One of the Nuer leaders attending the conference asked bitterly: 'If all the Nuer and Dinka are killed, who are Garang and Riek going to be leaders of?'[54] As 1999 was drawing to an end, it was quite unclear whether John Garang still enjoyed the confidence of the majority of Southerners, and consequently both the NIF regime, the opposition parties and the southerners were hopelessly split.

During May 2000 President Bashir pursued reconciliation efforts. He invited Muhammad 'Uthman al-Mirghani to join in the negotiations of his government with NDA leaders, and the latter responded favourably. Egypt, which at the time was leading the Egyptian–Libyan peace initiative, seemed to be behind these moves. It also initiated efforts to bring John Garang into the negotiating process. Garang visited Cairo and following his talks it was announced at a press conference that he did not favour an independent South. Rather he wanted a 'New Sudan', with a new constitution wherein equality was granted to all citizens.[55] Al-Sadiq al-Mahdi came to the following conclusion:

Legitimacy of government in the Sudan can neither be based on dynastic credentials, nor on the credentials of a Revolution which had, through its accomplishments achieved national recognition. The only feasible basis for legitimacy in the Sudan, is democratic legitimacy.[56]

[53] *Al-Musawwar*, 24 Mar. 2000, 12.
[54] Jok & Hutchinson, *Militarization of Nuer & Dinka Ethnic Identities*, 143.
[55] 'War and politics: after long hesitation el Mirghani warms up to Khartoum', *SDG*, 120 (June 2000): 2.
[56] Sadiq, *Second Birth*, 67.

Al-Sadiq al-Mahdi returned to Sudan from his self-imposed exile on 23 November 2000. In his Friday sermon at the Wad Nubawi mosque, he pledged his word to an audience of about one million Ansar that the Umma party would remain committed to all its pledges regarding self-determination for the southern Sudanese. He also stated that 'there is not going to be an Islamic state in a country as religiously and culturally divided as Sudan'.[57]

However, it seemed that real reconciliation was as far away as ever. In December 2000 'Umar Hasan al-Bashir was elected to a second term as President, winning 86.5 per cent of the vote. But voting was boycotted by most opposition parties, which denounced the election as undemocratic. Furthermore, on 31 December President Bashir declared the extension of the State of Emergency in Sudan, first imposed on 12 December 1999. At the time it was believed that the State of Emergency was introduced in order to curb the influence of Hasan al-Turabi and his supporters, who had formed their own opposition party challenging President Bashir. Bashir even stated that the State of Emergency would not violate any of the constitutional articles nor the individual freedoms guaranteed by the constitution. The reason he gave for the extension of the State of Emergency was that it would enable Sudan's National Council to amend the constitution in preparation for general elections.[58] Whether or not the long-promised national reconciliation and the return to a multiparty democracy would indeed be achieved remained as unclear as ever.

---

[57] 'El Mahdi returns to a tumultus public welcome in Khartoum', *SDG*, 126 (Dec. 2000): 5–6.

[58] *Reuters*, Cairo, 10 Jan. 2001, quoting President Bashir's interview with Middle East News Agency (MENA).

18

ISLAM AND DEMOCRACY

In a study of 'plural societies' Arend Lijphart noted that in 'societies that are sharply divided along religious, ideological, linguistic, cultural, ethnic, or racial lines . . . the flexibility necessary for majoritarian democracy is absent'. He concluded:

> Under these conditions, majority rule is not only undemocratic but also dangerous, because minorities that are continually denied access to power will feel excluded and discriminated against and will lose their allegiance to the regime.[59]

John Esposito and John Voll seem to take a different view in their book *Islam and Democracy*. Its central theme was introduced as follows:

> Religious resurgence and democratization are two of the most important developments of the final decades of the twentieth century. In many areas, movements of religious revival coincide with and sometimes reinforce the formation of more democratic political systems.[60]

While neither of the studies quoted above singled out Sudan, nor did the study of Esposito and Voll deal with ethnic diversity, their predictions are relevant both to Sudan and to other multiethnic or multireligious countries. The following questions therefore seem relevant: first, if a majority imposes its religious convictions, whatever they may be, on a minority by force of numbers, can it be defined as democratic? Secondly, is the status of *ahl al-dhimmah* offered to non-Muslims in an Islamic state by Islamists a democratically acceptable one? Finally, can ethnic nationalism based on the Islamic–Arabic ideal, which has been dominant in Sudan's political life since independence, lead to coexistence within democratic institutions? Or is territorial nationalism more amenable to minority rights and therefore more suited to countries like Sudan?[61]

In *Islam and Democracy* Esposito and Voll offer the following analysis:

> The conflict, in principle, is not between Islam and democracy in Sudan. The Islamists have long participated in democratic politics, and define their desired political system in democratic terms. The real conflict is between different options for defining the relationship between Islam and democracy in the Sudanese context. The established relationship is the failed system of sectarian politics. The

---

[59] Lijphart, *Democracies*, 22.
[60] Esposito and Voll, *Islam and Democracy*, 3.
[61] See Lesch, *Contested National Identities*, 21–4.

option of a secular political system seems improbable under current conditions. The kind of option remaining is to create a nonsectarian system that is both Islamically identifiable and able to include, voluntarily, secularists and non-Muslim Sudanese.[62]

There seems to be no dispute with regard to the failure of sectarian politics in Sudan up to the present. Apart from naïve well-wishers, there also seems to be no disagreement regarding the improbability of secularism in Sudan in the foreseeable future. Unfortunately, Esposito and Voll's remaining option of creating a non-sectarian Islamic system [state?] that will be tolerant enough to include secularists and non-Muslims as equal citizens in an Islamist state, also seems highly unlikely.

In conclusion we will quote a number of Sudanese scholars and politicians who have expressed their views on these issues. In an article analysing the reasons leading to the failure of democracy in Sudan Muhammad Ibrahim Khalil, a professor of Islamic Law and a past Speaker of the post-1986 Parliament, argued that advanced societies marked by a high level of education have better chances of stable democratic rule. However, this was, in his view, not a precondition and the success of democracy in India and other non-Western democracies proved that, while education and progress might help, they were not essential.[63] As to whether democracy was consistent with Islam, Khalil argued that only fundamentalist Muslims question the compatibility of Islam and democracy

adopting, as they do, a literal, narrow interpretation of Islamic scriptures and vaunting a slavish idolization of pristine governmental and administrative institutions and practices . . . A liberal interpretation of Islamic doctrine would justify that Islam is perfectly compatible with democracy.

Furthermore, in contrast to many Western and Middle Eastern scholars, Khalil maintained that 'even a cursory reading of the Quran would reveal that it contains the fabric out of which democracy and constitutional government are woven'.[64] Taking into account that even progressive liberal Muslim thinkers reject a secular constitution, Khalil claimed that the provisions required for a democracy may be embodied in an Islamic constitution that need not be secular. The failure of democracy, according to Khalil, was not the fault either of traditional culture or of Islam, but lay with the failure of the educated class and the political parties. He therefore concluded: 'While Islam is not inimical to liberal constitutionalism, the fundamentalist interpretation of its scriptures is'.[65]

Al-Sadiq al-Mahdi, who was Prime Minister until the 1989 coup claimed that his removal was not caused by the failure of democracy in Sudan but

[62] Esposito and Voll, *Islam and Democracy*, 101.
[63] Khalil, *Democratic Experiment*, 105.
[64] *Ibid.*, 107.
[65] *Ibid.*, 108.

that he was overthrown by a limited military revolt, led by a small fraction of the antidemocratic political forces who had always supported Numayri's Islamist programme and who consequently rejected the peace proposals with the south.[66] However, a decade later al-Mahdi argued that the one-man one-vote majoritarian system fails to accommodate two social forces, which in the underdeveloped stage of Sudan constitute a minority. The first are the educated, who 'feel that the one man one vote system does not give them a voice commensurate with their real social power'. The same holds true for 'cultural minorities which are sufficiently conscious of a separate identity, and which feel that the majoritarian system somehow constrains them'. Al-Sadiq therefore concluded: 'Democracy needs to be qualified by certain balancing measures to absorb these frustrations without seriously undermining the one-man one-vote basis of representative democracy.'[67] The question is whether such a concept of democracy can prevail in Sudan or in other states that define their national identities in accordance with religious or ethnic loyalties. Hasan al-Turabi's publications and political statements over the last two decades suggest that he has basically remained true to his beliefs expressed in the 1980s and 1990s. He continues to support the nation–territorial state; he propagates a decentralized Islamic unity, without jeopardizing the national concept of individual states; and finally, he sees no contradiction between an Islamic state and democracy. The corruption of this ideal in present-day Sudan is blamed by al-Turabi and other Islamists on fraudulent politicians, such as President al-Bashir of Sudan, and does not disprove the validity of an Islamic democratic state. We are thus presented with the views of three prominent northern Sudanese politicians and Islamist scholars, who see no real contradiction between Islam and democracy and who blame its failure on a variety of factors, but not on Islam itself.

Francis Deng, a politician and scholar of Dinka origin, views the problem of democracy from a different vantage point. He has argued that democracy, although universally endorsed and accepted on principle, is problematic in its application in African states, owing to the ethnic, religious and racial diversity prevailing in them.

Africans tend to vote on the basis of their politicised ethnic or religious identity, democracy risks becoming a dictatorship of numbers. This enables an automatic majority to impose its will on the minority with impunity.

To overcome this predicament Deng suggested that African democracies have to be based on the devolution of power and to 'apply democracy on a non-racial, non-ethnic and non-religious basis a truly uniting concept of

---

[66] Jadin, *Taqyim al-tajriba al-dimuqratiyya*, 325, quoting from al-Sadiq al-Mahdi, 'Mihnat al-Islam fi al-Sudan', *al-Sharq al-Awsat*, 15 Mar. 1993.

[67] Sadiq, *Second Birth*, 91.

nationhood'.[68] Deng seems to favour a territorial rather than ethnic concept of nationhood.

All these comments, made by knowledgeable and experienced politicians and scholars, tend to ignore the real predicament. Assuming that a state based on Islam can be democratic, why has democracy failed repeatedly both in Sudan and in other Islamic states? Mohamed Ahmed Mahgoub, a leading member of the Umma party and Prime Minister of Sudan in the 1960s, stated in his book entitled *Democracy on Trial* that 'democracy has been on trial not only in Sudan but all over the African continent' and has failed everywhere. The reasons, in his view, included the failure of politicians to formulate a cohesive policy. 'Personal and sectarian rivalries and intrigue held full sway, and short-term personal power became predominant.' Consequently, throughout Africa, tribal and sectarian divisions dominated the political scene, people abused the freedoms brought to them by democracy, while the press indulged in destructive criticism.[69]

There are two important factors that make Sudan's experience different from that of other Muslim states. First, its initial experiment in statehood in 1881–98 was in the shape of an Islamic–Mahdist state. Secondly, Islamic sectarianism, largely the consequence of neo-Mahdism, played a dominant role both under colonial rule and in post-independence politics. Many Sudanese and Western scholars, as well as many Sudanese politicians – blame 'sectarianism' and not Islam for the failure of democracy in Sudan. However, it seems irrelevant whether Islam or sectarianism is to blame for democracy's failure, since, under prevailing conditions and against all predictions, sectarianism has outlived all its foes, be they military, Islamist or secular, and seems to move into the twenty-first century as strong as ever. Since 1989, when Sudan emerged as a militant Sunni-Islamist state under the guidance of Hasan al-Turabi, the question whether the Islamic political tradition as expressed in its Islamic constitution is compatible with democracy has remained unanswered. Sudan's Islamist experiments, in both the nineteenth and twentieth centuries, were under autocratic rule. It is therefore as impossible to appraise the relative strength or popular support of the Ansar or the Khatmiyya if free general elections were held in the near future. However, based on recent evidence and on current reports, it seems safe to assume that the sectarian political parties would gain considerable popular support and possibly emerge victorious if free general elections were held. In addition one has to take into account that the ethnoreligious basis of Sudanese nationality and statehood has dominated the political and socio-economic scenes since the nineteenth century. It is therefore questionable whether a drastic shift from sectarian loyalties to territorial nationhood, which implies secularism, is likely to happen in the foreseeable future.

[68] Quotations from Deng, *Democracy*, 11–12.
[69] Mahgoub, *Democracy*, 297–8.

An interesting example is quoted by Elie Kedourie in his study *Democracy and Arab Political Culture*, namely an opinion poll conducted in Egypt by *al-Ahram* in 1991. In it, nearly 5,000 people responded to two questions related to this problem in the following manner: 56 per cent favoured the introduction of Western-style democracy, while 52.3 per cent demanded the application of the shari'a. In other words, there seemed to be no contradiction between Islam and democracy in the minds of Egyptians or Sudanese and one may assume that this holds true for other Muslim states as well. None the less, it is generally admitted, even in Muslim countries, that democracy has so far failed throughout the Islamic world. Kedourie ascribed the failure to prevailing political traditions, which implied that autocracy and passive obedience reigned supreme.[70] Bernard Lewis, on the other hand, seems more optimistic with regard to the ability of Muslim states, if they rely on Islamic norms, to keep within the limits of justice. Quoting from the writings of Namik Kemal, the Young Ottoman ideologue he ascribes this primarily to the principle of consultation (*shura*) and to the oath of allegiance (*bay'a*). Namik Kemal regards the latter as guaranteeing the sovereignty of the people. While these in no way correspond to democracy as practised in other parts of the world, they none the less help to guard the separation of powers and limit autocratic tendencies to a certain extent.[71] When relating to the twentieth century nation-state, Lewis has sadly agreed that the tolerance practised under traditional Islam has all but vanished and that 'non-Muslim minorities, while enjoying complete equality on paper, in fact have fewer opportunities . . . than under the old Islamic yet pluralistic order'.[72] However, Lewis does not see an inherent contradiction between Islam and democracy. The Islamic doctrine is autocratic but not dictatorial and the rulers are according to this doctrine, not above the law since the *bay'a* compels them to seek the people's agreement to their rule.[73]

[70] Kedourie, *Democracy*, 1, 103.
[71] Lewis, *Islam in History*, 275–6.
[72] Lewis, *Islamic World*, 51.
[73] B. Lewis, interview in *Haaretz*, 23 Mar. 2001, 60.

BIBLIOGRAPHY

*listed alphabetically according to the abbreviations used
in the footnotes*

Abbas, *British Views* – 'Abbas Ibrahim Muhammad 'Ali, 'Contemporary British Views on the Khalifa's Rule', *SNR*, 51 (1970): 31–46.

Abbas, *Slave Trade* – Abbas Ibrahim Muhammad Ali, *The British, the Slave-Trade and Slavery in the Sudan 1820–1881* (Khartoum University Press, 1972).

Abu Salim, *Athar* – Muhammad Ibrahim Abu Salim, *Al-athar al-kamila li'l-Imam al-Mahdi*, 7 vols (Khartoum: dar jami'at al-Khartum li'l-nashr, 1990–4).

Abu Salim, *Dawr al-'ulama'* – Muhammad Ibrahim Abu Salim, 'Dawr al-*'ulama'* fi nashr al-Islam fi al-Sudan' in Muddathir and al-Tayyib, *Islam*, 31–42.

Abu Salim, *Haraka* – Muhammad Ibrahim Abu Salim, *Al-haraka al-fikriyya fi al-Mahdiyya*, 3rd edn (Khartoum: dar jami'at al-Khartum li'l-nashr, 1989).

Abu Salim, *Ma'alim* – Muhammad Ibrahim Abu Salim (ed.), *Min ma'alim ta'rikh al-Islam fi al-Sudan* (Khartoum: dar al-fikr li'l-tiba'a wa'l-nashr wa'l-tawzi', n d.).

Abu Salim, *Manshurat* – Muhammad Ibrahim Abu Salim, *Manshurat al-Mahdiyya* (Beirut: dar al-jil, 1979).

Abu Salim, *Murshid* – Muhammad Ibrahim Abu Salim, *Al-murshid ila wath'aiq al-mahdi* (Khartoum, n.d.).

Abu Salim, *Nasihat al-'Awwam* – Muhammad Ibrahim Abu Salim, 'Nasihat al-'Awwam wa'l-'alaqa bayn al-thawratayn al-mahdiyya wa'l-'urabiyya' (unpublished manuscript, n.p.; n.d.).

Abu Salim and Vikör, *The Man Who Believed* – Muhammad Ibrahim Abu Salim and Knut S. Vikör, 'The Man Who Believed in the Mahdi', *Sudanic Africa*, 2 (1991): 29–52.

Affendi, *Turabi's Revolution* – Abdelwahab El-Affendi, *Turabi's Revolution: Islam and Power in Sudan* (London: Grey Seal, 1991).

Ahmed Uthman, *Ideology* – Ahmed Uthman Ibrahim, 'Some aspects of the Ideology of the Mahdiya', *SNR*, 60 (1979).

Alier, *Southern Sudan* – Abel Alier, *Southern Sudan: Too Many Agreements Dishonoured* (London: Ithaca, 1990).

'Ali Taha, *Al-Haraka al-Siyasiyya* – Faysal 'Abd al-Rahman 'Ali Taha, *Al-haraka al-siyasiyya al-sudaniyya wa'l-sira' al-misri al-baritani bi-sha'n al-sudan, 1936-1953* (Cairo: dar al-amin, 1998).

'Am 'ala tatbiq al-shari'a – *'Am 'ala tatbiq al-shari'a al-islamiyya fi al-Sudan* (Khartoum: majlis al-sha'ab, 1984).

Anderson, *Law Reform* – J.N.D. Anderson, 'Law Reform in Egypt: 1850-1950' in Holt, *Political and Social Change*, 209–30

Anderson, *Modernization* – J.N.D. Anderson, 'The Modernization of Islamic law in the Sudan', *Sudan Law Journal and Reports* (1960): 295–302.

Anderson, *Recent Developments* – J.N.D. Anderson, 'Recent Developments in Shari'a Law in the Sudan', *SNR*, 31/1 (June 1950): 82–104.

Atiyah, *An Arab* – Edward Atiyah, *An Arab Tells his Story* (London: John Murray, 1946).

Bakheit, *Native Administration* – Jafar M.A. Bakheit, 'Native administration in the Sudan and its Significance to Africa' in Hasan, *Sudan in Africa*, 256–78.

Barclay, *Hindiyya* – H.B. Barclay, 'A Sudanese religious brotherhood: al-Tariqa al-Hindiya', *The Muslim World*, vol.53 (1963): 127–37.

Bechtold, *Politics in Sudan* – Peter K. Bechtold, *Politics in Sudan: Parliamentary and Military Rule in an Emerging African Nation* (New York: Praeger, 1976).

Bedri, *Hayati* – Babikr Badri, *Ta'rikh hayati*, 3 vols (Omdurman: matba'at Misr [Sudan], 1959–61).

Bedri, *Memoirs* – Babikr Bedri, *The Memoirs of Babikr Bedri*, vol. 1 (Oxford University Press, 1969); vol. 2 (London: Ithaca Press, 1980). Translation of vols 1 & 2 of the Arabic version.

Bell, *Shadows* – Sir Gawain Bell, *Shadows on the Sand: the Memoirs of Sir Gawain Bell* (London: Hurst, 1983).

Beshir, *Education* – Mohamed Omer Beshir, *Educational Development in the Sudan, 1898-1956* (London: Oxford University Press, 1969).

Beshir, *El Jabri* – M.O. Beshir, 'Abdel Rahman Ibn Hussein El Jabri and his Book "History of the Mahdi" ', *SNR*, 44 (1963): 136–9.

Beshir, *Southern Sudan* – M.O. Beshir, *The Southern Sudan: Background to Conflict* (London: Hurst, 1968).

Birks, *Pilgrimage* – J. Birks, *Across the Savannas to Mecca: The Overland Pilgrimage route from West Africa* (London: Hurst, 1978).

Björkelo, *Prelude to the Mahdiyya* – Anders Björkelo, *Prelude to the Mahdiyya: Peasants and Traders in the Shendi Region, 1821-1885* (Cambridge University Press, 1989).

Björkelo, *Turco-Jallaba Relations* – Anders Björkelo, 'Turco-Jallaba Relations 1821–1885' in Manger, *Trade*, 81–107.

Bruce, *Travels* – James Bruce, *Travels to Discover the Source of the Nile*, 2nd edn (Edinburgh: 1805).

Burckhardt, *Travels* – John L. Burckhardt, *Travels in Nubia*, 2nd edn (London: 1822).

Collins, *Southern Sudan* – R.O. Collins, *The Southern Sudan, 1883-1898* (New Haven, CT: Yale University Press, 1962).

Cudsi, *Islam and Politics* – A.S. Cudsi, 'Islam and Politics in the Sudan' in J.P. Piscatori (ed.), *Islam in the Political Process* (Cambridge University Press, 1983).

Daly, *Imperial Sudan* – M.W. Daly, *Imperial Sudan: The Anglo-Egyptian Condominium, 1934-56* (Cambridge University Press, 1991).

Daly, *Modernization* – M.W.Daly (ed.), *Modernization in the Sudan: Essays in Honour of Richard Hill* (New York: Lilian Barber Press, 1985).

Daniel, *Islam & Europe* – Norman Daniel, *Islam Europe and Empire* (Edinburgh University Press, 1966).

Davies, *Camel's Back* – Reginald Davies, *The Camel's Back* (London: John Murray, 1957).

Davies, *Mahdism 1926* – Reginald Davies, 'Note on Mahdism', 7 Apr. 1926, FO 371/11613.

Davies, *Memorandum* – 'Memorandum on the policy of the Sudan Government towards the Mahdist Cult' by Reginald Davies, *SSIR*, 7, 11 Dec. 1926, FO 371/ 11613.

Dekmejian and Wyszomirski, *Charismatic Leadership* – R.H. Dekmejian and M.J. Wyszomirski, 'Charismatic Leadership in Islam: The Mahdi of the Sudan', *Comparative Studies in Society and History*, 14 (1972): 193–214.

Deng, *Democracy* – F.M. Deng, 'Globalisation and Localisation of Democracy in the African Context', *SDG*, 96 (May 1998).

Deng, *Seed* – Francis Mading Deng, *Seed of Redemption: A Political Novel* (New York: Lilian Barber Press, 1986).

Dhaher, *Al-Mirghani* – Dhaher Jasim Mohammed, 'The Contribution of Sayed 'Ali al-Mirghani, Leader of the Khatmiyya, to the Political Evolution of the Sudan, 1884–1968' (unpublished PhD dissertation, University of Exeter, 1988).

Dietrich, *Der Mahdi* – E.L. Dietrich, 'Der Mahdi Mohamed Ahmed vom Sudan nach Arabischen Quellen', *Der Islam*, 24 (1925): 199–288.

Duran, *Centrifugal Forces* – Khalid Duran, 'The Centrifugal Forces of Religion in Sudanese Politics', *Orient*, 26/4 (Dec. 1985): 572–600.

Duran, *Islam* – Khalid Duran, *Islam und politischer Extremismus. Einführung und Documentation* (Hamburg: Deutsches Orient-Institut, Sondernummer 11, 1985).

Esposito, *Modern Islam* – John Esposito (ed.), *The Oxford Encyclopedia of the Modern Islamic World* (New York: Oxford University Press, 1995).

Esposito, *Political Islam* – John L.Esposito (ed.), *Political Islam: Revolution, Radicalism, or Reform?* (Boulder, CO: Lynne Rienner, 1997).

Esposito, *Voices* – John L. Esposito (ed.), *Voices of Resurgent Islam* (New York: Oxford University Press, 1983).

Esposito and Voll, *Islam and Democracy* – John L. Esposito and John O. Voll, *Islam and Democracy* (New York: Oxford University Press, 1996).

Furman, *Minorities* – Uriah Furman, 'Minorities in Contemporary Islamist Discourse', *MES*, 36/4 (Oct. 2000): 1–20.

Gaddal, *Religion* – Muhammad Said al-Gaddal, 'Religion in a Changing Socio-Political Structure: a Case Study of Islam in Nineteenth-Century Sudan', in Daly, *Modernization*, 49–56.

GGR – *Reports on the Finances, Administration and Condition of the Sudan*. (These were annual reports submitted by the Governor General of Sudan to the British Consul General, later High Commissioner and, from 1936, Ambassador in Egypt. These reports should not be confused with the abbreviated version, compiled by the British Consul-General in Cairo, which were published as *Command Papers*.)

Ghandur, *Qissat al-Jaysh* – Muzamil Salman Ghandur, 'Qissat al-jaysh wal-sulta fi al-Sudan', *al-Tadammun*, 1 Feb.–8 Mar. 1986.

Grunebaum, *Modern Islam* – G.E. von Grunebaum, *Modern Islam: The Search for Cultural Identity* (New York: Vintage Books, 1964).

Gumaa, *African and Arab* – Gumaa Mohammed Ahmed, 'The Sudan: African and Arab' in M.O. Beshir (ed.), *Sudan: Aid and External Relations* (Khartoum: Graduate College Publications, University of Khartoum, 1984).

Hajj, *Al-Mahdiyya wa'athruha* – Muhammad Ahmad al-Hajj, 'al-mahdiyya wa'athruha al-dini fi al-Sudan' in Abu Salim, *Ma'alim*, 91–104.

Hale, *Women and NIF* – Sondra Hale, 'The Women of Sudan's National Islamic

Front' in J. Benin and J. Stork (eds), *Political Islam, Essays from Middle East Report* (Berkeley: University of California Press, 1997), 234–49.

Hale, *Sudan Civil War* – Sondra Hale, 'The Sudan Civil War: Religion, Colonialism, and the World System' in Joseph and Pillsbury, *Muslim-Christian Conflicts*, 173–8.

Hamdi, *Turabi* – Mohamed Elhachmi Hamdi, *The Making of an Islamic Political Leader: Conversations with Hasan al-Turabi* (Boulder, CO: Westview Press, 1998).

Harir, *Racism* – Sharif Harir, 'Racism in Islamic Disguise: Retreating Nationalism and Upsurging Ethnicity in Dar Fur, Sudan' in Hanne Veber *et al.* (eds), *Never Drink From the Same Cup*, Proceedings of the conference on Indigenous peoples in Africa, CDR-IWGIH Document No. 74 (Tune, Denmark 1993); 291–311.

Hasan, *Islam* – Yusuf Fadl Hasan, *The Coming of Islam to the Sudan* (Cambridge University Press, 1965).

Hasan, *Islamization of Sudan* – Yusuf Fadl Hasan, 'External Islamic influences and Progress of Islamization in the Eastern Sudan between the Fifteenth and Eighteenth Centuries' in Hasan, *Sudan in Africa*, 73–86.

Hasan, *Masar al-da'wa* – Yusuf Fadl Hasan, 'Masar al-da'wa al-mahdiyya kharij al-Sudan 'ala daw' rasa'il al-Mahdi wa-Khalifatihi' in Naqr, *Dirasat*, 166–82.

Hasan, *Sudan in Africa* – Yusuf Fadl Hasan (ed.), *Sudan in Africa* (Khartoum University Press, 1971).

Hassan, *'Abd al-Rahman* – Hassan Ahmad Ibrahim, 'Sayyid 'Abd al-Rahman al-Mahdi a Master of Manipulation Manipulated (1935–1944)', paper presented to the Fifth International Conference on Sudan Studies, University of Durham, England, 30 Aug.–1 Sept. 2000.

Hassan, *Al-Imam* – Hasan Ahmad Ibrahim, *Al-imam 'Abd al-Rahman al-Mahdi* (Omdurman: jami'at al-ahfad li'l-banat, 1998).

Hassan, *Mahdist Risings* – Hassan Ahmad Ibrahim, 'Mahdist Risings Against the Condominium Government in the Sudan, 1900-1927', *International Journal of African Historical Studies*, 12/3 (1979): 440–82.

Hassan, *Sayyid 'Abd al-Rahman* – Hassan Ahmad Ibrahim, 'al-Sayyid 'Abd al-Rahman al-Mahdi wa-bara'at al-munawarat al-siyasiyya', in Naqr, *Dirasat*, 193–202.

Haydar, *Azmat al-Islam* – Haydar Ibrahim 'Ali, *Azmat al-Islam al-siyasi, al-jabha al-Islamiyya al-qawmiyya fi al-Sudan namudhajan* (Rabat: markaz al-dirasat al-Sudaniyya, 1991).

Haydar, *Mahmud Muhammad Taha* – Haydar Ibrahim 'Ali (ed.), *Al-ustadh Mahmud Muhammad Taha, ra'id al-tajdid al-dini fi al-Sudan* (Al-Dar al-Bayda: markaz al-dirasat al-Sudaniyya, 1992).

Haydar, *NIF and SDF* – Haydar Taha, *Al-ikhwan wa'l-'askar, qisat al-jabha al-Islamiyya wa'l-sulta fi al-Sudan* (Cairo: markaz al-hadara al-'arabiyya li'l-i'lam wa'l-nashr, 1993).

Henderson, *Modern Sudan* – K.D.D. Henderson, *The Making of the Modern Sudan* (London: Faber & Faber, 1953).

Hill, *BD* – R. L. Hill, *A Biographical dictionary of the Sudan*, 2nd edn (London: Frank Cass, 1967).

Hill, *Christian Missions* – R. L. Hill, 'Governments and Christian missions in the Anglo-Egyptian Sudan 1899-1914', *Middle Eastern Studies*, 1/2 (1965): 113–34.

Hill, *Egypt in Sudan* – Richard Hill, *Egypt in the Sudan, 1820–1881* (Oxford University Press, 1959).

Hill, *Frontiers* – Richard Hill, *On the Frontiers of Islam: the Sudan under Turco-Egyptian Rule, 1822–1845* (Oxford: Clarendon Press, 1970).

Hill, *Giegler Pasha* – Richard Hill (ed.), *The Sudan Memoirs of Carl Christian Giegler Pasha, 1873–83* (London: published for the British Academy by Oxford University Press, 1984).

Hill, *Slatin* – Richard Hill, *Slatin Pasha* (Oxford University Press, 1965).

Hodgkin, *Mahdism* – T. Hodgkin, 'Mahdism, Messianism and Marxism in the African Setting' in Hasan, *Sudan in Africa*, 109–28.

Hofheinz, *Faki* – Albrecht Hofheinz, 'From Faki to Duktor: Changing Attitudes Towards Tradition Among Sudanese Rural Intellectuals', *Conference Papers, Second International Sudan Studies Conference*, vol. 3 (University of Durham, 1992), 96–106.

Hofheinz, *Idrisi* – Albrecht Hofheinz, 'More on Idrisi Influence in the Sudan', *Sudanic Africa* 2 (1991): 179–82.

Hofheinz, *Internalising Islam* – Albrecht Hofheinz, 'Internalising Islam: Shaykh Muhammad Majdhub, Scriptural Islam, and Local Context in the Early Nineteenth-Century Sudan' (unpublished PhD thesis, University of Bergen, 1996).

Holt, *EI* – P.M. Holt, 'Al-Mahdiyya', *Encyclopedia of Islam*, vol. V, new edn (Leiden: E.J. Brill, 1986), 1247–52.

Holt, *Funj Chronicle* – P.M. Holt, *The Sudan of the Three Niles: The Funj Chronicle 910–1288/1504–1871* (Leiden: E.J. Brill 1999).

Holt, *Holy Families* – P.M. Holt, 'Holy Families and Islam In The Sudan' in Holt, *Studies*, 121–34.

Holt, *Islamic Millenarianism* – P.M. Holt, 'Islamic Millenarianism and the fulfillment of Prophecy: A Case Study' in *Prophecy and Millenarianism: Essays in Honour of Marjorie Reeves* (Harlow: Longman, 1980), 337–47.

Holt, *Mahdia and Outside World* – P.M. Holt, 'The Sudanese Mahdia and the Outside World: 1881–9', *BSOAS*, 21/2 (1958): 276–90.

Holt, *Mahdist State* – P.M. Holt, *The Mahdist State in the Sudan 1881–1898*, 2nd edn (Oxford University Press, 1970).

Holt, *Political and Social Change* – P.M. Holt, *Political and Social Change in Modern Egypt* (Oxford University Press, 1968).

Holt, *Sons of Jabir* – P.M. Holt, 'The Sons of Jabir and their Kin: A Clan of Sudanese Religious Notables' in Holt, *Studies*, 88–103.

Holt, *Studies* – P.M. Holt, *Studies in the History of the Near East* (London: Frank Cass, 1973).

Holt and Daly, *History of Sudan* – P.M. Holt and M.W. Daly, *The History of the Sudan* (London: Weidenfeld & Nicolson, 1979).

Hunwick and O'Fahey, *ALA* – John Hunwick and Rex S. O'Fahey, *Arabic Literature in Africa*, vol. I (Leiden: E.J. Brill, 1994–5).

Idris, *Nemeiri and the Turuq* – Dr Idris S. El-Hassan, *Religion in Society, Nemeiri and the Turuq 1972–1980* (Khartoum University Press, 1993).

Islamic Banking – *Towards an Understanding of Islamic Banking in Sudan: the Case of Faisal Islamic Bank*, Monograph Series no. 21 (Development Studies and Research Centre, University of Khartoum, 1985).

Jackson, *Osman Digna* – H.C. Jackson, *Osman Digna* (London: Methuen, 1926).

Jadin, *Taqyim al-tajriba al-dimuqratiyya* – Muhammad 'Ali Jadin, *Taqyim al-tajriba al-dimuqratiyya al-thalitha fi al-Sudan* (Cairo: markaz al-dirasat al-Sudaniyya, 1997).

Johnson, *Religious Paradigms* – Nels Johnson, 'Religious Paradigms of the Sudanese Mahdiyah', *Ethnohistory*, 25/2 (1978): 159–78.

Jok and Hutchinson, *Militarization of Nuer and Dinka Ethnic Identities* – Jok M. Jok and Sharon E. Hutchinson, 'Sudan's Prolonged Second Civil War and the Militarization of Nuer and Dinka Ethnic Identities', *African Studies Review*, 49/2 (Sept. 1999): 125–45.

Joseph and Pillsbury, *Muslim-Christian Conflicts* – Suad Joseph and Barbara L.K. Pillsbury (eds), *Muslim-Christian Conflicts: Economic, Political, and Social Origins* (Boulder, CO: Westview Press, 1978).

Kabbashi, *Tatbiq al-shari'a* – Al-Mikashfi Taha al-Kabbashi, *Tatbiq al-shari'a al-Islamiyya fi al-Sudan bayn al-haqiqa wa'l-ithara* (Cairo: al-zahara' li'l-i'lam al-'arabi, 1986).

Karrar, *Sufi Brotherhoods* – Ali Salih Karrar, *The Sufi Brotherhoods in the Sudan* (London: Hurst, 1992).

Karsani, *Beyond Sufism* – Awad al-Sid al-Karsani, 'Beyond Sufism: the Case of Millennial Islam in Sudan' in Louis Brenner (ed), *Muslim Identity and Social Change in Sub-Saharan Africa* (London: Hurst, 1993), 134–53.

Kedourie, *Cairo and Khartoum* – Elie Kedourie, 'Cairo and Khartoum on the Arab Question' in E. Kedourie, *The Chatham House Version* (London: Weidenfeld & Nicolson, 1970), 13–32.

Kedourie, *Democracy* – Elie Kedourie, *Democracy and Arab Political Culture* (London: Frank Cass, 1994).

Keown-Boyd, *Good Dusting* – Henry Keown-Boyd, *A Good Dusting* (London: Leo Cooper with Secker & Warburg, 1986).

Kevane and Gray, *Kordofan* – M. Kevane and L. Gray, 'Local Politics in the Time of Turabi's Revolution: Gender, Class and Ethnicity in Western Sudan', *Africa*, 65/2 (1995): 271–96.

Khalid, *Nimeiri* – Mansour Khalid, *Nimeiri and the Revolution of Dis-May* (London: Kegan Paul International, 1985).

Khalil, *Democratic Experiment* – Muhammad Ibrahim Khalil, 'Sudan's Democratic Experiment: Present Crisis and Future Prospects', *North East African Studies*, I, 2–3 (New Series, 1994): 103–17.

Klein, *Awlad Jabir* – Haim Klein, 'The Awlad Jabir and their Land 1720–1900' (unpublished MA thesis, University of Haifa, 1984 [Hebrew]).

Kok, *Constitution* – Peter Nyot Kok, 'El-Turabi's Constitution: Islamic Totalitarianism in Neo-Liberal Garments', *SDG* 97 (June 1998): 10–11.

Kok, *Governance* – Peter Nyot Kok, *Governance and Conflict in the Sudan, 1985–1995, Analysis, Evaluation and Documentation* (Hamburg: Deutsches Orient-Institut, Mitteilungen 53, 1996).

Layish, *Legal Methodology* – Aharon Layish, 'The legal Methodology of the Mahdi in the Sudan, 1881–1885: Issues in Marriage and Divorce', *Sudanic Africa*, 8 (1997): 37–66.

Layish and Warburg, *Reinstatement* – A. Layish and G. Warburg, *The Reinstatement of Islamic Law in Sudan Under Numayri: an evaluation of a legal experiment in the light of its historical context, methodology and repercussions* (Leiden: E.J. Brill, 2002).

Lazarus-Yafeh, *Redemption in Islam* – Hava Lazarus-Yafeh, 'Is There a Concept of Redemption in Islam?' in J.Z. Werblowsky and C.J. Bleeker (eds), *Types of Redemption* (Leiden: E.J. Brill, 1970), 168–70.

Lesch, *Contested National Identities* – Ann M. Lesch, *The Sudan-Contested National Identities* (Bloomington: Indiana University Press, 1998).

Lesch, *Khartoum Diary* – Ann M. Lesch, 'Khartoum Diary', *Middle East Report* (Nov.–Dec. 1989), 36–8.

Lewis, *Islam in History* – Bernard Lewis, *Islam in History: Ideas, Men and Events in the Middle East* (London: Alcove Press, 1973).

Lewis, *State & Society* – Bernard Lewis, 'State and Society Under Islam', *Wilson Quarterly* (autumn 1989): 39–51.

Lijphart, *Democracies* – Arend Lijphart, *Democracies: Patterns of Majoritarian and Consensus Government in Twenty-one Countries* (New Haven: Yale University Press, 1984).

Lowrie, *Islam and the West* – A.L. Lowrie (ed.), *Islam, Democracy, the State and the West: a round table with Dr Hasan Turabi* (Tampa, Florida: The World and Islam Studies Enterprise, 1993).

McHugh, *Holy Men* – Neil McHugh, 'Holy Men of the Blue Nile: Religious Leadership and the Genesis of the Arab Islamic Society in the Nilotic Sudan, 1500–1850' (unpublished PhD thesis, Northwestern University, 1986).

Mahgoub, *Democracy* – Mohamed Ahmed Mahgoub, *Democracy on Trial: Reflections on Arab and African Politics* (London: André Deutsch, 1974).

Malwal, *People* – Bona Malwal, *People and Power in Sudan* (London: Ithaca Press, 1981).

Malwal, *Second Challenge* – Bona Malwal, *The Sudan: a Second Challenge to Nationhood* (New York: Thornton Books, 1985).

Mangarella, *Republican Brothers* – P.J. Magnarella, 'The Republican Brothers: A Reformist Movement in the Sudan', *The Muslim World*, 72/1 (1982): 14–24.

Manger, *Trade* – L.O. Manger (ed.), *Trade and Traders in the Sudan* (University of Bergen, Norway, 1984).

Manshurat II – *Manshurat al-imam al-mahdi*, vol. 2 (Khartoum: idarat al-mahfuzat, 1963).

Meinhof, *Kordofan* – K. Meinhof, *Eine Studienfahrt nach Kordofan* (Hamburg, 1916).

Moore-Harell, *Gordon* – Alice Moore-Harell, *Gordon and the Sudan: Prologue to the Mahdiyya 1877–1880* (London: Frank Cass, 2001).

Muddathir, *Arabism* – Muddathir 'Abd al-Rahim, 'Arabism, Africanism and self-identification in the Sudan' in Hasan, *Sudan in Africa*, 228-38.

Muddathir, *Imperialism* – Muddathir Abdel Rahim, *Imperialism and Nationalism in the Sudan, 1899–1956* (Oxford University Press, 1969).

Muddathir & al-Tayyib, *Islam* – Muddathir 'Abd al-Rahim & al-Tayyib Zein al-'Abdin (eds), *Al-islam fi al-Sudan, buhuth mukhtara min al-mu'tamar al-awwal li-Jama'at al-fikr wa'l-thaqafa al-islamiyya* (Khartoum: dar al-asala li'l-sahafa wa'l-nashr wa'l-intaj al-i'lami, 1987).

Mukhtar, *Kharif* – 'Abd al-Rahman Mukhtar, *Kharif al-farah asrar al-Sudan 1950–1970* (Khartoum, dar al-sahafa, 1978).

Na'im, *Apostasy* – 'Abdullahi Ahmed An-Na'im, 'The Islamic Law of Apostasy and its Applicability, a Case from the Sudan', *Religion*, 16 (1986): 197–224.

Na'im, *Islamic Constitution* – 'Abdullahi Ahmad An-Na'im, 'The Elusive Islamic Constitution: the Sudanese Experience', *Orient*, 26/3 (Sept. 1985): 329–39.

Najib, *Kalimati* – Muhammad Najib, *Kalimati li'l-ta'rikh* (Cairo: dar al-kitab al-namudhaji, 1975).

Naqr, *Dirasat* – 'Umar 'Abd al-Raziq al-Naqr (ed.), *Dirasat fi al-mahdiyya* (Khartoum: qism al-ta'rikh jami'at al-Khartum, n.d. [1983?]).

National Islamic Front, *Southern Sudan* – *'The Islamic National Front Presents: The Southern Sudan Question, Review, Analysis, Proposals'* (n.d.; n.p.) 1–34 (this pamphlet was probably printed in Khartoum in 1985).

National Islamic Front, *Sudan Charter* – National Islamic Front, *Sudan Charter, National Unity and Diversity* (Khartoum: 1 Jumada 1407 (Jan. 1987).

Numayri, *Al-nahj al-islami* – Ja'far Muhammad Numayri, *Al-nahj al-Islami limadha?* (Cairo: al-maktab al-Misri al-hadith, 1980).

Numayri, *Al-nahj al-islami kayfa?* – Ja'far Muhammad Numayri, *Al-nahj al-islami kayfa?* (Cairo: al-maktab al-Misri al-hadith, 1985).

Oduho and Deng, *Southern Sudan* – Joseph Oduho and William Deng, *The Problem of the Southern Sudan* (Oxford University Press, 1963).

O'Fahey, *Enigmatic Saint* – R.S. O'Fahey, *Enigmatic Saint: Ahmad Ibn Idris and the Idrisi Tradition* (London: Hurst, 1990).

O'Fahey and Radtke, *Neo-Sufism* – R.S. O'Fahey and Bernd Radtke, 'Neo-Sufism Reconsidered', *Der Islam*, 70/1 (1993): 52–87.

O'Fahey, *Religion and Trade* – R.S. O'Fahey, 'Religion and Trade in the Kayra Sultanate of Dar Fur' in Hasan, *Sudan in Africa*. 87–97.

O'Fahey, *Sufism in Suspense* – R.S. O'Fahey, 'Sufism in Suspense: the Sudanese Mahdi and the Sufis', Paper presented to the International Conference on Sufism and its Opponents, University of Utrecht, May 1995.

O'Fahey and Abu Salim, *Land in Dar Fur* – R.S. O'Fahey and M.I. Abu Salim, *Land in Dar Fur: Charters and Related Documents from the Dar Fur Sultanate* (Cambridge University Press, 1983).

Ohrwalder, *Ten Years* – Father Joseph Ohrwalder, *Ten Years' Captivity in the Mahdi's Camp, 1882–1892* (London: Samson Low, Marston, 1892), translated from the original manuscript by Major F.R. Wingate.

Osman, *Muslim Brotherhood* – Abdelwahab A.M. Osman, 'The Political and Ideological Development of the Muslim Brotherhood in Sudan, 1945–1986' (PhD thesis, Department of Politics, University of Reading, 1989). Printed version: Affendi, *Turabi's Revolution*.

Peters, *The Mahdi* – Rudolf Peters, 'Islam and the Légitimation of Power: the Mahdi Revolt in the Sudan', XXI Deutscher Orientalistentag Berlin, 23–29 Mar. 1980. *Ausgewaelte Vortraege*, ed. F. Steppat (ZDMG, Supplement V), 409–20.

Qaddal, *Ru'ya thawriyya* – Muhammad Sa'id al-Qaddal. 'Al-ru'ya al-thawriyya fi fikr al-Mahdi 1844–1885' in Naqr, *Dirasat*, 74–88.

Qaddal, *Siyasa iqtisadiyya* – Dr Muhammad Sa'id al-Qaddal, *Al-siyasa al-iqtisadiyya li'l-dawlah al-mahdiyya* (Khartoum: dar jami'at al-khartum li'l-nashr, 1986).

Rafi'i, 'Asr – 'Abd al-Rahman al-Rafi'i, *'Asr Muhammad 'Ali*, 3rd impression (Cairo: maktabat al-nahda al-Misriyya, 1951).

Ramadan, *Ukdhubat* – 'Abd al-'Azim Ramadan, *Ukdhubat al-isti'mar al-Misri li'l-Sudan* (Cairo: al-hay'ah al-misriyya al-'ama li'l-kitab, 1988).

Rogalski, *Republikanischen Brüder* – Jürgen Rogalski, 'Die Republikanischen Brüder im Sudan. Ein Eintrag zur Ideologiegeschichte des Islam in der Gegenwart' (Magister thesis, Freie Universität Berlin, 1990).

Rondinelli, *Administrative Decentralization* – Dennis A. Rondinelli, 'Administrative Decentralization and Economic Development: the Sudan Experiment with Devolution', *Journal of Modern African Studies*, 19/4 (1981): 595–624.

Sabry, *Sovereignty* – Hussein Zulfakar Sabry, *Sovereignty for the Sudan* (London: Ithaca Press, 1982).

Sadiq, *Islam and Change* – Al-Sadiq al-Mahdi, 'Islam–Society and Change' in Esposito, *Voices*, 230–40.

Sadiq, *Istiqlal* – Al-Sadiq al-Mahdi, *Jihad fi sabil al-istiqlal* (Khartoum: al-matba'a al-hukumiyya, n.d. [1965]).

Sadiq, *Mustaqbal* – Al-Sayyid al-Sadiq al-Siddiq al-Mahdi, 'Mustaqbal al-Islam fi al-Sudan' in Muddathir and al-Tayyib, *Islam*, 375–425.

Sadiq, *Second Birth* – Al-Sadig Al-Mahdi, *Second Birth in Sudan, in the Cradle of Sustainable Human Rights* (Khartoum: Umma Party, n.p.; Feb. 2000).

Sadiq, *Yas'alunaka* – Al-Sadiq al-Mahdi, *Yas'alunaka 'an al-mahdiyya* (Beirut: dar al-qadaya, 1975).

Sa'id, *Azhari* – Bashir Muhammad Sa'id, *Al-za'im al-Azhari wa-'asruhu* (Cairo: al-qahira al-haditha li'-tiba'a, 1990).

Salih, *Fading Democracy* – Kamal Osman Salih, 'The Sudan 1985-9: The Fading Democracy', *JMAS*, 28 (June 1990): 201–19.

Salih, *Sudanese Press* – Mahgoub Mohamed Salih, 'The Sudanese Press', *Sudan Notes and Records*, 46 (1965): 1–7.

Sanderson, *Sudanese Nationalism* – G.N. Sanderson, 'Sudanese nationalism and the independence of the Sudan', paper presented to a Symposium on Islamic North Africa, London, 14 Sept. 1971.

Shaked, *Sudanese Mahdi* – Haim Shaked, *The Life of the Sudanese Mahdi. A historical study of Kitab sa'adat al-mutahdi bi-sirat al-Imam al-Mahdi by Isma'il b. 'Abd al-Qadir* (New Brunswick, NJ: Transaction Books, 1978).

Shamuq, *Shakhsiyyat* – Ahmad Muhammad Shamuq, *al-Shakhsiyyat al-Sudaniyyah al-mu'asirah* (Khartoum: bayt al-thaqafa li'l-tarjama wa'l-nashr, 1988).

Shibayka, *Sudan fi qarn* – Al-Makki Shibayka, *Al-Sudan fi qarn 1819–1919* (Cairo: matba'at lajnat al-ta'lif wa'l-tarjama wa'l-nashr, 1947).

Shibeika, *British Policy* – Mekki Shibeika, *British Policy in the Sudan 1882–1902* (London: Oxford University Press, 1952).

Shukri, *Al-Hukm al-Misri* – Muhammad Fu'ad Shukri, *Al-hukm al-Misri fi al-Sudan 1820–1885* (Cairo: dar al-fikr al-'arabi, 1947).

Shuqayr, *Ta'rikh* – Na'um Shuqayr, *Jurjafiyyat wa-ta'rikh al-Sudan*, 2nd edn (Beirut: dar al-thaqafa, 1967).

Sidahmed, *Politics & Islam* – Abdel Salam Sidahmed, *Politics and Islam in Contemporary Sudan* (Richmond: Curzon Press, 1997).

Smith, *Islam* – Wilfred Cantwell Smith, *Islam in Modern Times* (New York: Mentor Books, 1957).

Spaulding, *Heroic Age* – Jay Spaulding, *The Heroic Age in Sinnar* (East Lansing: Michigan State University Press, 1985).

Spaulding *Land Tenure* – Jay Spaulding, 'Land Tenure and Social Class in the Northern Turkish Sudan', *International Journal of African Historical Studies* 15/1 (1982): 1–20.

Stevens, *Republican Brothers* – R.P. Stevens, 'Sudan's Republican Brothers and Islamic Reform', *Journal of Arab Affairs*, 1/1 (1981): 133–44.

Stiansen, *Imperialism* – Endre Stiansen, 'Overture to Imperialism' (PhD thesis, University of Bergen, 1993).

Stiansen and Kevane, *Kordofan Invaded* – Endre Stiansen and Michael Kevane, *Kordofan Invaded: Peripheral Incorporation and Social Transformation in Islamic Africa* (Leiden: E.J. Brill, 1998).

Sulayman, *Al-Yasar* – Muhammad Sulayman, *al-Yasar al-Sudani fi 'asharah a'wam 1954-1963* (Wad Madani, n.d.).

Symes, *Mahdism 1935* – G.S.S [Symes], 'Mahdism and El Sayed Abdel Rahman El-Mahdi K.B.E., C.V.O.', by Public Security Intelligence, Khartoum, 28 Apr. 1935, FO 371/19096.

Symes, *Mahdism 1937* – G.S.S [Symes], 'Memorandum on Mahdism and Government Policy', 22 Feb. 1937, the report was enclosed in Lampson to Eden, 5 Mar. 1937, FO 371/20870.

Taha, *Second Message* – Mahmoud Mohamed Taha, *The Second Message of Islam*, translation and introduction by 'Abdullahi Ahmed An-Na'im (Syracuse, NY: Syracuse University Press, 1987).

Talhami, *Suakin* – Ghada H. Talhami, *Suakin and Massawa Under Turkish Rule, 1865-1885* (Washington, DC: University Press of America, 1979).

Thawrat al-inqadh al-watani – *Thawrat al-inqadh al-watani fi 'am, watha'iq wa-haqa'iq* (Dar al-thaqafa li'l-tiba'at wa'l-nashr, n.p.; n.d. [Khartoum 1990?]). The book was a byproduct of 'Al-Sudan al-Hadith' and was edited by Muhammad Sa'id and Muhammad Ahmad Karrar.

Theobald, *'Ali Dinar* – A.B. Theobald, *'Ali Dinar, Last Sultan of Darfur, 1898-1916* (London: Longman, 1965).

Thomas, *Sudan* – Graham F. Thomas, *Sudan Struggle for Survival* (London: Darf Publishers, 1993).

Trimingham, *Islam* – J. Spencer Trimingham, *Islam in the Sudan* (repr. London: Frank Cass, 1965).

Turabi, *Mustaqbal al-Islam* – Hasan 'Abdallah al-Turabi, 'Mustaqbal al-Islam fi al-Sudan' in Muddathir and al-Tayyib, *Islam*, 427–45.

Turabi, *Secularism* – Hasan al-Turabi, 'We have eliminated secularism', interview in *The Middle East* (Sept. 1979); in Duran, *Islam*, 71–3

Turabi, *Sudanow* – *Sudanow*, interviews with Dr Hasan Turabi, Mar. 1982; Jan. 1983.

Umma, *Dimuqratiyya* – Hizb al-Umma, *Al-dimuqratiyya fi al-Sudan 'a'idat wa-rajiha* (Markaz abhath wa-dirasat al-umma, n.p. 21 Oct. 1990).

'Uthman, *Al-din wa'l-siyasa* – 'Uthman Sayyid Ahmad Isma'il, *Al-din wa'l-siyasa wa-nash'at wa-tatawwur al-khatmiyya wa'l-ansar* (Khartoum: matba'at al-tamaddun, n.d.).

Vatikiotis, *Nasser* – P.J. Vatikiotis, *Nasser and his Generation* (London: Croom Helm, 1978).

Volkov, *Minorities* – Shulamit Volkov, *Being Different: Minorities, Aliens and Outsiders in History* (Jerusalem: Shazar Center for Jewish History, 2000) [Hebrew].

Voll, *Britain & the 'Ulama* – John O. Voll, 'The British, the *'ulama'*, and Popular Islam in the Early Anglo-Egyptian Sudan', *IJMES*, 2 (1971): 212–28.

Voll, *Khatmiyya* – J.O. Voll, 'A History of the Khatmiyah Tariqah in the Sudan' (unpublished PhD dissertation, Harvard University, 1969).

Voll, *Revivalism*, John O. Voll, 'Revivalism and Social Transformation In Islamic History', *Muslim World*, 76 (1986): 168–80.

Voll, *Stateness* – John O. Voll, *Islam and Stateness in the Modern Sudan* (Montreal: McGill University, CDAS Discussion Paper no. 4), Mar. 1983.

Voll, *Sudanese Mahdi* – John O. Voll, 'The Sudanese Mahdi: Frontier Fundamentalist', *IJMES*, 10 (1979): 153–65.

Warburg, *Democracy* – G. Warburg, 'Democracy In the Sudan: Trial and Error', *Northeast African Studies*, 8/2–3 (1986): 77–94.

Warburg, *Historical Controversy* – G.R. Warburg, 'British Policy towards the Ansar in Sudan: A Note on an Historical Controversy', *MES*, 33/4 (Oct. 1997): 675–92.

Warburg, *Historical Discord* – G.R. Warburg, *Historical Discord in the Nile Valley* (London: Hurst/Evanston, IL: Northwestern University Press, 1992).

Warburg, *Islam and Communism* – G.R. Warburg, *Islam Nationalism and Communism in a Traditional Society: the Case of the Sudan* (London: Frank Cass, 1978)

Warburg, *Islam and State* – G.R. Warburg, 'Islam and State in Numayri's Sudan' in J.D.Y. Peel & C.C. Stewart (eds), *Popular Islam South of the Sahara* (Manchester: University Press, 1985), 400–13.

Warburg, *Islam in Egypt* – G. Warburg, 'Islam and Politics in Egypt', *MES*, vol. 18/2 (1982): 131–57.

Warburg, *Mahdist Ideology* – G. Warburg, 'From Revolution to Conservatism: Some Aspects of Mahdist Ideology and Politics in the Sudan', *Der Islam*, 70/1 (1993): 88–111.

Warburg, *Muslim Brothers* – G. Warburg, 'Muslim Brothers' in Esposito, *Modern Islam*, vol. I, 92–3.

Warburg, *Nile* – 'The Nile Waters, Border Issues and Radical Islam in Egyptian-Sudanese Relations, 1956–1995' in S. Beswick and J. Spaulding (eds), *White Nile Black Blood* (Lawrenceville, NJ: Red Sea Press, 1999), 73–90.

Warburg, *Shari'a* – G. Warburg, 'The Shari'a in Sudan: Implementation and Repercussions, 1983–1989', *Middle East Journal*, vol. 44/4 (autumn 1990): 624–37.

Warburg, *Sharif* – G. Warburg, 'Wingate and the Sharifian Revolt, 1915-1916', *Hamizrah Hehadash*, 19/4 (1969), 355–63, in Hebrew.

Warburg, *Social and Economic Aspects* – G. Warburg, 'Some Social and Economic Aspects of Turco-Egyptian Rule in the Sudan' in *Belleten*, CLIII, 49 (1989): 769–95.

Warburg, *Sudan and Egypt* – G. Warburg, 'The Sudan, Egypt and Britain 1899-1916', *MES*, 6/2 (1970): 163–78.

Warburg, *Sudan's Path* – G. Warburg, 'The Sudan's Path to Independence: Continuity and Change in Egypt's Policy Towards the Sudan' in S. Shamir (ed.), *Egypt From Monarchy to Republic* (Boulder, CO: Westview Press, 1995), 309–24.

Warburg, *'Ulama* – G. Warburg, ' 'Ulama', Popular Islam and Religious Policy in the Northern Sudan, 1899–1916', *Asian and African Studies*, vol. 7 (1971): 89–119; also in Hebrew in G. Baer (ed.), *'Ulama' and Religious Problems in the Islamic World* (Jerusalem: Magnes Press, 1971), 167–85.

Warburg, *Wingate* – Gabriel Warburg, *The Sudan under Wingate, 1899-1916* (London: Frank Cass 1970).

Weissbrod, *Turabi* – Amir Weissbrod, *Turabi: Spokesman of Radical Islam* (Tel Aviv: Dayan Center, 1999), in Hebrew.

Willis, *Religious Confraternities* – C.A. Willis, 'Religious Confraternities of the Sudan', *SNR*, 4/2 (1921), 175–94.

Wingate, *Mahdiism* – F.R. Wingate, *Mahdiism and the Egyptian Sudan* (repr. London: Frank Cass, 1968).

Wingate, *Wingate of the Sudan* – Ronald Wingate, *Wingate of the Sudan* (London: 1955). The biography of Sir Reginald Wingate by his son.

Woodward, *Islamic Radicalism* – Peter Woodward, 'Sudan: Islamic Radicals in Power' in Esposito, *Political Islam*, 95–114.

Yahya, *Al-thawra* – Jalal Yahya, *Al-thawra al-mahdiyya wa-usul al-siyasa al-Baritaniyya fi al-Sudan* (Cairo: maktabat al-nahda al-Misriyya, 1959).

Zaki, *Al-Qawl* – Husayn Muhammad Zaki, *Al-qawl al-fasl fi al-radd 'ala mahazil Mahmud Muhammad Taha* (Alexandria, 1406 h./1986 m.).

Zein, *Religion and State* – Ibrahim M. Zein, 'Religion, Legality, and the State: 1983 Sudanese Penal Code' (PhD dissertation, Temple University, 1989).

INDEX

Aba Island, 81–3, 88–95, 101, 108, 159, 172–5, 183
'Abbas (the Prophet's uncle), 2
'Abbas I, Viceroy of Egypt, 27
'Abbas Hilmi II, Khedive of Egypt, 73
'Abbasiyya (quarter of Omdurman), 99, 102
'Abbud, see Ibrahim 'Abbud
'Abd al-'Azim Ramadan, 8
'Abd al-Hamid II, Ottoman Sultan, 36
'Abd al-Karim al-Samman, 4
'Abd al-Majid, 113
'Abd al-Qadir Abu Qurun: 153–4, 157
  Abu Qurun sufi family, 153
'Abd al Qadir Hilmi, 38
'Abd al-Qadir Imam wad Habuba, 62, 75
'Abd al-Qadir al-Jaza'iri, 28
'Abd al-Rahman al-Mahdi, see Mahdi's family: 'Abd al-Rahman al-Mahdi
'Abd al-Rahman al-Nujumi, 47, 53
'Abd al-Rahman Suwwar al-Dhahab, 190, 194
'Abdullah 'Abd al-Majid, 185–6
'Abdallah al-Fadil, 99, 116–17, 119
'Abdullah Khalil, 86, 126, 133, 135, 203
'Abdel Rahman Ibn Hussein al-Jabri, 37 and fn. 40
Abdel Salam Sidahmed, 151, 162, 198, 206
Abdelwahab El-Affendi, 188
'Abduh, see Muhammad 'Abduh 36
'Abdullahi al-Dufani, 41
'Abdullahi b. Muhammad, the Mahdi's Khalifa, see Mahdi, khulafa'
Abel Alier, see Alier, Abel
Abu Diqn (shaykh al-'ulama'), 107
Abu Jummayza, Ahmad, 47
Abu Qurun, see 'Abd al-Qadir Abu Qurun
Abu Ruf, 117
Abu Salim, see Muhammad Ibrahim Abu Salim
Abyssinia (also Ethiopia), 45–7, 55
Adam 'Umar (king of jabal Taqali), 38
Addis Ababa Agreement (February 1972), 150, 160, 162, 165–6, 199, 204, 215

Advisory Council, 119–21, 124–8
Afafit, 50
al-Afghani, see Jamal al-Din al-Afghani
Afghanistan, Afghani jihad, 207
Africa(n): 17–21, 46, 51, 122, 144, 167–8, 202, 220, 224–6
  Central Africa, 6, 46
  East Africa, 118
  North Africa (Maghrib), 17, 37, 46
  partition of Africa, 51
  South Africa, 219
  West Africa, 15–17, 20, 46, 73–5, 89–90, 93, 101
  African Muslims, 195
  African religions, (traditional faiths) 169, 209; see also tribal religions, animists
Algeria, 153
Alliance of National Salvation, see Sudan: military and civilian coups
Ahd al-umma (pact of the Umma), 168
ahl al-bayt (people of the House, i.e. the Prophet's family), 22
ahl al-dhimmah, 222
Ahmad Abu 'Ali, 6
Ahmad 'Ali, 56
Ahmad al-'Awwam, 36 and fn. 39
Ahmad al-Basir, 4
Ahmad ibn Idris, 4–5, 9, 164; see also Sufi Orders: Idrissiya
Ahmad b. al-Hajj 'Ali al-Majdhub, 34
Ahmad 'Izzat 'Abd al-Karim, 28
Ahmad Jubara (qadi al-islam), 39, 55
Ahmad Mumtaz Pasha, 18–19
Ahmad al-Nur, 53
Ahmad Safi al-Din 'Awad, 146
Ahmad al-Salawi, 6
Ahmad Sulayman (amin bayt al-mal), 39, 52–4
Ahmad al-Tayyib wad al-Bashir, 4, 35
Ahmad 'Uthman al-Qadi, 86, 108
Ahmad Yasin, 54
Ahmad Yusuf Hashim, 117, 119
Ahmadu Shehu, 46
Alexandria, 189
Algeria, 152
'Ali, (fourth Caliph), 22

239

'Ali 'Abd al-Karim, 61
'Ali 'Abd al-Rahman al-Amin,
    137
'Ali Dinar, Sultan Dar Fur, 79
'Ali Mahir, 113–14 and fn. 194
'Ali al-Mirghani, al-Sayyid, 10, 35, 62–3,
    77–80, 85–8, 92, 96, 99, 104–41,
    145–6, 181, 196–7; *see also* Sufi orders:
    Khatmiyya
'Ali Muhammad b. Hilu, *see* Mahdi,
    khulafa'
'Ali 'Uthman Muhammad Taha, 187,
    207
Alier, Abel, 139
'alim, see 'ulama'
Allenby, Sir Edmund (Viscount), 84, 89,
    96–7
Alliance of National Salvation, 204
America, American(s), 8, 27; *see also*
    United States
amir, see umara'
Anglo-Egyptian Sudan: 35, 51, 55, 57–141,
    161, 170
    Anglo-Egyptian Treaty (1936), 104–5,
        110, (abrogation by Egypt), 129
    Governor-General of, 90, 110, 118, 132,
        139
    Sudan Political Service (SPS), 87–93, 96,
        104, 129–32, 134–5
    Civil Secretary, 110–11, 128, 139
    Legal Secretary, 64–8, 72
    see also Condominium, Britain, British,
        Advisory Council
animists, 1, 58, 144
Ansar, *see* Sufi orders and religious
    movements
Ansar, al-Sunna, *see* Sufi orders and
    religious movements
Antichrist (*al-dajjal*), 22, 88
Anwar al-Sadat, President of Egypt, 153,
    174, 183–4
apostasy (*ridda*), 163 and fn. 48, 188
Arab(s): 112, 122, 168–9
    nationalism, 158
    Socialism, 143
    tribal militias, 211 (*also* Popular Defence
        Force)
    unity, 105, 143
    the Arab world, 143
Arab League, 105
Arabia, Arabian Peninsula, 17, 37, 46
Arabic (language): 70, 114, 118, 168, 214
    language of the Qur'an, 209
Arabic-speaking Muslims, 202

Arabization, 27, 48, 140
    and Islamization of education, 211
Archer, Sir Geoffrey, 90 and fn. 110, 92
al-Ashiqqa', *see* political parties and
    organizations
ashraf (Prophet's descendants), 44, 48–9,
    51, 54–5
'Atbara, 25
Atlantic Charter, 118
'Awad al-Jid Muhammad Ahmad, 153–4;
    see also 'Abd al-Qadir Abu Qurun
'Awad al-Karim al-Muslimi, 50
al-'Awad al-Mardi, 54
awlad al-'arab (nomad tribes), 45; *see also*
    tribes
awlad al-balad (riverain [settled] tribes), 2,
    5, 7, 12, 24, 27, 44–7, 51–5; *see also*
    tribes
Awlad Jabir, 2; *see also* Sufi orders and
    religious movements
Awlad Hindi, *see also* Sufi orders:
    Hindiyya
awqaf, see waqf
al-Azhar, 8–9, 23, 35, 55–6, 58–62, 70, 182
    Azharite(s), 8–9, 20, 24, 66
al-Azhari, *see* Isma'il al-Azhari
'Aziziyya Misriyya Steamship Company,
    18

Babikr 'Awadallah, Chief Justice, 182
Babikr Bedri (Badri), 83, 127, 130
Babikr al-Dib, 135
Badrab school of Umm Dubban, 153–4
    and fn. 24; *see also* Yusuf wad Badur,
    al-khalifa
Bahr al-Ghazal, 6–7, 16, 23, 27, 39, 46, 48
Baker, Sir Samuel, 14
al-Bakri al-Mirghani, 35
al-Bakri, Shaykh, responsible for Sufi
    orders, 72
Balal Sabun, 41
Balkans, 202
Bandiagara, 46
Baqqara, *see* tribes
Bara, 5
baraka (blessing), 1, 9, 35
bash buzuq (irregular soldiers), 7
Bashir, *see* 'Umar Hasan al-Bashir
Bashir Muhammad Sa'id, 137
Ba'th, *see* political parties
bay'a (oath of allegiance), 157, 187, 267;
    see also Mahdi
bayt al-mal (treasury), *see* Mahdi
BBC overseas broadcasts, 108

Beja, *see* tribes
Berber, 9, 13, 16, 40, 45, 50, 60,
125
Bible, 166
Bireka, 211
Björkelo, Anders, 29
Board of Ulemas, *see* 'ulama'
Bonham Carter, Edgar, 70, 82; *see also*
Sudan Political Service, Legal
Secretary
booty (*ghanima*), 52, 54–5
Bornu, 46
Boyle, Harry (British Oriental Secretary
under Lord Cromer), 67
Britain, British, 14–15, 20–1, 27, 36–7,
46–7, 51, 57–141, 161, 167, 170; *see*
also Anglo-Egyptian Sudan
Bruce, James, 3
Burckhardt, John, 3, 16
Bush, Vice-President George, 188
Butler, Stephen S., 63

Cairo, 3, 14–15, 27, 45, 73, 84–5, 107,
131–2, 134, 179, 219–20
Caliph(s), Caliphate, 32; *see also khalifa*
Cameroon, 89
Camp David Accords, 174
Cecil, Lord Edward, 62
Charter of Democratic Rally (October
1989), 208 and fn. 14
Christian(s) 22–3, 27, 32, 36, 38, 47, 61, 78,
144, 156, 163, 168, 209
colonialist powers, 24
missionaries, 20, 58
Christianity, 70, 157, 214
Churchill, Sir Winston, 132
CIA (Central Intelligence Agency), 187
Civil Transactions Act (1984), 156, 158
Communist, Communism, 128, 140, 148,
161–2, 209; *see also* Parties, Sudan
Communist Party (SCP)
Condominium: 52, 57–142, 161, 167
Agreement abrogated by Egypt, 130; *see*
also Anglo-Egyptian Sudan
Congo, 142
Constantinople, 37
Constitution: 144–52
Amendment Commission (1951),
139
Islamic, 140, 144–51, 181, 195–8,
(ratified June 1998) 151, 214–15, 216,
219–20, 221
Permanent (May 1973), 143–4, 148–50,
157, 166, 215

secular, 147, 149
transitional (temporary) (1956), 144–7
Constitutional Committee, (1956) 145
(1966–7), 147–8, 181
Constituent Assembly (1965–9), 133,
147–8, 182; (1989) 200, 217
(National) Constitutional Conference,
1986–9 (NCC): 150–1, 199
suggested in NIF's 'Sudan Charter', 169
Controller of Public Security, 105, 111,
115–18, 120–1
Copt(s), Coptic, 52, 162
Cripps, Sir Stafford, 118
Cromer, Lord, 57–60, 66–8, 73, 78, 97
Crusaders, 189
Currie, Sir James (secretary for education),
97 and fn. 131

da'irat al-mahdi, see Mahdi
al-dajjal (anti-Christ), *see* anti-Christ
Daly, Martin, 140
al-Damir, (al-Damar), 2–3, 12, 70–2, 125;
see also ma'had al-damir al-'ilmi
Danaqla, *see* tribes
Dar Fur, 2–7, 12–17, 24, 26–7, 34, 38–9,
44–8, 56–9, 75, 79, 82–3, 88–9, 92, 94,
148, 165–6, 196, 211
darb al-arba 'in (the forty days way), 16–17
al-Dardiri Muhammad 'Uthman, 130, 133
darwish, darawish, 33; *see also* sufi, sufism
Davies, Reginald, 88–9, and fn. 102, 110
and fn. 184
da'wa (propaganda), *see* Mahdi
Deng, Francis Mading, 154 and fn. 27,
224–5
dhikr (rythmical invocation of God's
names among sufis): 63, 95; *also* sufi,
sufism
Dinka Nuer Peace Conference, 220; *see*
also tribes, Dinka, Nuer
Director of Public Security, *see* Controller
of Public Security
diya (blood money), 198
Dongola (al-Urdi), 9, 15, 51, 63, 68, 95
al-Dueim, 71

East Africa, *see* Africa
Egypt, Egyptian: 4–21, 24–8, 32–3, 37–9,
46–7, 50, 57–142, 161–6, 179, 182,
200, 208, 210, 213, 220, 227; *see also*
Anglo-Egyptian Sudan
British conquest of (1881), 38
Crown, 87, 106, 122–3, 133
ma'had, 106

nationalism, 70, 83–7, 96
Free Officers, 104, 131, 179
Revolutionary Command Council
(RCC), 132–4, 136
Egyptian Gazette, see newspapers
Egyptian Sudan, *see* Turco-Egyptian Sudan
elections to parliament, *see* Sudan: *majlis
al-sha'ab*
Elliot, Sir Henry, 15
El Fasher, *see* Fasher
El Obeid (al-Ubayyid), *see* Obeid
Emin Pasha (Eduard Schnitzer), 48
English, 68–9, 168; *see also* Britain,
British
Equatoria, 48
Equatorial Corps, 140
Eritrea, 108
Esposito, John L., 222
Ethiopia, 33, 47, 172; *see also* Abyssinia
Europe, European(s), 8, 13, 18–19, 27, 33,
46, 51, 217

Fadl al-Mawla Muhammad, 48
fallata (West African Muslim pilgrims in
Sudan), 16–17, 73–5, 93–4, 99
faqih, fuqaha' (jurists, exponents of the
shari'a): 1–3, 29, 163–4, 197
al-faqih al-kabir, 3
fiki (colloquial corruption), 1, 5, 7–9, 17,
25, 58–9, 64, 67, 75–8, 96
faqir, fuqara' (Arabic equivalent of
derwish, Mahdi's followers), 1, 9, 12,
23–4, 33
Faruq, Abu 'Isa', 216
Faruq, King of Egypt, 104–17
Fascism (Italian), 108
Faysal, King of Sa'udi Arabia, 159–60
El-Fasher, 47
Fashoda (Kodok), 58
Fez, 45
fiki, see faqih
First World War, *see* World War I
Forced labour, 19
France, French, 46
Frankfurter Allgemeine, 215
Freemasons, 189
Free Officers, *see* Egypt
Fulani, 46
Funj, Sultanate (*see also* Sultanate of
Sinnar), 1, 2, 5–6, 8, 25, 29, 47, 64
Province under Condominium, 82–3, 92,
94
'Funj' Chronicle (*katib al-shuna*), 6
Fur, *see* tribes; *also* Dar Fur

Garang, Dr John, 168–9, 196–200, 218,
219–20
George V, King, 86, 102
German, Germany, 19, 76–8
Gessi, Romolo, 39
Geteina, 93
Gezira (al-Jazira), 4, 37, 39, 44, 54, 76–7,
93
cotton scheme, 84, 140
Ghabush, Father Philip 'Abbas, 216
ghanima, see booty
Giegler Pasha, Carl Christian, 14, 38
Gillan, Sir Angus, 105 and fn. 164, 106–7,
110–11 and fn. 184
Gondar, 16, 47, 92
Gordon, General Charles, 15, 27, 34, 36,
40
Gordon College, 66, 69–71, 98, 110–11,
171; *see also* Khartoum University
Gorst, Sir Eldon, 73
graduates' club (1919), 86, 96–9
Graduates' Constituencies, 181–2, 213
Graduates' General Congress, 108–41,
147, 161
Grant, J.A., 14
Grenfell, Francis Wallace, 102
Greece, Greek, 20
Gulf states, 185
Gulf War (1991), 213

Hadarat al-Sudan, see newspapers
Hadariba, *see* tribes
hadith (formal tradition deriving from the
Prophet), 22–3, 31, 35
hadra nabawiyya, see Prophetic colloquy
hajj, see pilgrimage
al-Hajj Hamad Muhammad Khayr, 28 and
fn. 15
al-Hajj Muhammad 'Uthman Abu Qarja,
48
Hajj 'Umar (ruler of Segu), 46
Hakimiyyat Allah (sovereignty of God),
182
Halawiyyin, *see* tribes
Hale, Sondra, 210–11
Hamaj Regent, 4
Hamad ibn Muhammad al-Majdhub: 2–3
(fn. 8); *mawlid of*, 71
Hamdan Abu 'Anja, 47
Hammad Salih, 86
al-Hamra mosque (near Cairo), 163
hanafi (madhhab), 64, 66
Hasan al-Banna, 176, 185
Hasan al-Hudaybi, 185

Hasan ('Abdallah) al-Turabi, 147–8, 155–6,
161–2, 167–9, 176–222, 224–6
Hashimab brothers, clan, 83, 117
Hashimite-Fatimid family, 170
Hawkesworth, Desmond, 131
Hayatu Ibn Sa'id (Sultan of Sokoto), 45–6
Haydar Ibrahim 'Ali, 217–19
Haydar Taha, 206
Henderson, K.D.D., 130 and fn. 262
al-Hibr Yusuf Nur al-Da'im, 186
Hicks, Colonel William, 37–9
Hijaz, 1, 16, 45, 73–4
Hijra (migration), 46–7, 100
to Jabal Qadir, 38, 52–3, 77; *see also*
pilgrimage
al-hijra mosque, 176
Hindiyya, *see* Sufi orders; *also* Yusuf al-
Hindi, al-Sharif
'Historical Compromise' (*Musawamah
Tarikhiyyah*), 217–19
Horn of Africa, 142
Holt, P.M., 28 and fn. 15
holy families (men), 1, 2, 6–9, 12, 17, 26,
114, 127; *see also* Sufi orders
House of Lords, 78
Howe, Sir Robert, 132 and fn. 264
Huddleston, Sir Hubert, 118, 125
hudud (Qur'anic punishments), 155–60,
163, 174–7, 187–9, 192, 198
Husayn Abu Salih, 190
Husayn Dhu al-Faqar Sabri, *see* Sabry
Husayn Ibrahim wad al-Zahra, 100 and fn.
147
Husayn Muhammad Zaki, 162

Ibn al-Baz, Shaykh, 164
Ibrahim 'Abbud, General, 145–6, 161, 171,
189, 203
Ibrahim Ahmad, 117–19, 125, 133
Ibrahim Bedri, (Badri), 130
Ibrahim Muhammad 'Adlan, 54
Ibrahim Ramadan, 54
'id al-fitr (1953), 134
al-'id al-kabir, 93
Idrisiyya, *see* Sufi orders
Idrisi tradition, 5
ightirab (out-migration), also *mughtarib(in)*,
190
ijma' (consensus of the *fuqaha'*), 41
ijtihad (legal reasoning), 41, 149, 174
ilham (Prophetic inspiration), 40–1
'ilm, 2–3
Illyas Umm Birayr Pasha, 16, 55
imam: 67–8, 101, 157, 187

of al-Ansar, 170–3
'. . . and commander of the faithful', 187
India, Indian subcontinent, 17, 37, 79, 222
indirect rule, *see* Native Administration
Indonesia, 4
International Islamic Conference
(Khartoum 1984), 152
International Monetary Fund (IMF), 159
Iran, Iranian, 152, 191, 207, 209
Iraq (Mesopotamia), 37, 45, 191
Islam, Islamic: *passim*
and democracy 213, 223–7
army, 189
bank(ing), 158
constitution, *see* constitutions
economy, 158–60, 177;
endowments, *see* waqf
law(s) and custom(s), 166, *see also*
Shari'a
evolution, 213
republic, 197
state, 143–4, 160–1, 175–83, 190,
195–225; (Islamic-Mahdist state), 225
Islamic African Center, 212–13
Islamic Charter Front (ICF), *see* political
parties
Islamic College Omdurman, *see* al-ma'
had al-islami
Islamic Conference Organization, 213
Islamic da'wa, 161, 191, 210–12
Islamic Da'wa Organization, 212
Islamic Legal Codes (1991–8), 213
Penal Code (March 1991), 198, 209
Islamic legislation (1983–4), 157, 192
Civil Procedures Act, 156
Civil Transactions Act, 156, 158
Code of criminal procedure, 156
law of inheritance, 161
penal code, 156
zakar and taxation act, 156, 158, 195
Islamic Path (*al-nahj al-islami*), *see* Islamist
Laws (September 1983)
Islamic Revival Committee, 158, 197
Islamic unity, 225
Islamic World League, 164
'Islaminomics', 185; *see also mughtaribin*
Islamist Laws (September 1983), 150, 152–
222
Islamization: 6, 103, 140, 187–8; of south,
168, 192
Isma'il, Khedive of Egypt, 6, 14–21, 23, 27,
48
Isma'il b. 'Abd al-Qadir, 30 and fn. 22,
32

Isma'il al-Azhari, 99, 111, 115–25, 133–8, 161, 171, 218 and fn. 50
Isma'il al-Faruqi, 25
Isma'ili traditions, 22
Isma'iliyya, *see* Sufi orders
Israel, 174
Italy, Italian, 108
ivory, 7

Ja'aliyyin, *see* tribes
Ja'far Numayri (Nimeiri), President 1969–85: 144, 149–50, 152–97, 201–4, 207, 216–19, 224
    unseated 6 Apr. 1985, 192
Ja'far Shaykh Idris, 185
jallaba (merchants), 7, 12–13, 16, 24
Jama'at al-fikr wa'l-thaqafa al-islamiyya (society of Islamic thought and civilization), 187
Jama'at Islami (Pakistan), 145
Jamal 'Abd al-Nasir (Nasser), President of Egypt, 104, 134, 143, 179, 184
Jamal al-Din al-Afghani, 36
al-Jazuli Dafa'allah, 190, 194
Jedda, 16–21, 159
Jerusalem, 45
Jesus: *jewich, see nabi 'isa*
Jew(s), 77, 169, 208
Jihad (holy war): 21, 31–3, 36, 38–9, 43–9, 53–5, 77–80, 101–3, 163, 203, 206–7, 210–11
    jihad al-nafs (exertion to purify one's soul), 102
    'Jihad fi sabil al-istiqlal', 94
    jihadiyya, 39, 51
John (Johannes) IV, Abyssinian king, 47
Juba Conference (1947), 104, 138–40

karama (saintliness), 9
Kaolack, 196
Karamallah Muhammad Kurkusawi, 48
Karari (battle of, 2 Sep. 1898), 51, 81
Kassala, 18–20, 34–5, 62, 71, 82, 94, 108
Kedourie, Elie, 226
Kenrick, J.W., 135
Kenya, 142
Keown-Boyd, Alexander, 84
Khalafallah Khalid, 133
Khalid Farah, 198
Khalid, Mansur, 160, 164
khalifa, khulafa' (*also* caliph) 4–5
khalifat rasul allah, 30–1; *see also* Prophet Muhammad

Khalifa 'Abdullahi b. Muhammad al-Ta'aishi, *see* Mahdi *khulafa'*
al-Khalij, see newspaper
khalwa, (Qur'anic school), 2, 9, 62; *see also kuttab*
Khalwatiyya, *see* Sufi orders
Khartoum, 12, 14, 21, 27, 29, 35–6, 40, 45, 50, 52, 62, 72–3, 75, 87, 90, 95, 105, 108, 119, 130–2, 135–7, 140, 149, 152, 156, 160–3, 170, 199, 204, 213, 217, 220
Khartoum University (*also* Gordon College), 178–83
    Student Union (KUSU), 178–80, 186
khatim al-awliya' (the seal of the saints), 42 and fn. 51
Khatmiyya, *see* Sufi orders; *also* 'Ali al-Mirghani, Muhammad 'Uthman al-Mirghani
'Khomeini-like revolt', 186, 195
Khurshid Pasha, Governor General, 7
Kitchener, Lord, 58
Kobar Mosque, 163
Kok, Peter Nyot, 150
Kordofan, 4–5, 12, 16–17, 26, 33–4, 38, 45, 47, 58, 71–2, 82–3, 89, 92, 94–5, 108, 165, 196, 211
Kosti, 94
al-Kufa, 45
KUSU, *see* Khartoum University Student Union
kuttab (Qur'an School), 9, 24, 68–71; *see also khalwa, madrasa*

Labour Party, 104, 118
Lajnat muraja 'at al-qawanin li 'tatamasha ma'al-shari'a, 155
Lampson, Sir Miles (Lord Killearn), 97–8, 107
Lebanon, Lebanese, 207
Legislative Assembly, 128–30, 139
Lethem, G.B., 89
Lewis, Bernard, 226
Libya, Libyan, 173, 187, 194, 207, 220
Lijphart, Arend, 222
Liwa' al-Islam, see newspapers
Lloyd, Selwyn, 132
London, 76, 97, 179, 184
Luce, Sir William, 134

Machar, Riek, 220; *see also* Dinka Nuer peace
madhhab, madhahib (the four schools of Sunni Islam), 40–1, 64

ma'dhun, 68–9

madrasa (Muslim boarding school attached to mosque), 3; *see also kuttab, khalwa*

Maffey, Sir John, 90–3

Maghrib, *see* Africa, North Africa

al-ma'had al-'ilmi (college of science), 69–70

ma'had al-damir al-'ilmi, 70–1

al-ma'had al-Islami (Omdurman Islamic College, later University), 107–8, 113

Mahdi (lit. 'the rightly guided one'): 10–11, 22–59, 62, 64, 152–3
   death of, 43, 60, 100–3, 170, 196

Mahdiyya, Mahdism, Mahdist state: 3, 11, 12, 15, 22–57, 59–62, 70, 74–80, 100–3, 116, 126, 135, 142, 152, 167

Muhammad Ahmad b. 'Abdallah al-Mahdi (*khalifat rasul allah*), 3–4, 10–11, 15, 21, 26, 28, 30–42, 61, 142

al-mahdi al-muntazar (the expected mahdi), 10
   manifestation (*zuhur*) 29 June 1883, 31

Mahdi's supporters:
   akbar al-mahdiyya (core supporters), 44
   Mahdi's *khulafa'* and their flags: 10, 30, 39, 44
      Abdullahi b. Muhammad al-Ta'aishi (*khalifat al-siddiq* black [blue] flag), 24, 30, 33, 35, 39, 43–56, 59–61, 64, 75, 81, 102
      'Ali Muhammad b. (wad) Hilu (*khalifat al-faruk* green flag), 30, 39, 44, 48, 51–3; Muhammad Sharif b. Hamid (*khalifat al-karrar*, red flag), 30, 39, 44, 48–9, 51–3, 81; *khalifat* 'Uthman, offered to Muhammad b. al-Mahdi al-Sannusi (May 1883), 30–1; Mahdist *umara', amir* (commanders), 10, 24, 44, 46–9, 50–1; Mahdi's *ansar*, 29, 33, 35–9, 41, 43, 47, 51–2, 77–8, 100; *also* Sufi orders: Ansar [neo-Mahdist]; *bay'a* (oath of allegiance), 32–3, 43, 86, 100–1; *see also bay'a*

Mahdi's financial system:
   bayt al-mat, 52–5, 100
      bayt mal khums al-khalifa (the Khalifa's Privy Treasury), 54–5
      bayt mal al-umum (General Treasury), 54–5
      bayt mal al-mulazimin (Orderlies' Treasury), 54

amin bayt al-mal (Commissioner of Treasury), 39, 53–5

da'wa (propaganda), 32–5, 100

da'irat al-mahdi (Mahdi's domain), 99, 101

Mahdi's ideology and legal methodology: ideology (doctrine), 22–3, 99–103, 111, 173
   legal methodology, 40–1 and fn. 48–9

Mahdi's prayer book (*ratib al-Mahdi*), 37, 81–3, 86, 99–100

Mahdi's proclamations (*manshurat al-imam al-mahdi*), 37, 46, 50, 64, 99–102

Mahdi's *shura* council (*al-majlis al-a'ala li'l-shura*), 44; *see also shura*

Mahdism, neo-: 78, 81–143, 152, 170–7, 225

Mahdist daira (*da'irat al-mahdi*), 99, 101, 127, 170

Mahdist *da'wa*, 170

'Mahdist tents', 95, 128; *see also* Sufi orders and religious movements, Ansar

Mahdi's sons and family: 148, 172–3, 195, 210
   al-Fadil and al-Bushra, Mahdi's sons killed in 1898 by government troops, 81 and fn. 78
   'Abd al-Rahman al-Mahdi, al-Sayyid, *imam al-ansar*, 37, 77–141, 145–6, 170–1
   Fadil al-Mahdi, 120, 170
   al-Hadi al-Mahdi, 148, 171–3
   al-Sadiq al-Mahdi, 36 and fn. 39, 102–3, 147–8, 152, 156–7, 161, 164, 167, 170–83, 192–201, 204–25
   al-Siddiq al-Mahdi, 107, 116, 119–20, 133–5, 170–1, 179, 182–3

Mahgoub, *see* Muhammad Ahmad Mahjub

Mahir, 'Ali, *see* 'Ali Maher

Mahmud Ahmad, 47

Mahmud Muhammad Taha, 160–5, 188

Majdhubiyya, Majadhib, *see* Sufi orders and religious movements

al-Majdhub, Hamad ibn Muhammad, 2

Majdhub Jalal al-Din, 70–1

majlis al-shura, see shura, Mahdi: *al-majlis al-a'la li'l-shura*

majlis al-sha'ab (people's assembly), *see* Sudan *majlis al-sha'ab*

Makerere University, 138

Malaysia, 4

Mallam Jibril Gaini, 46

Mali, 45
Maliki (madhhab), 2, 6, 64
Malwal, Bona, 167 and fn. 59
manshurat al-imam al-mahdi, see Mahdi
Maraghi, *see* Muhammad Mustafa al-Maraghi
Marakesh, 45
Marghibi school, 31
Marxism, Marxist, 169, 186
Maryam b. Hashim al-Mirghani, 35
Masallamiyya, 62, 75
Massawa, 4, 15, 18–19
al-Matamma, 4, 12
Mauritania, 45
mawlid (birthday), 128
mawlid al-nabi, see Prophet
May 1969 Revolution, *see* Sudan: military coups, *also* Ja'far Numayri
Maymuna Mirghani Hamza, 28 and fn. 15
Mecca, 2–5, 16–20, 37, 57, 73, 77, 159, 164, 168
Medina (al-Madina; Yathrib), 4, 18,20, 38, 45, 57, 73, 77, 100, 168–9
Mediterranean ports, 19
Mekki Abbas, 11
Middle East(ern), 104–5, 224
al-Mikashfi Taha al-Kabbashi, 163–4, 188 and fn. 104
Military Coups in Sudan, *see* Sudan
al-Mirghani family: 108; al-Sharifa 'Alawiyya, 108; *see also* Sayyid 'Ali al-Mirghani, Sayyid Muhammad 'Uthman al-Mirghani
Mirghanists, 120, *also* Sufi orders: Khatmiyya
Mirghanist Shirt Movement, *see* Sufi orders, Khatmiyya *shabab al-Khatmiyya*
Mirghani Hamza, 113, 133, 135–6
Mirghani al-Makki, 129
missionaries, *see under* Christian
Mohammedan Law Courts: Ordinance (1902), 64; Organization and Procedure Regulations (1915), 66
Morocco, Moroccan, 70
Mu'ammar al-Qadhafi, 187
Mubarak, Husni, President of Egypt, 165
al-Mudawwi 'Abd al-Rahman, 62
Muddathir al-Hajjaz, 61, 69
mufti (expert in Islamic law), 65
mughtarib(in) (living away from home), 190–1 and fn. 109; *also ightirab*, Islaminomics
muhajirun (migrant), 94, *also fallata*

Muhammad 'Abdallah (Mahdi's brother), 39
Muhammad 'Abduh, 36, 66–7
Muhammad Ahmad b. 'Abdallah, *see* Mahdi
Muhammad Ahmad al-Hajj, 29
Muhammad Ahmad Mahjub (Mahgoub), 94, 135, 146–9, 171, 182, 224
Muhammad b. 'Abd al-Karim al-Samman, 4; *also* Sufi orders, Sammaniyya
Muhammad 'Ali Pasha (Ottoman Wali of Egypt, 1805–49), 5, 8, 17, 23, 27
Muhammad al-Amim al-Darir, 60
Muhammad al-Amin al-Hindi, 41
Muhammad al-Azhari, 216
Muhammad al-Badawi, 60
Muhammad Bello Mai Wurnu, 46
Muhammad Fu'ad Shukri, 7
Muhammad Harun, 66
Muhammad Hasan Diyab, 109
Muhammad al-Hasan al-Mirghani, 5, 9–10; *also* Sufi orders, Khatmiyya
Muhammad Ibrahim Abu Salim, 1, 41
Muhammad Ibrahim Khalil, 223
Muhammad Isma'il al-Makki, 33
Muhammad Khalid, 44, 47
Muhammad al-Khalifa Sharif, 86, 120
Muhammad al-Mahdi al-Sannusi, 31, 45; *see also* Mahdi *khulafa'*
Muhammad al-Majdhub, 50
Muhammad al-Makki, 64
Muhammad Mustafa al-Maraghi, 66, 106
Muhammad Najib (Nagib), President of Egypt after 1952 revolution, 131–6
Muhammad Najib al-Muti'i, 162–3
Muhammad Nur al-Din, 133, 136
Muhammad Ra'uf Pasha, 14, 38
Muhammad Sadiq al-Karuri, 183
Muhammad Sa'id al-Qaddal, 32–3, 54
Muhammad Salah 'Umar, 183
Muhammad Sharif b. Hamd, *see* Mahdi, *khulafa*
Muhammad Sharif Nur al-Da'im, 4
Muhammad Sirr al-Khatim II, 34–5
Muhammad al-Tahir al-Tatli, 50
Muhammad al-Tayyib al-Basir, 4, 31, 35, 38
Muhammad 'Umar al-Banna, 53
Muhammad 'Uthman al-Mirghani, 4–5, 34; *also* Sufi orders; Khatmiyya
Muhammad 'Uthman al-Mirghani II, 9–10, 34–5; *also* Sufi orders; Khatmiyya
Muhammad 'Uthman al-Mirghani, (head of Kahtmiyya since 1968), 177,

194–200, 206, 212–13, 216–17, 220, *also* Sufi orders: Khatmiyya
Muhammad Yusuf al-Maqrif, 187
mujahidin (fighters of holy war), *see jihad*
mulazimin, mulazimiyya (Khalifa's bodyguard), 51, 56, 59
musawamah tarikhiyyah, see 'Historical Compromise'
al-Musawwar, see newspapers
musharaka (cooperation), 207
Muslim, Islam: *passim*; jurists, 1, law, *see shari'a*; Missionaries, 113, *also da'wa*; non-Muslim minorities, 161, 168, 214, 223, 226
Muslim Brothers, *see* political parties
Mustafa al-Maraghi, *see* Muhammad Mustafa al-Maraghi
al-Mu'tamar, see newspapers
al-Mu'tamirin al-Ahrar, see political parties

nabi 'isa, 22, 75–6, 88–9
al-nahj al-islami, see Islamic path, *also* Ja'far Numayri
'al-nahj al-islami limadha?' (Why the Islamic way? Cairo 1983), 152
'al-najh al-islami kayfa?' (How the Islamic way? Cairo 1985), 152
Najib (Nagib), *see* Muhammad Najib
Namik Kemal, 226
Nasser, *see* Jamal 'Abd al-Nasir
Nasserism, 152
Nasir b. Muhammad Abi Likaylik, 4
National Congress, *see* political parties
National Agreement Government (*wifaq watani*), 198
National Constitutional Conference (NCC), *see* Constitution
National Democratic Alliance, (NDA), *see* political parties
National Front, (NF), *see* political parties
National Reconciliation (July 1977), 150, 155, 173–5, 178, 184–5, 195–7, 204, 218
National Salvation Government, 200, 206
Native Administration, 95–7
al-Nayil 'Abd al-Qadir Abu Qurun, 154–5; *also* 'Abd al-Qadir Abu Qurun
al-nizam al-sirri, see political parties: Muslim Brothers
NDA, *see* political parties: National Democratic Alliance
neo-Mahdism, *see* Mahdism
Newbold, Sir Douglas, 110–14, 117

newspapers and journals:
al-Ayyam, 137
Egyptian Gazette, 84
Hadarat al-Sudan (al-hadara), 86, 96
al-Khalij, 216
al-Khartum, 217
liwa al-Islam, 208
al-Mu'tamar, 115
al-Musawwar, 216–17, 219–21
al-Nil, 99, 107, 108, 114–15, 117–18, 125, 134
Sawt al-Sudan, 109, 114–15
al-Siyasa, 198
Sudan Democratic Gazette, 218
Sudanow, 186
Sudan Times, 78
al-'urwa al-wuthqa, 36
al-Umma, 126
Nigeria, 89
al-Nil, see newspapers
Nile: 12, 14, 16–17, 24, 38–9, 81, 137, 202; Blue Nile, 12, 62, 75, 81, 82–3, 92–4, 101; White Nile, 12, 27, 31, 39, 71, 77, 82, 91–4, 101, 108; Nile valley, 2, 13, 17–21, 29, 71, 75, 99, 135, 142, 184; Nile valley, unity of the, 84, 86, 105–6, 131–3; Nile waters, 142
Nuba mountains, 7, 38, 48, 58, 76–9, 148, 165, 195, 216
Nubar Pasha, 20
Nujumi, *see* 'Abd al-Rahman al-Nujumi
Numayri, *see* Ja'far Numayri
al-Nur Ibrahim al-Dijirayfawi, 54–5 (*amin bayt al-mal*, 1890–93)
Nyala revolt (1921), 75, 88–9

Obeid, El-Obeid (al-Ubayyid), 12–13, 39, 43, 45–6, 51–5, 72
Oliphant, Sir Lancelot, 97–8
Omdurman (Ummdurman), 4, 40, 43–4, 48, 50, 68–9, 70, 77, 81–2, 87, 95–9, 109, 116, 119, 135, 175
Omdurman Islamic University, 203; *see also al-ma'had al-Islami al-'ilmi*
Orthodox Islam, 59–80
Ottoman(s): 6, 25, 64, 893; *see also* Turkey; Ottoman Caliph (Sultan), 15, 19–20, 36, 38, 76–9; Young Ottoman, 227, *see also* Namik Kemal
Oxford, 171

pagan, *see* animist
Pakistan, 145
Palmer, H.R., 89

pan-Islam(ic), 28, 77
Paris, 36, 179
PDF, *see* Popular Defence Force
Penny, J.C., 110
'People of the Book', 209
People's Assembly, *see* Sudan: *majlis al-sha'ab*
Peoples' Democratic Party (PDP), *see* political parties
Polotical Association Bill, (*qanun al-tawali al siyasi*), 215–19
pilgrimage, 59, 73–4, 89, 93, 101, 153, 159
political parties and fronts:
  al-Ashiqqa', 119–29
  al-Ahrar, 125
  al-Ba'th, 192
  Democratic Unionist Party (DUP), 143, 150–1, 182, 190–200, 204–7, 212, 215–19, 221
  al-mu'tamarin al-ahrar, 117
  Muslim Brothers, 128, 144–7, 151, 153–62, 167–8, 175–93, 206–7
    al-murshid al-'am (general guide or leader), 185, 194–5, 198, 201, 207
    Shura Council (Supreme), 180–1, 185
    AFFILIATED MOVEMENT AND INSTITUTES
    al-nizam al-sirri, 189, 207
    raidat al-nahda', 191
    shabad al-bina', 191
    shabab al-watan, 211; *see also* Popular Defence Force, Arab tribal militias
  Islamic Liberation Movement (ILM), 179
  Islamic Charter Front (ICF), 147–8, 161, 179–82
  National Congress, 214–15, 219
  National Islamic Front (NIF), 144, 150–1, 159, 167–9, 186, 190–3, 195–201, 203, 205–17, 221
  National Front (NF), 133, 172–3, 183–4, 197, 218
  National Democratic Alliance (NDA), 203, 208, 216–21
  National Unionist Party (NUP), 130, 133–7, 144, 147, 172, 179, 212
  Peoples' Democratic Party (PDP), (*hizb al-sha'ab al-dimuqrati*), 109, 136–7, 181
  Republican Brothers, *see* Sufi and Religious movements
  al-qawmiyyun, 125
  al-Sha'ab, 125
  Socialist Republican Party (SRP), 130–1

Southern Front, 146
Southern Liberal Party, 139
Sudan Communist Party's (SCP), 145, 152, 159, 161, 178–83, 186, 189, 192, 195–7, 201, 203, 215–16
Sudan People's Liberation Movement (SPLM), 196–200, 206, 220
Sudan Socialist Union (SSU), 149, 153–5, 185
al-Umma, 86, 126–32, 134, 144, 146, 148–51, 161, 167, 170–7, 179–83, 192–205, 207–8, 212, 216, 218–21, 226
White Flag League, 84–6
Popular Defence Force (PDF), 210–11; *see also* Sudan: military coups; 1989 Islamist coup
Popular Islam, 59–80, 151; *see also* sufi(sm), Mahdism, neo-Mahdism
Popular Islamic and Arabic Conference (PIAC, 1991), 212–13
Popular Police Corps, 210; *also* Sudan: military coups, 1989 Islamist coup
Port Sudan, 178
'Prompt Courts', 158
Prophet (Muhammad Rasul Allah): 22, 30–3, 35–6, 38, 43, 73, 100, 164, 168–9
  Prophetic colloquy (*hadra nabawiyya*), 31
  Prophet's biography (*sirat al-nabi*), 100
  Prophet's birthday (*mawlid al-nabi*), 63, 153, 172
al-Qadarif, (Kedaref), 7, 34, 94, 179
Qadhafi, *see* Mu'ammar al-Qadhafi

qadi (pl. *qudat*) (judge of a shar'i or civil court): 6, 20, 64–71, 76
  qadi al-Islam (head of shar'i judiciary in Mahdist state), 39, 55–6
  qadi al-qudat (head of shar'i legal system during Condominium), 64–8
Qadir, Jabal (*hijra* to), 33, 38, 41, 44, 52, 62, 77–8, 81, *also* Nuba Mountains
Qadiriyya, *see* Sufi orders
qa'id al-mu'minin (Commander of the Faithful), 157
al-Qallabat, 47
qanun al-tawali al-siyasi, *see* Political Association Bill
Qasim Amin, 66
qisas, (retribution), 41, 163, 198
al-Qurashi wad al-Zayn, 4, 10, 31
Qur'an, 2, 5, 23, 30–1, 34–5, 40–1, 55, 68–71, 145, 160, 162, 166, 174,

177, 195, 209, 224; *see also kuttab-*
'*Qur'an contest*', 153

Rabih ibn Fadl Allah (Zubayr), 46
al-Rajjaf, 48
Ras al-Fil, 16
al-Rashid al-Tahir Bakr, 179–80 and fn.
82, 184, 189
ratib al-Mahdi, see Mahdi
RCC, *see* Egypt, Revolutionary Command
Council
Red Sea, 4, 13–21, 26, 64, 148, 165, 195
Regional Government Act (1980), Shari'a
Reid, M.J., 91
Republicans, *see* Sufi orders and religious
parties: Republican Brothers
Revolutionary Command Council (RCC),
see Egypt
Al-risala al-thaniya min al-Islam
(The second message of Islam),
161–3 and fn. 48, *also* Mahmud
Muhammad Taha
Rizayqat, *see* tribes
Robertson, Sir James, 128, 130, 139
Round Table Conference (March 1965),
147, 168

Sabry, Husayn Dhu al Faqar Sabri, 132–3
Sa'd Zaghlul, 83–4
sadaqa, 100; *see also zakat*
Sadat, *see* Anwar al-Sadat
al-Sadiq al-Mahdi, *see* Mahdi family: al-
Sadiq al-Mahdi
Sa'id Pahsa, Egyptian Viceroy, 27
Sa'id b. Hayatu, 89
Salah Salim, Col., 134–7, 179
Sammaniyya, *see* Sufi orders
Sanusiyya, *see* Sufi orders
saqiyya (water wheel), 12–13
SAM, *see* 'Ali al-Mirghani
SAR, 107 fn. 172; *see also* Mahdi, 'Abd al-
Rahman al-Mahdi
Satiru rebellion (1906), 46
Saudi Arabia, 153, 159–60, 184, 210, 213
Sawakin (Suakin), 13–21, 35, 39, 74
Sawt al-Sudan, see newspapers
Sayed Abd El Rahman, *see* Mahdi, 'Abd
al-Rahman al-Mahdi
Sayed Ali El Mirghani, *see* 'Ali al-Mirghani
Sayyid(s), *see* Mahdi, 'Abd al-Rahman al-
Mahdi; 'Ali al-Mirghani
SDF, *see* Sudan Defence Force
Second World War, *see* World War II
Self-Government Statute (April 1952), 130

Sennar, *see* Sinnar
shabab al-ansar, see Sufi orders and
religious movements: Ansar
shabab al-Khatmiyya, see Sufi orders and
religious movements: Khatmiyya
Shadhiliyya, *see* Sufi orders and religious
movements: Shadhliyya
shafi'i, 6
Sha'iqiyya, *see* tribes
Shakaba, 80
Shaked, Haim, 30 and fn. 22
Shakha, 56
(uncodified Islamic law), 55, 64–8, 143–
5, 155–64, 168, 174–7, 192, 194–222
courts, 59, 64–8, 72, 162
Supreme Shari'a Court, 65
al-Sharif Yusuf al-Hindi, *see under* Yusuf
Sharifian family, 4 *also* Ashraf
Shatta dam, 19
Shaykan (battle of 5 Nov. 1883), 30
Shendi (Shandi), 13, 16
Shi'a, Shi'ite, Shi'ism, 22, 157, 170
Shibeika (Shibayka) Mekki, 28, 37–8
shirk (polytheism), 100
Shuqayr, Na'um, 28
shura (consultation), 227
majlis al-shura (consultative council),
157–8, 171
Sidahmed, *see* Abdel Salam Sidahmed
al-Siddiq al-Mahdi, *see* Mahdi family:
al-Siddiq al-Mahdi
Sinnar, 1–6, 13–17, 92–4, *see also* Funj
Singa, 94
Sinka, 99
sirat al-mahdi, see Mahdi
Sirr al-Khatm al-Khalifa, 71, 179, 204
Slatin, Rudolf C. von, 39, 56–81
slaves, slavery: 2, 8, 13, 16–17, 27
trade, traders, 7, 14–15, 16, 24, 27,
167–8
Convention for the Suppression of
Slave-Trade (1877), 15
Sokoto caliphate, 45–6, 89
Somali coast, 14, 18
South Africa, 218
Southern Sudan, *see* Sudan
Speke, John Hanning, 14
SPLA, *see* Sudan, South: Sudan People's
Liberation Army
SPLM, *see* political parties: Sudan People's
Liberation Movement
SPS, *see* Anglo-Egyptian Sudan
SSIR, see Sudan: *Sudan Secret Intelligence
Reports*

Stack, Sir Lee, 83, 85, 89, 110
Stanley, Sir Henry, 48
Sudan, *passim: see also* Anglo-Egyptian
    Sudan; Condominium; Turco-
    Egyptian Sudan (First Turkiyya):
  majlis al-Sha'jb (Parliament; National
    [or People's] Assembly), 135, 156–8,
    165–6, 171, 179, 182, 187–8, 216, 218
    1953 elections: 129, 133–4, 137, 139,
      181
    1965 elections: 147, 171, 179
    1968 elections: 182
    1986 elections: 186, 195–7, 214
    1996 elections: 213–14
  military coups (regimes) and civilian
    uprisings: 143
    1958–64, Ibrahim 'Abbud, 142,
      145–7, 179–80
    1959, abortive anti-'Abbud coup,
      179, 189
    October 1964, civilian revolution,
      161, 179–80, 203
    1969–85 Ja'far Numayri also May
      Revolution, 142, 148, 160, 162,
      172, 183, 206, 218
    Free Officers, May 1969, 159
    July 1971, abortive Communist
      coup, 152, 159, 179, 183–4
    April 1985, anti-Numayri uprising,
      167, 176, 192, 203
    June 1989, 'Umar Hasan al-Bashir,
      also Islamist coup, 142, 190, 201,
      205–22
  'Sudan Charter' (NIF 1987), 169
Sudan Defence Force (SDF), 37, 84, 89–90
  (fn. 108), 173, 178, 189, 190, 204, 211
Government Acts:
    Decentralization Act (1980), 166
    Regional Government Act (1980), 166
  'Sudan for the Sudanese', 105, 112, 125–6,
    133, 135
    intelligentsia, 96–9, 103, 105, 110–41,
      143, 151
    National Council, 221
    nationalism, 29, 104–41
    Sudan Political Service, *see* Anglo-
      Egyptian Sudan
    Sudan Railways, 19
Sudan Republic (Jan. 1956), 142
Sudan Secret Intelligence Report (SSIR),
    90
Sudan Times, see newspapers
Supreme Court, 182
television, 163

umma, 187
Sudanese Student Union in Britain,
    179
Sudanization Commission, 139
Sudanow, see newspapers
South(ern) Sudan: 58, 104, 111, 138–41,
    149, 165–9, 176, 180, 192, 195, 200,
    207, 212, 214–15, 220–2, 225
  Southern conflict, civil war, 140, 156,
    176, 192, 198, 201–4
  Southern mutiny at Torit (18 Aug.
    1955), 138–9
  Southern fears of Islamization, 192
  Islamic Association of Southern Sudan,
    168
  maginalized regions, 144, 165
  non-Muslim and non-Arab minorities,
    144, 219–20, 223, 227; *jahili* status of
    non-Muslims, 189, 219
Southern Muslims, 168–9
Southern policy, 117, 138–41, 166–9; *see
    also* Juba coference
Southern Regional Assembly, 165
Sudan People's Liberation Army, 193,
    199–200, 208, 219–20
Sudan Political Liberation Movement,
    SPLM, *see* political parties
Suez campaign (1956), 179
Suez Canal, 18–21
sufi, Sufism: 1–11, 29, 37, 57–141, 151–5,
    158, 162, 186
  sufi dhikr, 62, 95–6
  sufi order(s) *tariqa, turuq*, 1–11, 22, 24–
    5, 33–5, 38–9, 41, 57, 76–80, 95–6,
    128, 137, 143, 147, 153–5, 196
  sufi ulama' (shaykhs), 1, 21, 31
Sufi orders and religious movements:
  Ahmadiyya, 95
  Ansar (twentieth century), 77, 82–148,
    151, 152–3, 159, 161–2, 170–86, 192,
    195–200, 204, 207, 210–14, 222, 225;
    see also neo-Mahdism
    shabab al-ansar, 109
    Ansar al-Sunna, 154, 181
    awlad Jabir, 2, 25
  Hindiyya (*awlad hindi*), 85, 172
  Idrisiyya, 9, 63, 95, 125
  Isma'iliyya, 33–4, 64, 95, 128, 153
  Khalwatiyya, 4
  Khatmiyya, 3–5, 8–11, 14, 24, 26, 29,
    34–5, 62, 85–8, 91, 95–6, 100 and fn.
    145, 104–44, 151, 153, 159, 161, 177,
    180, 183, 192, 195–201, 204, 207,
    210–14, 225

itihadat al-khatmiyya, 109, 137
shabab al-Khatmiyya, also
  Mirghanist Shirt Movement,
  108–9
Majdhuviyya, Majadhib, 2–3, 21, 23,
  25–6, 34–5, 40, 50, 64, 71, 72
Niasisyya, 196
Qadiriyya, 1, 4, 153, 181
Republican Brothers, 153, 160–5, 186–8
Sammaniyya, 3, 4, 10–11, 31, 33, 38, 41,
  95, 153, 181
Sanusiyya, 31, 40
Shadhiliyya, 1, 2, 5
Tijaniyya, 10, 33, 181
Wahhabiyya, 40, 154
Ya'qubab, 4
Sulayman al-Hajjaz, 56
Sunna, sunni, 20, 30, 40–1, 55, 66, 145, 154,
  156, 163–4, 174–7, 225
Suwwar al-Dhahab, *see* Abd al-Rahman
  Suwwar al-Dhahab
Symes, Sir Stewart, 78, 91 3 and fn. 113,
  97–8, 107, 112 4
Syria, 213

Ta'aisha, *see* tribes
Ta'aishi, *see* Mahdi: Khalifa 'Abdullahi
  al-
Taha, *see* Mahmud Muhammad Taha
al-Tahir Ahmad (Sultan of Sokoto), 46
al-Tahir al-Tayyib al-Majdhub, 40, 50; *see
  also* Sufi orders: Majdhubiyya
tahaluf (alliance), 207
Taj al-Din 'Abdallah Fadl, 190
tajdid, 100
Talodi, 81
Taqali, Jabal, 38; *see also* Nuba Mountains
taqlid (imitation), 40, 174
tariqa, see Sufi order
Tawfiq Pasha, Khedive, 32, 36, 38, 40
tawhid (doctrine of unity of God), 41
Al-Tayyib Ahmad Hashim, 61, *also*
  Hashimad family (clan)
Tijaniyya, *see* Sufi orders
Tokar, 72
Torit, 138–9
Toski, *see* Tushki
Transitional Military Council 1985–6
  (TMC), 192
treasury, *see bayt al-mal*
tribal religions, 168; *see also* African
  religions; animists
tribes:
  'Arakiyyin, 14

Baqqara, 13, 26, 34, 38, 44, 48, 51, 54,
  99
Beja, 20–1, 26, 165, 202
Danaqla, 2, 12–13, 27
Dinka, 168, 220, 224
Fur, 47, 202
Hadariba, 20
Halawiyyin, 4, 31
Ja'aliyyin, 2, 4, 7–8, 12–14, 23, 27, 29, 34
  Ja'aliyyin revolt (1822–3), 7, 13, 55,
  71
Nilotic, 1, 2
Nuer, 220
Nuba, 38, 202
Riverain, 2, 5, 7, 12, 27; *see also awlad
  al-balad*
Rizayqat, 48
Sha'iqiyya, 5, 7–9, 14, 24
Ta'aisha, 44, 48, 54
Turabi, *see* Hasan al-Turabi
Turco-Egyptian Sudan (First Turkiyya),
  4–21, 23, 25–30, 34–5, 43, 52, 56,
  58–60, 62, 72–80
Turkey, Turkish, Turks: 21, 26, 29, 31, 41,
  46, 55, 76–80, 82, 167
  Turks (described by Mahdi: *a'da' al-din
  wa-kuffar* [enemies of God]), 32
  Young Turks' revolution (1908), 76
Tushki (battle of August 1889), 47, 49, 102
Tuti Island, 124

Uganda, 138, 142
'ulama' (sing. *'alim*), (Muslim scholars),
  1–3, 6–9, 17, 23–4, 29, 32, 36–7, 40,
  44, 57–105, 163, 174–6, 197, 208–9
  'ulama' al-su' ('scholars of evil',
  denounced by al-Mahdi), 23, 32, 35
Ulemas, 'Board of Ulemas', 60–4, 69,
  79–80
'Umar Hasan al-Bashir, President (1989-),
  151, 189, 201–3, 205–22, 224
'Umar Muhammad al-Tayyib, Numayri's
  vice-president, 163, 187–8
'Umar Nur al-Da'im, 201
umara', (sing. *amir*), *see* Mahdi
Umm Dubban Rural Council, 153
umma (the Muslim community), 22, 25, 55
Umma party, *see* political parties
United Parties Committees, 123
United States of America, 8, 187–8, 192,
  210, 217
'Urabi Revolt, Ahmad, 21, 26, 28, 32
'urf (cutomary law), 64
al-'urwa al-wuthqa, see newspapers

'ushr, (tithe, tax levied at one tenth of income), 54
'Uthman Adam, 47
'Uthman Diqna, 10, 24, 40, 44, 50
'Uthman Nur al-Din, 45
'Uthman b. al-Khalifa 'Abdullahi, (*shaykh al-din*), 49, 51
'Uthman Jarkas (al-Birinji), 12
'Uthman Sayyid Ahmad Isma'il, 23

Victoria, Queen, 62
Voll, John O., 223
Wad Habuba, *see* 'Abd al-Qadir Imam wad Habuba
Wad Madani, 12, 92
Wad Nubawi mosque, 221
Wadi Halfa, 47, 61
Wafd, 80, 83–6, 129
Wahhabiyya, *see* Sufi orders and religious movements
waqf (plur. *awqaf*, religious endowment): 71–3
  waqf ahli (family endowment), 71
  Ministry of Endowments (*awqaf*), 153
Washington, DC, 191
West Africa, *see* Africa
Williams, C.W. (director of education), 138
Willis, C.A., 88 (fn. 102)
White Flag League, *see* political parties
Wingate, Sir Reginald, 57–80, 110
World War I, 59–60, 62, 64, 67, 74–80, 82, 91, 110, 134

World War II, 91, 103–4, 109, 128
Wunlit, 220

Yahya al-Fadli, 99, 117
Ya'qub ibn Muhammad (Khalifa's brother), 49, 54, 56
Yathrib, 38, 44; *see also* Medina
Yemen, Yemenite, 37
Young Ottomans, 226
Yusuf Fadl Hasan, 46
Yusuf Hasan al-Shalali, 38
Yusuf Ibrahim (royal Fur clan), 47
Yusuf Muhammad al-Amin al-Hindi, Sayyid (head of the Hindiyya and one of the 'Three Sayyids'), 80, 85
(al-Sharif) Yusuf al-Hindi, 172, 183–4
  death, (1978), 197; *see also* DUP and NF
Yusuf wad Badur, Badrab Khalifa, 153–4

Zaghlul, Sa'd, *see* Sa'd Zaghlul
zakat (shar'i alms tax levied on cattle and crops), 52, 54–5, 155, 159, *also* Islamic legislation
  zakat (paid to Sayyid 'Abd al-Rahman by the Ansar), 82, 93; *see also sadaqa*
  Zakat and Taxation Act (1984), 155, 158
Zanzibar, 15
zawiya (small, usually private mosque), 1, 59, 62, 72, 153
Zein El-'Abdin El-Hindi, 216
Zionists, 189
Zoroastrian, 22